C000220893

NARRATIVE CRIMINOLOGY

ALTERNATIVE CRIMINOLOGY SERIES

General Editor: Jeff Ferrell

Narrative Criminology

Understanding Stories of Crime

Edited by Lois Presser and Sveinung Sandberg

NEW YORK UNIVERSITY PRESS

New York and London

NEW YORK UNIVERSITY PRESS
New York and London
www.nyupress.org

© 2015 by New York University
All rights reserved

References to Internet websites (URLs) were accurate at the time of writing. Neither the author nor New York University Press is responsible for URLs that may have expired or changed since the manuscript was prepared.

Library of Congress Cataloging-in-Publication Data
Narrative criminology : understanding stories of crime / edited by Lois Presser and Sveinung Sandberg.
pages cm. — (Alternative criminology series)
Includes bibliographical references and index.
ISBN 978-1-4798-7677-8 (cl : alk. paper) — ISBN 978-1-4798-2341-3 (pb : alk. paper)
1. Criminology. 2. Criminal behavior. 3. Narrative inquiry (Research method) I. Presser, Lois. II. Sandberg, Sveinung.
HV6025.N32 2015
364.072'3—dc23 2015001637

New York University Press books are printed on acid-free paper, and their binding materials are chosen for strength and durability. We strive to use environmentally responsible suppliers and materials to the greatest extent possible in publishing our books.

Manufactured in the United States of America

10 9 8 7 6 5 4 3 2 1

Also available as an ebook

CONTENTS

FOREWORD: NARRATIVE CRIMINOLOGY AS THE NEW MAINSTREAM

SHADD MARUNA

The movement toward narrative criminology is radical in its insights and implications. As a genuine departure from and viable alternative to mainstream criminology, the work showcased in this remarkable collection is likely to create serious waves in criminology that will be unruly and difficult to contain.

The irony, of course, is that there is nothing radical about narrative criminology at all. Throughout this book, the authors draw on a sophisticated array of leading thought in psychology, philosophy, cultural studies, and elsewhere. The so-called narrative turn in the social sciences (Brown et al. 1994) has characterized these other fields of enquiry for decades with its understanding, adopted from Sartre, that the human being is fundamentally a storytelling creature—or "homo narrativus" (Ferrand and Weil, 2001). Using the male-centered language of his time, Sartre ([1938] 1965, 61) wrote: "A man is always a teller of tales, he lives surrounded by his stories and the stories of others, he sees everything that happens to him through them; and he tries to live his life as if he were recounting it."

Over the last two decades, this notion that identity is an internal narrative has achieved a privileged place in the social sciences and humanities, with adherents like Paul Ricoeur, Dan McAdams, and Charles Taylor. The distinguished Harvard psychologist Jerome Bruner (1987, 15) argues: "Eventually the culturally shaped cognitive and linguistic processes that guide the self-telling of life narratives achieve the power to structure perceptual experience, to organise memory, to segment and purpose-build the very 'events' of a life. In the end, we become the autobiographical narratives by which we 'tell about' our lives."

The equally distinguished London School of Economics sociologist Anthony Giddens (1991, 54) agrees, arguing that in modernity, "a person's identity is not to be found in behavior, nor—important though this is—in the reactions of others, but in the capacity to keep a particular narrative going." Theodore Sarbin (1986, vii) even suggests that the narrative should be seen as the "root metaphor" for the entire field of psychology. As crime is simply a form of human behavior, it makes sense that criminological knowledge and understanding would follow closely (if perhaps lagging slightly) behind developments in these wider fields of understanding human relationships and cultures.

Far more radical, then, is the much wider field of nonnarrative criminology. How is such a thing even possible? As Scott and Lyman (1968, 62) have argued: "Since it is with respect to deviant behavior that we call for accounts, the study of deviance and the study of accounts are intrinsically related, and a clarification of accounts will constitute a clarification of deviant phenomena—to the extent that deviance is considered in an interactional framework."

Our criminal courts are full of stories; police work largely involves the collection of stories. The same is true of offender rehabilitation. Religions—the traditional realm of sin and punishment (and redemption)—explicitly explain right and wrong through parables and other stories. Indeed, all cultures appear to rely on mythologies and legends to teach morality. There may be no other way to teach it. Good and bad, crime and justice, deviance and punishment: These are not concepts that belong naturally to the realms of science, quantification, calculus, or accounting. They are, at heart, narrative concepts, belonging only and always to the field of stories and storytelling; they can appear ridiculous and hollow outside of this light.

The late Jock Young, a trained mathematician and one of criminology's looming geniuses, makes this case in his characteristically fearless and often hilarious magnum opus *The Criminological Imagination* (2011). Young's argument is not that crimes are not measurable or contain no empirical reality. Rape, murder, robbery, and assault may all be social and linguistic constructs, but this is cold comfort for the victims of such acts whose physical experiences of crime are most certainly real. Counting, measuring, and utilizing statistical probability models for predicting such acts were among the most radical and important of enlightenment inventions.

Yet, it has to be remembered that this sort of approach to understanding the social psychology of crime is just as counterintuitive today as it was in the nineteenth century. When human beings, in every culture, seek to understand "why did she do it?" the answer is not a mathematical formula but a story: "First, this happened, then that happened, and then she decided to do X." Moreover, despite two hundred years of nonnarrative criminology, human beings around the world continue to tell such stories for why they did what they did or do what they do.

These stories are not the literal or complete truth (if such a thing exists), nor are they in and of themselves the sole explanation for criminal behaviors, but they are an unmistakable source of evidence, the elephant in the room. Indeed, the most radical aspect of nonnarrative criminology is not the elevation of quantification which amuses Young so much, but rather the remarkable dismissal of these narrative data that are everywhere around us in the buildup to and aftermath of crimes. Leaving aside the ethics of this, what could be the scientific rationale of ignoring the stories of those human beings we have assigned to the construct of victim, offender, or family member in our analyses? If quarks and waves could talk, you can bet that physicists would be doing qualitative research as well.

The contributions to this crucial new volume demonstrate the value of doing so, both by force of the rich qualitative material itself (although this is hardly new) and through the engagement with psychosocial theories that can point to new strategies for interpreting these data. In doing so, the chapters also expose the considerable difficulty in analyzing self-narratives in criminology. We find that our versions of quarks and waves are not reliable recorders of some objective truth. Their narratives are biased (albeit often in ways that expose useful patterns of thought), they are influenced by the circumstances and audience of the telling, and they are, above all, complicated, nonlinear, and unique (if familiar through cultural conventions of storytelling).

One does not finish this book and conclude "we are almost there" in the quest to understand crime and punishment; far from it. Such false hopes for certainty may plague nonnarrative criminology with its goals of uncovering what works in controlling crime (at long last). Yet, narrative criminology aims at understanding and confronting rather than prediction and control. The conclusion from the essays in this book, or this author's conclusion at least, is not that we have almost cracked the mysteries of crime and justice, but that at least we are now asking the right questions.

REFERENCES

Bruner, Jerome S. 1987. "Life as narrative." *Social Research* 54 (1): 11–32.

Ferrand, Nathalie, and Weil, Michèle, eds. 2001. *Homo Narrativus, Recherches Sur la Topique Romanesque dans les Fictions de Langue Française Avant 1800*. Montpellier, FR: Presses de l'Université Paul-Valéry.

Giddens, Anthony. 1991. *Modernity and Self-Identity: Self and Society in the Late Modern Age*. Stanford, CA: Stanford University Press.

Sarbin, Theodore R. 1986. *Narrative Psychology: The Storied Nature of Human Conduct*. New York: Praeger.

Sartre, Jean-Paul. (1938) 1965. *Nausea*. Translated by Robert Baldick. Harmondsworth, UK: Penguin.

Scott, Marvin B., and Stanford M. Lyman. 1968. "Accounts." *American Sociological Review* 33 (1): 46–61.

Young, Jock. 2011. *The Criminological Imagination*. Cambridge, UK: Polity Press.

Introduction

What Is the Story?

LOIS PRESSER AND SVEINUNG SANDBERG

Narratives are central to human existence. By constructing our lives as stories, we forge connections among experiences, actions, and aspirations. We know ourselves as *one* over time—one consistent moral actor or one unified group of moral actors—however numerous or varied the cultural story elements that we access and integrate into our self-stories. Our self-stories condition what we will do tomorrow because whatever tomorrow brings, our responses must somehow cohere with the storied identity generated thus far. Criminologists have made ample use of offenders' narratives, mainly, albeit not exclusively, as vehicles for data on the factors that promote criminal behavior. The idea that narratives or stories themselves shape future action has not been exploited for the sake of understanding criminal behavior. Enter our approach, narrative criminology (Presser 2009; see also Presser 2012; Sandberg 2010, 2013).[1] Narrative criminology is any inquiry based on the view of stories as instigating, sustaining, or effecting desistance from harmful action. We study how narratives inspire and motivate harmful action, and how they are used to make sense of harm. In granting primacy to narrative in human action, narrative criminology follows a well-trodden path in psychology, sociology, history, literature, and cultural studies. Narrative criminology also hews to a critical perspective on power and agency as constituted discursively.

Narrative criminologists view narrative texts as foundational objects of inquiry and the study of those texts as "a useful corrective to the reductive tendencies that other analyses, rooted in individual disciplines, can manifest" (Andrews et al. 2004). The approach is a constructionist one. We do not view offenders' narratives as accurately—or

inaccurately—describing events. We do not consider narratives as vehicles for thoughts or as suppressed voices. What, then, is narrative?
Where does narrative criminology come from theoretically and what
does it look like methodologically? What can narrative criminology help
us to achieve?

The Nature of Narrative

Narrative is just one discursive form. Other forms include reports,
chronicles, expositions, metaphors, dialogues, and arguments. Generally speaking, a narrative is a type of discourse that follows events or
experiences over time and makes some point. William Labov and Joshua
Waletzky (1967, 20–21) famously set out the first characteristic of narrative, temporal sequencing, as central: "The basic narrative units that we
wish to isolate are defined by the fact that they recapitulate experience
in the same order as the original events." Labov and Waletzky assigned
a somewhat less vital role to the evaluation of a narrative, which "estab-
lishes the importance or point" (32), although by now scholars generally
agree that narratives, however subtly, always make a morally transcendent point (Bruner 1990; Mishler 1986; Polkinghorne 1988; Polletta et al.
2011). When the protagonist of the narrative is oneself or one's group,
the point typically concerns who the self or the group is in the world.
Hence the fairly recent view of identity or self as something constructed
via storytelling (see Bruner 1990; Chanfrault-Duchet 2000; Kerby 1991;
Linde 1993; Somers 1994).

Labov (1972, 363) is also responsible for a classic model of the well-
formed narrative, which includes six essential elements: abstract, orientation, complicating action, evaluation, result or resolution, and coda.
An abstract says something about the theme, the orientation introduces
the context, the complicating narrative action introduces an event, and
an evaluation makes the point clear. The result tells audiences what ultimately happened, while the coda signals that the story has come to an
end. In recent decades narratologists have questioned the faithfulness
of stories to the classic model. For example, whereas narrative is said to
include an evaluation, evaluative ambiguity is a resource some narrators use to influence others (see Polletta et al. 2011). Similarly, Sandberg
(2009) has noted multiple, even contradictory, evaluations in a single

narrative. A storyteller may not even signal an end to the story; instead she or he may allow or invite interlocutors to continue it—sometimes from rather sparse beginnings (Fairclough 1992). Nonetheless, however much a particular story diverges from conventionality, audiences seem to recognize it as a story when they hear or read it.

Narratives themselves take many forms. Literary scholars distinguish between comedy, romance, tragedy, and irony (McAdams 1993). Hankiss (1981) claims that most life stories are dynastic (a good past gives birth to a good present), antithetical (a bad past gives birth to a good present), compensatory (a good past gives birth to a bad present), or self-absolutory (a bad past gives birth to a bad present). The narrative literature is replete with similar typologies.

Michel Foucault's (1972) discourse is a collection of many genres including narratives.[2] Discourses are ways of structuring areas of knowledge and social practice that systematically form the objects of which they speak. Discourses are embedded in, emerge from, and uphold social institutions. A discourse can achieve hegemony in particular historical times, where certain *épistèmes* and narrative structures dominate (Foucault 1970); there may even be several competing discourses, each with its own set of narratives (Foucault 1978). Viewing narratives as embedded within larger discourses highlights their power and the power relations in which they are implicated. It also highlights and contextualizes the limits of the individual narrator's agency.

Narrative and Experience

Narrative is closely related to experience, yet the relationship is highly problematic. First, experience is constantly changing, thus narrative must change as well. We have no once-and-for-all life story. Nor does the story of an event remain exactly the same with the passage of time: the evaluation or plot, if not the events themselves, is subject to change. Second, narratives vary with the circumstances of their telling. They are tailored to interlocutors—Michael Polanyi (1985, 33) neatly states that "the teller must 'recipient design' his story"—and shaped by interlocutors: narratives may be collective productions, as suggested above. They are also tailored to the purposes of storytelling, a fact that engenders suspicion about the truthfulness of people's stories.

The question of the truthfulness of stories comes to the fore where the stories of offenders are concerned. The public commonly presumes that offenders lie—either by nature or to avoid or mitigate formal and informal sanctions. Criminologists often share the view of offenders' narratives as suspect, belied by their methodological concern with whether storytellers are "telling the truth" (Sandberg 2010). Yet, many critical scholars espouse an apparently opposite view of the stories marginalized offenders (and victims) tell. They take these to reflect heretofore silenced truths about oppression and subaltern existence. Hence, some ethnographers say they are allowing those informants to speak their own truths through narrative excerpts. Whether offenders' stories are seen as potentially fictional or as offering a unique vantage point on truth, the implication is the same: narrative is epistemologically subordinate to experience. For philosopher Paul Ricoeur (1984) that is but one of the ways that the relationship between narrative and experience may be conceptualized.

Ricoeur describes three basic views of that relationship. First, narrative may be seen as an objective representation of experience—a historical record of what happened. Second, narrative may be seen as a subjective interpretation of experience. As in the first conceptualization, narrative as interpretive statement reveals what happened but through a subjective lens. Third, narrative may be seen as shaping experience. In this conceptualization, experience is always understood and acted upon as it has been storied.[3] Narrative criminology adopts this third view, which may be called constitutive.

We venture that the constitutive view—the view that narratives produce experience even as experience produces narratives—is foreign to most criminologists, a fact that owes a good deal to the discipline's individualism, its connection to the criminal justice system, and its limited forays into social theory. Criminologists study individual action far more than they do mass harms. Whole categories of mass harm, causing untold casualties, have been virtually ignored, including genocide and institutionalized animal abuse (see Beirne 2009; Day and Vandiver 2000; Hagan and Rymond-Richmond 2009). Yet, outside of criminology, scholars routinely bracket individuals' inner realities in order to theorize collective behavior. Such scholars have gone far in explaining collective violence in terms of the narrative constructions of would-be offenders and victims (see Cohn 1987; Huggins, Haritos-Fatouros, and

Zimbardo 2002; Mason 2002; Smith 2005; Sternberg 2003; Vetlesen 2005). Case studies demonstrate that stories matter a great deal for the mobilization of terrorism and war, development of nuclear weaponry, participation in corporate pollution, and the like, as well as smaller-scale group actions like gang rape and drive-by shootings by warring drug dealers. Few would think to assert that the inauthenticity of those collective stories undermines their mobilizing effects.

The weightiness of what people say is only more evident—not more salient—where group action is concerned. Consider that the human capacity to interpret experience depends upon language. People's verbalizations thus affect their behavior by affecting what they are able to think. Of the discursive—indeed, narrative—nature of thought David Polonoff (1987, 47) states: "Even the private consultation with recollection issues in a kind of narration in which temporal gaps are elided and the continuous succession of experiences is organized as movement to and from significant episodes or markers." What we take to be reality necessarily takes narrative form.

Some, in fact, view events themselves as narrative in form. Donald Polkinghorne (1988, 68) relates that aspects of experience are "presented originally as they appear in the narration and that narrative form is not simply imposed on preexistent real experiences but helps to give them form." This radical position is consistent with postmodern thought. However, narrative criminology need not go to that extreme. We need only bracket so-called actual conditions in the world to focus on the role of narrative constructions in influencing behavior. In adopting the constitutive view, in any of its forms, the researcher theoretically and methodologically focuses on storied experience, not experience per se.

Related Concepts from Criminology

Narratives bear a likeness to established criminological concepts, namely, neutralizations, thinking errors, identities, and situational interpretations. Each of these constructs is something actors are said to borrow, more or less, from their culture to construct the world and themselves, with the result being misconduct. The gap between these criminological concepts and narrative colors our vision of narrative criminology, as we will show.

Gresham Sykes and David Matza's (1957) techniques of neutralizations—denial of responsibility, denial of injury, denial of the victim, condemnation of the condemned, and appeal to higher loyalties—are the best known of these concepts. Neutralizations are verbalizations actors use to tell themselves that their actions are not in violation of the norms they are otherwise committed to. The parsimony of Sykes and Matza's typology has fostered a tendency toward excessive reduction in research on what offenders say (see Maruna and Copes 2005), just as it assured the prominence of neutralizations over similar though more theoretically intricate earlier work by C. Wright Mills (1940) on vocabularies of motive and Donald Cressey (1953) on the justifications of embezzlers. Nor has Matza's 1964 book *Delinquency and Drift*—which offers a more complex theory of how the individual youth conceives of her- or himself as drifting into delinquency under the spell of a "mood of fatalism" (88)—received nearly as much attention as the 1957 article.

Unlike narratives, neutralizations attend only to the offense, not to a lifetime of criminal and noncriminal actions. The neutralizing actor focuses on the illegitimate act alone, giving little indication—as narrative does—of who she or he, allegedly, will be in the future. Such indication informs the narrator's criminal project. Narrative criminology advocates a more constitutive and all-encompassing understanding of language than the concepts of neutralization, justification, and excuses allow for.

More reductive still are thinking errors, which are the focal points of a hegemonic program of offender rehabilitation in the West (Ellis 1973; Yochelson and Samenow 1976). Thinking errors, such as attribution of intent to harm to one whose action was accidental, are similar to narratives in that they feature protagonists engaging with the world. They differ from narratives in that rehabilitation scholars view thinking errors as (1) discrete cognitions unrelated to a fuller sense of self in the world through time, and (2) internal, psychic phenomena, with no requirement of verbalization. Only in the treatment setting must the erroneous thoughts purportedly be expressed or narrated for purposes of effective intervention. In addition, from the perspective of narrative criminology narratives are never erroneous. Finally, narrative criminology attends to individual and collective narratives and action, whereas thinking errors are individual phenomena used to explain individual offending only.

A third criminological concept that informs narrative criminology is identity. Among criminologists labeling theorists have given the most sustained attention to identities, investigating their impact on criminal behavior. As a notion that individuals construct about who they are and how they see themselves by making meaning of available resources (i.e., social roles and personal attributes), identity shares common conceptual ground with self-narratives. However, identities as traditionally conceived are not narratives. Rather, labeling theorists have represented deviant identities as marks or stigmata, or, more realistically, as a criminal record. A label, not a story, is imposed, and the consequences of that label form the basis for one's identity. Indeed, part of the actor's problem with labeling is that others deny her or his stories altogether, constructing the individual instead as one-dimensional—as only the label (Garfinkel 1956). Whereas the labeling perspective brackets the authenticity of who people are and what crime is, the fact of labeling is taken to be real. Labeling theorists have not emphasized a story (or even a perception) of having been labeled.

Finally, many criminological theories deem important, if not primary, the would-be offender's interpretations of (1) situations antecedent to the crime and (2) the situation for the crime. Strain theories consider how actors interpret their life circumstances—as, for example, thwarting goals or not; learning theories look at how actors interpret the outcomes of their conduct—as favorable (and thus reinforcing) or unfavorable (and thus punishing); rational choice theories are concerned with the actor's perception of the benefits and costs of the criminal act; structured action theory attends to the actor's performance of the "appropriate" gender, which may entail criminal action depending on the resources the actor deems available in particular settings and situational threats to gender performance.

Interpretations differ from narratives in important ways. First, as was also true of neutralizations, interpretations are principally *about* an event or situation, whereas narratives are more comprehensive. Second, situational interpretations may avoid referencing the self, whereas narratives are fundamentally concerned with the self.[4] Finally, interpretations need not be communicated to have the criminogenic effect. In contrast, narratives are essentially verbalizations. The ways in which we assemble and verbalize our stories are paramount to narrative criminology.

Broader Theoretical Context

The main sources of guidance for narrative criminology are theoretical traditions that, for the most part, lie beyond the discipline. Construction-ist approaches all, they include narrative psychology, ethnomethodology, cultural structuralism, and postmodernism in its various forms. As demonstrated below, these approaches differ along lines of agency and structure, and unity and fragmentation, which are all important aspects of narratives. We are also inspired by criminologies influenced by postmod-ern thought—constitutive criminology and cultural criminology.

Narrative Psychology: The Study of a Unified Self-Narrative

Narratives may be seen as the creative and artful construction of coher-ence and consistency. Such is the approach generally taken by narrative psychologists (e.g., László 2008; Crossley 2000; McAdams 1993; Polk-inghorne 1988). Dan P. McAdams (1993, 11–12) emphasizes that "each of us constructs, consciously and unconsciously, a personal myth" which makes every individual unique. In his groundbreaking book *Making Good*, Shadd Maruna (2001, 85) argues that to desist from crime, ex-offenders must create a coherent prosocial identity in story form. Thus he writes: "If such an enormous life transformation is to be believed, the person needs a coherent narrative to explain and justify this turnaround."

Borne of psychology, it is not surprising that agency and coherence are featured in these approaches. Psychological inquiry begins and ends with individuals and the field largely accepts individuals' needs to see themselves as unified, to eliminate contradiction and thus to reduce cog-nitive dissonance (Festinger 1957). Consider that the formation of mul-tiple self-identities is a diagnosis of mental disorder. Similarly, agency is central, at least in part, because the tradition emerges from clinical set-tings. This raises the question of whether coherence and agency are not so much in the nature of self-narratives as they are the goals of psycho-logical therapies that reconstruct them. In any case, the approach from narrative psychology reminds us that agency is an undeniable fact of social life. Yet, the narrative coherence and consistency that contempo-rary storytellers pursue may be treated as historical phenomenon rather than intransigent fact.

Ethnomethodology: Narration as Self-Presentation

Because sociologists study cultural and social structures, their narrative analyses tend to depict greater cultural and societal determinacy than do those of psychologists. However, human agency and creativity are still important, at least in the American sociological tradition. Erving Goffman (1959), for example, describes actors' near-constant shifts between different roles as they forge presentations of self. Likewise concerned with shifts, though not with assumed roles, ethnomethodologists (e.g., Garfinkel 1967) and conversation analysts (e.g., Sachs 1995) understand talk as involving constant and strategic moves between different, sometimes competing, narratives. Like narrative psychologists, ethnomethodologists are concerned with agency—in this case the active accomplishment of selves (among other things) through symbolic gestures—but they do not search for altogether unified self-narratives. Rather, narratives like other speech acts are local productions; they can only be understood in particular social settings: "they are features of the very scenes which they describe" (Wieder 1977, 4).

D. Lawrence Wieder's (1974) book *Language and Social Reality* is the most important ethnomethodological contribution to criminology thus far. Wieder describes halfway house residents' articulations of the so-called convict code during interviews as a continuous constitutive activity, and the code as a device in conversation. According to Wieder (1974, 175) the narrative is "more a method of moral persuasion and justification than it is a substantive account of an organized way of life." Such artful creativity and the importance of storytelling context are both important insights for narrative criminology.

Cultural Structuralism: The Prewritten Narrative

A narrative is essentially a structure and narrative analysis is a search for that structure in the cultural structural traditions that have emerged in continental Europe. Michael Roemer (1997) argues that every story is over before it begins because we know how it will end. In other words, if characters were altogether free there would be no story. Other approaches similarly emphasize that self-narratives are determined by the social context and probe the structure of the narrative itself. These draw inspiration from Ferdinand de Saussure's (1974) linguistic structuralism, according to which language is a relatively closed and determinist system, and the early writings of Foucault (1970), which described overarching cultural structures as shaping every aspect of society.

In *Discipline and Punish*, Foucault (1977) recounts the history of the penal system as one in which the target of punishment went from the body to the soul, discourses closely connected to institutions became a means of disciplining subjects, and self-narratives were targeted for intervention. Such interventions are launched in the first instance by a full confession to the psychologist, doctor, or rehabilitation officer; these agents police the "right" narrative (see Fox 1999). Whereas Foucauldian studies of narrative scrutinize language use, the emphasis is on structural constraint and domination rather than human agency. Moreover, the emphasis is on the role of narrative for the larger system of meaning, or discourse, and not the particular narrative text. The important insight for narrative criminology is that narratives are part of larger meaning-making structures and that these are embedded in social institutions.

Postmodernism: Narrative as Multidimensional Space

Postmodernism has been one of the most important trends in the human sciences of the last three decades. Postmodernism, while oriented toward the structural level of meaning, emphasizes diversity and fragmentation. Jean-François Lyotard (1984), for example, famously described meta-narratives as increasingly supplanted by an array of "language games" (Wittgenstein 1972), where "questions, requests, assertions and narratives are launched pell-mell into battle" (Lyotard 1984, 17). From a postmodern perspective, a narrative can be described as a multidimensional space where different genres, discourses, and vocabularies merge and clash.

Postmodern thinkers view narratives as drawing on diverse cultural repertoires, representations, and discourses that originate in diverse social contexts. Norman Fairclough (1992, 1995), one of the founders of critical discourse analysis, describes these multiple origins as the interdiscursivity of texts. Derived from Mikhail M. Bakhtin's (1981) notion of intertextuality, this concept describes the process by which a speaker or a text draws on multiple discourses to construct meaning. In this regard Norman Fairclough (1992, 101–102) observes that "texts and utterances are shaped by prior texts that they are 'responding' to, and by subsequent texts that they 'anticipate'" and notes that "utterances . . . are inherently intertextual." Postmodernists see intertextuality and complexity where others see uniformity; thus they endorse multiple interpretations of any one narrative. As Jacques Derrida (1988) points out, when the context of some discourse changes, its meaning also changes. A narrative is never the same from one appearance to another. No essential story is ever told. This hybridity, or fragmentation, can be considered a problem for narrative analysis. It can, for example, be argued that a hybrid or fragmented narrative is a failed narrative. However, these characteristics can be resources. The space left open for interpretation may make a story more effective upon reception (Polletta 2006). Speakers may also take advantage of that quality to achieve goals of, say, acceptance, as an ambiguous narrative is harder to prove wrong. Certainly the hybridity of narratives is more in line with depictions of human agency, of both narrator and interpreter, than is either the determinist language system of structuralism (Saussure 1974) or Labov's (1972) components of the classic narrative.

These four theoretical traditions bring important insights to bear on narrative criminology. Narrative psychology reminds us that a speaker is an agent who seeks coherence, ethnomethodology that speakers use narratives as devices in particular social contexts, cultural structuralism that narration is essentially reproductive, and postmodernism that narratives are often fragmented and hybrid. Where others might see incompatibility, we arrive at the unifying idea that narrative criminologists should understand self-narratives dialectically—as agency conditioned by context (see Bourdieu 1990; Giddens 1984)—and as attempts at coherence that draw on a wide variety of cultural narratives and discourses.

Related Criminological Traditions

With the foregoing lessons in mind, we believe that narrative criminology can add something to the two established criminological traditions closest to our project: constitutive criminology and cultural criminology. Both observe that mainstream, positivistic criminology has neglected the cultural significance and signification of what is called crime. Both thus promise a provocative engagement with the narrative criminological project of explaining harm.

Constitutive Criminology

In part because they question postmodernists' radical break from modernism and order, Stuart Henry and Dragan Milovanovic (1996, 6) call their constitutive criminology postpostmodern. They state that constitutive criminology "directs our attention to the way law, crime and criminal justice are conceptualized and implied as though they are objective realities having real consequences, consequences that we attribute to their claim, but that they do not possess in any intrinsic sense" (96). Because crime is no essential thing, it cannot be said to have causes: "crime is not so much caused as discursively constructed through human processes of which it is one" (170). Elsewhere Henry and Milovanovic do codify crime and therewith a (proximate) cause: crime is "the harm resulting from any attempt to reduce or suppress another's position or potential standing through the use of power that limits the other's ability to make a difference" (13; see also 116).

Constitutive criminology shares common ground with narrative criminology, given their joint emphasis on the discursive aspect of action. Henry and Milovanovic's insights on the dialectics of crime and discourse chart a promising path for a nascent narrative criminology: whereas we have emphasized its primary task as discerning harm-promoting narratives, we might discern harm's effects on narratives. Narrative criminologists sensitive to narrative fluidity should endorse the constitutive criminologists' belief in the human capacity for change. However, in its explicit concern to distinguish causes of crime, narrative criminology stands within the realist tradition of the discipline, which constitutive criminology unequivocally rejects. A compromise might come from the notion that narrativists stand to recognize the fluid and therefore provisional nature of story causes—that is, researchers may treat stories as static for the sake of researching them, but that is not their essential nature.

Cultural Criminology

Cultural criminology, also borne of postmodern thought, has stimulated far more research than constitutive criminology has, which is not surprising given that its mandate is more of an empirical one (see

Ferrell and Hamm 1998; Katz 1988; Presdee 2000). Cultural criminologists specialize in describing particular criminalized or transgressive activities, but with a larger cultural context in view (Ferrell 2007). Jeff Ferrell (1999, 396) calls cultural criminology "an emergent array of perspectives linked by sensitivities to image, meaning, and representation in the study of crime and crime control." A unifying concept is image, with images of crime—especially those disseminated in the mass media—seen as reciprocally shaping offenders' experiences. Hayward and Young (2004, 259) thus state that cultural criminology "attempts to make sense of a world in which the street scripts the screen and the screen scripts the street."

Narrative criminology's explicit emphasis on discourse and its methodological commitment to studying discourse seem to differentiate it from cultural criminology. Consider that Lyng (2004, 360) positions cultural criminology against mainstream criminology's emphasis on "the mind, discursive practices and rationality." And yet, Jack Katz (1988, 302), forefather of cultural criminology, saw the violent offender as playing out a moral tale of one sort or another, mindful of "the narrative possibilities" of violent action. Katz's brand of narrative criminology advances the action as helping the individual to realize the story. The notion that doing speaks is an inversion of the discourse analytic axiom that speaking does or performs (Austin 1962). It is not incompatible with a narrative criminological project, as long as *doing* is not privileged over *speaking*. Clearly, narrative criminology shares an affinity with cultural criminology's view of "crime and the agencies of control as cultural products" (Hayward and Young 2004, 259). Finally, cultural criminology's insistence on the seductions of crime is something narrativists can get behind, by understanding those seductions as mediated by language.

Doing Narrative Criminology

To do narrative criminology is to study "narrative reality," to use Gubrium and Holstein's (2009) expression, by mapping narratives or elements thereof onto patterns of crime. Narrative criminologists can relate narrative forms (e.g., tragedy, comedy) to criminal behavior. They can consider how linguistic moves within self-stories, such as passive versus agentive structures, function to assert license to harm or conversely to deny responsibility for harm. They can study the role of metaphors (Lakoff and Johnson 1980), nominalization (Fairclough 1992), nodal points (Laclau and Mouffe 1985), symbolic boundary drawing (Lamont and Molnár 2002), and floating signifiers (Levi-Strauss 1987) in constructing the excusable harm and the blameworthy victim.

As our review suggests, narrative criminologists may choose to emphasize either narrative creativity or narrative conditioning, unity or fragmentation, depending on their theoretical interests and the available or potential data. Regardless, careful research designs and methodologies are crucial. The questions and prompts one poses, for example, will depend upon whether one is searching for common life stories, story elements of members of a group, or the multiple stories that individuals tell.

Beyond these early choices as to research emphasis, the work of narrative criminology will not be straightforward, practically or politically. Researchers working with transcripts of interviews know that a narrative can be hard to distinguish. Narrative is generally coproduced by the research participant and the researcher, if not during the interview then certainly in the process of analyzing data later. Oftentimes a narrator only hints at a narrative, and the listener—the researcher or someone else—grasps a fuller narrative and its meaning. Narrative is seldom *there* in the classic (e.g., Labovian) form. Analysts can and do use intimations of narrative as texts, perhaps investigating how the narrative was produced collaboratively (e.g., Presser 2004). In this regard, reflexivity and the analyst's disclosure of what she or he calls the narrative and why are crucial. That is to say, one should tell the story of the research.

For researchers accustomed to digging beneath words to locate their "true" meaning, the experience of privileging the story may feel strange. The researcher should forge ahead, even if the story sounds put on, canned, like a press release (Wiersma 1988). As we have argued, for narrative criminology, the fictive character of offenders' narratives poses no problem. The story may be developed and told for strategic purposes, or the storyteller may truly believe it; the narrative criminological proposition is that either way, the story is consequential for teller and others. But do we go too far in our focus on the fictive? Do we pay too little attention to the so-called real world? We think not.

Narrative criminologists do take tangible oppressive structures into consideration. We perceive them as important in their own right and as conditioning discursive processes (Sandberg and Pedersen 2 but we also see them as discursively constructed and aim to stud ways in which they are plotted and given meaning in different social contexts. That is, we investigate hegemonic stories and limitations on creative storytelling due to social context, class, race, gender, and so on. We also recognize that the narratives of oppressed persons can subvert hegemonic understandings of the world (see Ewick and Silbey 1995; Polletta 2006).

A Collective First Step toward Narrative Criminology

In this book fifteen prominent scholars share their work in narrative criminology. They examine the narratives of offenders collected through qualitative interviews, ethnographic fieldwork, or written sources, or write theoretically about research that does so. They scrutinize the structure and meaning of offenders' narratives including plots, metaphors, symbolic boundary drawing, and identities. They also consider how offenders' narratives are linked to and emerge from the narratives and culture of mainstream society or particular subcultures or subsocieties. In each of these works narratives are ways of constructing (or deconstructing) criminal behavior, actually or symbolically. Each of the chapters reveals important insights and elements for the development of a framework of narrative criminology. The result is a collective first step toward establishing the field of narrative criminology.

We hope the book inspires reflection and further research on the role of stories in criminal or harmful behavior. Part I of the book examines stories that construct proper selves. Based on fieldwork in prison, the first two chapters illuminate the moral identities that prisoners strive to achieve narratively. Thomas Ugelvik (chapter 1) examines the stories that male prisoners in Norway tell about violence toward and social marginalization of rapists which allow them to forge righteous selves. Jennifer Fleetwood (chapter 2) looks at female prisoners in Ecuador who see themselves as noncriminal story protagonists caught up in smuggling operations. Jody Miller, Kristin Carbone-Lopez, and Mikh Gunderman (chapter 3) show that imprisoned women draw from gendered narratives to make sense of their shifting involvement with methamphetamine. And Janice Victor and James Waldram (chapter 4) investigate the storied stigma management efforts of men who were released from prison after their participation in sexual offender treatment programs.

Part II relates how stories animate and mobilize or curb harmdoing. Robert Keeton (chapter 5) reveals the impact that religious narratives had in inspiring Indian removal policies and related atrocities in nineteenth-century America. Sveinung Sandberg and Sébastien Tutenges (chapter 6) discuss the similarities between contemporary stories of addiction and bad trips, and ancient folktales and myths, arguing that even tragic drug stories can motivate drug use. Patricia O'Connor (chapter 7) clarifies the discursive devices that drug users and maximum security prisoners use to change their storylines and their lives.

Part III highlights narrative creativity and reflexivity. Fiona Brookman (chapter 8) advances a view of narratives as ever changing and inherently ambiguous, and discusses the theoretical implications of such narrative incoherence. Kester Aspden and Keith Hayward (chapter 9) assess the relationship between cultural and narrative criminology, and offer autoethnographic insight into the reflexive nature of storytelling. Carlo Tognato (chapter 10) illuminates cultural shifts in the shared story of tax evaders in Italian culture and argues that convincing performances of that story are crucial to public acceptance. Finally, to conclude our story of a transformative dialogue of ideas for a transformative criminology, we summarize the insights from each of our contributors and discuss the way forward for narrative criminology.

NOTES

1. Here and throughout the book we use the terms *narrative* and *story* interchangeably, although an alternative view posits the former as more all-encompassing and the latter as more episode-oriented (see Presser 2008).

2. Foucault treats discourse differently than do most linguists, for whom it simply means spoken or written language use (see, e.g., Fairclough 1995).

3. More generally Fairclough (1992, 41–42) describes the distinction between "referential" and "constitutive" views of the relationship between language and reality.

4. One exception is Lonnie Athens's theory of violence, where a self is evoked in making an interpretation. According to Athens (1997, 98–99), "the type of self-image that people hold is intimately connected to both the range and character of the situations that they will interpret as calling for violent action, underscoring that their self-images are congruent rather than incongruent with their interpretations." As such, identities constrain how one defines a situation

among myriad possibilities. Another exception is Messerschmidt's (1993, 1997) structured action theory, where the actor is primarily concerned with self-identification: the situations as the actor interprets them help her or him to enact identities.

REFERENCES

Andrews, Molly, Shelley Day Sclater, Corinne Squire, and Maria Tamboukou. 2004. "Narrative Research." In *Qualitative Research Practice*, edited by Clive Seale, Giampietro Gobo, Jaber F. Gubrium, and David Silverman, 109–124. London: Sage.

Athens, Lonnie. 1997. *Violent Criminal Acts and Actors Revisited*. Urbana: University of Illinois Press.

Atkinson, Paul, and Amanda Coffey. 2003. "Revisiting the Relationship between Participant Observation and Interviewing." In *Postmodern Interviewing*, edited by Jaber F. Gubrium and James A. Holstein, 109–122. London: Sage.

Austin, J. L. 1962. *How to Do Things with Words*. Cambridge, MA: Harvard University Press.

Bakhtin, Mikhail M. 1981. *The Dialogic Imagination*. Austin: University of Texas Press.

Beirne, Piers. 2009. *Confronting Animal Abuse*. Lanham, MD: Rowman and Littlefield.

Berger, Peter, and Luckmann, Thomas. 1967. *The Social Construction of Reality: A Treatise in the Sociology of Knowledge*. New York: Anchor Books.

Bourdieu, Pierre. 1990. *The Logic of Practice*. Stanford, CA: Stanford University Press.

Bruner, Jerome. 1990. *Acts of Meaning*. Cambridge, MA: Harvard University Press.

Chanfrault-Duchet, Marie-Françoise. 2000. "Textualisation of the Self and Gender Identity in the Life-Story." In *Feminism and Autobiography: Texts, Theories, Methods*, edited by Tess Cosslett, Celia Lury, and Penny Summerfield, 60–75. London: Routledge.

Cohn, Carol. 1987. "Sex and Death in the Rational World of Defense Intellectuals." *Signs: Journal of Women in Culture and Society* 12 (4): 687–718.

Cressey, Donald R. 1953. *Other People's Money: A Study in the Social Psychology of Embezzlement*. Glencoe, IL: The Free Press.

Crossley, Michele L. 2000. *Introducing Narrative Psychology: Self, Trauma, and the Construction of Meaning*. Buckingham, UK: Open University Press.

Day, L. Edward, and Margaret Vandiver. 2000. "Criminology and Genocide Studies: Notes on What Might Have Been and What Still Could Be." *Crime, Law and Social Change* 34 (1): 43–59.

Derrida, Jacques. 1988. "Signature, Event, Context." In *Limited Inc*, 1–25. Evanston, IL: Northwestern University Press.

Ellis, Albert. 1973. *Humanistic Psychotherapy*. Secaucus, NJ: Lyle Stuart.

Ewick, Patricia, and Susan S. Silbey. 1995. "Subversive Stories and Hegemonic Tales: Toward a Sociology of Narrative." *Law and Society Review* 29 (2): 197–226.

Fairclough, Norman. 1992. *Discourse and Social Change*. Cambridge, UK: Polity Press.

———. 1995. *Critical Discourse Analysis*. London: Longman Group Limited.

Ferrell, Jeff. 1999. "Cultural Criminology." *Annual Review of Sociology* 25 (1): 395–418.

———. 2007. "For a Ruthless Cultural Criticism of Everything Existing." *Crime, Media, Culture* 3 (1): 91–100.

Ferrell, Jeff, and Mark S. Hamm. 1998. *Ethnography at the Edge: Crime, Deviance, and Field Research.* Boston, MA: Northeastern University Press.

Festinger, Leon. 1957. *A Theory of Cognitive Dissonance.* Stanford, CA: Stanford University Press.

Foucault, Michel. 1970. *The Order of Things.* New York: Pantheon.

———. 1972. *The Archaeology of Knowledge.* New York: Pantheon.

———. 1977. *Discipline and Punish.* New York: Pantheon.

———. 1978. *The History of Sexuality.* Vol. 1. New York: Pantheon.

Fox, Kathryn J. 1999. "Changing Violent Minds: Discursive Correction and Resistance in the Cognitive Treatment of Violent Offenders in Prison." *Social Problems* 46 (1): 88–103.

Garfinkel, Harold. 1956. "Conditions of Successful Degradation Ceremonies." *American Journal of Sociology* 61 (5): 420–424.

———. 1967. *Studies in Ethnomethodology.* Englewood Cliffs, NJ: Prentice Hall.

Giddens, Anthony. 1984. *The Constitution of Society.* Berkeley: University of California Press.

Goffman, Erving. 1959. *The Presentation of Self in Everyday Life.* New York: Doubleday.

Gubrium, Jaber F., and James A. Holstein. 2009. *Analyzing Narrative Reality.* London: Sage.

Hagan, John, and Wenona Rymond-Richmond. 2009. *Darfur and the Crime of Genocide.* New York: Cambridge University Press.

Hankiss, Agnes. 1981. "Ontologies of the Self: On the Mythological Rearranging of One's Life History." In *Biography and Society: The Life History Approach in the Social Sciences,* edited by Daniel Bertaux, 203–209. Beverly Hills, CA: Sage.

Hayward, Keith J., and Jock Young. 2004. "Cultural Criminology: Some Notes on the Script." *Theoretical Criminology* 8 (3): 259–273.

Henry, Stuart, and Dragan Milovanovic. 1996. *Constitutive Criminology: Beyond Postmodernism.* London: Sage.

Huggins, Martha K., Mika Haritos-Fatouros, and Philip G. Zimbardo. 2002. *Violence Workers: Police Torturers and Murderers Reconstruct Brazilian Atrocities.* Berkeley: University of California Press.

Katz, Jack. 1988. *Seductions of Crime: The Moral and Sensual Attractions of Doing Evil.* New York: Basic Books.

Kerby, Anthony Paul. 1991. *Narrative and the Self.* Bloomington: Indiana University Press.

Labov, William. 1972. *Language in the Inner City: Studies in the Black English Vernacular.* Philadelphia: University of Pennsylvania Press.

Labov, William, and Joshua Waletzky. 1967. "Narrative Analysis: Oral Versions of Personal Experience." In *Essays on the Verbal and Visual Arts,* edited by June Helms, 12–44. Seattle: University of Washington Press.

Laclau, Ernesto, and Chantal Mouffe. 1985. *Hegemony and Socialist Strategy. Towards a Radical Democratic Politics.* London: Verso.

Lakoff, George, and Mark Johnson. 1980. *Metaphors We Live By*. Chicago: University of Chicago Press.

Lamont, Michele, and Virag Molnár. 2002. "The Study of Boundaries in the Social Sciences." *Annual Review of Sociology* 28: 167–195.

László, János. 2008. *The Science of Stories. An Introduction to Narrative Psychology*. London: Routledge.

Levi-Strauss, Claude. 1987. *Introduction to Marcel Mauss*. London: Routledge.

Linde, Charlotte. 1993. *Life Stories: The Creation of Coherence*. New York: Oxford University Press.

Lyng, Stephen. 2004. "Crime, Edgework and Corporeal Transaction." *Theoretical Criminology* 8 (3): 359–375.

Lyotard, Jean-Francois. 1984. *The Postmodern Condition: A Report on Knowledge*. Minneapolis, MN: University of Minnesota Press.

Maruna, Shadd. 2001. *Making Good. How Ex-Convicts Reform and Rebuild Their Lives*. Washington, DC: American Psychological Association.

Maruna, Shadd, and Heith Copes. 2005. "Excuses, Excuses: What Have We Learned from Five Decades of Neutralization Research." *Crime and Justice: A Review of Research* 32: 221–320.

Mason, Carol. 2002. *Killing For Life: The Apocalyptic Narrative of Pro-Life Politics*. Ithaca, NY: Cornell University Press.

Matza, David. 1964. *Delinquency and Drift*. New York: Wiley.

McAdams, Dan. P. 1993. *The Stories We Live By: Personal Myths and the Making of the Self*. New York: Guilford.

Messerschmidt, James W. 1993. *Masculinities and Crime: Critique and Reconceptualization of Theory*. Lanham, MD: Rowman and Littlefield.

———. 1997. *Crime as Structured Action: Gender, Race, Class, and Crime in the Making*. Thousand Oaks, CA: Sage.

Mills, C. Wright. 1940. "Situated Actions and Vocabularies of Motive." *American Sociological Review* 5 (6): 904–913.

Mishler, Elliot G. 1986. "The Analysis of Interview-Narratives." In *Narrative Psychology: The Storied Nature of Human Conduct*, edited by Theodore R. Sarbin, 233–255. New York: Praeger.

Polanyi, Livia. 1985. *Telling the American Story: A Structural and Cultural Analysis of Conversational Storytelling*. Norwood, NJ: Ablex.

Polkinghorne, Donald E. 1988. *Narrative Knowing and the Human Sciences*. Albany: State University of New York Press.

Polletta, Francesca. 2006. *It Was Like a Fever: Storytelling in Protest and Politics*. Chicago: University of Chicago Press.

Polletta, Francesca, Pang Ching Bobby Chen, Beth Gharrity Gardner, and Alice Motes. 2011. "The Sociology of Storytelling." *Annual Review of Sociology* 37: 109–130.

Polonoff, David. 1987. "Self-Deception." *Social Research* 54 (1): 45–53.

Presdee, Mike. 2000. *Cultural Criminology and the Carnival of Crime*. London: Routledge.

Presser, Lois. 2004. "Violent Offenders, Moral Selves: Constructing Identities and Accounts in the Research Interview." *Social Problems* 51 (1): 82–101.

———. 2008. *Been a Heavy Life: Stories of Violent Men*. Urbana and Chicago: University of Illinois Press.

———. 2009. "The Narratives of Offenders." *Theoretical Criminology* 13 (2): 177–200.

———. 2012. "Getting on Top through Mass Murder: Narrative, Metaphor, and Violence." *Crime, Media, Culture* 8 (1): 3–21.

Ricoeur, Paul. 1984. *Time and Narrative*. Translated by Kathleen McLaughlin and David Pellauer. Chicago: University of Chicago Press.

Roemer, Michael. 1997. *Telling Stories. Postmodernism and the Invalidation of Traditional Narrative*. Boston, MA: Rowman and Littlefield.

Sacks, Harvey. 1995. *Lectures on Conversation*. Malden, MA: Blackwell.

Sandberg, Sveinung. 2009. "Gangster, Victim, or Both? Street Drug Dealers' Interdiscursive Construction of Sameness and Difference in Self-Presentations." *British Journal of Sociology* 60 (3): 523–542.

———. 2010. "What Can 'Lies' Tell Us About Life? Notes Towards a Framework of Narrative Criminology." *Journal of Criminal Justice Education* 21 (4): 447–465.

———. 2013. "Are Self-Narratives Unified or Fragmented, Strategic or Determined? Reading the Manifesto of A. B. Breivik in Light of Narrative Criminology." *Acta Sociologica* 56 (1): 65–79.

Sandberg, Sveinung, and Willy Pedersen. 2009. *Street Capital. Black Cannabis Dealers in a White Welfare State*. Bristol, UK: Policy Press.

Saussure, Ferdinand de. 1974. *Course in General Linguistic*. London: Fontana.

Smith, Philip. 2005. *Why War? The Cultural Logic of Iraq, the Gulf War, and Suez*. Chicago: University of Chicago Press.

Somers, Margaret R. 1994. "The Narrative Constitution of Identity: A Relational and Network Approach." *Theory and Society* 23 (5): 605–649.

Sternberg, Robert J. 2003. "A Duplex Theory of Hate: Development and Application to Terrorism, Massacres, and Genocide." *Review of General Psychology* 7 (3): 299–328.

Sykes, Gresham M., and David Matza. 1957. "Techniques of Neutralization: A Theory of Delinquency." *American Sociological Review* 22 (December): 664–670.

Vetlesen, Arne Johan. 2005. *Evil and Human Agency: Understanding Collective Evildoing*. Cambridge: Cambridge University Press.

Wieder, D. Lawrence. 1974. *Language and Social Reality: The Case of Telling the Convict Code*. Lanham, MD: University Press of America.

———. 1977. "Ethnomethodology and Ethnosociology." *Mid-American Review of Sociology* 2 (2): 1–18.

Wiersma, Jacquelyn. 1988. "The Press Release: Symbolic Communication in Life History Interviewing." *Journal of Personality* 56 (1): 205–238.

Wittgenstein, Ludwig. 1972. *Philosophical Investigations*. Oxford, UK: Blackwell.

Yochelson, Samuel, and Stanton E. Samenow. 1976. *The Criminal Personality: A Profile for Change*. New York: Jason Aronson.

PART I

Stories Construct Proper Selves

1

The Rapist and the Proper Criminal

The Exclusion of Immoral Others as Narrative Work on the Self

THOMAS UGELVIK

Understood as a moral space, a prison symbolically positions its prisoners as a group of immoral others. Everyday life behind bars has
numerous ways of communicating that most basic of the prison's messages to its prisoners: you are not to be trusted. All forms of interaction
in the institution will be structured by prison officers' professional focus
on the worst case, and their multiple efforts to keep it from becoming
reality. The result is that day in and day out prisoners are reminded of
the fact that being a prisoner is being a member of a group of immoral
people who cannot be trusted. Many prisoners experience this ascribed
group affiliation as an attack on their self-image, and thus as one of the
pains of imprisonment (Sykes 1958). They are frustrated by and often
protest against this institutionalized lack of trust. Brede,[1] a prisoner in
remand (imprisoned pretrial) in Oslo Prison, put it like this: "Is everything we say just lies, then? Is that it, just 'cause we're here in prison, does
that mean we only tell lies?"

Reacting to the unwanted change of moral status imprisonment entails, many prisoners claim that the fact that one has broken a rule does
not mean that one has no rules. This chapter explores one of the strategies prisoners employ to adapt to and assuage this particular pain of
imprisonment. I will analyze how practices of exclusion and hierarchy
building may be interpreted as part of the self's work on itself. More specifically, I will show how narratives about violence against and exclusion
of rapists and sex offenders are used by prisoners to counter the ascribed
stigma of immorality and symbolically reposition themselves as morally
conscious proper criminals. The rapist, a narrative figure common in
prison culture, is used to signify true evil in stark contrast to a narrator

repositioned as a proper criminal with strong moral fiber. A byproduct is an important distinction between two types of crime: the rational (and defendable) crimes of the proper criminals and the immoral horrors perpetrated by so-called rapist monsters.

Appraising the truthfulness of the narratives is not relevant from this perspective (Sandberg 2010); rather, the focus is on exploring the dynamic of a specific kind of exclusion and its consequences, and on showing how such practices are essential for prisoners when they try to make sense of themselves and their own lives. I will not approach prisoners' narratives as records of what really happened, but—following Brookman, Copes, and Hochstetler (2011)—as means of identifying with (subcultural) expectations that arise from prison-specific identity threats. Inspired by narrative criminology (Presser 2004, 2009) and a narrative understanding of self-making (inter alia Ricoeur 1992; Bruner 1997; Harré and Langenhove 1999; Davies and Harré 2001), narratives and accounts may be understood in their performative capacity (following Butler 1993, 1997, 2006). What you *do* and what you *say* you do is clearly not the same, but stories are not just talk. Following a narrative understanding of self-making, narratives are speech acts that performatively reposition the narrator; tales reflect back on the teller.

Thus understood, narratives are central to human existence. By continuously telling and retelling our life stories (in the widest possible understanding of the term), we recreate ourselves as consistent moral actors across settings and over time. An individual constructs continuity and stability through the social construction of culturally acceptable life stories; this process thus connects the individual, the social, and the cultural (Geertz 1973). A chaotic mess of experiences is thus transformed into a (somewhat) coherent and culturally legible narrative.

Context and Research Methodology

Oslo Prison is Norway's largest penitentiary. With a capacity of 392 prisoners, it houses over one tenth of the total national prison population. The all-male facility originally was built on a hillside outside Oslo. Today, it is located in the eastern part of the city center, skirted by a multiethnic residential area. The facility has two major units. The oldest one, a Philadelphia-style penitentiary that opened in 1851, houses prisoners with sentences of up to two years. The newer buildings, which until 1939 accommodated a brewery, are predominantly for prisoners held on remand (imprisoned pretrial). On Norwegian remand wings, you will mostly find prisoners suspected of violent crimes, drug crimes, and sexual offenses.

As part of a larger ethnographic study on power relations and identity work in prison, I collected observation and interview data on two connected wings in the brewery part of the prison over a period of one year (May 2007–May 2008). The majority of the prisoners in this part of Oslo Prisons, between 80 and 90 percent, were on remand. Most of those prisoners, who had received a final verdict, were in the process of being transferred to facilities considered better suited for prisoners with longer sentences. The approximate fifty prisoners (the exact number of occupied cells varied, as a number of cells were undergoing ad hoc renovation) shared a small common area with a large TV set, pool, and Ping-Pong tables as well as a small weight training area. The cells—albeit sparse, gloomy, and somewhat reminiscent of the 1930s rebuilding process—have sanitation facilities and a TV set.

I was given free access to both wings, could come and go as I pleased, and talk to any prisoner I wanted to without going through the officers first. Conversations mainly took place in the small, shared common area or in the privacy of a cell together with one or two prisoners. Like the prisoners, I wore civilian clothes. In addition, I had a visible ID card identifying me as a university employee, a single key on a sturdy chain to unlock the gates between the two wings, and an assault alarm on my belt. Quickly realizing that there are only three reasons for wearing a collared shirt in prison—you are on your way either to court or to a funeral, or you are an officer—I deliberately tried to dress down. As I had no official role in the prison system and no cell keys, I spent most of my time hanging around, drinking coffee, playing pool, and talking with anyone about whatever they wanted to talk about. What Geertz (1998, 69) has called "deep hanging out"—"localized long-term close-in vernacular field research"—worked well as a research strategy in an environment where people have a lot of time on their hands and not a lot to do, although it did provoke a lot of jokes about my seemingly endless break from "real work."

I never took notes while in the presence of prisoners, believing that it might inhibit my participation in the interaction with them. Prisoners in general are suspicious of strangers. A notepad would potentially add to this sentiment and make initial meetings difficult. Instead, I wrote down my observations on the same or the following day, with an effort to reflect meaning, language, tone, and style, as well as the relevant context of the words spoken.

Most of the prisoners I interacted with over the course of my year in Oslo Prison would self-identify as so-called proper criminals, that is, prisoners who have done the kinds of crimes that are validated in the prison culture. Property crimes are accepted, as long as they are on a certain level—stealing shiny sports cars is OK, stealing bicycles is not. Violent crimes are also acceptable, at least when you refrain from hurting those manifestly weaker than you, and you have a good and believable (and rational) reason. Drug crimes may be acceptable, unless you are known to sell drugs to children or you use a lot of drugs yourself. Mindful of the potential ethical problems associated with prison researchers imposing themselves on incarcerated research objects, I deliberately took a passive role when meeting new arrivals. I let participants make a first move by showing an active interest in participating in the study. Prisoners who were known rapists or sex offenders hardly ever did; they often isolated themselves in their cells and declined to participate in the everyday interaction on the wings. The material analyzed here thus reflects only the self-identifying proper criminals' talk about the rapists, not the feelings and thoughts of those individuals labeled as rapists.

Prisoner Hierarchies and Moral Superiority

Prison hierarchies have long been the focus of prison research (e.g., Clemmer 1940; Sykes and Messinger 1960; Jewkes 2002; Crewe 2009; Trammell 2012). Seeing hierarchy building as part of the self's work on itself is not an entirely novel thought: Jewkes (2002, 145), for instance, describes how a "key feature of the prison hierarchy is the need for convicted criminals to feel morally superior to someone." One could extrapolate that this feeling of moral superiority might influence self-image and perception of self-worth—which is the connection I would like to explore: narratives in support of the prisoner hierarchy may result in feelings of moral superiority, which again means that they may be employed as part of a wider process of collective moral sense making and self-making.

Individual and collective identities are the results of ongoing processes in which relations of difference and similarity are established between the individual and the group and designated others (Böss 2011). A moral subject can only have high morals in contrast to immoral others. A moral community is thus constituted in relation both to a shared moral code and to out-groups of immoral others who must be controlled, excluded, or sanctioned. In this perspective, subjectivity is to a certain extent the result of what the subject *is not*, that is, its *constitutive outside*.[2] That which is put on the outside acts as a constitutive border post, constituting the inside. Butler (1993, 72) puts it like this: "The subject is constituted through the force of exclusion and abjection, one which produces a constitutive outside to the subject, an abjected outside, which is, after all, 'inside' the subject as its own founding repudiation."

In his later works, Foucault studied the subject's work on her- or himself with the aim of turning her- or himself into an ethical subject (Foucault 1990a, 1990b; 1992). Becoming an ethical subject is all about different ways of getting to know oneself as an example of an ethical subject in and through practice. According to Foucault, it is a case of moving the well-known Delphic imperative (know thyself) back into its original context of a much broader set of practices of forming and reforming good relations with yourself (Foucault 2005; cf. Flynn 1985). On this practical level, morality is about the ways individuals adapt to and act out a given moral code, and the techniques they employ to tell and retell the stories about themselves as people with morals, whatever that might mean in a given context (Foucault 1997a, 1997b).

Connecting all the dots between these theoretical positions, I will argue that morality narratives about exclusion of immoral others may be reconceptualized as part of what Foucault called the techniques of the self.[3] The specific culturally accepted and validated techniques of the self available may differ extremely between moral systems (Edel and Edel 1959). Confession, self-flagellation, and religious fasting are all examples analyzed by Foucault, but it is quite possible that any kind of act may work, as long as it is possible to infuse it with moral significance and relate it to a specific moral code. The important thing is that every moral action, qua moral action, will always tell a story about how the specific person acting in a certain way fits hand in glove with the moral system articulated. At the same time, the moral acts of moral subjects reconstitute the entire moral system as a social fact. Such an analysis of moral self-making in practice could concentrate on how people narratively create or talk themselves into being ethically conscious, if not ethically superior, people in a given socio-cultural context, and how nonconformist behavior is understood, explained, and possibly sanctioned. According to Foucault, ethical narratives are fundamentally social and relational. They are social because their purpose is to connect a single act to a larger set of conventions, something which must be social in nature, and they are relational because the ethical practices presuppose an other to give the acts the meaning of ethical acts—confession is not worth much as technology of the self unless someone listens and has the power to absolve. Put differently, the government of self by the self is necessarily articulated in the self's relationship with others (Foucault 1997a).

The gist of this argument, then, is that the stories people tell are tools used in the everyday work on the self they engage in as part of their encounters with other people. I will show how one important narrative figure frequently encountered in a prison context, the rapist, is used as symbolic boundary marker in the ethical self-work of prisoners who thereby can recreate themselves as proper criminals: straight-up, trustworthy professionals, miles away from the honorless evil rapist of prison culture. The narrative articulation of an ethical code thus works as a dividing practice (Foucault 2000a); it is constitutive of the difference between good and bad people. I will now turn to one facet of this process as it is played out in Oslo Prison—the narrative exclusion of rapists and sex offenders.

Narratives about the Rapist and the Proper Criminal

In Oslo Prison, it was hard to find the sort of (more or less) clear-cut prisoner hierarchies described by others (e.g., Clemmer 1940; Sykes 1958). Instead, several competing hierarchies seemed to be operating simultaneously. Drug traffickers argued that they are smart and savvy businessmen far superior to the simple and brutal violent offenders, while the violent offenders claimed that drug traffickers are cynical profiteers lacking a sense of honor. Who occupied the bottom tier of the different hierarchies was indisputable, however. Even below the universally shunned figure of the snitch, one could always find the rapist or sex offender.

In narratives about rapists and sex offenders, the prisoner who is an ethical other marks a fundamental and radical difference from the narrator. Rapists hurt people who are weaker than they are, an act generally frowned upon both behind prison walls as well as in society in general; and to make matters worse, they hurt women. The innocent, defenseless woman is a necessary implicit constitutive figure when the category of the rapist is talked into being in prison. In such narratives, regular or proper prisoners are driven by their search for easy profit; they are professionals wanting money. This goes for both the proper criminal drug traffickers and violent offenders. The rapist, on the other hand, is evil, perverse, sick, and insane—a monster that the prisoner society, like the society outside, needs to identify and exclude. In contrast to this figure, professional/proper criminal prisoners can position themselves not far from regular wageworkers, at least as far as motivational structures and ethics are concerned.

The resulting discursive division between proper criminals and perverts is of central importance in the prisoners' ethical self-work. The practices of exclusion are many. For example, I'm hanging out in the common area with Tom. A young prisoner on the gallery above us points a finger at a third prisoner, aiming it like he would a pistol. He "shoots" at him with the imaginary weapon, the illusion bolstered by an accompanying loud sound resembling a gunshot. Tom talks me through what we just observed:

> TOM: That guy [the one who got "shot"], you know, he's one of those rapists. Damn, he took a seventeen-year-old girl and raped her for hours. Fuck! But he got what he deserved, too; an Albanian guy in here, he has the body mass of me and you combined, took him out. One blow, that was it. He stayed down. Another guy, he was put in the washing machine. They have these big machines down at the laundry. They just threw him inside and started the cycle.

THOMAS: What? But that could kill him?

TOM: Heh, heh, that's right, that could kill you, no doubt, it gets hot as hell. And it takes a few minutes to stop the machine once it's started. And you can't open the door right away, there's a time stop. But he made it that time.

Violence narratives are generally common among prisoners. In my data material, they are often exchanged in friendly contests of one-upmanship. These stories were so common and were told so loudly that it must have been very difficult for those who were known rapists to ignore them. Such stories may thus also work as poorly veiled threats. Loudly banging on a closed cell door every time you walk past it was another common practice aimed at known rapists. It serves as a sort of signal, a form of communication telling the person that he must not forget that "we know what you have done."

Revenge on behalf of the victims is seen not only as a legitimate action but also as the moral thing to do. For those prisoners unfortunate enough to have to live with the rapist brand, this has tangible consequences in everyday life. Not that beating up rapists is a usual pastime; in fact, such violence is relatively rare in Norwegian prisons (Hanoa 2008). However, this does not remove any symbolic weight from the commonplace exchange of such violence narratives between ethically self-positioning proper criminals. There is an important difference between discourse and practice here: beating up rapists is not the same as talking about doing it. But talking about it is not just talk. The imaginary violence made legitimate in the culture among prisoners is fundamental to prisoners' creation of an ethical community:

From the open cell door one can hear Tom's disgruntled sounds. He has been assigned the work of readying the empty cell for its next inhabitant. . . . A group of prisoners in the middle of their afternoon workout congregate outside the door to keep Tom company as he does the cleaning.

ERIK: So the rapist has finally moved? Fuck, what a relief! We can't have people like that here. It's fucking sickening!

NAVEED: No, fuck, that's so true. I've remained calm, I didn't want to sabotage my own case, you know, but once I have a final verdict . . .

ERIK: I agree! If someone like that comes to the wing, we'll just [demonstrates a hard elbow punch in his hand with a loud sound].

They're both grinning; both are hyped up by the workout. The sweat is running, they are together, part of a community of people who would like to hurt the sick rapists. Tom nods inside the cell. Living with someone like that on the wing is thankfully a thing of the past. It's been hard. Outside, the conversation develops into a friendly fight. Erik and Naveed are in a good mood, and high kicks and playful ninja sounds typical of Hong Kong movies fill the air.

Proper criminals come together and become a community of proper criminals through the exchange of narratives about what they see as righteous violence. But the exclusion of rapists also has other forms. Rapists are excluded from most types of regular everyday interaction with proper criminals. The following excerpt from my field diary is illustrative of this pattern:

I'm giving the pool table another go. And I'm losing as always. The winner stands at the table, so I walk over to the guys in the sofa. They haven't been following the game. "Next," I tell them. Morten is up. "No," he answers, "I won't play with that guy." He looks in the opposite direction, they all do. The winner just stands there with the pool cue in his hand, without a willing opponent. They're not interested. One does not play pool with a rapist, unless one is a clueless researcher, that is. He hangs around a little longer, smiling, but unsure of the situation, before he lays down the cue and concedes the table. After a couple of minutes, two of the other prisoners from the sofa have started a new game. The rapist is alone in his cell.

This kind of social exclusion is part of the normal, everyday life on the wings. Rapists are not accepted as part of the community of like-minded proper criminals doing time together. One certainly does not engage in any sort of game or other activity with such immoral scum.

The prison and its officers cannot explicitly condone this exclusion, even though the officers are aware of what is going on. One example from the data gathered is particularly illuminating. The prison education department had arranged for a group of prisoners, one representing each class, to come together to discuss school-related issues. Each class has chosen its own representative. According to most prisoners, one class chose poorly. One of the other representatives went to both school and prison management to try to argue for a change in representation:

> PRISONER: In the first group meeting, that rapist guy downstairs turned up, the guy from Somalia, like it was the most natural thing in the world. But nobody wanted to have anything to do with him. Which makes cooperation a bit difficult. They should probably choose another representative.
>
> TEACHER: Oh, was that it? I thought the problem was just about language?
>
> PRISONER: Well, that too, he hardly speaks any Norwegian. But it was first and foremost about him being a rapist, he went to court the day before and got six years for rape, and then he just shows up in the group meeting like nothing happened? That doesn't fly.
>
> SCHOOL MANAGEMENT REPRESENTATIVE: That doesn't work, we can't all of a sudden take something like that into account, who has done that sort of thing, that's not possible.
>
> PRISON MANAGEMENT REPRESENTATIVE: No, we can't worry about something like that. To us, you are all the same, that sort of thing is irrelevant. We can't take things like that into account.

Later, I talked to the prisoner in the privacy of his cell. He was frustrated and angry not only because he had to continue to associate with the Somali rapist, but also because both managers refused to acknowledge the obvious moral difference between rapists and proper criminals like himself: "It's just stupid, you know? Nobody wants to have anything to do with him. We found out what he has done, that he got six years the day before, and then he just sits there, smiling. No one wants to talk with him, we all sat there with our backs turned. They say we are all the same, yeah, well, well, that's fine. The hell we are! And that makes it nine versus one in the group. Do you think that's a good idea?" When management tells the prisoners they are all equal, in moral terms it tells them they are *equally bad*. The prisoners who see themselves as proper criminals are put, against their will, into the same uncomfortable box as deviant and perverted individuals.

Toward the end of my fieldwork, something happened that put the division between rapists and proper criminals on its keenest edge. Through courtroom newspaper accounts, the prisoners discovered that one among them in reality was a rapist. The prisoner in question had told everyone that he was put on remand for his role in a "completely ordinary" episode of drunken violence—an act of a proper criminal (albeit a rather stupid one). But when the court date arrived, his story was challenged by the newspaper reports. The courtroom reporters tried to maintain his anonymity as best they could, but their articles provided more than enough information for the prisoner collective to put two and two together. All of a sudden, the disclosure was all anybody talked about. One prisoner, Flamur, put it this way:

It's the worst, the most fucked up, you know, that he has said something else all this time, that he has been taken in like one of the guys. He seemed like a nice enough bloke, but fuck, what a pig, a bastard like that, but he will get what's coming to him, this will explode, mark my words. We are all pissed off at him, [prisoner X] is really pissed off, he went to school with him in the same class, they talked, you know. Of course, we wondered about the whole thing, we figured something was wrong, you know, just broken up a fight and wiped up some blood, and up for six years? Something didn't quite add up.

Later, I talked with the former classmate of the rapist in disguise:

I hate being tricked like that! It would have been a different story if he had told us right away, so that we could keep our distance, but now, we became attached to him. I thought he was a good guy, with a good sense of humor, and then he turned out to be the lowest of the low. I hate violence, but sometimes it's necessary in my line of work, you know. But it's another guy, always a man and someone who's part of the same life. And when it happens, it's necessary; I get no joy from it, quite the opposite, it's just sometimes necessary for people in my business. But women and children who are weaker than you? Pedophiles and rapists should be in a separate wing, and they should stay there for a long time. A really long time. We can't hurt him physically now, not in here; the officers are watching him. But I'm going to hurt him in other ways. Fuck, he should be so embarrassed of himself, he should just crawl underneath his bed and disappear. I want him to think, not forget, not think that he's all that. I'm going to make sure that he remembers what he's done. Fucking, fucking rapist! I get physically sick almost, just talking about him.

The worst thing for the prisoners was that they were tricked into including a rapist in the community of proper criminal equals. Being associated that closely with rapists is painful. It is as if they are afraid that the rapists might be morally contagious (Cohen and Taylor 1981; Goffman 1963). The maximum distance had to be produced between the narrator and these "evil perverts."

Prisoners as Ethical Subjects

In *Discipline and Punish*, Foucault (1995) describes the parallel development of the prison as a modern institution and discipline as a form of power specific to modernity. The prison is described as a factory producing self-disciplining subjects who are not only micro-managed through various disciplinary techniques, but constituted as subjects precisely through being made the objects of the disciplinary machine in this particular way.

Here, Foucault's debt to his old teacher Althusser is easy to spot. One of Althusser's contributions to the social science vocabulary comes from his take on that fundamental problem of all social science: How should one think of the relationship between individuals and the social structure? Or, in the Marxist vocabulary of Althusser, how does ideology actually enter into and shape people? His answer is that ideology calls out to or *interpellates* us, and we answer it, and are positioned as subjects of ideology in the process. In Althusser's (1971) original discussion of the term *interpellation*, he describes a meeting between a police officer and a suspect in the street. The police officer recognizes the man, follows him, and calls out to him to make him stop. The man immediately understands that the call is meant for him. He turns and faces the officer, thereby acknowledging his position as a subject interpellated by state power, simultaneously positioning the police officer as a representative of the state. For Althusser, this is an example of how ideology is reproduced through forms of everyday interaction where individuals are positioned as different kinds of state subjects.

When it comes to the practical particulars of becoming a subject of state power, however, Althusser's account is a bit unclear. He has been criticized for not giving the individual turning around much say in the matter (Butler 1995; McNay 2000; Laclau and Mouffe 2001). Likewise, the Foucault of *Discipline and Punish* has been read as making his imprisoned subjects of discipline only a passive effect of power, lacking any possibility for agency. Critics have claimed that real prisons and real prisoners are not like that (e.g., Alford 2000). Whether this is an entirely fair critique is debatable.[4] Nevertheless, it was a form of critique he seemingly took seriously in his later works. The subject of the later Foucault is also a power effect, but not in the purely negative or passive manner of (some critical readings of) *Discipline and Punish*. In the later works, Foucault's subject actively constitutes her- or himself through engaging with and reacting to different technologies of power. The subject of discipline in *Discipline and Punish* could be reformulated in such a perspective as being interpellated by the disciplinary machine as a docile object of the panoptic gaze, a form of power, which nevertheless must play itself out on the practical level in a local setting with active subjects able to adapt to and resist the interpellation attempt.

In Butler's (1995, 1997) reinterpretation of Althusser's theory, she places this possibility for agency, adaptation, and resistance at center stage. Returning to the example of the man and the police officer in the street, Butler discusses the self-evident acceptance and the automatic result in Althusser's original. The subject's choice between situated alternatives becomes central for Butler. It is all the choices one makes when confronted by multiple and diverging interpellative calls, which are constitutive for the subject. What she calls the sovereign voice of the law does not in any simple way determine the individual subject producing an answer:

> He [Althusser] does not consider the range of disobedience that such an interpellating law might produce. The law might not only be refused, but it might also be ruptured, forced into a rearticulation that calls into question the monotheistic force of its own unilateral operation. Where the uniformity of the subject is expected, where the behavioural conformity of the subject is commanded, there might be produced the refusal of the law in the form of the parodic inhabiting of conformity that subtly calls

into question the legitimacy of the command, a repetition of the law into hyperbole, a rearticulation of the law against the authority of the one who delivers it. (Butler 1993, 122–23)

In the example, the man turned and faced the law, making himself into a state subject. The question is whether this was his only option. In Butler's use of the interpellation concept, the situation where individuals and forms of power meet and subjects are produced is complex and dialogical, not deterministic. The individual's choice between available positions connected to alternative interpellation attempts and the different possible ways of articulating such positions, or perhaps resisting them altogether, open up, for many, different kinds of subjects as possible results. An advantage of Butler's version is that it acknowledges the constitutive force of the social environment, but keeps a space open for individual agency, choice, and variation. I have shown how the ascribed status may be painful for prisoners interpellated as immoral others. As Butler says of interpellation attempts in general, however, this is only a place to start. The prisoners engage with the interpellative voices; they adapt to them and narratively recreate them in ways that open new and less painful subject positions in the process.

Morality is part of the social glue of a community (Edel and Edel 1959); it is about the continuous renewal of the solidarity between members of moral communities through the exclusion of immoral others.[5] The self-work described in this chapter may be seen as intimately tied to a particular context, namely that of a specific contemporary Norwegian prison. The narratives provided here make sense in a prison environment. They can therefore be used to say something (but not everything) about that context. The narratives and practices described here are not exclusive to prison environments, however. They can also be found outside the prison walls. But I argue that they are shaped in specific ways by being played out inside a prison, understood as a kind of moral space that tags inhabitants as unethical and immoral people.

Conclusion

What can the practices and narratives of exclusion tell us, then, about the prison context in which they are put to work? If the techniques of the self are situational, what is it about the prison as a moral space that validates some accounts and not others? The prison, as an administrative system, will see the prisoner as part of a group of prisoners who are equal and of the same category. The officer's use of cell numbers to refer to prisoners is one of many examples of how prisoners are reduced to numbers in a series of similar units. On one hand, prisoners mostly agree that they are equals. The need for in-group solidarity makes the construction of a collective of proper criminals necessary. In a prison, the perpetual conflict (Sparks et al. 1996; Lindberg 2005) between prisoners and prison officers makes the questions of group identity and in-group loyalty particularly significant. Prisoners and officers alike strive to keep up a united front vis-à-vis the opposite group. On the other hand, the problem for prisoners is the added normative value: When all prisoners are equal, in effect, they all are *equally bad*. Prisoners are, qua prisoners, positioned at or near the bottom end of the collective moral hierarchy of the society outside the prison walls (Cohen and Taylor 1981). In prison, then, individuals' work on their selves must be aimed at resolving one of the fundamental problems of the prison experience: namely that of being positioned as an immoral other by the society outside. From the perspective of that society, the prison is a place where, if you wear an officer's uniform, you are one of the good guys. If you do not, you are one of the bad guys. From this perspective, the prisoner status is a problem or challenge the imprisoned must try to meet. The kind of narrative work on the self described in this chapter is one way of accomplishing this.

Penal law thus works as a dividing practice drawing a line between lawbreakers and law-abiding citizens. A derogatory label is attached to the lawbreaker. If the mark of bad morals is already stamped on your forehead, if you are already known as part of society's most immoral minority, narratively reconstructing someone else as the *real* bad guy may be understood as a technique of the self. Much of the penal research literature focuses on the specific aspects of the prison hierarchy and the convict code. Being put in a jail entails at least to some degree a loss of self (Sykes 1958), a process of mortification (Goffman 1961) leaving individuals struggling to find their bearings in this new environment. No wonder reconstructing an identity in line with the prisoner code is a common preoccupation. This is not done in a vacuum; it is a form of work that must be done in accordance with the culture already present in the relevant arena. Prisoners take this challenge and reconstruct themselves as people with high moral standards. Morality, then, is not only about what is right or wrong. For Foucault, the question of ethics is always (also) an existential one. The fundamental moral question may be reconceptualized as who and what kind of (moral) person you would like to make yourself into, and who and what kinds of persons (constitutive immoral others) do you have to exclude to get there.

The ascribed stigma associated with being one of society's immoral others is a challenge that must be met, a form of powerful objectification to be resisted. Prisoners employ a variety of distinguishing techniques to reconstruct themselves as unique individuals when faced with the totalizing system. One effective measure is to articulate a difference between different kinds of prisoners based on morality. This narrative resistance amounts to the dismantling of the prison-made discursive connection: As one of the prisoners quoted in this chapter put it: "They say we are all the same. . . . The hell we are!" The ethical self-work, then, may be seen as a form of resistance, not directed at the prison as a social technology as such nor the prison guards, but at the results of the prison experience on the level of subjectification (Foucault 2000b). The prison context thus creates narratives that fortify the moral distinction between the proper criminal and the rapist. This distinction may instigate and promote violence, both on the local level of the prison wing in question—the violence fantasies may have to be acted out at some point—and more indirectly, because these narratives may serve to legitimize, from the prisoner's point of view, more rational and acceptable forms of violence as part of the proper criminal identity. Again, stories are not always "just talk"—narratives like the ones detailed in this chapter may promote harmful actions in the future.

NOTES

1. Pseudonyms are used throughout. I have tried to keep a sense of the ethnic origin of the prisoners through choice of names. Text in italics is taken from field diaries. Unless otherwise noted, such excerpts are translated from the Norwegian by the author.

2. This has been a central theme in poststructuralist analyses (inter alia Derrida 1981, 1988; Norton 1988; Laclau and Mouffe 2001; Søndergaard 2002; Butler 2006).

3. Defined as "the procedures, which no doubt exists in every civilization, suggested or prescribed to individuals in order to determine their identity, maintain it, or

transform it in terms of a certain number of ends, through relations of self-mastery or self-knowledge" (Foucault 1988, 88).

4. "If I had wanted to describe 'real life' in the prisons, I indeed wouldn't have gone to Bentham. But the fact that this real life isn't the same thing as the theoreticians' schemes doesn't entail that these schemes are therefore utopian, imaginary and so on. One could only think this if one had a very impoverished notion of the real. . . . It is absolutely true that criminals stubbornly resisted the new disciplinary mechanism in the prison; it is absolutely correct that the actual functioning of the prisons, in the inherited buildings where they were established and with the governors and guards who administered them, was a witches' brew compared to the beautiful Benthamite machine" (Foucault 2000a, 232–33).

5. This point is in fact widely recognized, not just in Foucauldian or poststructuralist scholarship. In his classic study of the society of captives, for instance, Sykes (1958) describes the strict code among inmates and the exclusion of nonconformers as a normative device for the production of group solidarity.

REFERENCES

Althusser, Louis. 1971. *Lenin and Philosophy, and Other Essays*. London: New Left Books.

Böss, Michael. 2011. "Stories of Peoplehood: An Approach to the Study of Identity, Memory, and Historiography." In *Narrating Peoplehood Amidst Diversity: Historical and Theoretical Perspectives*, edited by M Böss, 11–24. Århus: Aarhus University Press.

Brookman, Fiona, Heith Copes, and Andy Hochstetler. 2011. "Street Codes as Formula Stories: How Inmates Recount Violence." *Journal of Contemporary Ethnography* 40 (4): 397–424.

Bruner, Jerome. 1997. "A Narrative Model of Self-Construction." *Annals of the New York Academy of Sciences* 818 (June): 145–161.

Butler, Judith. 1993. *Bodies That Matter: On the Discursive Limits of "Sex."* New York: Routledge.

———. 1995. "Conscience Doth Make Subjects of Us All." *Yale French Studies* 88: 6–26.

———. 2006. *Gender Trouble: Feminism and the Subversion of Identity*. New York: Routledge.

Clemmer, Donald. 1940. *The Prison Community*. New York: Holt, Rinehart, and Winston.

Cohen, Stanley, and Laurie Taylor. 1981. *Psychological Survival: The Experience of Long-Term Imprisonment*. Harmondsworth, UK: Penguin.

Crewe, Ben. 2009. *The Prisoner Society: Power, Adaptation, and Social Life in an English Prison*. Oxford: Oxford University Press.

Davies, Bronwyn, and Rom Harré. 2001. "Positioning: The Discursive Production of Selves." In *Discourse Theory and Practice: A Reader*, edited by M. Wetherell, S. Taylor, and S. J. Yates, 261–271. London, Thousand Oaks, New Delhi: Sage.

Derrida, Jacques. 1981. *Positions*. Chicago: University of Chicago Press.

———. 1988. *Limited Inc*. Evanston, IL: Northwestern University Press.

Edel, May, and Abraham Edel. 1959. *Anthropology and Ethics*. Springfield, IL: Charles C. Thomas.

Flynn, Thomas R. 1985. "Truth and Subjectivation in the Later Foucault." *Journal of Philosophy* 82 (10): 531–540.

Foucault, Michel. 1988. "The Ethic of Care for the Self as a Practice of Freedom: An Interview with Michel Foucault on January 20, 1984." In *The Final Foucault*, edited by J. Bernauer and D. Rasmussen, 1–20. Cambridge, MA: MIT Press.

———. 1990a. *The Will to Knowledge: The History of Sexuality*. Vol. 1. London: Penguin.

———. 1990b. *The Care of the Self: The History of Sexuality*. Vol. 3. London: Penguin.

———. 1992. *The Use of Pleasures: The History of Sexuality*. Vol. 2. London: Penguin.

———. 1995. *Discipline and Punish: The Birth of the Prison*. New York: Vintage Books.

———. 1997a. "Subjectivity and Truth." In *Ethics, Subjectivity and Truth: Essential Works of Foucault 1954–1984*, edited by P. Rabinow, 87–92. New York: The New Press.

———. 1997b. "Technologies of the Self." In *Ethics, Subjectivity and Truth: Essential Works of Foucault 1954–1984*, edited by P. Rabinow, 223–252. New York: The New Press.

———. 2000a. "Questions of Method." In *Power: Essential Works of Foucault 1954–1984*, vol. 3, edited by J. D. Faubion, 223–238. New York: The New Press.

———. 2000b. "The Subject and Power." In *Power: Essential Works of Foucault 1954–1984*, edited by J. D. Faubion, 326–348. New York: The New Press.

———. 2005. *The Hermeneutics of the Subject: Lectures at the Collège De France 1981–1982*. New York: Picador.

Geertz, Clifford. 1973. *The Interpretation of Cultures*. New York: Basic Books.

———. 1998. "Deep Hanging Out." *New York Review of Books* 45 (October 22): 69.

Goffman, Erving. 1961. *Asylums: Essays on the Social Situation of Mental Patients and Other Inmates*. Harmondsworth, UK: Penguin.

Harré, Rom, and Luk van Langenhove. 1999. *Positioning Theory: Moral Contexts of Intentional Action*. Oxford: Blackwell.

Jewkes, Yvonne. 2002. *Captive Audience: Media, Masculinity and Power in Prisons*. Cullompton, UK: Willan.

Laclau, Ernesto, and Chantal Mouffe. 2001. *Hegemony and Socialist Strategy: Towards a Radical Democratic Politics*. London: Verso.

Lindberg, Odd. 2005. "Prison Cultures and Social Representations: The Case of Hinseberg, a Women's Prison in Sweden." *International Journal of Prisoner Health* 1 (2–4): 143–161.

McNay, Lois. 2000. *Gender and Agency: Reconfiguring the Subject in Feminist and Social Theory*. Cambridge, UK: Polity Press.

Norton, Anne. 1988. *Reflections on Political Identity*. Baltimore, MD: Johns Hopkins University Press.

Presser, Lois. 2004. "Violent Offenders, Moral Selves: Constructing Identities and Accounts in the Research Interview." *Social Problems* 51 (1): 82–101.

———. 2009. "The Narratives of Offenders." *Theoretical Criminology* 13 (2): 177–200.

Ricoeur, Paul. 1992. *Oneself as Another*. Chicago: University of Chicago Press.

Sandberg, Sveinung. 2010. "What Can 'Lies' Tell Us About Life? Notes towards a Framework of Narrative Criminology." *Journal of Criminal Justice Education* 21 (1): 447–465.

Sparks, Richard, A. E. Bottoms, and Will Hay. 1996. *Prisons and the Problem of Order*. Oxford, New York: Clarendon Press.

Sykes, Gresham M. 1958. *The Society of Captives: A Study of a Maximum Security Prison*. Princeton, NJ: Princeton University Press.

Sykes, Gresham M., and Sheldon L. Messinger. 1960. "The Inmate Social System." In *Theoretical Studies in Social Organization of the Prison*, edited by R. A. Cloward et al., 5–19. New York: The Social Science Research Council.

Søndergaard, Dorte Marie. 2002. "Poststructuralist Approaches to Empirical Analysis." *Qualitative Studies in Education* 15 (2): 187–204.

Trammell, Rebecca. 2012. *Enforcing the Convict Code: Violence and Prison Culture*. Boulder, CO: Lynne Rienner.

2

In Search of Respectability

Narrative Practice in a Women's Prison in Quito, Ecuador

JENNIFER FLEETWOOD

Rather than approach offenders' narratives as a record of events, narrative criminologists see talk as a form of social action (Presser 2009; Sandberg 2010, 2011). Building on Sykes and Matza's techniques of neutralization, research in this vein has mainly explored narrative in the construction of deviant or desisting identity (Maruna and Copes 2005; see also Copes et al. 2008; Sandberg 2011; Topalli 2005). Although important developments have been made, women offenders' narratives have been somewhat absent.[1] They arguably warrant special consideration: women's offending is less common, their offending careers are shorter, and they are less likely to have co-offenders than do their male counterparts (Gelsthorpe 2004). Furthermore, there is a lack of mainstream or subcultural norms that might support female offending (Lloyd 1995; Steffensmeier and Allen 1996).

This chapter explores why, when, and how women offenders construct narratives about themselves, and demonstrates the significance of gender for narrative practice.[2] Drawing on ethnographic observations and interviews with women imprisoned in Ecuador for drug trafficking offenses, I will connect geopolitics and gender politics with women's narrative practice as a way of exploring how, when, and why women construct accounts of themselves as offenders. I show that women's narratives about being a drug mule were a response to misrecognition and institutional demands that they give an account of themselves. I also explore the significance of speaking, and draw attention to the importance of silence. In doing so, I draw attention to wider questions about the gendered nature of crime narratives and suggest new directions for research at the intersections of feminist criminology and narrative analysis, especially around talk, gender, and agency.[3]

Narrative and Feminist Perspectives in Criminology

Feminist and narrative modes of research are premised on similar ontological assumptions. While narrative criminology puts offenders' accounts squarely in focus, feminist epistemologies value listening to women, situating them as subjects rather than objects of knowledge (Comack 1999). Nonetheless, research on women and crime has yet to employ a narrative approach (Presser 2012, 6). Arguably, narrative analysis may be of particular significance since it offers new ways of tackling structure/agency dualities that have characterized research on female offending (Burgess-Proctor 2006; Maher 1997). Narrative analysis may also be particularly useful for bridging divisions between "women of discourse" and "real women" outlined by Daly (2006).

Narrative theorists contend that experience is always known and interpreted through narratives that are made available according to the actor's social structural position (Presser 2009). Individuals act on the basis of culturally familiar stories in which they are the imagined protagonists. Furthermore, the offender's subject position (i.e., subject or agent) is constituted in and through narratives (McNay 2000; Presser 2009, 178–179). However, it is also important to understand the contexts in which narratives are constructed and the social functions narratives serve and to comprehend how some narratives may be supported more than others (Sandberg 2010, 2011; see also Wright Mills 1940). Gubrium and Holstein (1998, 164) refer to this as "narrative practice." They argue that analyzing why, when, and how narratives are constructed "allows us to see the storytelling process as both actively constructive and locally constrained." Furthermore, narratives are oriented to local structures of meaning that determine what kinds of narratives can be heard, and who is listened to (ibid.).

Social class, gender, and race make available particular discourses, and material circumstances limit what discourses can be told credibly (Sandberg and Pederson 2009; Rosenwald 1992). Sandberg (2009) links habitus and available narratives. The habitus is generative (as the embodiment of social structures, capitals, etc.) but does not simply determine behavior as individuals always have access to a limited number of possibilities (Bourdieu 1977). For McNay (1999, 2004), gender is embedded in and produced by the habitus. Therefore gender is not the passive enactment of embedded social structures in a deterministic way but an active, ongoing process (see also Krais 2006). Similarly poststructuralist (and postmodern) feminist linguists have been influenced by West and Zimmerman's (1987) claims that gender is a situated accomplishment, and contend that gender is accomplished in and through speech rather than preceding it (Weatherall 2002). The idea of "doing gender" prompted important theoretical shifts in feminist criminology. According to Messerschmidt (1993, 27) men can "do" crime as a way to accomplish masculinity since "the dividing line between what is masculine and what is criminal is at times a thin one." Presser (2009, 2012) found that violent men sought to construct heroic, masculine identities through their self-narratives. Men's talk about crime is arguably a situated accomplishment of hegemonic masculinity based on "situated normative beliefs" (Miller 2002, 434). Thus, male offenders may accomplish masculinity through talking about crime (Presser 2008).

Women have a different relationship to offending than men since "crime is almost always stigmatised for females" (Lloyd 1995; Steffensmeier and Allen 1996, 476). This asymmetrical positioning in relation to crime suggests that women may have difficulty employing discourses about crime to "accomplish" female gender through talk about crime. Indeed, some aspects of female deviance may not be voiced at all; Lisa Maher (1997), for example, found that sex-for-crack exchanges were surrounded by a cultural silence. Whilst gender may not always be the most significant social structure, it is arguably omnipresent (West and Zimmerman 1987). Gender does not exist alone but is always coconstituted by other social structures. In other words, individuals are situated at the intersections of multiple social structures (such as age, class, ethnicity, and nation), which offer multiple narrative possibilities for action (Miller 2002; Sewell 1992). These narrative possibilities also offer different subject positions (McNay 2000). However, as Byrne (2003, 37) notes: "the creation of subject-positions is not a free or voluntaristic process—it is produced through accessing available and material and discursive resources."

El Inca Prison

The women's prison in Quito, Ecuador—known as El Inca—was profoundly shaped by drug war politics at the time of my fieldwork

(2003–2007). In 2002 Ecuador signed a bilateral agreement in which the United States required a 10 percent increase in the number of people arrested for drug offenses (Pontón and Torres 2007). The result of this policy was a sharp rise in arrests for drug trafficking, although in reality users, dealers, and smugglers were all sanctioned under one drug law (Edwards 2003). The effects of this policy were especially evident in the women's prison: 75 percent of women in prison were serving sentences for drug offenses, compared to 33 percent of incarcerated men (Dirección Nacional de Rehabilitación Social 2005).[4] Reflecting the international nature of the trade, 23 percent of the female prison population were foreign nationals (Edwards 2011, 56).[5] Sentences for drug trafficking were the highest in the continent and were on a par with serious, violent offenses (Edwards 2003). Before 2002 prisoners were released automatically at the midpoint of their sentence, but the abolition of this policy effectively doubled sentences overnight (Pontón and Torres 2007). The sheer number of people arrested stretched the capacity of the courts to breaking point. Inmates often waited over a year (and sometimes up to three) to go to trial (Aguirre 2007).[6] This wait was unconstitutionally long. Furthermore the drug law was incompatible with the Ecuadorian constitution (Edwards 2003, 2011).

The impact of the drug war on El Inca was profound. In the space of a few short years, the prison became overcrowded with drug offenders, many of whom were waiting a very long time for trial. Almost everything was in short supply including beds, food, space, meaningful activity, and medical treatment (Fleetwood and Torres 2011; Pontón 2009; Torres 2008). The United Nations Minimum Rules for the Treatment of Prisoners (1955) were not met. Furthermore, the prison estate did not recognize women's distinct needs, thus compounding their suffering (Pontón 2008). For example, prison officials did not register the presence of children or provide for them. Women did not have access to gender-specific healthcare. Prison regime was minimal with very few opportunities available for meaningful occupation or rehabilitation activities. Prisoners were acutely aware that their imprisonment had little to do with rehabilitation and much to do with the war on drugs (Corva 2008). Inmates often said that the United States paid a bonus of ten thousand dollars to Ecuadorian police officers for each trafficker arrested. Regardless of whether or not this had a basis in fact, it reveals much about how inmates understood the geopolitical context of their incarceration.

Research Methodology

This research sought to understand women's role in the international drug trade, especially as so-called mules. I use this term here (as respondents did) to describe people who carry drugs belonging to others across international borders. As participants in transnational crime, their offending was characterized by movement across border and continents. Most respondents were not part of a criminal subculture, far less one rooted in a geographic locale, and few respondents had been involved in the cocaine trade prior to traveling to Ecuador. Given that their participation in the drug trade was short, hidden, and characterized by international travel, the only viable way to research this topic was through post hoc accounts. A wide variety of criminologically relevant phenomena can only be accessed this way, including serious violence (Presser 2008), crime that takes place virtually (for example, fraud and financial crimes), and victimization (Sandberg 2010). Undertaking research in prisons in Ecuador enabled me to access an extremely hard-to-research population. As stated above, around three quarters of women in prison were sentenced for drug offenses.

Fieldwork was broadly ethnographic, acknowledging the impossibility of full immersion in prison (Owen 1998). I spent four days a week in both women's and men's prison for a full year, in addition to several visits and revisits betwee 2002 and 2007 (Burawoy 2003).[7] I had unaccompanied access to most parts of the prisons which enabled me to listen to everyday narrative practice. In addition to ethnographic observation and participation in daily prison routines, I interviewed nineteen women and eighteen men sentenced for drug trafficking offenses. They came from all over the world, but mostly from North and South America, Europe, South Africa, and Southeast Asia. Everyone was given the opportunity to participate and although most were happy to speak about their experiences of imprisonment, a smaller number wanted to speak about their involvement in the drug trade. Ecuadorian women were the least willing to participate in an interview, mainly as it posed the highest risk to them. Interviews took place in a variety of settings, from cells to communal kitchens, corridors, and workshops. Sometimes they were conducted in private, even in secret, while others were done in public view. Some respondents took part in just one interview, while others chose to do several, sometimes years apart. Interviews were open-ended and led by respondents (Reissman 1993). Interviews often began with a single question: what led you to be here? This usually elicited a narrative that was highly polished and had been practiced in various institutional settings. Acknowledging the importance of narrative for respondents' psychological survival in prison, I gently prompted my subjects about aspects of their account. Long-term presence in prison also enabled me to interview respondents several times and observe multiple retellings of their accounts to visitors, missionaries, and other inmates. I also spoke about my own deviance as a way of building mutual trust. I wanted to make clear that respondents would not be judged or experience stigma through the interview process.

As I will show, giving an account of oneself was not simply an opportunity for self-expression but was often required by the institution (Stanley 2000; Steedman 2000). Thus, concerns about power and voice informed how the research was undertaken. Women likened imprisonment to being buried alive. As one inmate said with conviction: "You've got to be visited; you've got to be seen and heard!" Here, where speaking was often an act of resistance, listening could be an act of solidarity (Harding 1987). Guided by feminist principles of reciprocity in research, I made myself available as a listener. Entire weeks were spent hanging out, chatting, and listening to anyone who wanted to take advantage of my presence. We talked about lots of things, most prominently family, cellmates, gossip, money worries, legal problems, relationships, news from home, and reminiscences of better times. I speak Spanish more or less fluently, but I also draw on research by local academics whose fieldwork coincided with mine (Pontón and Torres 2007; Pontón 2008; Torres 2008).

Situating Narratives: Gender, Stigma, and Imprisonment

The following section explores women's narrative practice in El Inca, drawing on ethnographic observations and interviews with respondents.

Throughout I demonstrate that women negotiated conflicting demands to produce an account of themselves. The institutional context of prison supported some narratives but not others, paying special attention to the kinds of subject positions and gender these offered. Women's narratives were not stable; they were crafted depending on who the intended listener was and were situated accomplishments of the speaker's gender. This process was complicated by the lack of "fit" between discourses about female gender and serious offending.

Misrecognition, Femininity, and Protest Selves

Between 2002 and 2008 prisoners in Ecuador campaigned against judicial and constitutional injustices, human rights abuses, overcrowding, and inhumane living conditions in prison. Protests—including public campaigns, strikes, and taking visitors hostage—were coordinated nationally by a network of inmate committees (a democratically elected assembly of inmate representatives).[8] Although protests took place simultaneously nationwide, each prison planned and managed protests according to local priorities. In El Inca, narrative identity was an important resource for protest and the drug mule was adopted as emblematic, both by the committee of inmates and by the women themselves. Visitors were often told "everyone here is a mule" (Torres 2008). The typical mule story justified women's involvement in trafficking through poverty and emphasized lack of choice. For example, Amanda stated: "I had to pay my rent in a week or the marshal was gonna come 'n padlock my door; I had nowhere to go. My mother was being evicted too so I, if I was gonna go live with my mum, she was gonna get kicked out also so . . . everybody would be in the doghouse."[9] Interestingly, prison guards and administrative staff reiterated the same discourse: "You will see for a fact that the majority of the population in this centre are here for drug trafficking. The majority of them are mules, people that have been *used* to carry the drugs and perhaps they did this because at that time they were *forced* to do that work out of economic necessity. It is simply a person with a need who they [traffickers] offer the world" (Torres 2008, 89, interview with an administrator; my translation and emphasis). Both accounts highlight the gendered nature of poverty: specifically due to women's role as primary careers for children, and their responsibilities as head of household. The discourse of no choice due to family needs emphasizes the moral connectedness of the woman in relation to her family, and her responsibility for others (Gilligan 1982), and appeals to normative ideals about maternal sacrifice.

These publicly iterated narratives tended to appeal to ideas of absolute poverty, but individual accounts reflected women's diverse backgrounds and interpretations of financial need. For example, one woman wanted to be able to send her child to school (she had only received basic education), another wanted to move to a different house where her daughter could have her own room. Although women were also motivated by the wish to provide for parents, grandparents, and siblings, the most commonly circulated stories centered on motherhood, perhaps due to the centrality of motherhood to normative femininity (Bosworth 1999, 148), especially in the Ecuadorian context (Pontón 2008). This discourse served to render women's participation as passive and "inoffensive" (Torres 2008, 113). In a survey of inmates only 27.5 percent of the women in El Inca self-identified as mules and in fact around 40 percent of women were mothers (Torres 2008). Thus identification as mule did not reflect an objective kind of truth, but rather a collective adoption of an effectual identity.

Other standard narratives existed in addition to the narrative of the drug mule forced into such work by poverty. These included women who were unknowingly set up by men. There were variations on this trope, for example being asked to mail a parcel or carry a package containing drugs. A similar storyline included women who had been arrested with boyfriends who were carrying drugs (although again, they did not know this). Stories about women who are disposed by men or boyfriends were iterated quite commonly, although only a handful of women actually claimed to have been set up. When speaking to visitors, women often said things like: "none of us are really traffickers, there is one woman here who was arrested with five kilos her boyfriend put in her suitcase without her knowing." Despite the fact that accounts of this kind were dismissed in court (where possession of drugs was evidence of guilt), they were rarely questioned in prison.

Less commonly, women's involvement in drug trafficking was explained through discourses of romantic love (see Torres 2008). Indeed, the story of the woman led astray is a recognizable cultural script (Fraser

2005). This discourse differed from the above in which the woman did know she (or her boyfriend) was carrying drugs. It appealed to natural and universal facets of femininity (since love is supposedly timeless). Interestingly, this narrative offered both passive and active subject positions: women could be "caught up in the moment" or could be active players in ensuring the future of the relationship. Nonetheless, the stories that were most heard were those in which women were not culpable and therefore blameless.

The collective adoption of the drug mule as a symbolic figure is worth reflecting upon. The kinds of stories that were widely circulated tended to be characterized by normative conceptions of femininity and featured women passively involved in drug trafficking, either through being tricked into trafficking by men or coerced into it by poverty. This strategic adoption of victimhood can be interpreted as a collective form of (gendered) repair work (Goffman 1968). It was also an attempt to counter misrecognition, which "is to be denied the status of full partner in social interaction and prevented from participating as a peer in social life—not as a consequence of distributive inequality . . . but rather as a consequence of institutionalised patterns of evaluation that constitute one as comparatively unworthy or respect or esteem" (Fraser 1995, 280). Women in El Inca were subject to various misrecognitions. First, the law treated them as drug traffickers (even those who were arrested for possession or dealing). The usual minimum sentence of eight years designated them as particularly dangerous or serious offenders on a par with serious violent offenses (Edwards 2003). Second, the title of drug trafficker (or even drug dealer) was experienced as highly shameful and stigmatizing. Sarah describes how she felt when she was arrested: "I was getting angry cause they [police] kept calling me a *mula* [mule] and I was getting very upset about it. I was getting really, really upset about that, they weren't thinking the type of person I was, you know, the job, the lifestyle I had and then someone catch me in a foreign country with drugs, that was shameful, you know I felt very embarrassed. Very . . . very."

This stigma was doubly felt since women had not only transgressed the law, but also transgressed gender norms (Lloyd 1995). However, the resulting misrecognition compounded their inability to campaign against and challenge the injustices they experienced: as criminals (and therefore gender deviants) their protests would simply not be heard.

Thus, their public protest relied upon the construction of a nondeviant identity. Because femininity is a cultural imperative (Skeggs 2001, 299), women could not construct a nondeviant identity without countering their gendered deviance. The kind of femininity that women collectively sought to undertake drew on cultural scripts that were natural and time-less, for example, caring for children and romantic love. Furthermore, "when you have restricted access to small amounts of capitals, femininity may be better than nothing at all" (ibid). However, strategically adopting victim status may not have been that successful. Goffman (1968) notes that even victim identities carry stigma, and as Skeggs (2004) notes, the value of femininity is limited.

Considerable effort was invested in maintaining this collective nar-rative, particularly from the committee of inmates. In addition to par-ticipating in national-level negotiations and protests, the committee organized day-to-day life in the prison as well as special events. These were key events for public representation and protest. For example, they organized an annual "Queen of the prison" pageant, which was attended by local dignitaries, friends, and family and was covered by national newspapers. In addition to catwalks, dresses, and dancing, women spoke out about the pains of imprisonment, emphasizing their gendered, car-ing responsibilities and the minor nature of their offending. This was just one occasion of many throughout the year at which women were encouraged to tell their stories publically. These public accounts were self-conscious performances of the kind of female gender that adhered to normative discourses—a public appeal for both entitlement to prison reform and participation in public debate about it. Establishing them-selves as respectable was not solely a matter of talking the talk but was backed up by an embodied performance of femininity. The inmates' committee also played an important role in mandating everyday con-duct. For example, on visit days everyone had to be properly dressed (no pajamas, no flip-flops).

The committee also attempted to influence my research. Halfway through fieldwork, when I began interviewing women who were not considered respectable (lesbians, drug users, and serious criminals), the committee tried to block my access to prison through the prison direc-tor. The director ruled that my tape recorder was a security risk, and that he should listen to any interviews I recorded. This incident made clear that some women were not considered entitled to represent the experience of women in prison. This is a neat example of "formal narrative control" whereby the committee exercised control over the kinds of stories that could be told to outsiders (Gubrium and Holstein 1998, 175). It was also notable that the formal control came from inmates, rather than the director.

Although this chapter focuses on women's narratives, it is worth noting how different they were from those in the men's prison. Identity played almost no role in men's protests. Instead, human rights, the unfairness of the prison system, and the pains of imprisonment took center stage (Sykes 2007). Protests employed theological imagery to highlight these pains: for example, inmates staged crucifixions (Garces 2010).[10] Although having a loose tongue or openly boasting about oneself was frowned upon, at the level of corridor talk anecdotes about trafficking feats were circulated nonetheless. The contrast was stark: narratives in the men's prison emphasized autonomy; women's accounts emphasized victimization and relationships. These narrative constructions say more about how women and men are supposed to be than what they actually did. In fact, interviews with imprisoned women and men revealed that many more men were mules than would have been anticipated on the basis of corridor talk.

Crime Networks and the Code of Silence

Talking about involvement in trafficking was discouraged by a code of silence connected to trafficking networks. These were a powerful, albeit hidden presence in prison. Violating the code of silence by speaking to outsiders had very real consequences: one of my respondents was poisoned after speaking to an Interpol officer. This silence, or, in Hallsworth and Young's (2008) terms, absent presence, is an important aspect of discourse. However, in this context, speaking about one's experience (and being *seen* to do so) was a way of claiming a particular kind of identity. For example, Caroline claimed, "There's a code of privacy, because if you're so high up they'll kill you [for talking]. But what am I? A drug mule—nobody cares about me." And Paula mentioned, "I don't think if it's a person from the outside . . . they're [other women] going to talk about it, like to you. But I've never heard of them talking to any visitors. We're more open to talk to people who we don't know about what happened. But they did it many times and it's kind of dangerous for them; they're mixing with these people still." For Caroline and Paula being seen to do an interview was a way of publicly demonstrating that they were not like connected, criminal others. By doing an interview publically, Paula claimed a particular subject position for herself: as the unknowing mule. Some women chose to do interviews in public view, for example, on the shared patio or in the kitchen. Where interviews were done in private, they made it known that they were doing an interview. In contrast, I interviewed three women who had considerable experience in the trade: one worked in partnership with her boyfriend for several years and it was widely known that she was a real trafficker. Our interviews were conducted in secret, at her request. Two respondents publicly claimed to be mere mules, even though in fact they were much more involved in the drug business, having recruited or minded others working as drug mules.[11] Unlike in the men's prison, they had little to gain from publicly admitting being involved in trafficking in any willing capacity.

Audit Selves

Although the code of silence discouraged women from speaking about trafficking, they were required to give an account of themselves to various functionaries, including social workers and psychologists. According to Scott and Lyman (1968, 46) an account is a "linguistic device employed whenever an action is subjected to valuative enquiry." Accounts are therefore a particular type of narrative. Women's accounts mainly functioned to explain their involvement in crime, particularly the drug trade. Stanley (2000) and Steedman (2000) note that women (especially poor women) have been required to give a narrative account of themselves ever since the establishment of the burgeoning welfare state in the United Kingdom, contrasting starkly with the romantic ideal of self-narratives as artful self-expression. Stanley (2000, 49) refers to self-narratives produced through organizational encounters as "audit selves," which she claims are "constrained or compelled by organisational purposes and functions." El Inca was one such institution (see also Fox 1999; Guo 2012).

Shortly after arriving in prison women met a psychologist who assessed them and placed them in one of three buildings. Amanda explains: "We have to speak to the psychologist and he has to determine like, I guess try to get into our minds on what kind of people we are, where we come from, what kind of background, character, personality, everything in one, he tries to summarize. . . . So I was being observed because I'm here for trafficking and they always send the drug traffickers to the middle *pabellón* [pavilion] for three months to check out how you are and collect the data on you, or whatever." As Amanda describes, the basis for the assessment was the respondent's account (Scott and Lyman 1968), rather than any formal classification such as remand/sentenced, time served, or offense. Women could be placed in one of the three buildings. The newest (and best) pavilion mainly housed educated, middle-class women, including many foreign nationals. The oldest pavilion housed women who were seen to be troublesome or violent. Women in this pavilion were overwhelmingly poor and Afro-Ecuadorian. How women were categorized had a lasting effect on how they were perceived by prison officials; it also impacted the kinds of resources they could expect to receive from the prison estate.

Being one of the "girls from the back" (the oldest pavilion) brought with it a great deal of stigma, even from other women prisoners. They were seen as violent and unruly. Furthermore, these categorizations were self-perpetuating. Since resources were in short supply, access was limited to the most deserving. The view of residents in the oldest wing as troublesome limited their access to meaningful occupation, training, and health care. The result was a worsening of their poverty and subsequent reduction of capital—both symbolic and material—to construct themselves as respectably feminine within the prison. Thus, giving an account of oneself had material consequences that further impacted which narratives could be credibly told about oneself. Women's ability to tell the right narrative was constrained by material inequalities. Their ethnic, national, and class backgrounds played an important role in how they were categorized; this was often inscribed in people's bodies and was related to how well they could perform a reformed, traditional femininity.

As with protest narratives, women drew upon normative scripts of gender as a way of denying deviance: becoming involved because of love, being compelled because of family need, and so on. Additionally, audit narratives also highlighted remorse (see Guo 2012). Pontón (2008) examined how disciplinary power operated on and was resisted by women in El Inca. She notes that the Catholic Church had responsibility for delinquent women up until 1982, and religious doctrine continued to shape ideas about women's rehabilitation. Specifically, the reformed woman was supposed to be "docile, demure, submissive and selfless" (Pontón 2008, 320, my translation). These moral expectations were imbued with class and race prejudices.

Stanley (2000, 54) notes that audit selves are not solely performative, "people may feel or may actually be constrained to perform the characteristics of the audit selves with which they are associated because of the surveillance consequences involved." Women iterated audit narratives even when officials were not present, for example weekly pavilion meetings began with a group prayer often thanking God for his help for keeping them on the right path. The meeting also included poems, prayer, and plays; for example, one inmate performed a play about her drug use and recovery. As with protest selves, narratives about finding God were important. These public performances of audit narratives reproduced discursive formats connected to the prison in spaces not under the purview of guards, psychologists, or any other institutional surveillance.

Yet, although institutional power played out on women's bodies and narratives (Pontón 2008), resistance was possible. Indeed, those women who were seen to be the most troublesome (residing in the oldest pavilion) experienced the most minimal intervention. They were not invested in constructing themselves in relation to institutional discourses about femininity (see Skeggs 2004) and developed counternarratives about what it really meant to be decent and feminine. They mocked women in the better pavilions for being "bitchy and fake" and assembled alternative forms of respectability based on being up front and looking out for one another. Marta was a foreign national who lived in the oldest pavilion with her girlfriend. She smoked crack openly, and thus was barred from being housed elsewhere. She describes life in the oldest pavilion and draws together discourses about gender and class (loosely conceived) to construct femininity differently:

"Oh the girls from the back are gonna come, be careful!" [Have you] ever heard that in the new pavilions? The girls here, if you don't mess with them, they don't mess with you. . . . When there's a fight, there's a fight and it's called a fight. It's a good fight, you know . . . and they're happy again ten minutes later. But a lot of the women here are street women. They all sell their drugs outside, they're always on the roads late, and the roads outside on Quito aren't very safe, aren't very nice so they're all roughnecks, you know. But they're really down to earth, you know, you can talk to some of them and they'll give you such . . . what's the word in English . . . good advice . . . I'm forgetting my English, dude. . . . Yeah, they'll give you some amazing advice that you'd never think they'll be able to give you. Like people think these are the stupid people but no, man . . . and when you find a friend you really find a friend, you know.

Although research has explored the inmate code in men's prisons, there is a lack of similar research on women's prisons (McGuire 2011). Nonetheless, it is clear that Marta draws on aspects of street code such as being street-smart, standing up for oneself and taking care of (criminal) business. Interestingly, this discourse was only adopted by a small section of the prison population that was not invested in constructing selves drawing on dominant discourses within the institution.

Men in prison were not required to give an account of themselves to prison psychologists. Instead room placements were organized by elected representatives from each pavilion who ran an informal market in which cells were bought and sold, although cell owners were required to share their cell. Thus, the institutional requirement placed on women to give an account of themselves reflects wider social norms about gender and deviance. Whereas men's offending did not require an explanation, women's apparent deviance was doubly problematic, as criminal and gender deviance. Ironically, although men's crimes were of a greater scale (they were much more likely to be imprisoned for violence than women), women's gender deviance justified much greater involvement in their day-to-day living from prison psychologists, for example. Thus, being required to give an account of oneself reflected not only institutional power but also gender power.

Dealing with Imprisonment

Lastly, women used narrative as a way of reestablishing a meaningful sense of self. Maruna et al. (2006) note that imprisonment can produce a crisis of self-narrative, and examine the ways that (male) prisoners used narrative to make sense of imprisonment. Respondents frequently spoke of experiencing disorientation when they were arrested. This was especially the case for those who had previously defined themselves through being and doing motherhood: imprisonment made this impossible and left them without the usual material resources through which to make themselves meaningful. In addition to being cut off from family, Amanda faced depersonalization from the prison or her embassy:

> Explaining to you what happened to me and how I dealt with it the first couple of weeks I was here, it's like . . . it's hard to explain sometimes, Sometimes, I get like . . . when people get writer's block. I . . . I can't explain because it's . . . it's like a harsh . . . the way they treat people here, it's . . . it's like you're being totally wiped off the face of the earth, it's like you're not here, you're not in the world, it's like you don't exist anymore especially if you're from a foreign country, such as myself, 'n the, like your Embassy comes to visit and they don't actually pay no mind to you and they just come and just give you vitamins and magazines?!

Being unable to care for children often resulted in feelings of guilt and anger (Clark 1995). Involvement with the drug trade was highly stigmatizing and had a great impact on women's families. For example, Sarah's husband lost his job after her arrest was reported in the local papers. Families also bore the financial brunt of legal proceedings and even paid for the flight home. Relationships with boyfriends often fell apart after imprisonment. The collapse of these relationships was keenly felt. Tisha was arrested with drugs her boyfriend had hidden in her suitcase. She remembers the time shortly after being arrested: "All these charges are starting to come. . . . All the accusations and they're painting this picture and their talking these words about author and all and I'm starting to learn what they're talking about and they're telling me [I'd get a prison sentence of] twelve years. . . . I had not time to even mend a broken heart."[12] In short, narratives were a key way to maintain agency in circumstances that were particularly disempowering (Jackson 1998), especially given the unlikelihood of being able to enact material change in their lives.

Narrators needed listeners: while women told their narratives to each other, they particularly appreciated telling their stories to a visitor. The contexts of these stories varied and included testimonials at church services, confessions at narcotics anonymous, informal conversations in the corridors or bedrooms, and conversation and interviews with me. These settings provided different formats and different systems of meaning for making sense of one's experience. In addition to discourses about family and love mentioned above, religion offered an important way for the women to make sense of imprisonment and their involvement in crime (Maruna et al. 2006). For example, it was common to hear the phrase, "I am not guilty but I must have done something for God to have me here" (see also Torres 2008, 124). Tisha incorporates this into her personal narrative:

> TISHA: I don't know why I'm here but for whatever reason . . . I've been using that time to talk as much as I can, to explain, to show, to give proof of something and make a difference. I'm here in prison but there's something inside me driving me to do that. I don't know. Well I know where the energy comes from but I'm tapped into it and I'm digging it!
>
> JF: You're talking about energy from God?
>
> TISHA: Yeah, I don't understand everything, but I know I understand that much.

Others have commented on the format of religious testimonials, noting that the conversion enables the narrator to separate the deviant act from the self and claim moral authority (Maruna 2001; Maruna et al. 2006). Interestingly, this format also enabled women to reframe their experiences in a completely different way to the account of offending demanded by the courts or prison. For example, women often began the story before becoming involved in trafficking at a moment when they felt that their faith in God had faltered. For example, Tisha explains: "I did stop seeking [God] for some time and that's when I made choices that . . . [There were] so many obstacles in my way to come here. In hindsight, I can see the 'do not go' signs, but I was determined, not realizing there was a trap. Even when I wasn't seeking, the forces were working on my behalf." Such accounts did not end with arrest but instead were resolved with their return to recognizing God. The subject position offered by this kind of discourse is complex. God plays an all-powerful role: he could put the narrator into prison; however, the narrator has agency insofar as she could work hard on her faith. Importantly, shifting the goalposts from an appeal to legal innocence to an appeal for divine forgiveness took place in the context of a legal and criminal justice system that was overwhelmingly corrupt and unlistening. As noted above, women found the experience of prison (and their dealings with the Embassy system and other officials) deeply depersonalizing. Many described their relationship with God as deeply personal and comforting.

In sum, then, women's narratives about offending were a response to, and shaped by, micro- and macro-level politics: the war on drugs, the prison regime, and gender expectations. These politics shaped when, why, and how women produced narratives about themselves and what they could and could not say. Although it has been recognized before that prisoners use narrative to make sense of imprisonment (Maruna at al. 2006), and that prisoners' narratives are organized by prison protocols (Fox 1999; Guo 2012), ethnographic immersion helps us to understand the connections between the imperatives to speak or stay silent and the politics that support some discourses more than others. The opportunity to give an account of oneself was generally valued since storytelling could be a site of agency, positioning the women as interpreters of their own experiences. Despite spending around twenty hours a week in prison, my time was constantly in demand from women inviting me to hang out, chat, and listen to their stories. Many commented that they really enjoyed speaking to someone from the outside as it gave them the chance to feel normal for a while.

Dominant discourses, connected to prison and female gender, did not solely repress or constrain individuals but produced ways of interpreting events as well as suggesting subject positions (Fox 1999). Although dominant discourses explaining women's offending could sometimes permit active subject positions (for example, women could be protectors of their families or relationships), passive subject positions were the most commonly voiced. As a result, discourses could potentially support aspects of their experiences that were not validated in court such as coercion and control, abusive relationships, or fraudulent lovers. Nonetheless, available discourses also limited the subject positions that could be claimed. Despite the diversity of inmates' backgrounds (class, race, and nationality), available discourses coalesced around traditional, respectable kinds of femininity (Pontón 2008; Skeggs 1997). The institution encouraged women to present selves as reformed, newly conformed to Catholic, Ecuadorian ideals of femininity: passive, submissive, and demure. Thus, the ways in which women could speak about themselves as agents of crime were limited. For example, discussing actual participation in the drug trade was taboo (see also Torres 2008) and the women described themselves as mules whether they were or not. This narrative was supported by the inmates' committee, which adopted the mule as emblematic in their protests. Furthermore, strategically adopting victimhood overlapped with institutional demands that women account for themselves as *women*.

Conclusion

This chapter looked at the narratives of women drug mules imprisoned in Ecuador. Focusing on women's narrative practice raises questions about the role of gender in shaping when, why and how women produce accounts about their offending. By way of conclusion, I highlight several key points that have emerged in adopting a narrative criminological framework.

First, silence was an important aspect of discourse: "The make up of discourse has to be pieced together, with things both said and unsaid, with required and forbidden speech" (Foucault 1981, cited in Hallsworth and Young 2008, 133). Silence was especially significant in the women's prison. Although trafficking networks punished those who spoke out to the wrong person, women were also compelled to tell their story to prison officials. At the same time, gender played a key role in shaping available discourses and therefore what could and could not be said. For example, both the committee of inmates and the prison institution supported discourses about womanhood that emphasized passivity and sacrifice. A cultural silence surrounded any instance of talking about active involvement in crime due to the reality of trafficking networks; institutional discourses also meant that talking about trafficking was taboo.

These cultural silences are particularly important for understanding the narratives that contribute to women's offending (Presser 2009). I suggest that constructing crime narratives is a gender-differentiated project.

In general women had little to gain by including their offenses in their narratives, and much to gain by describing themselves in terms of normative femininity. It was also notable that women described their offending in passive terms, or as having no choice, which poses interesting questions about the relationships between gender, narrative, and agency. Men may also adopt passive subject positions in their narratives (Maruna 2001; Presser 2008; Sandberg and Pederson 2009), however my research found discourses about female gender tended to suggest passive subject positions encouraged by the institution. In contrast, Fox's research on male offenders found that cognitive programs discouraged men from adopting passive subject positions in their narratives (Fox 1999).

Second, many of the narratives employed by women emphasized connectedness in the form of relationships with husbands, partners, children, and parents. For example, women described their motivations in ways that emphasized benefits for others (for example, relatives and boyfriends) as well as by ideas of collective benefit (Eakin 1999). Remember that Amanda felt she had to take action or "everybody would be in the doghouse." These connected narratives may reflect the fact that women's lives are characterized by a greater focus on relationships (Gilligan 1982). However, Somers takes a critical view and contends that discourses for "doing" femininity emphasize connectedness as a key aspect of female gender, and thus, emphasizing collective needs may be a way for women to construct their offending in gender-appropriate ways. For Somers (1994), cultural scripts of femininity offer little opportunity for women to narrate themselves as autonomous actors. Importantly, these narratives of collective benefit challenge orthodox explanations for crime since they are premised on the idea of the rational actor. Davies (2003) contends that the concept of rationality is rooted in masculinist vocabularies and is ill equipped for understanding female offending. Narrative methods are well placed to move beyond rational choice perspectives in order to understand the significance of others in women's narratives. It may be important for narrative criminology to explore agency in a way that is not limited to individual action (see McKenzie and Stoljar 2000).

Finally, my research shows that gender is accomplished situationally in/through talk/narrative, coconstituted by other social structures such as sexuality, class, ethnicity, and age (Weatherall 2002). Drawing on the "doing gender" approach is advantageous as it avoids reifying gender: "Specifically, recognizing gender as situated action allows for recognition of agency, but does so in a way thoroughly grounded in the contexts of structural inequalities such as those of gender, sexuality, race, class and age" (Miller 2002, 434). Furthermore, paying attention to the situations in which narratives are constructed bring the importance of place and time into focus. My research reveals the significance of the discursive landscape in supporting some kinds of narratives but not others—and indeed some narrators more than others. Research based on one-off interviews has tended to present a static view of offending, motives, and justifications. Introducing offenders' own constructions allows space to recognize and make sense of the fact that offending was often a mistake rather than an inevitable consequence of social structural disadvantage. According to McNay (2000, 73), "highlighting the active role played by the subject in the construction of a coherent identity allows a more nuanced concept of agency to emerge." For example, narrative analysis reveals the multilayered aspects of agency, and in the process exposes the agency involved in constructing an account, including the strategic adoption of passive subject positions. Thus, understanding how women construct themselves and their offending behavior in and through discourses and gender (as well as class, ethnicity, age, and nationality) may offer a new way to breach the divide between the "women of discourse" and "real women" by recognizing that neither experience nor interpretation are necessarily prior to the other (Daly and Maher 1997, 6). Thus, narrative criminology may offer useful theory and methodology for better understanding structure and agency in women's offending.

NOTES

1. Research has examined female victims' (but not offenders') use of neutralizations (Maruna and Copes 2006, 66).
2. I acknowledge Dirección Nacional de Rehabilitación Social, Ecuador for granting research access; FLACSO, Ecuador, for hosting me during fieldwork; and Andreina Torres for drawing my attention to the importance of narrative in prison. Thanks to the women who participated in this research. This research was funded by a 1+3 studentship (PTA-030-2004-00460) from the Economic and Social Research Council of Great Britain.

3. There are a variety of feminist perspectives in criminology (Gelsthorpe and Morris 1998; Chesney-Lind 2006; Rafter and Heidensohn 1995).

4. Between 2002 and 2009, the proportion of women imprisoned for drug offenses rose from around 60 percent to around 80 percent, outpacing equivalent changes in the men's prison (Edwards 2011, 55).

5. According to a survey of the women's prison: "16.4% of all inmates said that they had been involved in international trafficking of drugs, 13.4% for trafficking at a regional/national level and 13.1% said they had been detained for consumption of drugs" (Pontón and Torres 2007, 67, my translation). Ten percent of those serving sentences for drug crime in Ecuador are women (66).

6. According to the Ecuadorian constitution, offenders cannot be imprisoned without trial for longer than six months for the most serious offenses. This category includes drug offenses (Edwards 2003).

7. I first visited prisons in 2002, then returned in 2003 as a researcher. I also visited the prison for several months during 2005 and 2007, and again in 2010. This has enabled me to understand historical and institutional changes.

8. A documentary about one such protest in 2004 was made by FLACSO (Herrera 2005).

9. This was the first account of being a drug mule that Amanda shared with me. Over subsequent interviews we discussed what led her to that work and multiple conflicting narratives emerged. This should be considered a public statement of self as much as an explanation for her offending.

10. Women also engaged in this physical form of protest, not in the capital Quito, but in Ecuador's second city Guayaquil.

11. These two women were traveling with mules to watch over them to make sure they followed the instructions they were given.

12. Tisha would want me to also record here that she did mend her heart. She gained parole, left prison and finally returned home.

REFERENCES

Aguirre, Flores. 2007. "La detención en firme: Crítica de un continuo fraude a la Constitución y a la Ley de la República del Ecuador." *URVIO: Revista Latinoamericana de Seguridad Ciudadana* 1: 23–30.

Allen, Hilary. 1998. "Rendering Them Harmless: The Professional Portrayal of Women Charged with Serious Violent Crimes." In *Criminology at the Crossroads: Feminist Readings in Crime and Justice*, edited by Kathleen Daly and Lisa Maher, 54–68. New York and Oxford: Oxford University Press.

Bewley-Taylor, Dave, Chris Hallam, and Rob Allen. 2009. *The Incarceration of Drug Offenders: An Overview.* London: Beckley Foundation.

Bourdieu, Pierre. 1977. *Outline of a Theory of Practice.* Cambridge: Cambridge University Press.

Bosworth, Mary. 1999. *Engendering Eesistance: Agency and Power in Women's Prisons.* Brookfield, VT: Ashgate.

Burawoy, Michael. 2003. "Revisits: An Outline of a Theory of Reflexive Ethnography." *American Sociological Review* 68 (October): 645–679.

Burgess-Proctor, Amanda. 2006. "Intersections of Race, Class, Gender, and Crime: Future Directions for Feminist Criminology." *Feminist Criminology* 1 (1): 27–47.

Byrne, Bridget. 2003. "Reciting the Self: Narrative Representations of the Self in Qualitative Interviews." *Feminist Theory* 4 (1): 29–49.

Chesney-Lind, Meda. 2006. "Patriarchy, Crime, and Justice: Feminist Criminology in an Era of Backlash." *Feminist Criminology* 1 (1): 6–26.

Chesney-Lind, Meda, and Jocelyn M. Pollock. 1994. "Women's Prisons: Equality with a Vengeance." In *Women, Law, and Social Control*, edited by Alida V. Merlo and Joycelyn M. Pollock, 155–175. Boston, MA: Pearson Education.

Clark, J. 1995. "The Impact of the Prison Environment on Mothers." *Prison Journal* 75 (3): 306–329.

Comack, E. 1999. "Producing Feminist Knowledge: Lessons from Women in Trouble." *Theoretical Criminology* 3 (3): 287–306.

Corva, Dominic. 2008. "Neoliberal Globalization and the War on Drugs: Transnationalizing Illiberal Governance in the Americas." *Political Geography* 27: 176–193.

Cosslett, Tess, Celia Lury, and Penny Summerfield. 2000. Introduction to *Feminism and Autobiography: Texts, Theories, Methods*, edited by Tess Cosslett, Celia Lury, and P. Summerfield. London: Routledge.

Daly, Kathleen. 1997. "Different Ways of Conceptualizing Sex/Gender in Feminist Theory and Their Implications for Criminology." *Theoretical Criminology* 1 (1): 25–51.

Daly, Kathleen, and Lisa Maher. 1998. "Crossroads and Intersections: Building from Feminist Critique." In *Criminology at the Crossroads: Feminist Readings in Crime and Justice*, edited by K. Daly and L. Maher, 1–20. Oxford: Oxford University Press.

Davies, Pamela A. 2003. "Is Economic Crime a Man's Game?" *Feminist Theory* 4 (3): 283–303.

Dirección Nacional de Rehabilitación Social. 2005. "El sistema penitenciario Ecuatoriano en cifras." Unpublished bulletin.

Eakin, Paul John. 1999. *How Our Lives Become Stories: Making Selves*. Ithaca, NY: Cornell University Press.

Edwards, Sandra G. 2003. "Illicit Drug Control Policies and Prisons: The Human Cost." Washington, DC: Washington Office on Latin America.

———. 2011. "A Short History of Ecuador's Drug Legislation and the Impact on Its Prison Population." In *Systems Overload: Drug Laws and Prisons in Latin America*, edited by Pien Metaal and Coletta Youngers, 50–60. Amsterdam/Washington, DC: Transnational Institute/Washington Office on Latin America.

Fleetwood, Jennifer, and Andreina Torres. 2011. "Mothers and Children of the International Drug War." In *Children of the Drug War*, edited by Damon Barrett, 127–141. London: International Harm Reduction Association/Idebate Press Books.

Fox, Kathryn J. 1999. "Changing Violent Minds: Discursive Correction and Resistance in the Cognitive Treatment of Violent Offenders in Prison." *Social Problems* 46 (1): 88–103.

Fraser, Heather. 2005. "Women, Love, and Intimacy 'Gone Wrong': Fire, Wind, and Ice." *Affilia* 20 (1): 10–20.

Fraser, Nancy. 1995. "From Redistribution to Recognition? Dilemmas of Justice in a 'Postsocialist' Age." *New Left Review* 212: 68–94.

Garces, Chris. 2010. "The Cross Politics of Ecuador's Penal State." *Cultural Anthropology* 25 (3): 459–496.

Gelsthorpe, Loraine. 1990. "Feminist Methodologies in Criminology: A New Approach or Old Wine in New Bottles?" In *Feminist Perspectives in Criminology*, edited by L. Gelsthorpe and A. Morris, 89–106. Milton Keynes, UK: Open University Press.

———. 2004. "Female Offending: A Theoretical Overview." In *Women Who Offend*, edited by Gill McIvor, 13–37. London: Jessica Kingsley Publishers.

Gelsthorpe, Loraine, and Allison Morris. 1988. "Feminism and Criminology in Britain." *British Journal of Criminology* 28 (2): 93–110.

Giddens, Anthony. 1991. *Modernity and Self-Identity*. Stanford, CA: Stanford University Press.

Gilligan, Carol. 1982. *In a Different Voice: Psychological Theory and Women's Development*. London: Harvard University Press.

Goffman, Erving. 1968. *Stigma: Notes on the Management of Spoiled Identity*. London: Penguin.

Gubrium, Jaber F., and James A. Holstein. 1998. "Narrative Practice and the Coherence of Personal Stories." *The Sociological Quarterly* 39 (1): 163–187.

Guo, Jing-ying. 2012. "'Anyone in my shoes will end up like me': Female Inmates' Discourse of Responsibility for Crime." *Discourse and Society* 23 (1): 34–46.

Hallsworth, S., and T. Young. 2008. "Crime and Silence: 'Death and life are in the power of the tongue' (Proverbs 18:21)." *Theoretical Criminology* 12 (2): 131–152.

Harding, Sandra G. 1987. *Feminism and Methodology: Social Science Issues*. Bloomington: Indiana University Press.

Herrera, M. 2005. *El Comité: La Toma del ex Penal Garcia Moreno*. Documentary. Quito, EC: FLACSO.

Jackson, S. 1998. "Telling Stories: Memory, Narrative, and Experience in Feminist Research and Theory." In *Standpoints and Differences: Essays in the Practice of Feminist Psychology*, edited by Karen Henwood, Christine Griffin, and Ann Phoenix, 45–64. London: Sage.

Krais, Beate. 2006. "Gender, Sociological Theory and Bourdieu's Sociology of Practice." *Theory, Culture and Society* 23 (6): 119–134.

Lloyd, Ann. 1995. *Doubly Deviant, Doubly Damned: Society's Treatment of Violent Women*. London: Penguin.

Maher, Lisa. 1997. *Sexed Work: Gender, Race, and Resistance in a Brooklyn Drug Market*. Oxford: Clarendon Press.

Maruna, Shadd. 2001. *Making Good: How Ex-Convicts Reform and Rebuild Their Lives*. Washington, DC: American Psychological Association Press.

Maruna, Shadd, Louise Wilson, and Kathryn Curran. 2006. "Why God Is Often Found Behind Bars: Prison Conversions and the Crisis of Self-Narrative." *Research in Human Development* 3 (2): 161–184.

Maton, Karl. 2008. "Habitus." In *Pierre Bourdieu: Key Concepts*, edited by Michael Grenfell, 49–66. Durham, NC: Acumen.

Mackenzie, Catriona, and Natalie Stoljar, eds. 2000. *Relational Autonomy: Feminist Perspectives on Autonomy, Agency, and the Social Self*. New York and Oxford: Oxford University Press.

McGuire, M. Dylan. 2011. "Doing the Life: An Exploration of the Connection between the Inmate Code and Violence Among Female Inmates," *Journal of the Institute of Justice and International Studies* 11: 145–158.

McKendy, John P. 2006. "'I'm very careful about that': Narrative and Agency of Men in Prison." *Discourse and Society* 17 (4): 473–502.

McNay, Lois. 2000. *Gender and Agency: Reconfiguring the Subject in Feminist and Social Theory*. Cambridge, UK: Polity Press.

———. 2004. "Agency and Experience: Gender as a Lived Relation." *Sociological Review* 52: 173–190.

Messerschmidt, James. 1993. *Masculinities and Crime: Critique and Reconceptualization of Theory*. Lanham, MD: Rowman and Littlefield.

Metaal, Pien, and Sandra Edwards. 2009. "Pardon for Mules in Ecuador: A Sound Proposal." *Series on Legislative Reform of Drug Policies*, no. 1. Washington, DC: Washington Office on Latin America.

Miller, Jody. 2002. "The Strengths and Limits of 'Doing Gender' for Understanding Street Crime." *Theoretical Criminology* 6 (4): 433–460.

Owen, Barbara. 1998. *"In the Mix: Struggle and Survival in a Women's Prison*. Albany: State University of New York Press.

Personal Narratives Group 1989. *Interpreting Women's Lives: Feminist Theory and Personal Narratives*. Bloomington: Indiana University Press.

Phoenix, Joanna. 2000. "Prostitute Identities." *British Journal of Criminology* 40 (1): 37–55.

Plummer, Ken. 1995. *Telling Sexual Stories: Power, Change and Social Worlds*. London: Routledge.

Pontón, Jenny. 2008. "Mujeres, cuerpo y encierro: acomodo y resistencias al sistema penitenciario." In *Estudios sobre sexualidades en America Latina*, edited by Kathya Aruajo and Mercedes Prieto, 309–330. Quito, EC: FLACSO.

Pontón, Jenny, and Andreina Torres. 2007. "Cárceles del Ecuador: los efectos de la criminalización por drogas." *URVIO: Revista Latinoamericana de Seguridad Cuidana* 1: 55.

Presser, Lois. 2008. *Been a Heavy Life: Stories of Violent Men*. Urbana: University of Illinois Press.

———. 2009. "The Narratives of Offenders." *Theoretical Criminology* 13 (2): 177–200.

———. 2012. "Getting on Top through Mass Murder: Narrative, Metaphor, and Violence." *Crime, Media, Culture* 8 (1): 3–21.

Rafter, Nicole, and Frances Heidensohn. 1995. "Introduction: The Development of Feminist Perspectives on Crime." In *International Feminist Perspectives in Criminol-*

ogy, edited by Nicole Hahn Rafter and Frances Heidensohn, 1–14. Buckingham, UK: Open University Press.

Reissman, Catherine Kohler. 1993. *Narrative Analysis*. London: Sage.

Rosenwald, George C. 1992. "Conclusion: Reflections on Narrative Self-Understanding." In *Storied Lives: The Cultural Politics of Self-Understanding*, edited by George C. Rosenwald and Richard L. Ochberg, 265–290. New Haven, CT: Yale University Press.

Sandberg, Sveinung. 2008. "Black Drug Dealers in a White Welfare State: Cannabis Dealing and Street Capital in Norway." *British Journal of Criminology* 48 (5): 604–619.

———. 2009. "A Narrative Search for Respect." *Deviant Behavior* 30 (6): 487–510.

———. 2010. "What Can 'Lies' Tell Us about Life? Notes towards a Framework of Narrative Criminology." *Journal of Criminal Justice Education* 21 (4): 447–465.

———. 2012. "Is Cannabis Use Normalized, Celebrated, or Neutralized? Analysing Talk as Action." *Addiction Research and Theory* 20 (5): 372–381.

Sandberg, Sveinung, and Willy Pederson. 2009. *Street Capital: Black Cannabis Dealers in a White Welfare State*. Bristol, UK: Policy Press.

Scott, Marvin B., and Stanford M. Lyman. 1968. "Accounts." *American Sociological Review* 33 (1): 46–62.

Sentencing Council. 2011. "Drug Offences Guide: Public Consultation." London: Sentencing Council. http://sentencingcouncil.judiciary.gov.uk/docs/Drug_Offences_Guideline_Public_Consultation_.pdf.

Sewell, W. H. 1992. "A Theory of Structure: Duality, Agency, and Transformation." *American Journal of Sociology* 98 (1): 1–29.

Sim, J. 2006. "Tougher Than the Rest? Men in Prison." In *Prison Readings: A Critical Introduction to Prisons and Punishment*, edited by Y. Jewkes and H. Johnston, 100–120. Cullompton, UK: Willan.

Skeggs, Beverley. 1997. *Formations of Class and Gender: Becoming Respectable*. London: Sage.

———. 2001. "The Toilet Paper: Femininity, Class and Misrecognition." *Women's Studies International Forum* 24 (3–4): 295–307.

———. 2004. "Exchange, Value and Affect: Bourdieu and the 'Self.'" In *Feminism after Bourdieu*, edited by Lisa Adkins and Beverley Skeggs, 75–95. Oxford: Blackwell Publishers.

Smart, Carol. 1989. *Feminism and the Power of Law*. London: Routledge.

Somers, Margaret, R. 1994. "The Narrative Construction of Identity: A Relational and Network Approach." *Theory and Society* 23 (5): 605–649.

Spender, Dale. 1980. *Man Made Language*, London: Routledge.

Stanley, Liz, ed. 1990. *Feminist Praxis: Research, Theory, and Epistemology in Feminist Sociology*. London: Rutledge.

———. 2000. "From 'Self-made Women' to 'Women's Made-selves': Audit Selves, Simulation and Surveillance in the Rise of the Public Woman." In *Feminism and*

Autobiography: Texts, Theories, Tethods, edited by Tess Cosslett, Celia Lury, and Penny Summerfield, 40–60. London: Routledge.

Steedman, Carolyn. 2000. "Enforced Narratives: Stories of Another Self." In *Feminism and Autobiography: Texts, Theories, Methods*, edited by Tess Cosslett, Celia Lury, and Penny Summerfield, 25–39. London: Routledge.

Steffensmeier, Darrell, and Emilie Allen. 1996. "Gender and Crime: Towards a Gendered Theory of Female Offending." *Annual Review of Sociology* 22: 459–487.

Sykes, Gresham M. 2007. *The Society of Captives: A Study of a Maximum Security Prison*. Princeton, NJ: Princeton University Press.

Torres, Andreina. 2008. *Drogas, cárcel y género en Ecuador: la experiencia de mujeres mulas*. Quito, EC: FLACSO.

United Nations. 1955. *Standard Minimum Rules for the Treatment of Prisoners*. Vienna, AT: United Nations.

Weatherall, Ann. 2002. *Gender, Language and Discourse*. London: Routledge.

West, Candace, and Don H. Zimmerman. 1987. "Doing Gender." *Gender and Society* 1 (2): 125–151.

Wright Mills, C. 1940. "Situated Actions and Vocabularies of Motive." *American Sociological Review* 5 (6): 904–913.

3

Gendered Narratives of Self, Addiction, and Recovery among Women Methamphetamine Users

JODY MILLER, KRISTIN CARBONE-LOPEZ, AND MIKH V. GUNDERMAN

Narrative criminology, with its ethnomethodological influences, has much in common with feminist theoretical frameworks that concern themselves with uncovering the constitutive nature of gendered practices, including speech (Butler 1990; Connell 2002; Stokoe 2006; West and Zimmerman 1987). If narratives provide us, as analysts, a window into how individuals "organize views of themselves, of others, and of their social worlds" (Orbuch 1997, 455), then a critical facet of narrative analysis involves investigating how "women are constructed or construct themselves" within them (Daly and Maher 1998, 4). Narratives impart essential messages about gender, with the structure, content, and usage of language emerging as important components in the constitution of gender and gender inequality. In particular, "gender dualism"—the assumption that there exist two distinct and opposite genders—shapes narrators' own beliefs and behaviors, as well as the ways in which they articulate them (Cameron 1998).

Our concern in this chapter is with the functions and uses of gender-based categorizations among offenders. We examine these issues by investigating women methamphetamine users' narratives of self, addiction, and recovery. How, when, and in what forms do categorizations based upon gender (dualism) appear in women meth users' accounts of their drug use? How do these characterizations shape women's own understanding of the progression of their methamphetamine use and plans for the future? Methamphetamine has taken its place, along with heroin and crack cocaine before it, as a drug whose pharmacological properties are said to cause immediate and long-term addiction. Meth is distinct, however, because as an amphetamine it can also be constructed—like many prescription drugs—as a "mother's little helper," facilitating, at least for a time, women users' successful performance of normative gender expectations (Campbell 2000). This opens up space within women's narrative stories of meth use for claims (to themselves and others) of a moral gendered self, even while contradictory depictions of women's meth use as transgressive, immoral, irresponsible, and dangerous are pervasive (Boyd 2004, 51). Women's narratives about the place of methamphetamine in their lives, we argue, are constitutive of gender in the process of identifying motives for meth use and desistance.

Narratives of Crime, Narratives of Gender

Criminologists have long been interested in the narratives of offenders, even though there has been considerable variation in *how* such narratives have been used (Presser 2009). For some, narratives provide insight into offenders' experiences, offering a play-by-play recounting of what offenders do and the contexts in which they do it. Narratives are also used to investigate offenders' explanations (or excuses) for their actions. Such accounts have assisted criminologists in better understanding the impact of individual, family, and situational factors on criminal involvement (Agnew 2006). Narrative criminology suggests that narratives are more than a simple retelling of a particular event or post hoc (re)interpretation of one's behavior; instead, narratives may also shape and guide future behavior, because people tend to behave in ways that agree with the self-stories they have created about themselves (McAdams 1985). In fact, the creation of self-narratives can facilitate continued criminal behavior, particularly when the stories told provide a compelling rationale for one's actions (Presser 2009). At the same time, narratives can be used to come to terms with one's past and outline a convincing tale for change (Maruna 2001).

Thus, one important feature of narratives is that they are dynamic. Identity is a life-long project; stories about the self are routinely created and recreated, as one's motivations, goals, and social position change over time. New experiences may cause one to reinterpret behavior long past, increasing or decreasing the salience of past experiences for one's self-story. For example, offenders may point to traumatic experiences in their childhoods to explain their entry into and continued involvement in criminal behavior. In contrast, experiences initially perceived as traumatic or unjust may be redefined within one's narrative as necessary turning points on a path of redemption, thus creating positive meaning out of troubled or troubling pasts (Maruna 2001). Ultimately the stories we construct to make sense of our lives are an attempt to situate ourselves within society (McAdams 2008), and this is as true for offenders and ex-offenders as for anyone else.

Narratives also "echo gender and class constructions in society" and therefore "reflect . . . prevailing patterns of hegemony in the economic, political, and cultural contexts wherein human lives are situated" (McAdams 2008, 247). It is in this way that we see important parallels between narrative criminology's call for the treatment of narratives as constitutive and the lengthy tradition in feminist scholarship that recognizes gendered practices—including the construction and uses of narratives—as one of the very bases on which gender and gender inequalities are constituted (West and Zimmerman 1987). Garfinkel (1967, 180) first began this line of inquiry through his investigation, with a male-to-female transsexual individual, of how gender "is accomplished through witnessable displays of talk and conduct." His early insights were taken up by other scholars, and used to theorize that gender is best understood as socially produced in the ongoing interactions of everyday life (Kessler and McKenna 1978; West and Zimmerman 1987).

Viewing gender as situated accomplishment means recognizing that gender "is a mechanism whereby situated social action contributes to the reproduction of social structure" (West and Fenstermaker 1995, 21). Women and men "do gender"—or engage in gendered practices—in response to situated expectations about masculinity and femininity. These actions, according to West and Zimmerman (1987, 147), are the "interactional scaffolding of social structure," such that the performance of gender is not only a response to gendered social hierarchies and expectations but also reproduces and reinforces them. An important facet of this "doing" is the production, adoption, and utilization of gendered stories of self and others to make sense of and negotiate one's place in the world. These can perhaps best be understood as the *narrative scaffolding of social structure*.

Narrative criminologists, according to Sandberg (2010, 455, 458), "recognize that narratives are enacted and identities constructed through "shared narrative formats . . . [they are] *spoken* by individuals but also *spoken through* them." An important facet of these shared narrative formats are categorizations and the use of categories for the work of boundary maintenance (Small, Harding, and Lamont 2010). As Stokoe (2006, 474–476) explains, "categories are *inference rich*": They contain cultural knowledge about those qualities members of categories are expected to "perform or possess" and "allow for a host of consequential moral assumptions" to be articulated. Given the centrality of gender dualism in the discursive construction of social life (Cameron 1998; Connell 2002), it should come as no surprise that gender-based categorizations are thus particularly entrenched features of narratives: "speakers categorize and position themselves and others in relation to particular conceptions of gender" (Stokoe 2006, 477; see also Anderson and Umberson 2001; Hollander 2001; Nilan 1994).

Saying and Doing Gender in Women's Narratives of Crime

How do these narrative practices play out among women involved in crime generally, and female drug users specifically? A key feature of the constitution of gender through narrative and other social practices is *accountability*. It is not simply that individuals constitute gender through the stories they tell, but that they are held accountable for their gendered performances (speech and otherwise) in light of the gender order in which patterns of social life are arranged. This is true even as "the conduct produced in light of this accountability is not a *product* of gender; *it is gender itself*" (Connell 2009, 105; our italics; see also Martin 2003).

Although the ethnomethodology-inspired framework of "doing gender" has been influential in criminology, it has generally been a poor fit for explaining women's involvement with crime (see Miller 2002). Crime, and stories about crime, are often interpreted as resources for performing gender, and particularly for demonstrating masculinity (Copes and Hochstetler 2003; Messerschmidt 1993). Yet, applying the concept to women's and girls' participation in crime is typically ineffectual, since crime is often recognized as "doubly deviant" when engaged in by women: both a criminal violation and a violation of normative expectations for women. Rarely are women able to cull from the types of popular "gangster discourses" Sandberg (2009) and others describe male offenders routinely adopting: when women embrace such narratives of self they are held accountable as *failed* members of the category "woman."[1]

What options remain, then, for telling stories of crime that can constitute women as morally "good" gendered actors? Not surprisingly, categorization processes that depend on a character dichotomy between women and men are often deployed. It is through the enactment and telling of such dichotomous interpretations that many of the most persistent, yet often invisible, facets of gender inequality are reproduced (Connell 2002, 40). Consider Sandberg's (2009, 530) description of male drug dealers sometimes articulating an *oppression discourse*, which emphasizes such problems as "ethnic discrimination, racism, problems from migration, and psychological problems" in their narrative accounts of offending. Women likewise can draw from a range of oppression discourses, including an emphasis on the gendered blurred boundaries of victimization and offending (Gilfus 1992), as well as highlighting the pressures or coercion applied to (passively constructed) women by their male partners (see Klee et al. 2001, 17). These are popular storylines among some criminologists as well (Maher 1997; Miller 2001); however, as Sandberg (2009, 535) points out, for individuals who enact them, such discourses come "with a definite dilemma: the marginalized speakers have to see themselves as victims." Yet the popular acceptance of gender dualism makes victim narratives much more socially acceptable for women than for men.

Another discourse potentially available for women offenders is that of the "good mother" who commits crime to support and look after her family (Ferraro and Moe 2003). But motherhood is a category especially fraught with danger for female offenders to embrace. There is no question that motherhood is typically considered a defining role in women's lives, constructed and experienced within prevailing historical and political contexts (Ridgeway and Correll 2004; Ulrich and Weatherall 2000). Contemporary Western society has constructed the ideal of *mother* to be one of selfless-sacrifice directed toward the caring, nurturing, and protecting of one's children. Yet, such a lofty and idealistic definition of mother means that women who fall short of the prescribed standards of motherhood are formally and informally sanctioned for their perceived failings (Ettorre 1992). Thus, female offenders with children—especially those who use drugs—face intense scrutiny and condemnation as "bad mothers" (Baker and Carson 1999; see also Banwell and Bammer 2006). It takes particularly compelling stories to overcome such stigma. Because of its pharmacological properties, methamphetamine has the potential to offer one such compelling route, albeit unsustainably as we shall see.

Perhaps where such categorical claims may be most effective for women offenders, for their self-understandings and for how they seek to be understood by others, is in the form of redemption narratives. As Presser (2009, 180) suggests: "A person's narrative presupposes a moral self in the narrating present. . . . [B]y narrating, the moral deviant separates . . . herself from past wrongdoing. . . . The self-narrative communicates a complex character that has unfolded over time and thus has the potential for further change." It is often the case that women offenders, particularly those who are incarcerated, embrace motherhood as a form of redemption, with the goal of claiming an ideal mother/self guiding the quest for change. It is these issues we turn to now, investigating the plots that guide women methamphetamine users' narratives of self over time, and the place of categorizations in these processes.

The Study

Our examination of women's narratives of their methamphetamine use relies on qualitative in-depth interviews with forty incarcerated women court-ordered to participate in a correctional drug and alcohol treatment program during their stay in one of Missouri's two women's prisons.[2] The women we interviewed need not have been incarcerated for methamphetamine-related charges to be included in our sample. Instead, those who volunteered were asked to complete an initial screening, and were eligible to participate if they had considerable experience with the drug, including using, selling, or manufacturing it. Our goal—both in choosing to interview incarcerated women and in adopting broad screening criteria—was to capture a diverse group of meth-involved women who were sufficiently embedded in drug use, crime, and their consequences to offer a repertoire of narratives about their meth initiation, progression, and perhaps wished for—if not actualized—desistance.

Interviewing women who were incarcerated and in mandated treatment provided a unique vantage point from which to investigate women's narratives of self and meth use, as such settings facilitate, even demand, a reflective context. Interviews—as with all communications—are recognizably produced in an interdiscursive process, with the audience influencing those stories selected and told. It is noteworthy for our analysis that the second author—who led the recruitment of research participants and conducted some of the interviews—was eight and a half months pregnant at the time we commenced our investigation. It is undoubtedly the case that her obvious pregnancy emphasized the saliency of motherhood in these exchanges. At the same time, the women we interviewed did not have an "infinite pool of language and meaning" from which to draw their identities; instead they "rel[ied] on ways of self-presenting . . . that they have learned and used elsewhere" (Sandberg 2010, 455). The stories shared by women in our project provide a window into the complex ways in which gender operates as a guiding feature of their identities, decision-making, and performances as female meth users. They provide us with important insights into how women understood, explained, and gave meaning to the (gendered) place of meth in their lives (Mishler 1986; Orbuch 1997), while also providing details about the micro- and meso-level contexts in which their meth use took place (Miller and Glassner 2011; Short 1998).

We understand women's narratives as "taken from, and illustrative of" the gendered social contexts of their meth use (Sandberg 2010, 455), both of which changed over time. Although the women's accounts are drawn from a single interview, they nonetheless reveal important variations within their overarching story of meth use, particularly in how women make sense of their initiation, continued use, and addiction to methamphetamine, as well as their plans for desistance. By comparing the elements of the stories told by the women we interviewed, as well as tracing the multiple stories each woman told as a means of making sense of herself and the progression of her methamphetamine use, our analysis reveals when and how gendered understandings of self are most relevant, and thus, perhaps constitutive for women's meth use and their redemptive desires for desistance.

Women's Narratives of Meth Initiation: Age-Graded Gendered Contexts

As we discussed elsewhere (Carbone-Lopez and Miller 2012; Carbone-Lopez et al. 2012), women's narratives of initiation into methamphetamine use were diverse, but despite this diversity, gendered threads were apparent in their accounts. The majority of women we spoke with were in their late twenties or early thirties at the time of our interview. They reported their first meth use, on average, at the age of nineteen, although there was considerable variation in women's age of meth initiation. Specifically, just over a third of the women (fourteen of forty) reported that their first experience with meth came before the age of sixteen, while around half (twenty-one of forty) placed their onset in late adolescence or early adulthood, and just five began using meth somewhere between their late twenties and early forties. Age of first use seemed to impact heavily the repertoire of narratives from which the women drew.

Nearly all of the women who reported initiating meth in adolescence or early adulthood described youthful social contexts associated with precocious movement into adult roles or responsibilities (see Carbone-Lopez and Miller 2012), and these social contexts were reflected in their initiation narratives. Although approximately a third of the women we spoke with reported childhood sexual abuse, and the vast majority described other forms of childhood family dysfunction, very few adopted the narrative account popular among many feminist criminologists— that they initiated meth to "numb the pain" associated with the trauma of these victimization experiences. Barbara and Geri reported the earliest onset of meth use in our sample at ages twelve and eleven, respectively, and each drew on the victimization narrative to describe their meth initiation.[3]

Barbara was sexually abused by an uncle who lived with her family from the age of six onward and described first using meth when an older boyfriend suggested it would help her cope with the "things that were going on." She explained: "I wanted to hide the pain. . . . [Meth was] a way to hide my feelings, to numb myself." Geri's early initiation into meth use was forced; her father's best friend raped her and, in the process, injected her with methamphetamine. She said that at the time, "it took all the pain away. And I didn't even care anymore." Several years later she initiated meth use on her own when her earlier victimization became public. Again, she recalled that "it made me feel good [and] took away all the pain of the situation." Both of these accounts are in keeping with one popular feminist narrative of women's drug use and offending: that it is a traumatic response to gender-based victimization (see Miller and Mancuso 2004; Salisbury and Van Voorhis 2009). Thus what is surprising is how infrequently this cultural frame was used by the women we spoke with. One reason for this may be the increasing cultural impact in recent decades of both third-wave and postfeminist discourses that position women less as *victims* of oppression than as *survivors* who exercise agency, including in the negotiation of gender inequalities (Lamb 1999). These shifts have made available a "cultural stock of plots" (Polletta et al. 2011, 111) for women in which they can position themselves as active agents, including in adolescence.

Another gendered feature of early movement into adulthood was more common in the narratives of women who initiated meth in adolescence and early adulthood: teenage rebellion against perceived gendered control and strict parenting (see also Carbone-Lopez et al. 2012). Mackenzie, for example, said she "came from a loving family, no drugs, no alcohol. . . . I always felt like I got all the love and affection I needed." But as a teenager, she explained, "I started to have my own way of thinking and going around with friends I thought I had . . . I'd . . . run around with older guys and do drugs," including meth.

Kennedy described her mother as "just really controlling; she was too overprotective." She had her first child at age seventeen, moved out on her own, and began to "do everything I never really got to do." Her meth use began, she explained, when she started dating a young man who was a meth user. Again, in contrast to some feminist accounts, she did not see him as responsible for her initiation, but instead said she tried meth because she "wanted to know what it was like, what it made you feel like. . . . It was something to do." In explaining their meth initiation, then, these women drew from cultural definitions of adolescence and young adulthood as a period in life in which the move toward independence—and even rebellion—guided their behaviors.

Most often, however, precocious movement into adult roles and responsibilities was not described as the result of adolescent rebellion, but instead emerged as a result of family problems, including parental drug use, mental illness, domestic violence, and maltreatment or victimization. Women in these circumstances described having family, household, and childcare duties early in life—via taking primary responsibility for the care of younger siblings, moving out on their own to avoid dysfunctional family dynamics, or early motherhood. In fact, all but six of the women in our sample were mothers, and the majority (twenty-one of thirty-four) became mothers when they were eighteen or younger. Consequently, a number of the women drew on cultural themes in their narratives about motherhood and family to make sense of their meth initiation by emphasizing their discovery that meth could enhance their ability to be an effective caretaker while also framing their decision to use meth as a desire for "freedom," to escape the frustration and burdens of early adult responsibilities.

Lauren, for example, grew up with parents who used drugs and were frequently absent from the home. As an adolescent she described having assumed parental responsibilities for her siblings and, soon after, becoming a teenage parent herself: "I pretty much raised my brothers and sisters, and so, I was fourteen, well fifteen, and that's when I got pregnant and moved out." She described dealing with "just a lot of stress, being so young with kids, and I'd dealt with my parents . . . so I went through a lot of that as a teenager." Lauren's account of why she liked methamphetamine initially was thus grounded in her description of all of the responsibilities she had to juggle: "It gave me energy. I was able to stay awake. I was able to concentrate on things, my school work, my job. . . . I was always on top of everything. . . . [Before using meth] I was run down. I already had kids at that age and people told me it would help me wake up and keep me going, so I wanted to try it."

Mariah left home pregnant at age fifteen, after having been sexually abused by her stepfather for years. She brought her younger siblings with her. By age twenty-one, she was married with three children and was still caring for her sisters so that they would not have to return home. She described the pressure of caring for so many people becoming too much: "One day, after I turned twenty-one, I was like I didn't want that anymore. You know, I wanted to have a little bit of freedom! So I kicked my husband out, you know. And it was all downhill from there." When her younger sister offered her some meth, although she had never before used drugs, she "figured what the hell," and tried it. What started as a weekend thing, she recalled, "just got worse from there."

Although both Lauren and Mariah framed their meth initiation in relation to precocious entry into adult responsibilities, they traced their pathways in slightly different ways. Lauren emphasized how meth initially helped her meet cultural expectations of being a "superwoman," while Mariah's initiation narrative was more indicative of how unrealistic expectations associated with women's caregiving roles could negatively affect them and even lead to drug use as an escape. In her drug initiation account, we see the seeds of "destruction" that many women attribute to meth once their use became chronic; this is a theme we return to later, but it is noteworthy here that Mariah so quickly linked her gendered rebellion—the desire for freedom—with the "downhill" turn of her life.

Five of the women we interviewed initiated meth use relatively late in life. Each of their initiation narratives emphasized pursuit: a desire to begin using meth specifically because of the benefits—physical or relational—it appeared to offer. In Dorothy's case, meth seemed to give her the energy she needed to study: "It wasn't like I was trying to get high. I was really just trying to get my schedule, keep my 4.0, and keep my grades up." Rose was drawn to meth at the age of thirty-five because she felt it would help her deal with chronic depression and give her much-needed energy. She explained, "I feel like I'm sleeping my life away sometimes and meth kept me . . . awake, made me want to stay awake and be awake and do things to be more active." And while prior research suggests that the popularity of methamphetamine among women is at least partially related to its weight-loss and energy-enhancing qualities (Brecht et al. 2004; Dluzen and Liu 2008), only a handful of women in our sample—and specifically those who initiated meth use as adults— articulated initiation narratives that focused on their desire to lose weight. Donna was offered meth by a friend when she was in her early forties. After learning it was a stimulant, she decided to give it a try: "I heard it was good. . . . My friend next door said it was really good. And I'm like, 'What does it make you do?' and he said, 'It amps you up.' And I'm like, 'alright that's it,' because I don't like marijuana because it makes you sleep and eat all the time and I don't need to be getting no fatter because I used to weigh three hundred pounds." Recalling her first time using, she exclaimed, "I'm like 'oh my God, I like this stuff so much better, there's no sense in eating and getting fat!'" Notice that in all three of these accounts—despite their differences—the initiation narratives emphasized that their initial use was not in pursuit of a *high*, but instead of conventional goals: to feel normal, to lose weight, or to excel educationally.

Super Mom and Super Thin: Women's Narratives of
Continued Meth Use

While our investigation of women's initiation narratives revealed some diversity associated with age of initiation and life circumstances, women's explanations for continued meth use centered more around cultural narratives of motherhood, domesticity, and beauty, which they drew on to make sense of their use to themselves and others. These constructed explanations centered on the use of methamphetamine to accomplish daily tasks associated with motherhood and household responsibilities, provide energy, and assist with weight loss. As explanations for sustained use, such narratives were socially acceptable, as they directly resonated with gendered expectations for behavior; other narratives— such as using the drug for recreational reasons or to "get high"—did not. Yet, as we will see, women's narratives also reveal a number of contradictions about the extent to which they were able to maintain their desired performances as "superwomen." Instead, women's narratives present two opposing images of self—one good and one bad—which they linked to both the progression of their meth use and their hopes for redemption.

As women's methamphetamine use progressed, they initially found success in meeting cultural standards of motherhood and beauty. As a result, they could construct a narrative of their continued meth use that was directly tied to conventional gendered expectations. In short, they indicated that they could continue to use methamphetamine because it did not interfere with their responsibilities and even enhanced their ability to multitask. Rachel perhaps said it most succinctly when she told us that, "it seems like you can do anything when you're on meth . . . you feel like you can clean and go places. You don't need to worry about sleeping [or] eating. You have energy to do anything."

Thus, in many cases women extolled the benefits of meth as it gave them energy to care for their children and households. For example, though Tracy's narrative of her meth initiation emphasized her attempt to solidify her relationship with her boyfriend in the hope that he would assist more with household chores—particularly taxing since she had four young children at the age of twenty-two, including premature infant twins—she described immediately recognizing that methamphetamine would help her to fulfill her role as mother. In her words: "I realized I could stay up all night. I could deal with my kids, even when I was left [alone]. So I just never quit."

Likewise, while Mackenzie reported that she quit using the drug while she was pregnant, she picked up the habit again when her daughter was about six months old because "it would help keep me going, keep me busy, taking care of the new baby." Tiffany also described how meth enabled her to care for her three children and stay "on top of everything." She continued using, she recalled:

Because people were actually bragging about how I was keeping things in order. And my house . . . everything was in its place, you know. My kids, I gotta say, I didn't eat. But my kids ate well. I was up to make them breakfast. I was up to get them little snacks. I wasn't sleeping or taking naps or letting depression keep me down. I was just on top of everything and people were proud of me for it. And it showed that they were proud of me for it. And it kept me wanting to do it.

The ability to stay "on top of things" often allowed women to hide their meth use from others. By all appearances, for a time they were successful in their gendered performances of motherhood and homemaking. Kathy described hiding her use from her daughter by maintaining a perfect front. Like Tiffany, she told us that even though she herself was not eating, she would "cook three meals a day, do all the dishes, and just constantly try and feed my kids and just try and be on point."

Alicia too indicated that the people in her life initially did not know about her meth use and she attributed their lack of awareness to the activities she engaged in with her children. "You know, me and my kids, we would make pancakes in the morning. I mean, it was always food in our house. My kids were always well taken care of. And we were always making cupcakes and I'd let them dye the icing and everything else, you know. Nobody ever knew." Kennedy even suggested that meth helped her to become more involved with her children. She recalled that she "was always at the park going walking. I went to all their school activities, their games." Because women often hid their drug use from their families, and especially their children (or so they believed), they felt that it did not affect their ability to effectively parent (Baker and Carson 1999). Lauren recalled, "I didn't see anything wrong with it. I was still able to take care of my kids, and do whatever I needed to do for them and I still felt like I was being a good mom and showing up for work, so I didn't see no harm in it."

Although motherhood and the performance of domestic duties are not one and the same, they often go hand in hand. Like motherhood, domestic duties are often seen as "woman's work" (Coltrane 2000). Thus the continued use narratives of the women in our sample also stressed the functional use of methamphetamine as a source of motivation and energy to perform domestic duties such as cleaning. For example, when asked what she would do after using meth, Tiffany noted that she would clean and organize constantly. She recalled: "Everything had to be organized. Everything had to be in its place." Similarly, Jade told us, "I could be moving my living room furniture and vacuuming at the same time. It [meth] almost gives you superhuman strength, like I can pick up my couch with one hand." And Christina, a mother of nine children, said that after using meth she could tackle even mundane cleaning tasks with vigor. She recalled feeling "like I could wash dishes, clean the house and everything just perfect. I was so crazy that I remember cleaning the bathroom over and over again. . . . I would literally take all of them [sliding shower doors] out and scrub 'em and scrub 'em for hours."

In addition, while women's narratives of their ongoing meth use were often centered on their mothering and domestic abilities, in some cases, they also drew on other cultural expectations for women to explain why they continued to use it. Though few women described the desire for weight loss as motivating their initiation into meth, many more recalled that their continued use helped them to lose weight; they told of quickly realizing that meth stopped their hunger, allowing them to control their weight easily. Jayda recalled being insecure about her body after having children, and said she continued to use meth to "lose weight and to keep my weight down really." She explained: "I still thought I had to use something to make me look like I did before I had kids, but you know, once you have kids, that's all she wrote, you know. So I'm just, I kept chasing the dream that I couldn't catch." Similarly, Mackenzie told us that she was "very, very heavy when I was younger and got made fun of a lot, I mean to the point where I was bulimic for two years." When she "started doing [meth] . . . the weight was just falling off and I thought I was looking good and that fueled it."

In sum, women relied much more heavily on accounts that emphasized their successful performance of gender to explain their continued meth use. While initial use—especially in adolescence and young adulthood—might be readily viewed as experimentation (and thus perhaps less stigmatizing), sustained use of the drug required more conventional normative explanations. Women's narratives of their continued methamphetamine use allowed them to construct themselves as morally "good" gendered actors—as women both devoted to and successful in their performances of childcare and domestic responsibilities, and concerned with improving or maintaining their physical attractiveness.

Not Like "Those" Women

By describing themselves as committed to maintaining their appearance, their home, and their children, the women we spoke with drew a sharp distinction between themselves and other substance-using women, whose drug addictions were depicted as leaving them morally "failed" women, unable to enact normative gender expectations successfully. Sheila spoke with disdain about the places where she and her boyfriend bought their drugs: "Just the people in there, just . . . I mean . . . totally disgusting. Sitting there, picking their faces, they wouldn't have food and water . . . [there were] kids, dogs running in and out of the house. Have a generator outside running so that they could have electricity in their house." Rose, too, was judgmental of a woman who "spent her entire child support checks on dope." This woman, she explained, "had a really way worse drug problem than I ever thought about having." Rose's remark implied that only a woman with a bad drug addiction would spend money intended for her children on drugs—a sign of moral degradation she was quick to note did not apply to her.

The tendency to pick at one's skin also was seen as an indication of a serious meth addiction, and consequently of the failure to properly attend to gendered appearance norms. Donna explained, "there's some of them that use for so long that they'll feel like bugs or whatever and then that's when the itching and the scratching come in. I've seen it more in women, that a sore will pop up and they will start picking and picking." Women also focused on the loss of sexual respectability in their gendered boundary maintenance, and linked it to physical deterioration as well. Erin described how she could recognize "crank whores"—women who traded sex for meth: "You just know those types of people because they got . . . pits in their face and they got holes and stuff in their arms. And you can just tell when they're there selling themselves for it."

Not surprisingly, the most scorn was reserved for women who used meth while pregnant: the ultimate example of violating gender norms of good motherhood. Valerie described what she believed to be the effects of in utero meth use:

> You could have a mutant child I am sure. I mean meth is so toxic, it's so caustic, it's just disgusting. I mean you chop up a line with a razor blade and it's not like the razor blade has no rust on it. And you've seen what it does to people who get burned cooking it? And that's what it does inside your body. I couldn't even [pause], I've lived with women who do meth when they're pregnant and it's just disgusting. I mean other drugs are bad, but meth is even worse. I'm surprised they don't have three-eyed kids coming out of them.

Despite such criticisms, the women did not necessarily abstain from drugs, and even meth, during their own pregnancies. In particular, the use of marijuana during pregnancy was not uncommon among would-be mothers in the sample. Tiffany told us that she quit using meth as soon as she learned she was pregnant, but continued to use marijuana. And Kathy's comment that "at least" she quit using meth exemplified the view held by many mothers in our sample that some drugs, such as methamphetamine, are much more harmful than others. By contrasting themselves with women who they depicted as clearly outside the social boundaries of acceptable behavior, the women in our sample asserted "a hierarchy of moral worth" (Small, Harding, and Lamont 2010, 17) that allowed them to maintain a self story of gendered respectability.

Not So Super After All: Women's Narratives of the Descent into Meth Addiction

Though the women we spoke with extolled the motivational and energizing properties of methamphetamine, they eventually recognized that there were serious unanticipated consequences to their use. As they became increasingly involved with the drug, their ability to function according to the gendered ideals they articulated was undermined. They found themselves unable and unwilling, without methamphetamine, to keep up the frenetic pace of their lives. More importantly, many of the women became separated from their children and families, making the good mother narrative unsustainable. Because of its destructive consequences in their lives, women's narratives of their use also included an unraveling of the interpretations they provided for their early continued use; many saw their meth use as a downward spiral that eventually resulted in their incarceration, as well as other significant losses in their lives. In this way, women's narratives included an account of a shameful past that became a necessary part of their story, as a prelude to redemption (see also Maruna 2001, 87).

Jade told us that she became dependent on meth to motivate her to take care of her responsibilities. In her words, "like I didn't want to clean my house unless I was high on meth. A lot of things like that, that are just normal everyday tasks, I just didn't want to do. . . . because I didn't have the extra energy." Liberty also suggested that eventually she could not get things done without using meth. She recalled, "I couldn't function, I started not being able to function. I had to have it to, in order to give me energy to go through the day." Ultimately, she said that meth "controlled my life. If I didn't have it, I would just sit there and my house would be dirty, my clothes wouldn't get washed, nothing would get done." In the peak of her use, Kelly was actually evicted from her home because she was unable to maintain it: "The house was always trashed. You'd think it wouldn't be livable. But, we were going too hard to even stop to pay attention." In this way, over time, women began to recognize those "other" drug-addicted women in themselves; they began narrating a life enslaved to the pharmacology of the drug.

In addition, though women suggested that initially they were good mothers, they acknowledged that their increased meth use eventually affected their ability to care for their children. In some cases, they described being unable to function as a mother without meth. Rachel remarked that, "it was the only way I had energy even to take my kids to the park. I'm tired, I need [meth] to help me." Some women described that over time they focused more on their drug use than their children. For instance, Erin's narrative of her early use contrasted with her evaluation of her later use. She said originally that she "liked [meth], it made me feel energetic, like I could clean my house and I could get a million things done all at once." Yet, she described "falling apart" after years of use. She continued: "Really the meth was keeping me down, I couldn't get along with anybody. . . . I was just depressed all the time. I wasn't the mom that I was before to the kids." Paige, likewise described her heavy meth use as eventually disrupting her ability to be a good mother: "I mean, I have been around my daughter, but it has kept me, I mean, I'm there physically, but mentally I'm just gone." And Sheila described physical absences associated with her escalating meth use: "I left my kids for months at a time just because I wanted to go get high. No trace, they didn't know if I was dead or alive."

Finally, as women's meth use continued, they described that their appearance suffered as well. The weight loss that was welcome early on was later seen as unhealthy, as women used increasingly larger amounts of meth. Lauren told us that at the peak of her use, "I mean I was sick looking. I was down to about ninety pounds and I'm five foot seven. I didn't eat, so I was very, very unhealthy." Similarly, Christina described her appearance at the peak of her use as "skinny and sucked up and just a total wreck." Extreme weight loss was not the only challenge to women's appearance as a result of meth use. Heather noted that because of her chronic meth use, "I only have six teeth on top [and have] wrinkles on my face." Kathy too lamented how meth "made a horrible difference in my face, the lines [and] the wrinkles."

Ultimately, the women's continued meth use meant that they looked less and less like the ideal woman they originally aspired toward, and more and more like a stereotypical drug-using female—hoary and worn-out. The original narrative by which they could interpret their meth use as enabling their attainment of cultural expectations of women eventually gave way to a narrative of failure. In their eyes, meth prohibited them from being the mothers and even the women they were intended to be. What is striking in all of this is how readily the women we spoke to situated their meth use in the context of a clearly articulated storyline of gendered conformity followed by destruction.

Women's Narratives of Redemption: Desistance from Meth and the Desire to be Normal

Because the women in our sample were clean—some by choice prior to prison and others compelled by their incarceration—their narratives of use also became narratives of change. They articulated reform narratives similar to those other scholars have identified (Maruna 2001; Presser 2008), but with a distinctly gendered flavor. Reform was not just about a future that did not include methamphetamine, but also was explicitly narrated as a return to respectable gendered selves. Drug use was described in their retrospective narratives as eventually a shameful, yet integral, part of their life history, with new narratives reembracing their roles as good mothers. For example, asked whether she thought she would return to meth use after her release, Alicia said, "I'm done. Because it's not . . . it's not worth it, you know. Because I have four kids at home that's waiting for me to come home. I'm all they got. And I can't let them, you know, be away from me again. And after almost four years clean, there's no way I can mess that up." Similarly, Georgia explained that postrelease "I'm going to take care of my little girls like a normal mom should and I'm just going to relax. I'm going to stay at home and relax, go to work, and come home and take care of my kids."

Just as women's narratives of early use involved boundary work differentiating them from "other" (failed) female drug users, and their accounts of their escalating use involved discovering themselves in the "other" they disdained, their narratives of redemption relied on drawing distinctions between their old and new selves, but also between themselves and their old drug partners and friends. Paige's comments are illustrative: "I just completely want out of the lifestyle. The people that I [was] around are horrible people. They have no morals, no values in life and I was one of those people too. I just don't want to be looked at like that anymore. I want to be a mommy and do things right and go to school and earn a career."

Ironically, though most of the women did not attribute their initial use to any undue influence associated with romantic relationships, instead focusing on their own motivations and agency, their future plans for redemption sometimes involved severing such relationships. This was particularly the case when these relationships were seen as counter to their return to the good mother role. Liberty, for example, told us she planned to divorce her husband because he continued to use meth. She explained, "he doesn't care. I mean, I care . . . so I choose my two little boys. I said I choose my two little boys." Though she was nervous about her ability to stay clean, she was determined to try: "I cannot guarantee one day from the next, but I can guarantee you I will give you my best to stay clean and to focus on life and my kids now."

The plan to abandon bad relationships was not an abandonment of the desire to be a wife *and* mother; indeed the two are tightly coupled in cultural ideals for women. Thus Tammy's plan for the future included not only divorcing her meth-using husband but also the hope for a potential new romance, with meth replaced by an idealized husband and home: "Of course, everyone wants to be, fall in love and get married. That's somethin' I've always wanted, that's been my dream. I always wanted what John Q. Public had: a house, picket fence and the kids, husband. I felt that was always out of my reach, always unattainable because of the people I ran with. You don't marry them, you know. . . . I don't want that. I'm not looking for that, you know, and I'm gonna find me a totally different kind of guy, I tell you that." Thus, as with their narratives of continued use, women often returned to gendered cultural stories as a means of articulating what their redeemed self would look like: a good and normal mother, and if they were lucky, a healthy romantic life and idealized home.

Conclusion

The women methamphetamine users we spoke with narrated a gendered chronological story of their meth initiation, continued use, descent into addiction, and finally, their (hoped for) recovery, and with it, redemption. The plots of women's stories varied with regard to contexts of initiation, but they converged in their explanations of continued use, drawing on their beliefs in the utility of the drug for their successful performance of so-called good womanhood and motherhood. Their initiation narratives were age-graded, with precocious movement into adult roles and responsibilities relevant for women who initiated at younger ages, as well as discourses about teenage rebellion not uncommon. Women who initiated in adulthood described their decision to try meth in the context of various pursuits—weight loss, meeting household obligations, to overcome depression, or to solidify romantic relationships—but often emphasized that their initial purpose was *not* to get high.

Interestingly, though many of these women initiated drug use with male romantic partners or peers, they did not embrace stories that implicated these men in their initiation. Likewise, despite many experiences with childhood abuse and trauma, very few women drew on victimization discourses to explain their meth initiation, with few framing their drug use as emerging from a desire to escape the pain of trauma. The agentic threads in women's initiation stories may be partly attributable to the greater social acceptability of drug experimentation than chronic use. And women's tendency to avoid victim narratives could reflect the influence in popular culture of "new versions of victims" that stress women's agency and survival (Lamb 1999), though it likely also was impacted by the situational context of their telling: a prison-based drug treatment program.

The continued chronology of women's meth use plots coalesced around stories about a morally good gendered self. Unlike with the use of many other drugs—and many other crimes, for that matter—women meth users appeared able to draw from an articulation of normative gender identities as a resource for "doing meth." They framed their continued use of the drug in normatively appropriate ways by emphasizing how its pharmacology assisted them in being good mothers and homemakers, and in embodying culturally idealized beauty by way of thinness. In this way, they attempted to reject the stigma of double deviance faced by women offenders. Yet, these women also had to account for how they ended up in prison and in a treatment program for drug addiction. The plot of their story thus incorporated both a fall from gendered grace and a redemptive future as good mothers who will perhaps be fortunate enough to enter into healthy relationships with healthy men.

We can't, of course, speak to whether women's gendered narratives about continued methamphetamine use were the same at the time we interviewed them as they were "in the moment," when their narratives would have spoken directly to their ongoing activities. Nor can we be sure that their stories of redemption will translate in any way to their actual decision-making about methamphetamine use or desistance upon release from prison. The particular gendered constructions used by women in our sample—and the plot which unfolded through their narrative accounts of meth initiation, use, addiction, and future redemption—demonstrate one set of gendered narratives available to them, but were also likely influenced both by the reflective environment of a prison-based treatment program, and the second author's visible pregnancy at the time. Such is the nature of retrospective interviewing, and the influence of context on the stories that get told (see Miller 2010).

Narrative criminology's quest to be a theoretical framework that can account for the constitutive nature of narratives for crime has such issues as a primary challenge, particularly given recognition that the narratives individuals tell themselves and others are recognizably "dynamic, emergent, local, variable, and shifting" (Martin 2003, 351). Thus, while we have no doubt that "stories shape self-awareness and chart action" (Presser 2009, 189), at what moment in time must we capture individuals' stories to identify their causal role in facilitating crime or desistance? This is a key methodological challenge for narrative criminology, particularly since most accounts collected by criminologists are retrospective (see Presser 2009, 193).

Critical interrogations of doing gender—concerned as it is with the nature of practices (including talk) for constituting gender—raise additional concerns of relevance for the development of narrative criminology (see Collins 1995; Deutsch 2007; Jones 2009; Miller 2002). Scholars have consistently found disparities when comparing how individuals *understand* and *represent* their and others' behaviors—including crime—compared with what they actually do (Bottcher 2001; Cobbina, Like-Haislip, and Miller 2010; Contreras 2009; Walker 1994). With regard to gender, for example, in practice there are both significant within-gender variations and cross-gender similarities that are often lost or downplayed in the gendered stories told. Moreover, gender differences in practice are often accounted for by social organization and individuals' accommodations to these in negotiating their strategies of action (Kandiyoti 1988). Thus, while interpretations of practice—particularly in the context of narratives and stories—often naturalize gender difference (Connell 2002), the behaviors themselves are likely less the result of *actual* (i.e., biological and character) gender differences than they are choices made in the contexts of gendered constraints (Miller 2002). Yet the cultural currency of gender duality means these explanations are rarely the content of self-stories.

In addition, we recognize that the stories individuals tell—like those told to us by women methamphetamine users—are guided by a plot, which is "the means by which what would otherwise be mere occurrences are made into moments in the unfolding of the story" (Polletta et al. 2011, 111). Yet, the use of probing questions in interview-based research can also reveal important gaps in individuals' stories, and these, too, can reveal contradictions between what people say and what they do. In this sense, interviewers' probes can themselves disrupt the plot of the stories being told. The implications for narrative criminology are twofold. First, as we have argued elsewhere, such disruptions and gaps provide important opportunities for theorizing about the meanings of such contradictions, raising questions about the explanatory power of narratives for understanding social action (Miller 2010; see also Sandberg 2010). In addition, narrative accounts can, in fact, impart important truths about social practices beyond the narratives themselves (Miller and Glassner 2011). It is thus important for narrative analysis to remain one of multiple ways we approach the social insights that can be gleaned from interview accounts.

Indeed, investigations of crime and criminalization must grapple with the social facts of inequality beyond their discursive production. Presser and Sandberg (this volume) suggest that narrative criminologists take "real oppressive structures into view . . . [by] consider[ing] them as discursively constructed and, furthermore, as conditioning discursive processes," noting the "limitations on creative storytelling due to social context, class, race, gender, and so on." This signals to us the import of moving beyond the study of narratives alone. As Winant (1995, 504) explains, while social structure is "dynamic and reciprocal," it also "has a formidable inertia, a historical weight, which is crystallized in innumerable institutions, customs and laws. It has been engraved in time and space, made into a truly 'deep structure'—a result not only of contemporary repetitions but also as a legacy." Thus, a primary limitation of a discursive treatment of such inequalities is that structure needs to be understood beyond that which is "constantly reproduced from moment to moment" (Winant 1995, 504). Ultimately, we would suggest that narrative criminology is indeed a useful theoretical tool. Yet it should remain only one of a complex range of tools in the toolkit we employ to understand the causes and consequences of crime.

NOTES

1. This is not to say such narratives of self are necessarily absent from women's and girls' accounts (see Jones 2010; Miller 2002), but rather to highlight that claiming such self-definitions comes with a gendered stigma that is not experienced by men and boys.
2. For a more detailed description of our research methods and data analysis, see Carbone-Lopez and Miller (2012).
3. All names used here are pseudonyms.

REFERENCES

Agnew, Robert. 2006. "Storylines as a Neglected Cause of Crime." *Journal of Research in Crime and Delinquency* 43 (2): 119–147.

Anderson, Kristin L., and Debra Umberson. 2001. "Gendering Violence: Masculinity and Power in Men's Accounts of Domestic Violence." *Gender and Society* 15 (3): 358–380.

Baker, Phyllis L., and Amy Carson. 1999. "'I Take Care of My Kids': Mothering Practices of Substance-Abusing Women." *Gender and Society* 13 (3): 347–363.

Banwell, Cathy, and Gabriele Bammer. 2006. "Maternal Habits: Narratives of Mothering, Social Position and Drug Use." *International Journal of Drug Policy* 17 (6): 504–513.

Bottcher, Jean. 2001. "Social Practices of Gender: How Gender Relates to Delinquency in the Everyday Lives of High-Risk Youths." *Criminology* 39 (4): 893–932.

Boyd, Susan C. 2004. *From Witches to Crack Moms: Women, Drug Law, and Policy.* Durham, NC: Carolina Academic Press.

Brecht, Mary-Lynn, Ann O'Brien, Christina von Mayrhauser, and M. Douglas Anglin. 2004. "Methamphetamine Use Behaviors and Gender Differences." *Addictive Behaviors* 29 (1): 89–106.

Butler, Judith. 1990. *Gender Trouble: Feminism and the Subversion of Identity.* London: Routledge.

Cameron, Deborah. 1998. "Gender, Language, and Discourse: A Review Essay." *Signs* 23 (4): 945–973.

Campbell, Nancy D. 2000. *Using Women: Gender, Drug Policy, and Social Justice.* New York, Routledge.

Carbone-Lopez, Kristin, and Jody Miller. 2012. "Precocious Role Entry as a Mediating Factor in Women's Methamphetamine Use: Implications for Life-Course and Pathways Research." *Criminology* 50 (1): 187–220.

Carbone-Lopez, Kristin, Jennifer Gatewood Owens, and Jody Miller. "Women's 'Storylines' of Methamphetamine Initiation in the Midwest." *Journal of Drug Issues* 42 (3): 226–246.

Cobbina, Jennifer, Toya Z. Like-Haislip, and Jody Miller. 2010. "Gang Fights Versus Cat Fights: Urban Young Men's Gendered Narratives of Violence." *Deviant Behavior* 31 (7): 596–624.

Collins, Patricia Hill. 1995. "Symposium: On West and Fenstermaker's 'Doing Difference.'" *Gender and Society* 9 (4): 491–494.

Coltrane, John. 2000. "Research on Household Labor: Modeling and Measuring the Social Embeddedness of Routine Family Work." *Journal of Marriage and Family* 62 (4): 1208–1233.

Connell, Raewyn. 2009. "Accountable Conduct: 'Doing Gender' in Transsexual and Political Retrospect." *Gender and Society* 23 (1): 104–111.

Connell, R. W. 2002. *Gender.* Cambridge, UK: Polity Press.

Contreras, Randol. 2009. "'Dam, Yo—Who's That Girl?': An Ethnographic Analysis of Masculinity in Drug Robberies." *Journal of Contemporary Ethnography* 38 (4): 465–492.

Copes, Heith, and Andy Hochstetler. 2003. "Situational Constructions of Masculinity among Male Street Thieves." *Journal of Contemporary Ethnography* 32 (3): 279–304.

Daly, Kathleen, and Lisa Maher. 1998. "Crossroads and Intersections: Building from Feminist Critique." In *Criminology at the Crossroads: Feminist Readings in Crime and Justice*, edited by Kathleen Daly and Lisa Maher, 1–17. Oxford: Oxford University Press.

Deutsch, Francine M. 2007. "Undoing Gender." *Gender and Society* 21 (1): 106–127.

Dluzen, Dean E., and Bin Liu. 2008. "Gender Differences in Methamphetamine Use and Responses: A Review." *Gender and Medicine* 5 (1): 24–35.

Ettorre, Elizabeth M. 1992. *Women and Substance Use.* New Brunswick, NJ: Rutgers University Press.

Ferraro, Kathleen J., and Angela M. Moe. 2003. "Mothering, Crime, and Incarceration." *Journal of Contemporary Ethnography* 32 (1): 9–40.

Garfinkel, Harold. 1967. *Studies in Ethnomethodology.* Englewood Cliffs, NJ: Prentice Hall.

Gilfus, Mary E. 1992. "From Victims to Survivors to Offenders: Women's Routes of Entry and Immersion in to Street Crime." *Women and Criminal Justice* 4 (1): 63–89.

Hollander, Jocelyn A. 2001. "Vulnerability and Dangerousness: The Construction of Gender through Conversation about Violence." *Gender and Society* 15 (1): 83–109.

Jones, Nikki. 2010. *Between Good and Ghetto: African American Girls and Inner City Violence.* New Brunswick, NJ: Rutgers University Press.

———. 2009. "'I was aggressive for the streets, pretty for the pictures': Gender, Difference, and the Inner-City Girl." *Gender and Society* 23 (1): 89–93.

Kandiyoti, Deniz. 1988. "Bargaining with Patriarchy." *Gender and Society* 2 (3): 274–290.

Kessler, Suzanne J., and Wendy McKenna. 1978. *Gender: An Ethnomethodological Approach*. Chicago: University of Chicago Press.

Klee, Hilary, Marcia Jackson, and Suzan Lewis. 2001. *Drug Misuse and Motherhood*. New York: Routledge.

Lamb, Sharon, ed. 1999. *New Versions of Victims: Feminists Struggle with the Concept*. New York: New York University Press.

Maher, Lisa. 1997. *Sexed Work: Gender, Race and Resistance in a Brooklyn Drug Market*. Oxford: Clarendon Press.

Maruna, Shadd. 2001. *Making Good: How Ex-Convicts Reform and Rebuild their Lives*. Washington, DC: American Psychological Association Books.

McAdams, Dan P. 1985. *Power, Intimacy, and the Life Story: Personological Inquiries into Identity*. New York: Guilford Press.

———. 2008. "Personal Narratives and the Life Story." In *The Handbook of Personality: Theory and Research*, 3rd ed., edited by Oliver P. John, Richard W. Robins, and Lawrence A. Pervin, 242–262. New York: Guilford Press.

Messerschmidt, James W. 1993. *Masculinities and Crime*. Lanham, MD: Rowman and Littlefield.

Miller, Brenda A., and Richard F. Mancuso. 2004. "Connecting Childhood Victimization to Later Alcohol/Drug Problems: Implications for Prevention." *Journal of Primary Prevention* 25 (2): 149–169.

Miller, Jody. 2001. *One of the Guys: Girls, Gangs, and Gender*. New York: Oxford University Press.

———. 2002. "The Strengths and Limits of 'Doing Gender' for Understanding Street Crime." *Theoretical Criminology* 6 (4): 433–460.

———. 2010. "The Impact of Gender when Studying 'Offenders on Offending.'" In *Offenders on Offending: Learning about Crime from Criminals*, edited by Wim Bernasco and Michael Tonry, 161–183. London: Willan Press.

Miller, Jody, and Barry Glassner. 2011. "The 'Inside' and the 'Outside': Finding Realities in Interviews." In *Qualitative Research: Theory, Method and Practice*, 3rd ed., edited by David Silverman, 131–148. London: Sage.

Mishler, Elliot G. 1986. *Research Interviewing: Context and Narrative*. Cambridge, MA: Harvard University Press.

Nilan, Pamela. 1994. "Gender as Positioned Identity Maintenance in Everyday Discourse." *Social Semiotics* 4 (1–2): 139–163.

Orbuch, Terrie L. 1997. "People's Accounts Count: The Sociology of Accounts." *Annual Review of Sociology* 23: 455–78.

Polletta, Francesca, Pang Ching Bobby Chen, Beth Charrity Gardner, and Alice Motes. 2011. "The Sociology of Storytelling." *Annual Review of Sociology* 37 (1): 109–130.

Presser, Lois. 2008. *Been a Heavy Life: Stories of Violent Men*. Urbana and Chicago: University of Illinois Press.

———. 2009. "The Narratives of Offenders." *Theoretical Criminology* 13 (2): 177–200.

Ridgeway, Cecilia L., and Shelley J. Correll. 2004. "Unpacking the Gender System: A Theoretical Perspective on Cultural Beliefs in Social Relations." *Gender and Society* 18 (4): 510–531.

Salisbury, Emily J., and Patricia Van Voorhis. 2009. "Gendered Pathways: A Quantitative Investigation of Women Probationer's Paths to Incarceration." *Criminal Justice and Behavior* 36 (6): 541–566.

Sandberg, Sveinung. 2009. "Gangster, Victim, or Both? The Interdiscursive Construction of Sameness and Difference in Self-Presentations." *British Journal of Sociology* 60 (3): 523–542.

———. 2010. "What Can 'Lies' Tell Us about Life? Notes toward a Framework of Narrative Criminology." *Journal of Criminal Justice Education* 21 (4): 447–465.

Short, James F. 1998. "The Level of Explanation Problem Revisited—The American Society of Criminology 1997 Presidential Address." *Criminology* 36 (1): 3–36.

Small, Mario Luis, David J. Harding, and Michèle Lamont. 2010. "Reconsidering Culture and Poverty." *The Annals of the American Academy of Political and Social Science* 629: 6–27.

Stokoe, Elizabeth. 2006. "On Ethnomethodology, Feminism, and the Analysis of Categorical Reference to Gender in Talk-in-Interaction." *Sociological Review* 54 (3): 467–494.

Ulrich, Miriam, and Ann Weatherall. 2000. "Motherhood and Infertility: Viewing Motherhood Through the Lens of Infertility." *Feminism and Psychology* 10 (3): 323–336.

Walker, Karen. 1994. "Men, Women, and Friendship: What They Say, What They Do." *Gender and Society* 8 (2): 246–265.

West, Candace, and Sarah Fenstermaker. 1995. "Doing Difference." *Gender and Society* 9 (1): 8–37.

West, Candace, and Don H. Zimmerman. 1987. "Doing Gender." *Gender and Society* 1 (2): 125–151.

4

Moral Habilitation and the New Normal

Sexual Offender Narratives of Posttreatment
Community Integration

JANICE VICTOR AND JAMES B. WALDRAM

Disruptive life events can shatter the complacent, routine, and unreflective nature of human existence, one's sense of what it means to be
normal and live a normal life (Becker 1997). Such events create narrative
turmoil, challenging our sense of self and identity, and the way in which
we choose to project these to the world at large (Garro and Mattingly
2000; Viney and Bousfield 1991). Troubling events force their way into
our personal narratives, and compel us to consider the value inherent in
acknowledging or hiding such events as we refashion our self-narratives
and confront a world that may—we are never sure—have knowledge
of these experiences. In this chapter we explore the narrative dilemmas
confronting individuals whose disruptive life experiences are quite dramatic, self-induced, and universally reviled: sexual offenders. Like any
other person, men convicted and treated for committing sexual offenses
desire a "normal" life (Waldram 2012), however defined. Yet their desire
for normalcy is that much more intense for their actions have thrust
them into a world where they can for a time be normal neither to themselves nor to society.

The concept of an authentic self is pervasive in Western society and is
embedded in folk psychologies and discourses on selfhood (Lindholm
2008; Shweder and Bourne 1994; Spiro 1993). The authentic self is believed to represent some core essence of one's personality that is stable
and unchanging, and acts as a moral compass guiding behavior. This
view of the self, however, does little to explain how those who consider
themselves as essentially good people commit acts that gravely hurt others. It has been suggested that individuals facing such existential dilem-

mas frequently employ *neutralizations*, self-talk designed to rationalize such inconsistent behavior in a manner that reinforces one's sense of morality (Sykes and Matza 1957). Narrative criminology encourages us to consider how neutralization is an unsatisfactory explanation for the broader narrative challenge that these morally abhorrent acts create for one's sense of identity, including both private and public presentations of the self (Presser and Sandberg, introduction, this volume). The offender here does not only grapple with this fragmentation of narrative identity privately; he also is confronted with a public discourse about sexual offenders that is essentialist in nature, cohering around moral notions that suggest his actions are de facto evidence of the existence of evil in the world, and that his aberrant or evil behavior is an intrinsic part of his selfhood that is immune to moral (re)habilitation (Waldram 2009; 2012).

We are not suggesting here that there is such a thing as an "authentic self," and instead tend to view this construct as a necessary illusion where the idea of self is a dynamic subjective and intersubjective representation constructed through multiple narratives that gather strength to further construct a narrative trajectory over time (de Munck 2000, 39). This discursive construction of selfhood is a means of creating coherence and consistency in one's life. The more it is employed, the more power it has to construct the appearance of a stable, authentic sense of self. The perception of selfhood as a coherent yet complex whole can become fractured when a significant life event takes place that forces the person to rethink who he or she is. Narrative, of course, is fluid, and challenges to one's narrative sense of self are characteristically met by efforts to refashion the narrative in a way that makes sense of the disruption (Becker 1997; Garro and Mattingly 2000). Narrativization— the ongoing construction and renovation of multilayered self-narratives of experience—brings some sense of order to the chaos as individuals reconstruct a story that hopefully helps them to derive positive meaning out of the experience.

Narrativization is problematic for sexual offenders because the stigma of their actions makes it more difficult to construct positive meaning from their convictions. Disruption, for these men, identifies the transformational experience and labored process that starts from the offense and includes arrest, conviction, imprisonment, and treatment, and eventually for most, community integration. Their *old* normal, a largely unreflective way of living their lives within a familiar social context prior to the commission of their sexual crimes, is no longer an option. This old normal is replaced by a *new* normal, a tension-riddled existential and intersubjective state of flux in which they seek a place in a community that reviles them for who they are as much as for what they have done. Many sexual offenders respond to the external imposition of an essentialized label—the evil, amoral sexual offender—through a process of narrativization that acknowledges rather than denies the crimes that they have committed. Exploring this process is key to understanding the contribution that a narrative criminology can make to forensic treatment's goals of "effecting desistance from . . . harmful action" (Presser and Sandberg, this volume).

Moral Habilitation: Transforming the Old Normal into a New Normal

Contrary to popular and state-sponsored discourses that promote the idea that prison treatment programs are designed to rehabilitate inmates, the primary aim of much offender treatment, including that for sexual offenders, is to *morally habilitate*. Moral habilitation is "the process by which individuals are morally remade into the image of certain ideals regarding appropriate social and ethical conduct so that they become 'fit' to be among us" (Waldram 2012, 101). Forensic treatment typically involves training offenders to accept responsibility for their actions instead of minimizing or denying accountability, thereby correcting the *cognitive distortions* that support offending behavior, and developing what is called a Relapse Prevention Plan (Abel, Becker, and Cunningham-Rathner 1984; Auburn and Lea 2003; Fox 1999; Mann 2004; Waldram 2010). Cognitive distortions are problematic from the perspective of narrative criminology because they posit "discrete cognitions unrelated to a fuller sense of self in the world through time" (Presser and Sandburg, this volume). Narrative criminology makes explicit the connectedness of time and self-construction. Moreover, the world portrayed in treatment as existing "out there" for the awaiting offender is unrealistic. Programs project a utopian view of society and prosocial behavior that fails to reflect the lived experience of even so-called normal individuals.

Relapse prevention is a typical component of treatment programs in which participants reflect on their life circumstances, thoughts, feelings, and patterns of social interaction prior to their offenses. Participants are required to prepare contingency plans and reconsider certain habits or patterns of behavior to avoid situations that might put them at high risk to reoffend when back in the community (simultaneously putting them at high risk of breaching court orders attached to their release). Contingency plans commonly include ongoing self-surveillance of thoughts and feelings; a customized collection of situations to avoid such as places where children might be found; and honoring curfews and prohibitions on the consumption of alcohol and gun possession. These practices are drilled into offenders in the name of risk management, and for the most part have a lowering effect on recidivism (Beech and Ford 2006; Hanson et al. 2009; Nicholaichuk et al. 2000). However, life in the community is unruly and cannot always be circumscribed by relapse prevention.

Like anyone who wants to improve, men convicted and treated for sexual offenses must accept a new way of thinking and acting in the world. Change can, and even *must*, be embraced, internalized, and then unreflectively enacted in daily life if the offender is to not reoffend. Treatment participants must be intrinsically motivated to redefine their selfhood, while also implementing their Relapse Prevention Plan consistently so as to routinize a new way of living. These changes, which are exacted through moral habilitation, constitute a transformation toward what we call the new normal.

For most sexual offenders, the old normal meant some level of psychosocial dysfunction that became exacerbated during times of stress or unhappiness. It is not uncommon for offenders to have experienced substance abuse, mental health troubles, marital or relationship dissatisfaction, childhood sexual abuse, or other situations that induced a high level of stress that they found unmanageable. Such dysfunction is typically familiarized and thus comforting. While some offenders may have very few positive influences in their lives, others can be seen from all outward appearances to be living ordinary lives with romantic relationships, children, friendships, and careers or employment. As Marshall (1996, 322) notes, they often appear as "everyman," largely indistinguishable from nonoffenders.

Informed by narrative psychology, the research presented here results from a person-centered ethnographic exploration of the community integration experiences of sexual offenders following imprisonment and treatment. Inspired by previous institutional ethnographic research of sexual offender treatment (Waldram 2012), we are interested in understanding how offenders utilize or enact treatment lessons from prison psychological programming and express the psychosocial and moral dimensions of their experiences after they have been released from prison. Eighteen men who had been treated for sexual offenses were recruited through various community organizations that provided specialized services for released sexual offenders. A narrative interview format was employed, where men were encouraged to share stories of their treatment and community experiences. Interviews were digitally recorded, transcribed, and analyzed using a variety of narrative and discourse analysis techniques. For this chapter we have selected data from four participants to demonstrate how narratives of self and social interaction are infused with discourses of authenticity that, combined with experiences of stigma in the face of an unruly society, inform the emergence of a new habilitated normal in past sexual offenders.

A cornerstone of sexual offender treatment programs in Canada eschews essentialism and invokes agency: sexual offenders are not bad people; they just made bad choices or decisions (Waldram 2012). This strategy is important for giving men hope that they can change and provides a goal toward which they can strive, that is, how to make more prosocial decisions. Many participants seem to embrace this idea, separating act from essence to reject the idea that they harbor some essential, inner badness (Waldram 2009). That said, perceptions of sexual offending behaviors are more complex than just a bad choice, in part due to the contempt society assigns to such acts. People make mistakes every day, some of which are even hurtful to others. Unlike ordinary mistakes, the ones that result in a sexual offense offer few options for redemption. Men convicted for such offenses may be stigmatized for a long time, finding it hard to escape the label of sexual offender. They are considered a permanent threat in the public eye because the essentialist discourse of selfhood fosters the assumption that these men harbor some inner defect through which they become solely defined. Essentialist perspectives of selfhood appear to take on a nuance when sexual offenders are struggling to construct a new life, while simultaneously working to hide their criminal label. In this transition from the old normal to the new normal, the desire for authenticity is undermined by confusion, uncertainty, and fear as selfhood and interpersonal interactions become filtered through the lens of stigma.

The transformation from the old to new normal involves two main tasks. First, offenders need to come to terms with their moral selfhood and make sense of their offenses. First-time sexual offenders may be especially disturbed by how their actions contrast so sharply with the views they hold of their "authentic" selves. Second, offenders have to learn to habilitate to a social world that falls significantly short of the prosocial ideal they heard about in prison, and where their stigmatized identities dramatically change their perceptions and expectations of interpersonal interactions. Each of these tasks may be resisted but must ultimately be embraced if one is to eventually find a new normal.

The Dissonant Self

Cognitive dissonance identifies a state of uncomfortable tension that is experienced when a person is faced with two or more contradicting cognitions about her or his self (Festinger 1957; Tavris and Aronson 2007). For the sexual offender, dissonance between his sense of self and his contradicting actions is very much a moral issue; at the heart of the discrepancy lie notions of what it means to be a good person. Not all sexual offenders believe that they are good people (Waldram 2009). Those that do must contend with the contradiction between their belief in themselves as basically good and their knowledge that they have committed bad, even horrific, acts. A key feature of the new normal is learning to overcome cognitive dissonance and accept their actions as one significant but not totalizing product of their self.

Kevin was a Caucasian man in his early forties who offended against his stepson. He ascribed to the psychological designation of homosexual pedophile and talked about how his life at the time of his offending was filled with a distress that left him feeling as if he was "drowning . . . in the deep end of the pool." At the time of the interview, Kevin had been out of prison for almost two years.

Kevin was still very troubled by his capability to hurt someone that he loved. When asked how he viewed himself now, Kevin responded:

> I *think* I've made a lot of positive things happen for myself. There's *a lot* of things that I've done right since the conviction but I'm still having a hard time balancing that with the things that I know I've done wrong. I think if I was a less caring person . . . [and] if I didn't care as much about what people thought about *me*, it would be easier; but I've always been a people pleaser and to let so many people down in such a big way has been a tough nut for me to swallow. Aside from the offending, I'd always had a fairly good opinion about myself, fairly good self-image, but . . . it's a bit more like a Picasso now. [Laughs.] There's pieces everywhere and some make sense and some don't.

Kevin elaborated on how therapeutic measures were helping him to make sense of his confusion and dissonance:

> I *did* do a lot of good things in the community. I am generally a good person. Take away the offending and I *am* a helpful, generous, kind individual. People love me and I love people in return . . . but there's the one area of my life where I failed to get help that I need to get. . . . There's constant reminders. I'll be sitting in a restaurant and see a dad with his son and I'll flash back to my time with my victim. Instantly there's this regret. Why couldn't I have been a better father? . . . If I *loved* him, how could I hurt him that way? And so then I have to balance that and say, "Well, the *whole* relationship wasn't about offending. There were many, many, many other aspects to that relationship."

One way Kevin was learning to deal with his dissonance was by accepting that he had a problem—his "deviant sexuality"—that he must learn to manage, much like everyone has problems that we need to overcome. He was starting to come to accept that his selfhood, although mostly good, also included parts that were shameful.

Carl's narrative bears similarities to Kevin's, particularly with regard to their experience of cognitive dissonance. Also a Caucasian man in his early forties, Carl had been convicted for fondling a young girl. Prior to his offense, he had been married with two daughters, a situation that ended in divorce and no visitation rights. He had been living back in the community for five years. When asked how he viewed himself, Carl responded, "I'm an easygoing, emotions-on-my-sleeve person. Very caring. Wants to help people. Disappointed in what I did and I guess I maybe beat myself up over it more than I think other people do." Like Kevin, Carl seemed aware that his actions did not match the other parts that comprised his self-concept. When asked if he viewed himself differently now compared to before his offense, he revealed just how perplexed he was about his "true" self:

> Basically the person I am now [is] the same person I was. I really haven't changed. I still help people, I still [am] very kindhearted, willing to listen. I have not changed. . . . I haven't really. The only thing I have changed is not to be around kids as much anymore. Still . . . I'd still like to be a father again. That's one thing I miss. . . . If I do get remarried, I'd like to have one more kid and be able to raise a kid and not be able to pass on the bad things about me. . . . Like there's the only compliment I ever had from my father, that I know of, is that I was a good parent, good father. I know I can do it. And that's the other weird thing. Why didn't I do anything to my own kids? What made me stop there?

Unlike Kevin, Carl insisted that he had not changed from who he was before his arrest. His self-concept was more stable, perhaps too much so considering he was having such difficulty constructing a new life for himself. At issue was Carl's cognitive dissonance between his loss of identity as a father and trying to understand how someone who was such a good father could abuse another's child.

Other men were more able to resolve their cognitive dissonance over time. Jason was in his early thirties and had been released from prison ten years prior. He briefly mentioned childhood sexual abuse by a boy slightly older than him. Jason had gone on to offend against an undisclosed number of boys. During treatment he learned to redirect his sexual arousal to age-appropriate men. Where Carl displayed a rigid sense of self, Jason's was flexible and adaptive. He represented himself as someone who invited a new way of being into his life, quickly throwing off the old normal to create a new normal for himself. He was immensely proud of the changes he wrought in himself, along with the fact that he had not even considered reoffending:

> I can't say it enough times. [Prison and treatment] was the *worst* piece of shit that ever happened to me, but it was also the *best* thing in my life because I learned so much. I changed my thought patterns, you changed your *feelings*, you change *habits*. Like all this just skewed sideways and I really did come out a different person. The old Jason died in one of the first beatings [in prison]. The new one was sort of born at that time. And by the time I got out, finished my parole, that's when I grew up. . . . *So* many things have changed. I mean mostly good, some bad, but mostly good things have come of it.

Jason's characterization of his sense of self suggested a fluidity that has facilitated his transformation into a new normal. When asked, "Who are you?" he simply responded with an emphatic, "I'm me!" Laughing, he continued:

> I hate that question. I really do because what do you want to hear? There's so many different things. . . . I am who I am. I see myself as a person who's just trying to make a life and try to be happy and be able to afford some things in life and find somebody, basically just like everybody else. I know a lot of other people who are tied to the stigmata and everything and so they never get out of that. But me, I've been able to move past that and just say, "I *am* who I am." I'm not an S.O. [sexual offender]. I'm not a . . . ex-convict. I'm not all this negative crap that . . . other people hold over you for years. And that's why I just say, "I am who I am," because I'm not *any* of this stuff that society says that I am . . . from the stigma. I'm just a normal person. I made some mistakes. I've had some poor coping skills. But I did my time and learned a lot and changed my life because of it.

Jason's response suggested that his sense of selfhood was less focused on ideas of authenticity and more closely aligned to a narrative self. Employing a cognitive device known as "containment" (Strauss 1990) or "compartmentalization" (Strauss 1997), he developed an understanding of his life in *chapters* that reflected more of an evolving self. Ten years after his release from prison, key chapters from Jason's life had come to a close while he had moved forward into new chapters, toward his new normal.

Self-Stigma

Collective representations of stigmatized identities ensure that those who are stigmatized are well aware of the stereotypes and personal attributes that others may be applying to them (Crocker and Quinn 2000). Their "spoiled identities" (Goffman 1963) are easily internalized. Sexual offenders are no different in this manner, accepting the con-code rankings of more and less acceptable sexual offenses and even going so far as to question the presence of other sexual offenders in their own neighborhoods (Waldram 2009; 2012). The men in this research generally gave indications that they too had internalized stigma associated with sexual offenders as sick perverts, for instance, and of no value to society. Of course the commission of their own crimes altered this perspective. Their knowledge of these negative discourses along with their experiences of cognitive dissonance, regret, and shame combined to form a self-stigma that impinged on their senses of self and created problems striving for their new normal.

Self-stigma can take a central role in adjusting to a new normal because it shapes men's experiences and social interactions. Describing his feelings of self-hate, Kevin talked about interpersonal projection, imagining what others saw and thought about him. This imagined perspective speaks directly to how moral discourses may be internalized: "The whole self-hate . . . [is] something I really have to battle. And I'm sure every offender in some way really struggles with the self-image. I think self-image is such a difficult thing to deal with because you can't help but look at yourself as . . . you think other people look at you. And the media and everything else certainly doesn't help in that either." Stigma became a lens through which the men viewed themselves and interpreted the world around them. Due to the very real risk of violence in prison if other inmates learn about their offenses, convicted sexual offenders experience near constant fear and anxiety (Waldram 2012). This fear continues in community life with less intensity, but in such a way that offenders feel as if their stigma is conspicuous to others. They construct a view of themselves based on what they think others might do if they knew about their conviction. This projection noticeably feeds into many aspects of sexual offenders' lives, creating a synoptic paranoia.

Shane, a Caucasian man in his late twenties, articulated his experience of stigma-induced fear. He had been convicted for possession of child pornography in two separate instances and was released from prison three and a half years prior to the interview. Shane's offenses were associated with significant mental health issues that stemmed from his own childhood sexual abuse. When asked if being labeled a sexual offender had affected who he was as a person, he responded with, "Yeah," and went on to explain further:

> It's affected me in the way I evaluate how other people are going to evaluate me. . . . Like when I go into a job interview, *now* I'm thinking, "Is he going to want to know? Is he going to find out I'm a sex offender?" So it affects the way I think about how other people are going to treat me. . . . I would go into a barber shop and I'd be like, "I don't know if I should get my hair cut today 'cause maybe he'll screw up my hair because he knows I'm a sex offender and wants me to look like an idiot 'cause he hates me." Seriously, that was how I was thinking for a while. It's just like everything was an opportunity for someone to judge me, which is unhealthy and came directly from them attaching that label to me. Because the label exists not only to me, but to everyone around me. . . . I can handle [the] label 'cause I know it's crap but they think the label is some kind of legitimate claim of who I am, and therefore they're going to treat me that way.

Shane received negative reactions early on in his community integration process, which sustained in him certain expectations for discrimination. The construction of his prospective life narrative included an exaggerated fear of being recognized, singled out, and discriminated against that bordered on paranoia. However, Shane's rejection of a label that he knew did not reveal anything about who he was, suggests that he experienced a more nuanced form of selfhood that could not be reduced simply to his good and bad parts.

The New Normal of Selfhood

Adjusting to a new normal appears to be more challenging when one strongly adheres to the concept of an unchanging, authentic self. In contrast to such essentialist conceptions of self, the narrative self may be seen as a collection of stories that construct a larger picture of how a person views her- or himself (Bruner 2002), which lends itself toward greater flexibility and adaptability. A common experience for research participants was to vacillate between feeling that their *true* self was something that did not include their offenses and feeling that their offenses had replaced their authentic self. Self-concepts rooted in ideas of authenticity seem to require more time to adapt to new circumstances than do those rooted in narrative.

For some sexual offenders, the stories of their crimes do not fit well with their other self-narratives. They may recognize the overall facts of the disruption as real, but cognitive dissonance makes it difficult to fathom how that story came to be theirs. Furthermore, if made public, the stigma assigned to sexual offenders from their shameful offense stories risks overshadowing all the other stories that make up the narrative self.

After a time, however, some men in this research did manage to move on by accepting the offense narrative through its compartmentalization as just one of many in a collection that was becoming integrated within older and newer stories. It becomes a chapter in his life that is reread and reimagined, often as a response to treatment programs that emphasize disclosure, and eventually merged as part of the emplotment of his life. With the advent of disruption, the perception of a unified self is temporarily fractured and replaced by discordance, disbelief, and confusion. After a time, the discordant story becomes less important and is accepted within the whole, restoring the experience of a coherent and unified self.

The cognitive dissonance expressed by participants' narratives was eased when the disruptive episode became more accepted within the broader mosaic of self-stories. Kevin's metaphor of his Picasso-like self-image is particularly astute: each of the cubist facets within a Picasso portrait might represent an episode in a life narrative. Their chaotic placement represents the discordance of those narrativized episodes that characterize the person's experience of disruption, much like the wild movement of particles in a snow globe after it has been shaken. Given some time, the chaos subsides and a new sense of order settles in. Very likely, Kevin will be less inclined to view his selfhood as a Picasso painting once he has come to accept his offenses as just another part of his past.

This process of finding comfort in a new normal is a progression that is as individualized as the person. Kevin, who had only been out of prison for two years, was working with a psychiatrist and appeared to be making steady progress in his moral habilitation. He was realistic about the effort he was going to have to expend, noting, "that this is going to be a lifelong project." Jason wholeheartedly welcomed a transformed self-hood and new normal. He had put the past behind him and internalized a new set of practices that would keep him and the community safe. Shane appeared to be having similar successes.

In contrast, Carl served as an example of the limitations an essentialist framework of selfhood present to moral habilitation. Carl started out by adapting as reasonably as might be expected but then he experienced a series of setbacks. First, health problems affected his ability to work in his previous profession, and then he learned that his ex-wife had become engaged. It hit home for him just how much he had lost because of his offense. Five years after his release, he still struggled with the agency to follow through on smaller acts like reaching out to people. Carl did not feel as if he had changed and his rigid sense of self appeared to hinder his ability to adapt to the new behaviors expected of past sexual offenders.

Authenticity and Self in the World

The new normal demands a new way of interacting in a world that views the offender's discredited personhood through the lens of stigma (Goffman 1963). This new way of being occurs in a context where control is exacted over the discredited person through moral regulation, synopticism, and panopticism. Moral regulation as defined by Hunt (1999, 6) is "the deployment of distinctively moral discourses which construct a moralized subject and an object or target which is acted upon by means of moralizing practices." Synopticism and panopticism are both forms of governing subjects to conform to desired behaviors. Where synopticism is executed via the public surveillance by many over the individual, panopticism is the surveillance of many by one such as the state (Foucault 1977; Waldram 2012). While moral discourses inform agents of an acceptable way to construct their subjectivities, the synoptic gaze monitors subjects' progress, quickly identifying when the individual falls short of expectations. Moral regulation operates from multiple structures where subjectivities can be formed from above through the panoptic actions of the state and state supported organizations, and from below through civil society groups and individual campaigns to expose and harass ex-offenders (Garland 1997; Hunt 1999).

For sexual offenders, state moral regulation is a panoptic force that is enforced through imprisonment or alternative sanctions, treatment, and the conditions of parole or probation. In the community, ex-offenders are often monitored by police and are required to meet a variety of scheduled check-ins. Moral regulation from below comes synoptically from pervasive stigmatizing discourses, new standards of behavior, and the suspicious eyes, real and imagined, of those surrounding the person, even hunting for him. Synopticism seems to be the most enduring and fear-ridden of the two forms of surveillance.

Social interactions for sexual offenders become a balancing act between a dissonant selfhood, prescribed enactments of moral habilitation that may be more or less coerced, and a stigmatized identity that must be hidden from the synoptic and panoptic gaze of others. With all these forces, Carl felt he could no longer be his authentic self:

> If things get known . . . you're completely shunned by all. But yet, the people who get to know you, if they know *who* you are . . . a lot of the times they will not care, unless they've had something done to them in the past and it brings back memories. It's the hardest thing . . . to try to get yourself to overcome and realize that you are still the same person. You just made a mistake. But yet, I can't be the same person because you never know if something might [happen], 'cause there's always people [who believe], "Once a pedophile, always a pedophile," kind of thing. . . . So you just don't know.

Stigma and moral regulation interact to problematize the development and acceptance of a new normal. The panoptic and synoptic systems of surveillance and regulation became overwhelming and Carl recounted his compulsion to be hypervigilant about his every thought, action, and motivation when he interacted with others, went to work, bought groceries, or even walked down the street. One of the characteristics of the new normal, hyper self-vigilance, prevents sexual offenders from behaving as what they might view as their authentic selves. Hyper self-vigilance and feelings of inauthenticity manifest through social interactions, especially those that involve potential disclosure of one's crimes, or situations where it becomes evident that the stigma incites feelings of mistrust from others.

Disclosure in an Unruly World

There is little doubt that society is hostile toward sexual offenders. State public notification policies that "out" sexual offenders in the community and provide online maps of their residences combine with the public's use of social media to monitor and harass released offenders. Not surprisingly, men convicted of sexual offenses are quite afraid of what could happen to them in the community (Waldram 2012). Sensationalized media accounts of assaults, harassment, or other forms of vigilantism construct the outside world as a dangerous place for sexual offenders. Lying about one's offenses begins in prison, if not earlier, and continues after release. The danger of being harassed and assaulted is very real for sexual offenders in prison. Once back in the community, where it is easier to hide one's criminal history and remove oneself from threatening situations, public disclosures can facilitate community ostracism and hostility directed at the offender and even his family, causing feelings of shame and loss of friends, employment, and housing (Zevitz and Farkas 2000). In light of these potentially destabilizing influences, the broad range of social interactions involved in daily life in the community turn the decision of whether to disclose one's offenses into an ongoing dilemma, even when such disclosure is court-mandated. A common situation where participants faced this debate occurred when seeking employment.

Discrimination against ex-offenders in hiring practices is commonplace; even low-end customer service jobs frequently require criminal record checks. Finding employment is an important factor for community integration, successful relapse prevention, and for settling into a new normal. Carl described the struggle he had with obtaining work and remaining employed: "You're looking for jobs [but] most people nowadays are asking for a criminal record [check]. You almost got to lie to get a job . . . and what do you do? You get found out, you're automatically fired. So you tell the truth. I've lost *four* jobs because I had . . . a criminal record . . . and they were good jobs. I nailed the interview. You can see in the guy's eyes, 'Okay, you're hired. Do you have a criminal record? Bye.'" Carl's perception of discrimination based on a criminal past is common among offenders. Perhaps surprisingly, he is reluctant to lie about his past, having learned through moral habilitation that truth-telling is a prosocial behavior. But the reaction of others to his truth is often considerably less prosocial, and creates for him considerable confusion and distress, plus the enticement to lie.

Kevin had a good job in a new profession but constantly feared the consequences of being found out. The threat of shame, embarrassment, loss of employment, and loss of friends was always hanging over his head:

I'm definitely more anxious than I used to be. It's a rare day that goes by where I don't worry that somebody's going to find out about my past and then, you know, will I lose my job? Will I lose everything that I have right now as far as work goes, and how well that's going? So that's kind of a constant in the back of my mind. It's like I wonder "is this my last day at work?" That'll often go through my head. Especially when I'm *really* happy. Then I'll think, "Oh gosh, you know, don't get too happy 'cause this could be your last day of work." Well that's kind of silly in a way but . . . if the wrong people . . . find out, if they decide to let me go right on the spot. The other guys in the shop may decide they don't want [me] working there, and put management in position where it's [a] him or us kind of thing. I don't know. Harassment could start. I'd like to think from the amount of time that I spent with these guys, that that wouldn't be the case, but I also know how strong people's feelings are about this issue. . . . A lot of the comments that I hear when I was at school and hear around work or whatever, things like, "Pedophiles should be taken out behind the barn and shot" or "If I ever met a pedophile, I'd kick the shit out of him" kind of thing. So stuff like that's kind of hard to hear.

"Stuff like that" also means that he cannot ever really trust someone until that person knows about his past, yet knowing about his past may create distrust. While Kevin was managing reasonably well in the social world, Carl had a harder time with the ongoing dilemma of whether to lie to a person or disclose his past. He had experienced enough confrontations that he learned it was just easier to withdraw from people. Carl lamented his confusion: "Is it safe to lie through life or be truthful? What do people want?"

Disclosure represents one of a multitude of ongoing moral and ethical dilemmas that sexual offenders are routinely confronted with in the community. According to Zigon (2007), moral breakdown occurs in a situation where one cannot automatically and unthinkingly resolve a dilemma of moral consequence. In moral breakdown, one is confronted by an ethical demand to act within a morally inflected situation and break into reflective contemplation about the best course of action. Ethical demand motivates the individual to work through the moment so that she or he can return to the internalized, "unreflective moral dispositions of everydayness" (Zigon 2007, 139). The routinization of moral breakdown and ethical demand is a central element of the new normal.

The men in this research would sometimes admit that they felt compelled to lie and hide their pasts even when reluctant to do so. "Well obviously I have to lie somewhat about my past and I really feel uncomfortable doing that," Kevin related. He learned to negotiate this ethical dilemma by giving people partial truths, telling people that he was not happy in his previous profession and that he "had an opportunity to retrain, so [he] took it." Moral dilemmas compound, of course: to meet the responsibilities expected of moral habilitation, including having a job, it is sometimes necessary to breach another element of moral habilitation, in this case by lying, which is viewed as a necessity in the new normal of postconviction life and community integration.

Hiding their past is problematic for it means that they cannot be honest, and this challenges their self-sense of authenticity. They fabulate stories to fill in the gap in time when they were in prison. They have to be careful how they respond to certain questions. They generate excuses as to why they are unable to participate in activities in otherwise innocuous locations like parks, schools, or bars. And they must consistently recall their fabulations and confabulations lest they be challenged for offering inconsistent narratives (Waldram 2012). These measures, when understood through the lens of cultural criminology, are all part of a daily interplay of their attempts to mediate, prevent, or enact damage control to their public self-representations, as opposed to the public representation of their crimes where the dehumanizing imagery of sexual offenders is "created and consumed by criminals, criminal subcultures, control agents, media institutions, and audiences" (Ferrell 1999, 397).

Synopticism: You Can't Be Yourself Even If You Want To

Social interactions in the new normal are replete with suspicion. Sexual offenders typically live in a state of hypervigilance, regularly second-guessing themselves until their new routine becomes normalized, which may never happen. Even when their crimes have not been disclosed, the internalized stigma hypersensitizes ex-offenders to the real or imagined gaze of others. It is through the sensation of knowing who knows, as well as not knowing who might know about their past, that their behavior is morally regulated. Foucault's (1977, 187) analysis is especially apt: "Disciplinary power . . . is exercised through its invisibility; at the same time it imposes on those whom it subjects a principle of compulsory visibility. In discipline, it is the subjects who have to be seen. Their visibility assures the hold of the power that is exercised over them. It is the fact of being constantly seen, of being able always to be seen, that maintains the disciplined individual in his subjection." This final section demonstrates how encounters with the synoptics of the social world forcibly require the offender to construct a new normal where moral regulation and moral breakdown are constant features. In particular, Carl's difficulty with this process is insightful for highlighting how stigma, moral regulation, and synopticism function in establishing a new morally habilitated normal.

Carl revealed what *normal* means for him and why he feels that the stigma is a barrier to living a normal life. "You're able to get back into society and help out," he explained, "become just a normal person back in society. . . . There's a few people that I've gotten to know that have been able to get back into society and nothing more for it. [For me], it's just getting yourself there is the biggest thing, [getting] back into your own self." When asked what he meant by this latter phrase, he clarified,

"Yeah, it is back to being who you used to be before you were charged . . . and I think that's . . . what most of us want to do is just get back to being who we were, not what we are." This begs the question, Is it possible to get back to that? Carl responded pessimistically. "I'm gonna have to say no because society . . . if they find out, they put so much condemnation on you." For Carl, *normal* meant being the person he was before the commission of his crimes. This person loved his role as a father and used to freely enjoy helping children, but these activities were part of his old normal and now had to be avoided. While such activities might be seen as normal behavior for anyone who likes to play with children, knowledge of Carl's offense changes the context and thus how his actions are judged.

Carl went on to give an example of how otherwise benign situations are now interpreted as threatening through the lens of his sexual offense:

> I had some friends that had younger kids. I was standing right there and we were trying to talk. . . . I went over to just . . . quickly [ask] for some advice and some things. I just reached down and tickled [their young daughter] and said, "Oh, gonna getchya," and right away I went, Okay, what are they going to think? He [the friend] confronted me [later], got really mad at me. . . . I'm going, "I'm not going to do anything. I'm just trying to have some fun, get back to normality," and that. Basically lost a friendship over it 'cause he knew the charges. And the weird thing is, the wife I'm still friends with 'cause she was there at the time [and] he wasn't.

What would otherwise be innocuous behaviors are viewed differently when the actor is a known sexual offender. Consequently, the new normal is not simply behaving as everyone else might. For sexual offenders, even innocent actions can raise the suspicions of others. These suspicions are exacerbated in a fearful society where people have become hypersensitized to any suggestion of potentially predatory behavior (Lancaster 2012). The new normal involves learning that one is more limited than the average person in the range of acceptable or appropriate behaviors; behaviors typically viewed as acceptable or normal for other individuals are prohibited for them or, perhaps worse, viewed as evidence of essential deviance. Carl was having difficulty because he had not accepted the full extent of these limitations in his life.

Carl was aware that he should avoid all contact with children, but resisted this advice because of his self-assurances that he would never re-offend. Moreover, he was reluctant to give up his interactions with children: "I'd bend over backward to give a helping hand to kids but I can't do that no more . . . 'cause you don't want to put yourself in a risky position even though . . . I know I'll never do it. Why tempt yourself? *That's* the part also that hurts, 'cause you're in a position [where] you know you won't do anything, you know you really *didn't* do anything, technically, that serious . . . but if somebody sees you that knows [about your offense], they go, 'Okay, what's he doing now? Why is he there?'" Carl recognized that being around children constituted a potentially high-risk situation according to treatment theory, but he exempted himself by both minimizing the seriousness of his offense and by declaring that he "knows [he] won't do anything." There are problems with this sort of rationalizing behavior. First, minimization, a forensic concept similar to one of Sykes and Matza's (1957) neutralization techniques—denial of injury—suggests that Carl may still be evading responsibility for his crimes. Although neutralization techniques have been rightfully critiqued as overly reductionist (Presser and Sandberg, this volume), one's evocation of minimization is a narrative strategy that bears implications for how that person has constructed his or her selfhood (Waldram 2010); it points to Carl's resistance to the lessons of moral habilitation and the necessary recourse to moral regulation to guide his behavior.

A second problem is with his overconfidence. Carl is so confident that he will never reoffend that he has become somewhat relaxed about relapse prevention. He eschews the hypervigilant activities other past offenders tend to adopt to prevent reoffense. This over-confidence seems firmly embedded in his sense of his authentic self, someone for whom children are a treasure, for instance, and not to be harmed, ever.

It became clear that Carl had not willingly embraced change. His resistance demonstrates that he was forced to morally habilitate by virtue of having the synoptic gaze imposed upon him. In other words, it was the fear of being constantly surveilled that motivated change: "You really don't know what you can do. And if you do something that is out of the context, they'll be thinking, 'Now what's he doing? Why is he doing it?' Always second-guessing. Especially if there's kids involved. I mean how can you live back to being normal when you got somebody second-guessing you all the time when you're around something?" As much as Carl trusted himself to not do anything, he failed to acknowledge the extent of the mistrust others, parents especially, hold toward him. Instead, he lamented how it is difficult to move on with his life when he is the subject of suspicion with people second-guessing his motives and actions. No longer on probation, he was on guard now primarily because he was concerned about how others would perceive his actions. Any changes he had made in his behavior appeared to be motivated more by the external surveillance of others—what they think and perceive about him—than by his own internal motivation or change in beliefs. This observation further indicates that Carl's behavioral changes are more due to moral regulation than they are the moral habilitation intended by treatment programs.

Moral regulation is an extrinsic motivator that synoptically reinforces past lessons of moral habilitation. For Carl, who admittedly "shut down" during treatment due to lack of therapeutic rapport, the lessons of moral habilitation were not strongly integrated into a new pattern of being. When asked if he would want to go back to that normal place where he was before his offenses occurred, he responded, "To some degree, yes. I know there's areas I can't go because the people, like . . . you're always being second-guessed and that is the hardest. So what do you do?" He talked about being forced into a paradigm shift that required him to think and act differently. As much as he knew that there were things that he had to change, he was still resisting the idea that he must adapt and accept his new limitations.

Despite his strong sense of confidence in the inherent triumph of his authentic self, the synoptic gaze and suspicion from others had Carl frequently question his own behavior, providing an apt illustration of moral breakdown. As Carl related how sexual offender discourses affected him, we see how moral regulation can negatively impinge upon one's experience of authentic selfhood:

> Oh, [societal messages about sexual offenders] make me feel dirty . . . [that] I don't fit in, [and] what's the use sometimes. Especially when you go into a job situation and you get turned down. It snowballs right back in your face again and it's really tough. You got to be kind of choosey, where you go, what you do and I don't like that. You *really* can't be your-

self at times and I think that's what hurts. You don't know where or how far you can take things. . . . It hurts 'cause you can't be as open and be completely who you used to be. You got to be guarded. You got to watch what you do and just hold yourself back . . . from what you used to be.

Carl had lost the ability to act spontaneously in public life, at least until he learns to internalize and habitually adapt to a new normal. He had withdrawn socially in order to hide from the need to be constantly vigilant about his behavior. Carl was an example of someone who has had difficulty conforming to the changes expected of him. Having participated but not entirely bought into the regimen of moral habilitation administered through his treatment program, Carl was grudgingly changing in response to the moral regulation of the synoptic gaze. He was caught between wanting to go back to his old normal and knowing that his stigma now prevented that. His frequent reference to not being able to be himself illustrates how he longed for the freedom of the unreflective automaticity characteristic of embodied morality (Zigon 2007, 2009). "Not being himself" is a state of moral breakdown where he is torn out of mundane unintentional being and into a sustained process of self-monitoring where he must evaluate the implications of his various actions and decisions. The self-surveillance of the breakdown state elicits uncertainty and distress due to the potential harm that could come from the wrong choice. Carl needs to be on near constant guard when in public. The ongoing tension between the old and new normal, mediated by Carl's strong sense of his authentic self, is clearly evident.

For sexual offenders, successful moral habilitation and community integration requires a transition from an old normal to a new normal. The transition period in between these two states is characterized by routinely occurring moral breakdown where men must intentionally reflect on their inner state of being and their social interactions. What seemed to separate Carl from Kevin, Jason, and Shane is that Carl reflected back on his old normal with longing that was perhaps even a bit romanticized. His family meant everything to him and his pining for the past seemed to prevent him from accepting change and moving toward a new future. The other three men described in this chapter were different from Carl because their old normals were characterized by lack of fulfillment, chronic stress, general unhappiness, and mental health concerns for some. Kevin and Jason welcomed the opportunity to get help and develop a new normal. Shane, although critical of treatment, was following his own path to moral habilitation, part of which came from his strong identification with Christianity. It is no wonder that Carl struggled so much between the old and new normal; he perceived that he had very little toward which he could look forward. He had no long-term goals, except wanting to start another family. It was the positive prospective narrative—a vision of a happier future—that made the difference for Kevin, Jason, and Shane. It gave them something toward which they could strive.

Conclusion

Transitioning from an old normal to a new, habilitated normal involves several tasks for sexual offenders. They need to make sense of their crimes and come to terms with the cognitive dissonance between their authentic selves and the person who committed those crimes. Being able to understand and cope with, even reject, the stigma assigned to their label is an important step in this process. To be successful at community integration they must also learn the lessons of moral habilitation but adapt them to an unruly social world that fails to blindly accept shared notions of prosociality and refuses to accept sexual offenders in their communities regardless of treatment. They must also learn to embrace, rather than resist, the fact that their crimes make them a prime focus of public synopticism. When faced with the inherent contradictions of the process of moral habilitation, that society is considerably more unruly and less prosocial than they have been taught, falling back on moral regulation as a mechanism to maintain a crime-free life seems logical. However, moral regulation seems to engender anger at the limitations placed upon the individual when the preoffense version of an authentic self still holds sway.

As Quinn (2006, 368) suggests when referencing Conway and Pleydell-Pearce, individuals experience a "working self," that is, "a constantly changing dynamic on-line conception of the self and what it may become" that is built upon a platform of "recurrent themes about their lives." They "construct integrated life narratives around these themes." A narrative understanding of selfhood appeared to facilitate participants' recognition that their selfhood evolves over time, and that eventually some stories matter much less than they did when they occurred. It is not so much that they construct a "coherent narrative," as Maruna (2001, 85) suggests, but that the dynamic process of narrativization accounts for their criminal actions in a manner that allows them to move past both their crimes and the lifestyles that contributed to them. Rather than resisting the changes required of the new normal, offenders may be better off accepting moral habilitation and moral regulation as a path to crafting a new, nonoffending life for themselves. This task seems to involve rejecting notions of an authentic self in favor of re-storying their lives in a more dynamic fashion. Narrative criminology allows us to better understand how offenders engage with treatment, and provides keys to understanding the success of community integration. Specifically, it helps us understand the process by which some offenders make sense of their past and present while anticipating an offense-free, albeit altered, lifestyle of a new normal, or alternatively, continue to embrace an old normal that conflicts with community moral standards and legal prescriptions, and leads to continued trouble. It is in this direction that forensic psychology should aim, so that it is informed by a broader narrative approach to criminality that seeks to value the role of narrative in lives rather than expunge it.

REFERENCES

Abel, Gene, Judith Becker, and Jerry Cunningham-Rathner. 1984. "Complications, Consent and Cognitions in Sex between Children and Adults." *International Journal of Law and Psychiatry* 7 (1): 89–103.

Auburn, Timothy, and Susan Lea. 2003. "Doing Cognitive Distortions: A Discursive Psychology Analysis of Sex Offender Treatment Talk." *British Journal of Social Psychology* 42 (2): 281–298.

Becker, Gay. 1997. *Disrupted Lives: How People Create Meaning in a Chaotic World.* Berkeley: University of California Press.

Beech, Anthony, and Hannah Ford. 2006. "The Relationship between Risk, Deviance, Treatment Outcome and Sexual Reconviction in a Sample of Child Sexual Abusers Completing Residential Treatment for Their Offending." *Psychology, Crime and Law* 12 (6): 685–701.

Bruner, Jerome. 2002. *Making Stories: Law, Literature, Life.* Cambridge, MA: Harvard University Press.

Conway, Martin A., and Christopher W. Pleydell-Pearce. 2000. "The Construction of Autobiographical Memories in the Self-Memory System." *Psychological Review* 107 (2): 261–288.

Crocker, Jennifer, and Diane M. Quinn. 2000. "Social Stigma and the Self: Meanings, Situations, and Self-Esteem." In *The Social Psychology of Stigma*, edited by T. F. Heatherton, R. E. Kleck, M. R. Hebl, and J. G. Hull, 153–183. New York: Guilford Press.

de Munck, Victor. 2000. *Culture, Self, and Meaning.* Prospect Heights, IL: Waveland Press.

Ferrell, Jeff. 1999. "Cultural Criminology." *Annual Review of Sociology* 25 (1): 395–418.

Festinger, Leon. 1957. *A Theory of Cognitive Dissonance.* Stanford, CA: Stanford University Press.

Foucault, Michel. 1977. *Discipline and Punish: The Birth of the Prison.* New York: Vintage Books.

Fox, Kathryn. 1999. "Changing Violent Minds: Discursive Correction and Resistance in the Cognitive Treatment of Violent Offenders in Prison." *Social Problems* 46 (1): 88–103.

Garland, David. 1997. "'Governmentality' and the Problem of Crime: Foucault, Criminology, Sociology." *Theoretical Criminology* 1 (2): 173–214.

Garro, Linda C., and Cheryl Mattingly. 2000. "Narrative Turns." In *Narrative and the Cultural Construction of Illness and Healing*, edited by C. Mattingly and L. C. Garro, 259–269. Berkeley: University of California Press.

Goffman, Erving. 1963. *Stigma: Notes on the Management of a Spoiled Identity.* New York: Simon and Shuster.

Hanson, R. Karl, Guy Bourgon, Leslie Helmus, and Shannon Hodgson. 2009. "The Principles of Effective Correctional Treatment also Apply to Sexual Offenders: A Meta-analysis." *Criminal Justice and Behavior* 36 (9): 865–891.

Hunt, Alan. 1999. *Governing Morals: A Social History of Moral Regulation.* New York: Cambridge University Press.

Lancaster, Roger N. 2011. *Sex Panic and the Punitive State.* Los Angeles: University of California Press.

Lindholm, Charles. 2008. *Culture and Identity: The History, Theory, and Practice of Psychological Anthropology.* Oxford: Oneworld.

Mann, Ruth E. 2004. "Innovations in Sex Offender Treatment." *Journal of Sexual Aggression* 10 (2): 141–152.

Marshall, William. 1996. "The Sexual Offender: Monster, Victim, or Everyman?" *Sexual Abuse: A Journal of Research and Treatment* 8 (4): 317–335.

Maruna, Shadd. 2001. *Making Good: How Ex-Convicts Reform and Rebuild Their Lives.* Washington, DC: American Psychological Association.

Nicholaichuk, Terry, Arthur Gordon, Deqiang Gu, and Stephan Wong. 2000. "Outcome of an Institutional Sexual Offender Treatment Program: A Comparison between Treated and Matched Untreated Offenders." *Sexual Abuse: A Journal of Research and Treatment* 12 (2): 139–153.

Quinn, Naomi. 2006. "The Self." *Anthropological Theory* 6 (3): 362–384.

Shweder, Richard A., and Edmund J. Bourne. 1982. "Does the Concept of the Person Vary Cross-culturally?" In *Culture Theory: Essays on Mind, Self and Emotion*, edited by R. Shweder and R. Levine, 158–199. Cambridge: Cambridge University Press.

Spiro, Melford E. 1993. "Is the Western Conception of the Self 'Peculiar' within the Context of the World Cultures?" *Ethos* 21 (2): 107–153.

Strauss, Claudia. 1990. "Who Gets Ahead? Cognitive Responses to Heteroglossia in American Political Culture." *American Ethnologist* 17 (2): 312–328.

———. 1997. "Partly Fragmented, Partly Integrated: An Anthropological Examination of 'Postmodern Fragmented Subjects.'" *Cultural Anthropology* 12 (3): 362–404.

Sykes, Gresham M., and David Matza. 1957. "Techniques of Neutralization: A Theory of Delinquency." *American Sociological Review* 22 (December): 664–670.

Tavris, Carol, and Elliot Aronson. 2007. *Mistakes Were Made (but Not by Me). Why We Justify Foolish Beliefs, Bad Decisions, and Hurtful Acts*. Toronto: Harcourt.

Viney, Linda, and Lynne Bousfield. 1991. "Narrative Analysis: A Method of Psychological Research for Aids-Affected People." *Social Science and Medicine* 32 (7): 757–65.

Waldram, James B. 2009. "'It's Just You and Satan, Hanging Out at a Pre-School': Notions of Evil and the Rehabilitation of Sexual Offenders." *Anthropology and Humanism* 34 (2): 219–234.

———. 2010. "Moral Agency, Cognitive Distortion, and Narrative Strategy in the Rehabilitation of Sexual Offenders." *Ethos* 38 (3): 251–274.

———. 2012. *Hound Pound Narrative. Sexual Offender Habilitation and the Anthropology of Therapeutic Intervention*. Berkeley: University of California Press.

Zevitz, Richard G., and Mary Ann Farkas. 2000. "Sex Offender Community Notification: Managing High Risk Criminals or Exacting Further Vengeance?" *Behavioral Sciences and the Law* 18 (2–3): 375–391.

Zigon, Jarrett. 2007. "Moral Breakdown and the Ethical Demand: A Theoretical Framework for an Anthropology of Moralities." *Anthropological Theory* 7 (2): 131–150.

———. 2009. "Within a Range of Possibilities: Morality and Ethics in Social Life." *Ethnos* 74 (2): 251–276.

PART II

Stories Animate and Mobilize

5

"The Race of Pale Men Should Increase and Multiply"

Religious Narratives and Indian Removal

ROBERT M. KEETON

If we determine upon the immigration to the West, the
sooner [the Indians] know it, the better. That they may send
their Calebs and Joshuas to search out and view the new
promised land. . . . I wish the most eligible portion of it to
become a permanent home and habitation for the oppressed
and afflicted sons of Ishmael.
—Lumpkin ([1852] 1907, 56)

The above quote was taken from a speech that Wilson Lumpkin, US
Congressional Representative from the State of Georgia, delivered on
February 20, 1828, in support of a federal policy that would relocate
Native American tribes from the southeastern United States to federally
controlled lands west of the Mississippi River. Representative Lumpkin's references were drawn from the Exodus narrative found in the Old
Testament of the Christian Bible, and by framing his rhetoric in this
manner, he forged a clear connection between the story of the Israelites
and the situation of the Native Americans in the earliest decades of the
nineteenth century. The Book of Genesis introduces Ishmael, the son
of Abraham and his servant Hagar, who was banished into the wilderness and whose descendants became nomadic tribes of the region. The
Book of Numbers describes the arrival of the Israelites upon reaching
the Promised Land of Canaan. Joshua and Caleb were chosen as the
first to venture into Canaan to prepare for the settlement of God's chosen people. Lumpkin's words identify the Native American people as the
nomadic descendants of the banished Ishmael, who face an opportunity
to become "Calebs and Joshuas" by finding their own "promised land"

just as God's chosen people had done. Casting the Native Americans as characters in a biblical script, this framing legitimizes the harm of their removal. Similar references can be found throughout the literature endorsing the Indian Removal Act of 1830, and the goal of this chapter is to demonstrate how the use of biblical narratives was instrumental in rationalizing this act of mass harm.

As a collection of stories that has endured for centuries, the Christian Bible has undoubtedly had a tremendous influence on human society. Biblical scripture has inspired innumerable acts of humanitarianism, but it has also been used to justify policies of politically sanctioned mass harm including slavery, torture, and war. The disciplinary focus of criminology is the study of harm, and by understanding how religious narratives motivate human action, criminologists may gain insights into how religious and political ideology are used to promote acts of harm. Religious institutions and beliefs frequently hold preeminence over other institutions of social control; therefore, the presence of religious framing in public discourse, especially rhetoric legitimizing harm, is highly significant. The influence of biblical narratives is prominent within the political rhetoric used by supporters of the Indian Removal Act.

As with any narrative, Biblical stories communicate culturally relevant information, which shapes interpretations of the past and guides future action. The social significance of these religious narratives over the course of American history is undeniable and should not be overlooked. During the eighteenth and nineteenth centuries, the Bible was "the most imported, most printed, most distributed, and most read" text in North America, and its influence was "absolutely foundational" to the development of American society (Gutjahar 1999, 1). For supporters of Indian removal, stories from the Old Testament served as "moralizing tales" (Presser 2009, 192), which were familiar to the American public and could be used as a source of motivation necessary to gather popular support for the policy.

The Indian Removal Act of 1830 authorized the president of the United States to negotiate removal treaties with Native American tribes residing east of the Mississippi River, and to provide support for their emigration to land set aside for their relocation in what is now the state of Oklahoma. Between 1831 and 1842, over fifty thousand Native American people emigrated to the West in accordance with treaties signed under the Removal Act (see Prucha 1986, 80–87). The most notable of these emigrations is the removal of the Cherokee, which has come to represent what was a broader federal policy of forced relocation that affected over twenty other tribes in the eastern United States. In October 1838 American troops forcibly removed over fifteen thousand Cherokee from their tribal lands in northwest Georgia and relocated them to lands in Oklahoma. The journey resulted in the deaths of at least four thousand Cherokee people and became known as *Nunna daul Tsuny*, or "the trail where they cried." By examining the rhetoric used by supporters of Indian removal, this research demonstrates the promise of narrative criminology for the study of atrocity crimes, a category of mass harm that has received limited attention from criminologists (see Hagan and Rymond-Richmond 2009; Savelsberg 2010; Yacoubian 2000). By emphasizing the cultural significance of stories, narrative criminology provides a theoretical framework useful for explaining how social institutions are able to motivate individuals to engage in collective action and legitimize acts of mass harm.

This research examines how policymakers used religious narratives to motivate support for the Indian Removal Act of 1830. The Old Testament books of Genesis, Exodus, Leviticus, Numbers, and Deuteronomy—commonly referred to as the Pentateuch—are a collection of stories that served as a single cultural metanarrative for many early Americans, including supporters of Indian removal.[1] Three unique stories from the Pentateuch featured prominently within the removal debate. The first was the creation story in Genesis, where mankind is given the mandate to populate the world and cultivate the soil. The second story was that of the Israelites in their exodus from bondage in Egypt in their quest for the Promised Land. Finally, the narrative of Jacob and Esau was cited as evidence of the superiority of an agrarian society over that of the hunter-gatherer. These three narratives form a web of metaphysical understanding that influenced two centuries of colonial history in the New World, culminating in the internal colonization of the United States and the subjugation of the Native Americans.

Narratives and Atrocity Crime

Scholars from multiple disciplines have recognized the importance of storytelling within human society. Gottschall (2012, 15–18) suggests that human beings are "creatures of story," and we define our very existence through the stories we tell; indeed we are "soaked to the bone in story." Because humans perceive the world as a series of events progressing across time, the logical progressive causal order within the narrative allows the audience to use accounts of the past as a reference for predicting future outcomes. Stories are told "within particular historical, institutional, and interactional contexts . . . with particular interests, motives, and purposes in mind" (Ewick and Silby 1995, 206). As carriers of collective history and shared values, narratives are "highly culturally informed" social phenomena that can be used to reinforce valued cultural logics and influence human behavior (Monroe 2012, 325). Put more concisely, in a given society the "microcosm" of narratives represents the "macrocosm" of the dominant cultural framework (Franzosi 1998, 550). As a result, the social significance of a narrative is determined by the outcome of an interpretive process, which is bounded by the preexisting conditions of a given social environment (Bruner 1991). In this way, stories have a dialectical quality; they are beholden to the very social actors and cultural forces they simultaneously have the power to change. Presser (2009) argues for a "constitutive view of narrative" that views stories as highly symbolic representations of a socially constructed reality, through which social actors interpret facts that are used to formulate future action. These actions comprise criminal acts committed by individuals or groups, including atrocity crime.

Scheffer (2006, 238) describes atrocity crimes as "collectively executed crimes of such magnitude and destructive character" as to be "inconsistent with the protection of human rights and the maintenance of international peace and security." According to this definition, atrocity crimes may be committed by nation-states as well as "certain non-state organizations and groups" (238). Crimes that fall under this definition include genocide, crimes against humanity, war crimes, wars of aggression, and other violations of international humanitarian law. As Scheffer's definition suggests, atrocity crimes are typically perpetrated by powerful groups in society, and in many cases they are the outcome of intentionally crafted public policy. The Indian Removal Act is a historical example of a public policy that, based upon contemporary standards, would be classified as an atrocity crime, *to wit* ethnic cleansing.[2] By examining the role of religious narratives during the removal debate, this research demonstrates the promise of narrative criminology to help explain similar acts of harm perpetrated by powerful institutions.

Researchers have recognized the function of narratives within social discourse as a mechanism for maintaining social power and shaping public policy (see Fairclough 1992; Smith 2005; van Dijk 2006). Ewick and Silby (1995, 212) proposed that the very "structure, content, and performance" of narratives commonly reinforces "existing ideologies and hegemonic relations of power and inequality." In some cases, these "hegemonic tales" become cultural metanarratives, stories that are so persuasive and familiar that they "stifle" alternative interpretations of social reality (213). Similarly, Somers (1995, 234) describes a metanarrative as a "cultural schema" that has "gatekeeping power" over interpretations of reality, which "not only provides the range of acceptable answers but also defines both the questions to be asked and the rules of procedure by which they can be rationally answered." In short, the cultural metanarrative is a socially privileged story, so deeply embedded into a society's collective consciousness that it becomes the primary frame of reference through which all social action is interpreted, rationalized, and understood. Policymaking is a social act, the outcomes of which have the potential to impact negatively millions of lives, thus examining how cultural metanarratives influence the political process is a fruitful endeavor for criminologists interested in the study of mass harm.

Undoubtedly, the policymaking process is steeped in narrative. Narratives serve as an interpretive framework through which policymakers interpret past events, establish causality, assign blame, predict future outcomes, judge the legitimacy of a proposed policy, and square the debate with dominant moral standards. Shenhav (2006) suggested that politicians promote policies using carefully constructed "political narratives," which are stories that represent a particular interpretation of "political reality." Smith (2005, 8) demonstrated that narratives are a key part of a "claims-making" process guided by carefully "refined language games" used to rouse collective support for policy decisions, including war. Within political debate, narratives act as a "middle level intervening variable" or "cultural pointsman" that connects cultural ideology with determining appropriate social action (45). The influence of dominant cultural ideologies may result in similar "consensual paradigms" within competing political narratives (Shenhav 2006), or through manipulation of social discourse that promotes the interests of the social elite to the detriment of less powerful groups in society (van Dijk 2006). In either case, policymakers must tell a good story to rouse collective support; a good story is one that aligns with the dominant values, morals, and ethics of society and will stand up to public scrutiny (Smith 2005). The story does not need to be completely believable; it only needs to be good enough to outweigh doubt, neutralize guilt, or limit culpability for harm.

Although it is an extreme form of collective violence, warfare is frequently legitimized on the basis of a narrated threat posed by a recognized military force. In contrast, the decision to collectively engage in crimes of atrocity is challenging, hence the content of the supporting narrative becomes especially crucial. As Barnes (2005, 311) notes, "killing for killing's sake" is rarely sufficient motive for genocide; rather these crimes are carried out for the purpose of achieving specific political, economic, or strategic goals. Policymakers use narratives as a source of cultural logic to frame the pursuit of these functional motives as crucial action worthy of exceptional social investment. By framing social conflict as a struggle between good and evil with the very survival of society at stake, policymakers can identify urgent threats to group power, marginalize and reduce the status of target group, promote group solidarity, and legitimize the use of extreme measures to eliminate the threat posed by the target group (Barnes 2005; Boon 2005; Kelman, 1973; Presser 2013). When religious framing is added to political rhetoric–legitimizing harm, the connection between ideology and policy becomes more pronounced.

Throughout human history, religious doctrine has motivated countless cases of mass harm; as Kelsay (1999, n.p.) concisely states, "killing each other in the name of religion has never gone out of fashion." Within political discourse, the use of religious doctrine by policy advocates imparts a sense of greater significance to the policy being legitimized. In some cases, the policy may assume the status of a "transcendent mission" (Kelman 1973). Even those actions that violate prevailing standards of morality may draw public support because the transcendent mission allows individuals to be "part of something larger than the self" (Lifton 2003, 6). Lifton further suggests that this drive for "symbolic immortality" is especially powerful when historical circumstances are chaotic and the future is uncertain. Religious narratives provide a frame of logic wherein action is divinely inspired, and its legitimacy timeless and unfailing.[3]

At times when a social group faces a particularly substantial threat, religious narratives may take on an apocalyptic tone, where "not just individual but collective life and death becomes bound up with a cosmic process that claims dominion over 'the nature and purpose of history'" (Lifton 2003, 19). Narratives with an apocalyptic theme are especially effective at legitimizing violent action that would otherwise shock the conscience of society and render such action unacceptable (Smith 2005). Through the use of religious rhetoric, an individual can see him- or her-self "in alliance with a deity—or with history" sharing in the "ultimate power to destroy and re-create" (20). With this divine mandate, groups can justify engaging in "god-sponsored violence" in pursuit of success-fully completing "God's project" (22). In short, religious narratives pro-vide a ready-made appeal to higher loyalties (see Sykes and Matza 1957) that can be invoked in times of social conflict and can rationalize actions that would otherwise be judged as inappropriate. The invocation of a divine mandate to pursue a specific course of action transcends all other morally and legally established checks on social behavior. In nineteenth-century America, "God's project" was nation building through westward expansion in pursuit of what would later become known as America's "Manifest Destiny."[4]

The Indian Removal Act of 1830

Federal policy regarding the Native American tribes, including the Indian Removal Act of 1830, has a history that predates the establish-ment of the United States as an independent nation; it originates in the period when the nation was a colony of the British crown. During this history, numerous treaties were negotiated between the federal govern-ment and Native American tribes, but they were not sufficient to prevent the crisis that Andrew Jackson and other stakeholders faced during the 1820s and 1830s as a rapidly expanding American nation clashed with established Native American tribes.

Removal as a solution to the "Indian problem"[5] in the United States was first suggested during the presidency of Thomas Jefferson (1801–1809); however, it was not officially proposed until the administration of Andrew Jackson. Jackson first laid out his policy as part of his First Annual Message submitted to Congress in December 1829, in which he described the policy as a humanitarian endeavor with the goal of "preserving this much-injured race" (1829c, para. 63). The Indian Removal Act was introduced in both houses of Congress during February 1830 and it was debated from April to May of the same year. Despite considerable opposition, the bill passed both houses of Congress and was signed into law on May 28, 1830. The Removal Act permitted the president of the United States to secure treaties with the Native American tribes located in the eastern United States and relocate them to designated lands west of the Mississippi River. In exchange for moving to the western United States, the federal government promised to provide the tribes with supplies and logistical support during the relocation, compensation for the value of land and personal assets they left behind, and protection upon arrival in their new territory. The law indicated that removal was voluntary: it would only apply to "tribes or nations of Indians as may choose to exchange the lands where they now reside, and remove there" (Indian Removal Act 1830, 1136). As Prucha (1986, 70) notes however, the tribes were "adamantly" opposed to removal, and those familiar with the policy recognized removal by force "would be inevitable."

Following passage of the law, the Jackson administration immediately began to negotiate with tribes in an effort to gain their voluntary relocation. Eager to escape constant pressure from white politicians and intimidation from white settlers who encroached on tribal lands, the Choctaw, Creek, and Chickasaw tribes presented little resistance to removal. Other tribes were not so passive. Although a removal treaty was signed in 1832, many members of the Seminole tribe resisted removal until they were defeated in the Second Seminole War in 1842 (Prucha 1986). The Cherokee also vigorously resisted removal, but appealed to the federal courts for relief in favor of armed resistance. As history shows, however, they were ultimately unsuccessful in their efforts to avert removal.

The condition of the Cherokee people decayed as the State of Georgia encouraged white settlers to seize the property, crops, and livestock owned by the Cherokee people. Members of the Georgia militia would periodically attack Native Americans who attempted to fend off starvation by hunting for wild game (Rogin 1975). To avert what was seen as the total destruction of Cherokee society, a group of Cherokee leaders led by Major Ridge agreed to the Treaty of New Echota on December 29, 1835. Many within the Cherokee nation were enraged that the treaty had been signed without their consent, and an opposition group led by Cherokee Chief John Ross continued to resist removal efforts. The Cherokee who affiliated themselves with Ridge's "treaty party" voluntarily emigrated without difficulty in 1837. The group led by John Ross was relocated by force in 1838 during the administration of Martin Van Buren, who had also served as Jackson's vice president (Prucha 1986; Satz [1975] 2002). This phase of the Cherokee removal became known as the Trail of Tears and is perhaps the single most tragic event of the Indian removal era.

In May 1838, armed federal troops entered Cherokee territory with orders to "evacuate" Native Americans in accordance with the Treaty of New Echota. General Winfield Scott (1838) ordered that the Cherokee should be gathered with "the least possible distress," but the grim reality of the process led one participant to describe the event as "the most brutal order in the history of American Warfare [sic]" (Burnett [1890] 1978, 181). The Cherokee were rounded up by force and held in captivity until October 1838 when the group departed Ross's Landing for the journey to the west. Historians have generally estimated that fifteen thousand Cherokee were subjected to forced removal, and approximately four thousand Cherokee died during the journey (Satz 1989; Thornton 1984). Though an analysis of demographic data for the Cherokee between 1808–1852, Thornton (1984) suggests the death toll may be closer to eight thousand people, and these losses resulted in an estimated demographic decline of an additional ten thousand people in the years following removal. Although skeptical of these estimates, noted historian Francis Paul Prucha acknowledges that the Trail of Tears "reaped a heavy harvest of misery and death" on the Cherokee people (1986, 87). The harm inflicted by the policy of removal can be explained through examination of narratives that are identifiable within the political debate surrounding the Indian Removal Act of 1830.

Biblical Narratives in the Removal Debate

During 1829 and 1830, the debate over the Indian Removal Act was at the forefront of American political discourse. Those in favor of the policy found themselves facing intense resistance from political opponents as well as religious groups who organized to support Native Americans in their efforts to resist removal. Jackson's ascendency to the presidency solidified the power of his supporters, collectively called Jacksonian Democrats, and thus paved the way for adoption of the Indian removal policy. Jackson and his supporters utilized their collective political power to influence the debate surrounding Indian removal via Old Testament stories. Using these narratives as a frame of reference, removal supporters defined the grievances between Native Americans and white society, rhetorically segregated the target group, reduced their standing in society, and denied the harmful outcomes of removal policy.

Had the Bible included a proclamation from God telling white settlers to "go ye forth into the wilderness of the New World, subjugate the wandering savages of the forests, subdue and cultivate all the land, for you shall be fathers of a great nation that extends from sea to sea, and this nation shall become the New Israel for my chosen people," the task of explaining the rationale for Indian removal would have been much easier. Although references to Old Testament narratives are clearly discernible within the political rhetoric, understanding how these stories were adapted and applied to the "Indian problem" requires more effort. For this task, we can turn to narrative criminology as a tool for examining how social actors used biblical narratives to guide the policymaking process in response to their interpretation of the "Indian problem." As Presser (2009, 191) notes, "narrative is a vehicle for self-understanding" and its role in motivating criminogenic action is frequently dependent on other social factors. Recalling the previous discussion of narratives and policymaking, the interplay between stories, policy, and society is one that involves a constant process of interpretation, action, and reinterpretation. Shenhav (2006, 54) describes this as a "complex metabolic exchange" through which "political narratives imitate a 'political reality' that [in turn] imitates political narratives." Using this perspective, researchers can treat narratives as an intervening variable that connects individual experience to the social world. Applied to Indian removal, we can see that the worldview of removal supporters was the product of a social reality shaped by Old Testament narratives, and hampered by these ideological blinders, the hegemonic influence of these same narratives was reproduced and reinforced through the political process.

America as the New Israel: The Exodus Story

The Exodus story served as the ideological foundation for policies related to the exploration and settlement of the North American continent. As the dominant narrative within the Pentateuch, it is a historical account of the Israelites that begins with God's promise to Abraham that he would become the patriarch of a great nation. After suffering four centuries of oppression in Egypt, Moses freed the Israelites from bondage and led them to the Promised Land in Canaan. During the journey, which lasted forty years, the Israelites endured multiple trials and tribulations for their failure to keep God's commandments. The Israelites ultimately reconcile with God and he rewards them for their renewed obedience. The narrative ends with the death of Moses after their successful arrival in the Promised Land. The story of the Israelites teaches us that through faith and obedience to God, we will be rewarded with favor and salvation; a lack of faith and disobedience will result in misery and destruction. The repetition of this dominant moral theme was combined with a belief that white Europeans were an extension of the Israelites, and the New World was a new Promised Land.

From the moment the first Puritan settlers arrived on the North American continent, they set the goal of expanding white Christian society. The Puritans of Massachusetts Bay Colony viewed themselves as God's chosen people occupying a new land that would become the "Promised Land for [God's] True Church, his New Israel" (Collins 2007, x). Citing the presumed "supremacy of the cultivator over the hunter" the Puritans justified dispossessing the Native Americans of their land because they were not "cultivating the earth as God had commanded" (Prucha 1986, 6). By the early nineteenth century, westward expansion was viewed as part of God's plan to create this kingdom and thus served as a transcendent mission for American society. As policymakers grappled with resistance to expansionist policy and disputes over the legal status of Native American tribes, many supporters of removal returned to long-standing legal precedents to justify their extending state control over tribal lands. The Doctrine of Discovery is perhaps the most commonly cited.

The Doctrine of Discovery was a natural law concept that gave ownership of newly discovered lands to the nation under whose flag it was "discovered." Hence it was believed that Europeans, and Americans later on, had a natural right—a Christian duty—to claim, settle, and cultivate uninhabited lands. Upon finding the Americas and its indigenous occupants, European powers interpreted the doctrine to mean that the "civilized" European nations had a natural right to claim title to the lands occupied by "uncivilized" indigenous people (Fitzpatrick 2002). Although the Doctrine of Discovery allowed the indigenous people of a newly discovered territory to retain their natural rights to occupy the land, they were obligated to submit to the sovereignty of the discovering nation. Should the indigenous people resist efforts to bring civilization and Christianity to these new lands, European powers assumed the authority to administer law through force (Fitzpatrick 2002).

The Roman Catholic Church legitimized the use of the Doctrine of Discovery through various papal bulls issued during the fifteenth century.[6] In one such decree entitled *Dum Diversas* (1452),[7] Pope Nicholas V granted King Don Alfonso of Portugal the authority to "subjugate Saracens, pagans, and all other enemies of Christianity" in addition to placing all non-Christian inhabitants of discovered lands in a state of "perpetual servitude" (Sweet 1997, 157). This declaration was cited as a moral justification for harsh treatment of indigenous people by all other European conquests of the globe. By the 1700s, colonial powers had further manipulated the doctrine to portray Native Americans as uncivilized tribes who were not granted the legal status as legitimate occupants of discovered lands (Miller 2010). These legal interpretations are significant because they established a formally sanctioned power relationship between whites over the native peoples of North America.

By the nineteenth century, the Doctrine of Discovery had become part of international law, including policies implemented in the United States related to the Native Americans. The US Supreme Court affirmed the doctrine in the case of *Johnson v. M'Intosh* (1823).[8] There, Chief Justice John Marshall described the Native Americans as "in a state of nature, and have never been admitted into the general society of nations" (567). The Johnson decision reinforced the subordinate status of the Native American tribes, and removal supporters cited the case in subsequent years. This legal decision was also influenced by what Seifert (2004, 304) describes as "two conflicting perceptions of the New World: on one hand, the notion of an Edenic world free of original sin where

Europe could begin anew, and on the other hand a reiteration of the various virtues and vices of the hunter versus the farmer." As a legal concept that blended religious ideology with public policy, the Doctrine of Discovery undoubtedly led to tragic consequences for the native tribes of North America.

Although Western European and American political thought was primarily the outcome of Enlightenment philosophy that emphasized rational over religious models of the human condition, religious logics survived and endured to shape public policy. Indeed, the emphasis on individual rights and the human capacity for rational thought so hailed by Enlightenment philosophy were seen by many in early America as gifts from God. The blending of religious narrative and Enlightenment rationality led to a "democratization" of Christianity in America that reached its zenith during the Second Great Awakening (Hatch 1989).[9] Lyman Beecher, a fiery Presbyterian evangelical minister of the period, regularly promoted the idea of "God's great plan" for the United States and "consecrated the American nation as a New Israel" that would lead "a millennial and democratic renovation of human existence" (Abzug 1994, 56). For those believers who saw themselves as playing an active part in fulfilling God's plan for humanity, the blending of Christian religious doctrine and public policy was unavoidable.

Subduing Tribal Lands: The Story of Creation

Jackson's ascendency to the presidency solidified the power of his supporters, collectively called Jacksonian Democrats, and thus paved the way for adoption of the Indian removal policy. Jackson and his supporters utilized their collective political power to influence the debate surrounding Indian removal via Old Testament stories. Policies of westward expansion, including the Indian Removal Act, owe much of their perceived legitimacy to narratives within the book of Genesis. The Creation story was commonly referenced as the source of a mandate given by God to humankind: "And God blessed [Adam and Eve], and God said unto them, 'Be fruitful, and multiply, and replenish the earth, and subdue it, and have dominion . . . over every living thing that moveth upon the earth" (Genesis 1:28). Through this statement, humankind is given the divine mandate to inhabit the land and cultivate the earth. The command appears again in various sections of the Bible including twice in Genesis chapter 9, which tells the story of Noah and the Great Flood. References to this command appear multiple times in nineteenth-century rhetoric and serve as a common justification for expansion and displacement of the native people.

One such reference is found in a speech supporting the Indian Removal Act made by Georgia Representative Richard Henry Wilde (1830) in Congress on May 19, 1830: "The European settlers [of North America] founded their title on the rights of discovery. . . . They quoted the divine law: The earth, they said, was given to man for his inheritance, and was destined by the Creator to sustain the greatest portion of life and happiness." Lewis Cass, who would become Andrew Jackson's Secretary of War in 1831, referred to the creation narrative explicitly: "Planted, as our ancestors were, in the course of Providence, upon the skirts of a boundless forest, they gradually subdued it by toil in industry. Year after year, the cultivated border advanced, bearing before it the primitive people . . . who could not stop their progress. The decree had gone forth, that the race of pale men should *increase and multiply*, and they did *increase and multiply*" (1830, 107; emphasis in the original). These quotes demonstrate how the supporters of removal approached the "Indian problem" as one framed by divine mandate outlined in the Book of Genesis, and as expected with any cultural metanarrative, the solution was conceived under the same paradigm. Cass's statement in particular is an excellent example of how many removal supporters combined biblical narratives with the Doctrine of Discovery and the representation of European settlement as God's providential plan for mankind as a conceptual reality.

Ironically, many opponents to removal also referred to God's providence. They emphasized God's mandate to "Go ye into all the world, and preach the gospel to every creature" (Mark 16:15) and to do so through the preexisting federal policy of Christianization. However, removal supporters, like Thomas McKenney, spoke of the failure of the policy, using biblical narratives to frame their position. In his address to the New York Indian Board on August 12, 1829, McKenney (1829b, 31) proclaimed that Native Americans are characterized by "indolence" and "aversion . . . to intellectual exertion" due to their uncivilized state, and are therefore "precluded from the benefits which civilization confers." As a result, removal was justified because the United States, "in the plans of the Eternal, was to be the empire of freedom and of the mind" (35) and because the policy of civilizing the native population did not "harmonize with the acknowledged principles of our union, [it] must be defective" (36). Without removal, "it will be difficult, if not *impossible*, to control their *degradation* and *extermination* will be inevitable!" (37; emphasis in the original). These statements demonstrate how McKenney, like many other supporters of removal, were able to conceptualize the relationship between the native population and white Americans as a conflict between God's chosen people and an uncivilized race of indigenous people who stood in the way of progress. This view of reality was reinforced by another narrative that is found within the Exodus story: the story of Jacob and Esau.

Reducing the Target and Denying Harm: The Story of Jacob and Esau

The biblical narrative most commonly referenced by removal supporters is the story of Jacob and Esau that begins in Genesis chapter 25, featuring twin brothers born to Isaac and his wife Rebekah. The story goes that while in Rebekah's womb, the twins would "struggle together" leading her to ask God, "If [my pregnancy] be so, why am I thus?" To this, God replied, "Two nations are in thy womb, and two manner of people shall be separated from thy bowels; and the one people shall be stronger than the other people; and the elder [Esau] shall serve the younger [Jacob]" (Genesis 25:23). This part of the narrative serves as foreshadowing for what is to come. Esau, the firstborn, was described as being "red, all over like a hairy garment" and "a cunning hunter, a man of the field." Jacob was described as a "plain man, dwelling in tents" referring to a life of a farmer (Genesis 25:25–27). Later in the story, Esau returns from an unsuccessful hunt and asks his brother Jacob for food; Jacob provides it in exchange for Esau's birthright. In Genesis chapter 27, Jacob pretends to be Esau in order to receive Esau's blessing from their blind father, Isaac. When the deception is discovered, Isaac tells Esau that "by the sword shalt thou live, and shalt serve thy brother" Jacob (Genesis 27:40). The contrast between these two lifestyles becomes the foundation of the moral lesson to be taken from the story.

Rogin (1975) suggests that the Jacob and Esau story "enshrined for Bible-reading Americans the right of the farming brother to claim the inheritance of the hunter" (126). This interpretation of the story is not unreasonable as God's preference for the lifestyle of the cultivator over the life of a hunter-gatherer is implied throughout the Pentateuch.[10] Elazar (1994, 297) describes the conflict between the two brothers as symbolic of "natural versus federal man," a dichotomy that contrasts the impulsive and wandering ways of Esau to the intelligent "sharpness" of mind that is associated with civil society. Elazar summarizes this point more bluntly stating that "the Esaus of the world, however attractive they may be . . . cannot assume the mantle of Abraham because of their personal deficiencies . . . the Jacobs are the lesser evil because they can be chastened, educated, and redirected" (296–297). Jacob's characteristics are consistent with the concept of "federal liberty" while "natural man simply cannot be restrained except by force" (297). Through this interpretation of the story, Europeans and early American settlers found rationalization for associating agriculture with prudence and civilization, and shunning the life of a wanderer as being irresponsible and barbaric. Further, disobedience to what was perceived as God's mandate to settle and cultivate the land would result in loss of the comforts and protections civil society provides.

During the Indian removal debate, the primary function of the Jacob and Esau narrative was to provide a moral justification for placing the agricultural lifestyle of Western Europeans above the hunter-gatherer lifestyle of indigenous tribes in America. Jacob was the symbol of white agrarian society and Esau represented the "red" man, the nomadic hunter who was destined to lose his birthright to those who would fulfill God's mandate to till the soil. In a letter dated January 8, 1830, from Alfred Balch to Andrew Jackson, this use of the Jacob and Esau narrative is evident: "These untutored sons of the Forest, cannot exist in a state of Independence, in the vicinity of the white man. If they will persist in remaining where they are, they may begin to dig their graves and prepare to die" (Balch 1830, 20). This logic allowed American society to reduce the status of the Native Americans to one that not only made removal justifiable but essential.

By the start of the nineteenth century, many Native Americans had come to adopt the Christian faith and some had even helped establish churches for the African slaves who lived among them (Minges 2001). By 1830 Vice President John C. Calhoun reported that the Cherokee "were all cultivators, with a representative government, judicial courts, Lancaster schools, and permanent property" (Finkelstein 1995, 36). This reality certainly proved to be a challenge for supporters of removal who needed to find some way to reconcile their desire to displace the tribes with the values of Christian fellowship and goodwill. The story of Jacob and Esau served as a frame of reference that removal advocates could use to portray the Christianization policy a failure. Whereas westward expansion and agricultural growth on the North American continent was seen as tantamount to fulfilling God's mandate, those native people who failed to adopt this lifestyle were doomed to give up their claim to the land, their birthright, just as Esau had done to his brother Jacob. On this point, Representative Richard Henry Wilde (1830, 1103) exhorted in Congress: "It's the order of nature we exclaim against. Jacob will forever obtain the inheritance of Esau. We cannot alter the laws of Providence . . . the earth was given for labor . . . not to the red, or to the white, but to the human race—and the inscription was, to the wisest—the bravest—to virtue—and to industry." Wilde's statement uses the narrative of Jacob and Esau to characterize the removal debate as one that is important to all humanity. It also alludes to the Creation story that provided the divine mandate to subdue the earth. This framing defines the removal issue as a moral imperative that justifies the use of extraordinary measures. It is not simply the desire of white society to conquer land; it is the "order of nature" that compels white society to expand westward. By portraying Native Americans as stubborn impediments to human progress, in accordance with the biblical mandate to cultivate the earth, removal supporters are able to justify their policy as being necessary to carry out society's transcendent mission.

The Jacob and Esau story reduced the standing of Native Americans and subjected them to the control of white society. On the possibility that the Cherokee would embrace an agrarian lifestyle, Representative Henry G. Lamar (1830, 1119) made his beliefs clear: "They are unfavorably situated to advance one grade above the wandering savage, to the life of a herdsman, which is the natural progress of society. . . . It is incompatible with their inclinations and habits of indolence." Georgia Representative James M. Wayne (1830, 1125) channeled similar rhetoric;

his words also contain references to the Doctrine of Discovery, as well as the Creation and Exodus narratives discussed previously:

> God in his providence, had been pleased to reveal himself to the man of another. . . . It was by this providence which gave our fathers the right to plant themselves by the side of the Indian . . . though the Indian roved through the forests of America contemporaneously with the wanderings of God's chosen people in their escape from Egyptian bondage—time could give them no right to more of the soil than he could cultivate; and the decree which denied him to be lord of the domain, was the Almighty's command to his creatures to till the earth.

When the story of Jacob and Esau is utilized in this manner, removal was justified as beneficial to society as well as beneficial for Native Americans. Thus was a narrative of differently favored brothers juxtaposed against that of the chosen people's exodus. White Americans are doubly privileged, and the native people's divinely decreed fate of subordination abundantly clear.

The Jacob and Esau story also became a source of logic for removal supporters to engage in what Cohen (2001, 7) called "implicatory denial." Cohen states, "officials do not claim that 'nothing happened,' but what happened is not what you think it is, not what it looks like, not what you call it" (7). Through the use of justifications, rationalizations, evasions, and deflections that minimize guilt for harm, actors are able to construct "good" and "believable" stories that relive the individual from "doing the 'right' thing" (9). Throughout the debate, Christianity and civilization were discussed as sharing in a lock-and-key relationship where the latter relies on the former. The story of Jacob and Esau reinforced the perception that Native Americans were uncivilized and barbaric people who were morally and intellectually incapable of adapting to the expansion of white society. Accordingly, removal was portrayed both as an act of benevolence as well as one that was necessary for the safety and prosperity of white society.

On this point, Superintendent of Indian Affairs Thomas McKenney (1829a, 13) spoke of "how utterly impractical it is to . . . fashion [Indian character] after the civilized form." Lewis Cass's (1830, 84) influential essay in the *New Republic* also promotes this argument stating that the native population possessed "habits and feelings" that make coexistence "impracticable." In particular, he warns of the Indians' proclivity for violence, declaring, "The sight of the war-flag, or the sound of the war-drum, operates instantly and intensely upon the warriors, and coinciding with their institutions and opinions, irresistibly impels them to war" (84). Later in the same essay, he disparages the "barbarous tribes," warning of those "who have neither religion or morality . . . to check their propensity for war; whose code requires them to murder and not subdue; to plunder and devastate . . . who acted from impulse more than from reason; whose customs required blood for blood, injury for injury . . . who had no permanent, settled residence . . . [and] whose young men were despised, until they had shed the blood of an enemy" (93). These "ruling motives" are used as justification for removal and "without going back to the question of right derived from conquest or discovery, or resorting to the received doctrine respecting the duty of cultivating the earth, it is enough for our present view . . . a just regard to the safety of both requires, that we should govern and they obey" (94). These statements clearly demonstrate how biblical narratives were used to portray removal as an act of necessity, thus denying the harm associated with their policy.

The influence of the Jacob and Esau story is also discernible in the paternalistic tone of removal supporters who portrayed Native Americans as uncivilized and thus childlike. During the early nineteenth century, paternalism was viewed as a "humane, Christian approach" to Indian policy, and policymakers presumed to know "what was best for the Indians according to white norms, which included . . . taking the Indians by the hand and leading them along the path to white civilization and Christianity" (Prucha 1986, x; see also Rogin 1975). As God's agent, Andrew Jackson assumes the role of a wise and just father who must inflict some harm upon his misguided "red children," but he does so for their own benefit. One famous example of this theme is found in Jackson's correspondence to the Creek Nation in 1829. There, with "permission of the Great Spirit of above" and "a father's love" he implored his "red children" to move west where he can "protect and foster" the members of the tribe (Jackson 1829a). The paternalistic theme is applied more directly in a correspondence between Secretary of War John H. Eaton and the Cherokee Nation dated April 18, 1829. In this document, Eaton (1829,

10) discusses Jackson's hope that the Cherokee will submit to removal and allow the government to "exercise over them a paternal, and superintending care" and once relocated "with the aid of schools . . . industry and refinements will take the place of those wandering habits now so peculiar to the Indian character, the tendency of which is to impede them in their march to civilization." In these examples, the biblical mandate to cultivate the soil is reflected in the assumed authority to suppress the rights of the Native American tribes.

Conclusion

Old Testament narratives were a cultural point of reference through which supporters of the Indian Removal Act portrayed the Native American tribes as deserving of relocation as people who failed to uphold the divine mandate to till the soil. Just as importantly, biblical narratives provided the cultural logic for colonizing North America and expanding westward, identifying these actions as part of a transcendent mission. Because America's indigenous tribes hindered the progress of this mission, biblical narratives also provided the justification for displacing Native Americans in furtherance of passing and implementing the Indian Removal Act. Removal supporters were not simply repeating biblical narratives or using them as a convenient prepackaged moral justification; rather they were referencing them as part of an assumed cultural logic that was reflected in political dialog. It was not necessary for policymakers to repeat these narratives for their meaning to be understood; the reference alone was sufficient to communicate the underlying message and influence the opinions of others. The analogy was self-explanatory and this is a testament to the hegemonic power of biblical narratives during the early nineteenth century. As cultural metanarratives, these stories shaped the very nature of social reality in the minds of individuals and help explain why removal supporters could be so blind to the harm caused by their policies. The case of Native American removal demonstrates that cultural metanarratives, especially those couched in religious themes, can have significant, indeed tragic, ramifications for members of society.

The findings of this research demonstrate the critical need for criminologists to study narratives and narrative influence on political policymaking. It is highly likely that the influence of culturally significant narratives, including stories gleaned from religious texts, can be discerned within the political rhetoric that leads to contemporary political violence, including war, genocide, and terrorism. It is important for criminologists to develop theoretical understandings about how these stories are used to marginalize target groups and gather the collective support that is necessary for the successful implementation of harmful policies.

The narrative criminology approach can also be applied fruitfully to developing policies intended to prevent and mitigate incidents of political violence. By analyzing the influence of cultural metanarratives used by social groups to further their harmful acts, the findings can be used as a means for constructing counterarguments that will be recognizable and deemed plausible to those who support these crimes. The challenge for social scientists will be to expose the hegemonic power of cultural metanarratives and use that knowledge to encourage policymakers and their constituents to look at an unfolding crisis in a different way. As other researchers in this book have demonstrated, narratives are an essential component of how individuals construct their own sense of identity and their own acts of criminal offending. These micro-level narratives are not constructed sui generis, but are heavily influenced by significant narratives reproduced and reinforced at the macro-level.

As in the days of Indian removal, Old Testament narratives are referenced today in a variety of ways. It is not uncommon to see public debate over the posting of the Ten Commandments in public facilities, and references to Old Testament scripture to justify harsher criminal punishments, withholding rights to same-sex couples, or justifying military conflict. Because these biblical narratives continue to influence contemporary American society, it is likely that continued study of Old Testament stories as a cultural metanarrative will pave the way for criminologists to better understand a multitude of harmful justice-related policies, including mass incarceration, capital punishment, or failures to consider alternative policies like restorative justice. To ignore the role of culturally significant narratives is to disregard the potential for reducing harm. It is my belief that this is an act of omission that criminologists should not be willing to accept.

NOTES

1. Although the Pentateuch is typically treated as a unified collection of stories, it is more accurately described as a collection of narratives lacking a "complete coherence of plot" that was written by multiple authors and compiled at different points in time (Brettler 2010, 3).
2. Ethnic cleansing is defined as "rendering an area ethnically homogenous by using force or intimidation to remove persons of given groups from the area" (United Nations 1994, 33).
3. Secular ideologies in the form of "civil religion" or "political religion" may also assume a similar sacred status (see Gentile 2005).
4. According to Pratt (1927), John L. O'Sullivan introduced the concept of manifest destiny in an editorial published in the July-August issue of the *Democratic Review* in 1845. Although the concept had not previously existed in common vernacular, its implied sanctification of westward expansion had, and pervaded the removal debate.
5. I use the word *Indian* here as it was the commonly used descriptor of Native Americans for much of US history. However, it is not an appropriate label today.
6. Papal bulls are documents issued by the Pope that typically conferred certain rights or privileges to those named in the document.
7. Translated: "Until Different."
8. *Johnson v. M'Intosh*, 21 US 543. 1823.
9. Between 1775 and 1845, Christianity in the United States became a "mass enterprise" as congregations swelled and the number of ministers increased from approximately 1,800 to nearly 40,000 (Hatch 1989, 4).
10. In fact, protagonists in the Pentateuch—including Adam, Noah, Abraham, Jacob, and Moses—were presented as cultivators of the land or livestock, whereas notable antagonists—Cain, Ishmael, and Esau—are characters cast as those punished to a life of wandering the wilderness for their disobedience. Following their disobedience, Adam and Eve were also cast out of the Garden of Eden and cursed to a life of wandering in the wilderness.

REFERENCES

Abzug, Robert H. 1994. *Cosmos Crumbling: American Reform and the Religious Imagination*. New York: Oxford University Press.

Balch, Alfred. 1830. Letter to Andrew Jackson, January 8. In *The Papers of Andrew Jackson*. Vol. 8, edited by D. Feller, T. Coens, and L. Moss, 18–20. Knoxville: University of Tennessee Press.

Barnes, Catherine. 2005. "The Functional Utility of Genocide: Towards a Framework for Understanding the Connection between Genocide and Regime Consolidation, Expansion, and Maintenance." *Journal of Genocide Research* 7 (3): 309–330.

Boon, Kevin Alexander. 2005. "Heroes, Metanarratives, and the Paradox of Masculinity in Contemporary Western Culture." *Journal of Men's Studies* 13 (3): 301–312.

Brettler, Marc Z. 2010. "Introduction to the Pentateuch." In *The New Oxford Annotated Bible, New Revised Standard Version with the Apocrypha*, 4th ed., 3–6. Oxford: Oxford University Press.

Bruner, Jerome. 1991. "The Narrative Construction of Reality." *Critical Inquiry* 18 (1): 1–21.

———. 1998. "What Is a Narrative Fact?" *Annals of the American Academy of Political and Social Science* 560 (November): 17–27.

Burnett, John G. [1890] 1978. "The Cherokee Removal through the Eyes of a Private Solder." *Journal of Cherokee Studies: Special Issue* 3 (3): 180–185.

Cass, Lewis. 1830. "Removal of the Indians." *North American Review* 30 (66): 62–121. http://digital.library.cornell.edu.

Cohen, Stanley. 2001. *States of Denial: Knowing About Atrocities and Suffering*. Cambridge: Polity Press.

Collins, Christopher. 2007. *Homeland Mythology: Biblical Narratives in American Culture*. University Park: Pennsylvania State University Press.

Eaton, John H. 1829. Correspondence to a Delegation of Cherokee. In *Documents and Proceedings Relating to the Formation of a Board in the City of New York, for the Emigration, Preservation, and Improvement of the Aborigines of America: July 22, 1829*. New York: Vanderpool and Cole.

Elazar, Daniel J. 1994. "Jacob and Esau and the Emergence of the Jewish People." *Judaism* 43 (3): 294–301.

Ewick, Patricia, and Silby, Susan S. 1995. "Subversive Stories and Hegemonic Tales: Toward a Sociology of Narrative." *Law and Society Review* 29 (2): 197–226.

Fairclough, Norman. 1992. *Discourse and Social Change*. Cambridge and Malden, MA: Polity Press.

Finkelstein, Norman. 1995. "History's Verdict: The Cherokee Case." *Journal of Palestine Studies* 24 (4): 32–45.

Fitzpatrick, Peter. 2002. "Doctrine of Discovery." In *A Companion to Racial and Ethnic Studies*, edited by D. T. Goldberg and J. Solomons, 25–30. Malden, MA: Blackwell.

Forsyth, John. 1830. *Speech of Mr. Forsyth of Georgia on the Bill Providing for the Removal of the Indians: Delivered in the Senate of the United States, May, 1830*. Washington, DC: Duff Green.

Franzosi, Roberto. 1998. "Narrative Analysis—Or Why (and How) Sociologists Should Be Interested in Narrative." *Annual Review of Sociology* 24 (1): 517–554.

Gentile, Emilio. 2005. "Political Religion: A Concept and its Critics–A Critical Survey." *Totalitarian Movements and Political Religions* 6 (1): 19–32.

Gottschall, Jonathan. 2012. *The Storytelling Animal: How Stories Make us Human*. Boston, MA, and New York: Mariner Books.

Gutjahar, Paul C. 1999. *An American Bible: A History of the Good Book in the United States, 1777–1880*. Stanford, CA: Stanford University Press.

Hagan, John, and Wenona Rymond-Richmond. 2009. *Darfur and the Crime of Genocide*. Cambridge: Cambridge University Press.

Hatch, Nathan O. 1989. *The Democratization of American Christianity*. New Haven, CT: Yale University Press.

Indian Removal Act of 1830. 1830. In *Gales and Seaton's Register of Debates in Congress*. 6:1135–1136.

Jackson, Andrew. 1829a. Talk to the Creek Indians. March 23. In *The Papers of Andrew Jackson*, vol. 8, edited by D. Feller, H. Moser, L. Moss, and T. Coens, 112–113. Knoxville: University of Tennessee Press.

———. 1829b. Letter to David W. Haley, October 15. In *The Papers of Andrew Jackson*, vol. 7, edited by D. Feller, H. D. Moser, L. Moss, and T. Coens, 494–495. Knoxville: University of Tennessee Press.

———. 1829c. First Annual Message to Congress. December 8. http://www.presidency. ucsb.edu.

———. 1830. Second Annual Message to Congress. December 6. http://www.presidency.ucsb.edu.

Kelman, Herbert C. 1973. "Violence without Moral Restraint: Reflections on the Dehumanization of the Victims and the Victimizers." *Journal of Social Issues* 29 (4): 25–61.

Kelsay, John. 1999. "Fighting the 'Good' Fight: The Return of the Religious War." *Research in Review*. Fall/Winter: n.p. http://rinr.fsu.edu/fallwinter99/features/religiouswar.html.

Lamar, Henry G. 1830. Speech in the United States House of Representatives. May 19. In *Gales and Seaton's Register* 6:1112–1120.

Lifton, Robert Jay. 2003. *Superpower Syndrome: America's Apocalyptic Confrontation with the World*. New York: Thunder's Mouth Press/Nation Books.

Lumpkin, Wilson. 1830. Speech in the United States House of Representatives. May 17. *Gales and Seaton's Register* 6:1016–1026.

McKenney, Thomas L. 1829a. Letter to Jeremiah Evarts, May 1. In *Documents and Proceedings Relating to the Formation of a Board in the City of New York, for the Emigration, Preservation, and Improvement of the Aborigines of America: July 22, 1829*. New York, Vanderpool and Cole.

———. 1829b. Address to the New York Board. August 12. In *Documents and Proceedings Relating to the Formation of a Board in the City of New York, for the Emigration, Preservation, and Improvement of the Aborigines of America: July 22, 1829*. New York: Vanderpool and Cole.

Miller, Robert J. 2010. "The Doctrine of Discovery." In *Discovering Indigenous Lands: The Doctrine of Discovery in the English Colonies*, edited by R. J. Miller, J. Ruru, L. Behrendt, and T. Lendberg, 66–88. Oxford: Oxford University Press.

Minges, Patrick. 2001."Beneath the Underdog: Race, Religion, and the Trail of Tears." *American Indian Quarterly* 25 (3): 453–479.

Monroe, Kristen Renwick. 2012. *Ethics in an Age of Terror and Genocide: Identity and Moral Choice*. Princeton and Oxford: Princeton University Press.

Pratt, Julius W. 1927. "The Origin of Manifest Destiny." *American Historical Review* 32 (4): 795–798.

Presser, Lois. 2009. "The Narratives of Offenders." *Theoretical Criminology* 13 (2): 177–200.

———. 2013. *Why We Harm*. New Brunswick, NJ: Rutgers University Press.

Prucha, Francis Paul. 1986. *The Great Father: The United States Government and the American Indians, Abridged Edition*. Lincoln: University of Nebraska Press.

Rogin, Michael Paul. 1975. *Fathers and Children: Andrew Jackson and the Subjugation of the American Indian*. New York: Alfred A. Knopf.

Satz, Ronald N. 1989. "The Cherokee Trail of Tears: A Sesquicentennial Perspective." *Georgia Historical Quarterly* 73 (3): 432–466.

Savelsberg, Joachim J. 2010. *Crime and Human Rights: Criminology of Genocide and Atrocities*. Los Angeles: Sage.

Scheffer, David. 2006."Genocide and Atrocity Crimes." *Genocide Studies and Prevention* 1 (3): 229–250.

Scott, Winfield. 1838. Orders No. [25] Head Quarters, Eastern Division Cherokee Agency, Ten[nessee], May 17, 1838. N.p. http://hdl.loc.gov/loc.rbc/rbpe.1740400a.

Seifert, Joshua L. 2004."The Myth of *Johnson v. M'Intosh*." *UCLA Law Review* 52: 289–332.

Shenhav, Shaul R. 2006. Political Narratives and Political Reality. *International Political Science Review* 27 (3): 245–262.

Smith, Philip. 2005. *Why War?: The Cultural Logic of Iraq, the Gulf War, and Suez*. Chicago: University of Chicago Press.

Somers, Margaret R. 1995. "Narrating and Naturalizing Civil Society and Citizenship Theory: The Place of Political Culture and the Public Sphere." *Sociological Theory* 13 (3): 229–274.

Sweet, James H. 1997. "The Iberian Roots of American Racist Thought." *William and Mary Quarterly* 54 (1): 143–166.

Sykes, Gresham M., and Matza, David. 1957. "Techniques of Neutralization: A Theory of Delinquency." *American Sociological Review* 22 (6): 664–670.

Thornton, Russell. 1984. "Cherokee Population Losses During the Trail of Tears: A New Perspective and a New Estimate." *Ethnohistory* 31 (4): 289–300.

United Nations. 1994. Letter from Secretary-General to the President of the Security Council (No. S/1994/674). May 21. http://www.icty.org/x/file/About/OTP/un_commission_of_experts_report_1994_en.pdf.

van Dijk, Teun A. 2006. "Discourse and Manipulation." *Discourse and Society* 17 (3): 359–383.

Wayne, James M. 1830. Speech in the United States House of Representatives. May 24. *Gales and Seaton's Register* 6:1123–1131.

Wilde, Richard Henry. 1830. Speech in the United States House of Representatives. May 19. *Gales and Seaton's Register* 6:1079–1103.

Yacoubian, George S. Jr. 2000. "The (In)Significance of Genocidal Behavior to the Discipline of Criminology." *Crime, Law and Social Change* 34 (1): 7–19.

6

Meeting the Djinn

Stories of Drug Use, Bad Trips, and Addiction

SVEINUNG SANDBERG AND SÉBASTIEN TUTENGES

What's destructive can also be positive, because it helps you
break something down.
—Maria, age 24

All societies have realms of darkness. The Kuranko people of Sierra
Leone, for example, have the bush, which they consider a place of wild
forces that both threaten and sustain the village and its rule-bound life.
The bush is where the djinn live—capricious creatures able to bestow
villagers with great powers but also to drive them insane. The djinn are
givers and takers of life, a source of vitality, adventure, and death. To
access and make proper use of the forces of the djinn requires ritual
technique and conceptual strategies (Jackson 1998, 51, 62). It is not an
option for the Kuranko to ignore, forget, or avoid the djinn: that would
drain social life of its vitality, things would come to a halt, and life would
become a bore. As Jackson puts it, "any social system tends toward stasis,
entropy, and death, unless its field of bound energy is periodically rein-
vigorated by the 'wild energies' and fecund powers that are associated
with extrasocial space and deep subjectivity" (Jackson 2002, 29).

In the Western world, magical creatures do not play a large role in social life, but there are other realms of darkness, including that inhabited
by criminals and deviants. This "other side" of social life is closely associated with a range of psychoactive drugs, such as cannabis, LSD, and
heroin. Drugs represent the forbidden, and to use them is symbolically
to move away from the rule-bound world of sanity and reason. Illegal
drugs signify transgression, excess, trouble, and fun, and the intake of
drugs signals such diverse personality traits as immorality, impulsivity,

and bravery. In much the same way as encounters with the djinn, the consumption of illegal drugs is a ritualized endeavor of great significance that brings people into contact with society's dark forces. In consequence, narratives about first-time use, bad trips, dealing, addiction, and other drug stories abound in Western society. As we shall see, such stories of substance use are more than simple pastimes; they address fundamental existential issues and play an important role in identity building, especially among youth (Fjær 2012; Tutenges and Rod 2009).

A narrative is essentially concerned with temporality and causality: events are put in a certain order, and the assumption is that the one leads to the other, making a plot that provides the moral of the story (Polletta et al. 2011; Riessman 2008). Labov (1972) famously distinguished between abstract, orientation, complicating action, evaluation, result or resolution, and coda in a narrative. He identified these elements in a variety of orally transmitted stories and argued that although the order was often chaotic, and in places may be missing altogether, it was the basic structure of the narrative. In stories of illegal drug use, the audience is told the reason for the story and supplied with certain essential information about those involved, time, place, and situation. Then some action takes place (use of a drug), there is a result (subsequent acts, feelings, experiences caused by the first event), and subsequently an evaluation of what happened (positive or negative) occurs. Finally, the coda returns the story to the audience and provides additional and more general meaning (such as what can be learned and why this is important). Drug experiences can be used to tell fun, entertaining stories, as well as stories about a different, relaxed lifestyle or opposition to mainstream society. They are widely used to convey edgy personality traits such as an attraction to alternative or rebellious lifestyles. However, drug stories may also be tragic, centered on addiction and psychological crises.

Recent scholarship on the subject of narratives has stressed that real-life narratives are less structured than Labov suggests (Polletta et al. 2011). Stories are dialogical, include multiple voices, and have several possible interpretations (Bakhtin 1981; Frank 2012). Stories are also fragmented, and the stories of illegal drug use that we have heard were often so well-known that narrators only had to hint at them for the listener to "hear" the full story. In familiar stories, learning minor details about acts of drug use and subsequent acts is often sufficient to enable the listener to understand the evaluation or coda. The presence of narratives in our data often took the form of cognitive cues (Zald 1996), or fragments of formula stories (Loseke 2001) or cultural stories (Polkinghorne 1991; Richardson 1990), directing the audience's attention in particular and familiar directions.

This chapter explores how drug cultures contain a multitude of stories and demonstrate how people can "realize a particular self-story" by using drugs (Presser 2009, 185).[1] We study stories to understand their functions and implications for storytellers. Rather than evaluating the stories according to their conformance to objective accounts of past events, we consider processes of storytelling to constitute instances of interpretation with existential implications (Tutenges and Rod 2009, 356). In line with narrative criminology (Presser 2009, 2012; Sandberg 2010, 2013a), we treat drug stories not simply as retrospective interpretations but as constructs that affect and shape people's actions. Narratives act as a "boomerang . . . thrown from the present into the past" and returning "with a force bearing it into the future" (Järvinen 2000, 385). We thus see them as motivating both abstinence from and use of drugs.

We pay particular attention to personal stories about addiction and bad trips, which we refer to as tragic drug stories, because they embody two characteristics in which we are particularly interested. First, these stories are highly ambiguous and challenge official discourses on illegal drugs. State-sponsored drug stories, for example, have the same complicating action as the tragic drug stories told among active drug users, but they have a very different evaluation and coda. Second, tragic drug stories represent the archetypal stories of meetings with dark forces in modern Western society. They concern not only crossing over (bad trips) but also being stuck on (addiction) the "other side." Tragic drug stories thus provide a window into not only the risks and dangers but also the fascination and excitement of substance use.

Research Methodology

This study is based on data collected as part of an extensive investigation of cannabis use in Norway between 2006 and 2010 (Sandberg and Pedersen 2010).[2] One hundred cannabis users were interviewed over a four-year period. Interviews were semistructured and flexible in thematic focus, and lasted between ninety minutes and three hours. Interviewees were recruited through social networks, university students with the assistance of an organization that lobbies for the legalization of cannabis, and an online advertisement. In addition, a number of smugglers and large-scale dealers were contacted in prison. All interviewees had used cannabis for long periods of time—some sporadically and recreationally, others regularly and more heavily. Some reported previous problems with the drug, but no one was recruited from clinical settings. All participants were white ethnic Norwegians, eighty-eight men and twelve women. The majority of respondents were in their twenties and thirties, but nine interviewees were in their fifties or sixties. Approximately one-third of the participants were employed, one-third were students, and one-third received unemployment or other state benefits.

Data for this chapter were partly based on previous categorizations identifying various themes in data, such as use of cannabis, use of other drugs, effects, or uses. In addition, we reread interview transcripts and searched for what we call addiction and bad trip stories. According to Lieblich and colleagues, narratives can be analyzed using four distinct strategies. A narrative can emphasize either content or form, and it can consider either the whole story or parts of it (Lieblich et al. 1998). In the following analysis, our aim is to combine these four analytical strategies. Our main focus is on content, describing influential and widespread cannabis stories as well as addiction and bad trip stories involving all kinds of illegal drugs. When relevant, we comment on their form. Narratives mainly emphasize a particular utterance or theme, but we include an analysis of a more complete narrative. We believe that all of these analytical strategies should be part of the methodological toolbox of narrative criminology. Used with discretion, they can assist researchers to develop the key stories of their research.

Cannabis Culture—A Pool of Stories

Culture consists of the symbolic forms that people use to express meaning. Examples include not only art and ceremonies but also less formal social phenomena such as gossip and everyday rituals (Swidler 1986, 273). Narratives are the essential building blocks of all cultures, including drug cultures. In the present study, we were interested in the culture surrounding cannabis and collected a wide variety of narratives from cannabis users. Many of the cannabis stories collected for this study depicted alternative states of consciousness and were linked to larger changes in the users' lives. Fredrik, for example, recounted that he had had a difficult upbringing but that his life changed when he started smoking hashish: "It has helped me manage to relax and instead let the solutions come to me. It has cleared up some confusing thoughts. A lot of fear has controlled me. I have been afraid since I was four or five years old, right up until my thirties." Fredrik described how cannabis helped him to relax and remove anxieties, a story embedded in the well-established language of the medical cannabis movement (Pedersen and Sandberg 2012). Another type of narrative about cannabis, associated with recreational use, was illustrated in an interview with Torsten.

> You think a bit differently, maybe the subconscious gets to percolate up more. It's impossible to talk about it without it sounding very peculiar (laughs). But it's like there is a thinner wall between dream and reality, that's the psychedelic effect. . . . That's what's been most attractive, the psychedelic bit. All the strange, funny things you can think of. And then there's that really beautiful feeling of things. Your senses open up. Just looking at the sky, it feels clearer, like a stronger impression. Listening to music can be a lot more interesting, and you feel that you understand it better.

Such stories about the psychedelic effects of cannabis were common. Several stated that cannabis makes you "more open to impressions" and capable of "concentrating on what's important." Others told stories about laughing, binge eating, relaxation, obtaining new insights, and changing personality (Sandberg 2012b, 2013b).

Many cannabis stories involve distanciation from the values of mainstream society. Mikael, for example, said about those not using cannabis: "I don't really like the conformist way of life. I feel they go round in their own circles like slaves." Cannabis users, on the other hand, "had a pretty relaxed view of life." Another pointed out that "holidays and hash smoking are the same lifestyle." Bjarke had considerable experience surfing and described how cannabis was an integral part of this scene, which revolves around "the holy trinity of snow, skate, and surf." He continued: "The surfing scene has something rather bohemian about it. It's like people who kind of drop out to be in the waves." Cannabis can help create a shared history and identity (Lee and Kirkpatrick 2005, 148–150), and cannabis stories play a decisive part in this process. Using cannabis may signal that one is not bound by the usual conformist lifestyle, with its emphasis on career and income, and telling cannabis stories can be a way of demonstrating commitment to a "subterranean world of play" (Young 1971).

The cultural context in which cannabis was introduced to large groups in the Western world influences how its effects are experienced. Gradually, the substance came to signalize an unforced, relaxed lifestyle. The youth culture of the hippies revolved around hedonism, expressionism, and spontaneity. Hippie culture was Dionysian; it required sexuality and other needs to be satisfied immediately. Actions were supposed to be spontaneous and unplanned. Hippies prolonged their childhood and play; they despised work and were interested in individuality and autonomy (Young 1971). The effects of cannabis, described as both relaxing and leading to creativity, fit in with this image.

Although use of cannabis has become much more common, cannabis still has an edge of rebellion to it. In Norway, as in many other Western societies, using cannabis symbolizes that one is not subservient to the dominant norms of society. It is a sign of autonomy, freedom, and opposition. Because it is illegal, it provides excitement and adds something extra to identity. Mats, for example, said that he used cannabis because "it's good and it's fun, and probably also because of that romantic bit. There is something bohemian about it. Still doing something criminal at the age of 32!" By smoking cannabis and integrating cannabis stories into his larger life story, he broke with an otherwise conventional identity. Cannabis use is symbolic consumption and can be seen as tightly and ritually linked to what can best be described as "cannabis culture" (Sandberg 2012b, 2013b). This culture is based on a vast pool of stories that cannabis users can dive into and use when constructing identities. The above examples are just some of the countless stories from which this culture is constituted. In short, using cannabis is a crucial aspect of the story that many tell about themselves to communicate edginess and subtle opposition to mainstream society.

The Authentic Storyteller

In his classic study of marijuana users, Becker describes three processes through which individuals pass to become users. Novice users need to learn to smoke the drug in a way that produces real effects, to learn to recognize these effects and to connect them with drug use, and to learn to enjoy the perceived sensations (Becker 1953, 242). "Becoming a marijuana user" thus demands engagement, commitment, and extensive use of the drugs in a supportive social context. We would like to add a fourth step to Becker's three-step model: in terms of identity and personal narratives, becoming a drug user is a process that often starts a long time before actual use of the substance. Cannabis users in this study, for example, often identified with "those who smoke weed" and knew a wide variety of cannabis stories long before they actually tried the substance. It was a part of their oppositional, rebellious, or nonconformist identity.

To embrace the identity of a cannabis user fully, however, and to join in telling cannabis stories effectively, they had to try the drug themselves. As previous studies have reported regarding teenage drinking, authenticity and sincerity are "an important part of one's performance" (Johnson 2012, 9), and to "over-claim," "pretend," "act hard" or make false claims of drug experience can lead to severe social sanctions from peers (Johnson 2012). A story thus promotes action (Presser 2009), but actions also tell a story (Jackson-Jacobs 2009; Katz 1988). Morten, for example, was sixteen when he first tried cannabis. He spoke of being part of a circle of friends who "had certain opinions and wanted to try the same stuff as the musicians we liked; it was kind of exclusive." They had planned and discussed it for years before actually trying the drug. For Morten, using the drug thus became an important ritual through which to realize a narrative of being a young musician, and others likewise treated cannabis use as a means to realize similar narratives. Far from being a hedonistic, here-and-now experience born of lack of self-control, drug use appeared to be well planned and reasoned. Perhaps novice cannabis users wanted a new experience, a pleasurable high, but their cannabis consumption was also a reflection of the story that they were developing about themselves (McAdam 1993).

Many described how initial use of the drug was embedded in a narrative landscape with which they were well acquainted. Thomas was introduced to cannabis at the age of fourteen. Initially he was afraid and avoided using it because he had been taught that it was dangerous. After a while, however, he said, "I had so many opinions about the drug that I wanted to try it for myself in order to know what I was talking about." A straightforward interpretation of this story would be that curiosity and exposure to the drug motivated Thomas's initial cannabis use. At the same time, having tried cannabis was also important in another sense. Without experiencing the substance, it was difficult for him to be taken seriously when his friends were discussing the drug. He could not tell cannabis stories, even the negative ones, without some experience of the substance.

In many drug stories, the emphasis was often on the experience of having tried a drug. Early on in our fieldwork, interviewees often would proudly volunteer lists of drugs they had tried. Sometimes this was in response to direct questions but also to less direct ones. Asked whether drugs could provide inspiration, Jonathan answered: "I think LSD is great. And 2CB, ketamine. More functional drugs such as cocaine and amphetamines do not inspire me. They keep me going." Similarly, Peter said, "I had a troublesome period when I was about twenty, where things got out of hand and I used ecstasy, a little LSD, mushrooms, valium, and other things; got through the whole spectrum." These cognitive cues (Zald 1996), or tropes, sometimes foreshadowed larger repertoires of more comprehensive and structured narratives about drug use to come; at other times they were simply left open for interpretation. Signe was quite explicit in respect of this important use of drug stories. Of her first cannabis experience as a fourteen year old, she said: "I was happy about having done it, to be able to say that I'd done it. That's the way it works." Later she smoked more, with a different rationale, but with regard to her first experience, the story of having tried it was a crucial aspect of her motivation.

Drug culture represents a pool of stories that can be used for multiple purposes such as entertainment and identity work. Drug stories are, for example, recounted as part of comprehensive life stories in intense and emotional personal meetings, or told as entertainment in social gatherings and everyday conversations. Sometimes, these stories were creatively interwoven into larger life stories; at other times they only seemed to spice up the conversation. However, an authentic storyteller needs to have tried the drug in question. Use of a drug provides access to a wide variety of drug stories and makes the storyteller credible. The value and uses of drug stories and the importance of being an authentic storyteller is thus crucial to the understanding of experimental and initial use of drugs.

Newsworthiness and Symbolic Boundary Work

We use the terms *narrative* and *story* interchangeably (Polletta et al. 2011). However, Riessman (2008) points to a sociolinguistic definition that separates the two, stating that narratives are the structure, while "real" stories, in the words of De Fina, "include some kind of rupture or disturbance in the normal course of events" (quoted in Riesman 2003, 13). Silverman (2006) indicates similar ruptures when describing what makes a story newsworthy in a conversation analytical framework. Without making a point of separating narrative and story, it is clear that a narrative with unexpected action and a rupture is more worthy of telling than one without.

When cannabis is used regularly and over a long period, the drug tends to lose some of its oppositional edge and newsworthiness. Some then move on to other illegal drugs to revive and cultivate their nonconformist identities and to be able to tell new stories. Several of the experienced cannabis users interviewed for this study emphasized that they had experimented with mushrooms, mescaline, and LSD. When we asked Jakob what drugs he had tried, he replied as follows.

> JAKOB: Mushrooms from many places, fly agarics (amanita muscaria, a poisonous mushroom), and LSD, and then, what's it called again, mescaline!
>
> INTERVIEWER: Sorry . . . ?
>
> JAKOB: Mescaline. It is often in plants, in cactuses. It is a cactus called Peyote, I'm sure you've heard about it. Mescaline is the active substance in those plants. And then you have St. Pedro, which is a big fat cactus that grows straight up in the air, twenty meters. What they do is they just cut it off and boil it for almost a day, and mix in a few other ingredients to make it taste better. Then it becomes some muddy, strange stuff. Disgusting, almost like jelly, tickles between the teeth.

Jakob seemed to enjoy telling this story, with all its details and special expertise. Having knowledge and first-hand experience of exotic drugs was a central feature of his life story. His storytelling also indicated a key difference between people. In much the same way as stories about socio-economic and cultural backgrounds and sexual history, stories about drug use say something about who we are. People identify themselves "in terms of similarity to some people and difference to others" (Copes et al. 2008, 256). Michael was even more explicit in this regard. He talked about films and described some of them as "acid movies." When we asked what he meant by that, he replied: "It's easier to understand if you have tried acid." He thus effectively established a dynamic symbolic boundary between those with and those without drug experience.

Barth (1969) argues that identity is created in meetings between groups and that boundaries drawn around a culture, not the "cultural stuff" they enclose, define a group. As with other narratives (Gubrium and Holstein 2009), the *us* and *them* in drug stories are critical. Boundary maintenance is an important part of drug stories, and it is difficult to understand the full meaning and function of drug stories without observing how they feature in active symbolic boundary work (Lamont and Molnár 2002). The distinction between insiders and outsiders may even be particularly strong and decisive in stories about illegal drugs because the position of an authentic storyteller requires a criminal act and a potentially dangerous and uncomfortable physical experience.

Balancing Addiction and Constructive Use

The importance of substance use for life stories can also be seen in more tragic stories, which typically serve to demonstrate that the narrator has been "out there," "lived life to the full," or knows the "hard life." Drug use adds a fascinating, sometimes dark and exotic dimension to the narrator's life story. In the Western world, just as in the villages of Sierra Leone, confronting the dark forces of existence can be both dangerous and rewarding. Tragic drug stories are often associated with heavily stigmatized drugs such as heroin, but they could also be discerned when users discussed less stigmatized drugs such as amphetamines, cocaine, and LSD. Even stories about a relatively soft drug such as cannabis sometimes involve dangers and psychedelic crises. Lars, for example, was unexpectedly dumped by a girlfriend because he had "smoked too much weed." He explained what happened next: "The sorrow I felt increased to irrational proportions because I smoked weed to become indifferent. I had to quit. And this spring I don't smoke much because some devil started speaking to me, in my head, and I didn't want to accept that. It was frightening. The moment you start believing: 'Shall I go for a walk with the dog or shoot myself?' 'I think I'll go for a walk.' Completely irrational voices in my head pop up." Lars indicated that his addiction to cannabis was the reason that he lost his girlfriend, and he made a clear link between cannabis and psychological problems. In this short quote, Lars touched upon the two types of drug stories that we study in detail in this chapter: stories of addiction (Reinarman 2005) and bad trips (Johnson and Stax 2006). Both are widespread in Western society.

Research participants in this study used cannabis on a regular basis, but none was recruited from clinical settings, and they were selected precisely because they were not problem users. However, during interviews, many of them mentioned negative experiences with cannabis. In what we describe as the tragic drug stories, there is often a thin line between constructive and destructive use. Speaking about cannabis addiction, for example, Erik said, "you start feeling that you lack creativity, right, the imagination disappears, it becomes harder to remember . . . it comes with a price, you know, you can't just push it, it needs to be planned to keep it under control." Henrik observed on a more general note: "Psychologically, I definitely think one can be dependent upon cannabis. It's dangerous to be dependent, it *can* be dangerous." Another interviewee described what happens when he stops smoking: "I will sweat like a pig, and then I will be aggressive for a couple of days." Yet another told several problematic stories and ended by saying that he "had respect for drugs." He still pointed out: "But I'm not afraid of them." This double meaning, to respect the potential dangerous forces of drugs but also to control and to be able to use them was the coda of many drug stories. For cannabis users, the balance between constructive and destructive use of drugs was a key element in the evaluation of their personal narratives.

Johannes was a musician, and when asked when he chose not to use cannabis, he said the following.

Well, there are no fixed rules [laughs]. I take it as it comes. But it's not as if I *have* to smoke, right, it's just that I want to. Many say that they get relaxed and dull, but that's not me. I'm more like, want to do exciting stuff. Everybody knows that it influences the way you experience sounds, right, so in that way it can be really good. But there is a problem, you do become a little bit . . . it can be difficult to finish things. There's a reason why the stereotypical cannabis smoker is portrayed as a sloth without a job, right.

Johannes presented a reasonable straightforward story until he came to the evaluation. He admitted to having smoked "*way* too much in some periods" and criticized the "Jim Morrison cliché" but still concluded: "I don't think you can take acid and be a genius. But I'm convinced that the alternative reality that drugs present can give you some perspective. When you play with different states of mind, you can get a different perspective than the one you had. You become less locked up in conventional thinking." Stories about physical and psychological addiction sometimes draw a line between beneficial uses of substances and more destructive uses. These stories may be considered a kind of risk management, or a "technique of risk denial" described by Peretti-Watel (2003) as scapegoating. Nevertheless, it is not that easy. Drug users may have become better acquainted and experienced with drugs, but in many of their stories, they never really controlled the substance. There was a sense of uncertainty and risk involved. Espen's conclusion was that experimenting with drugs was useful, but one should be careful with using drugs regularly.

> ESPEN: And then I tried mushrooms once, just for the fun of it, so that I know what it's like. I have tried LSD only once, and mushrooms a couple of times, just to check it out.
>
> INTERVIEWER: How was that compared with cannabis?
>
> ESPEN: It is completely freaky, even though intoxication from cannabis can be wild too. But not in the same way as LSD. It's different. But I only did it to check it out, and I only did it once.
>
> INTERVIEWER: Did you want to try again?
>
> ESPEN: No, it was fun once. But you can't do that stuff regularly. You'll go nuts.

Drug experiences were ritualized in the sense that they were right for particular occasions and followed established procedures, and breaking these "rules" could have serious implications. The balance between the destructive and constructive aspects of the realm of darkness was ongoing and continuous for many. Gunnar had used cannabis many years but still doubted his ability to control the drug.

> I'm strict about controlling use. Or—that's not the right way to put it because I feel that I'm still learning. I don't think I really know my own limits yet. And I know that many say I smoke too much. And at the same time, I think that they think it doesn't really matter because I work out, and stay fresh, I don't look tired or worn out at all. So I do feel that I have some kind of control, but I don't know my own limits well enough to really know.

Others had no doubt about their ability to control their drug use but were sure that it was time to quit. Sissel, for example, said: "Yes, I can really see that I have problems quitting now, to break with the routine I have. It's not 'heavy,' but it's enough so that I think that now it's time to quit." She continued to discuss friends that had problems with smoking too much before she said: "If you ask me whether one can be addicted, I say yes, I think you can. I do believe so. . . . You want the escape, that's what makes you dependent, I think, because it's fantastic."

As other stories, drug stories start from personal experiences to provide more general meaning. In this process, several narrative techniques are involved. In Sissel's account, for example, a generalized "you" is used to distance "the speaker from the act," and it "involves the audience and closes up the 'space' between the past act and the current understanding of that act" (O'Connor 2000, 77). To use Labov's (1972) concepts, the generalized you turns the complicating action (the action in a particular event) into a more general evaluation or coda. These evaluations are often expected and tightly connected to the plot. In tragic drug stories, however, the evaluation sometimes came as a surprise. Tragic drug stories such as bad trip and addiction stories are often used by representatives of mainstream society to warn potential users about the dangers of drugs, but these stories are also part of the fascination of drugs. Bad trip stories were particularly ambiguous.

Birgitte's Bad Trip Story

Birgitte recounted a bad trip on vacation in Denmark at the age of sixteen. The story was told with great verve and little hesitation, leaving the impression that she had told it many times before. We divided her story into three parts to insert our remarks clarifying the nature of bad trip stories.

> I remember I smoked that joint and we just laughed and laughed. We had so much fun. There was no end to it. I have never laughed so much; it was fantastic. But maybe halfway into that joint, I just looked at my friend and said, "You know what? I cannot smoke any more. I'm so high." And she just went, "I know what you mean." And then we stopped laughing, and we sat there for twenty minutes without saying anything. Then one of us said, "Shit, let's go get something to eat. We can't just sit here." We went to a 7–Eleven, and I remember I was going to buy something, and paid, and then suddenly I had no idea where I was. And I could hear my own voice, far away. The thing is, I was so high, right?

There is an abrupt mood change in the story. The laughter stops, and Birgitte and her friend are suddenly seized by silence and immobility. It is not entirely clear why this happens, but Birgitte emphasizes being "so high" (very intoxicated), which is a fragile state to be in. To enter states of intoxication is to depart from the reassuring familiarity of everyday experience. This transition can be pleasurable and rewarding, but also frightening and damaging, and many thus prefer to experiment with altered states of consciousness in a safe environment or in the company of trusted others (Fontaine and Fontana 1996, 21–22). Indeed, it is an "anthropological constant" that people seek the company of reliable and preferably like-minded others—people who can provide aid and support—when they transgress "into the margin" (Gauthier 2004, 76). However, Birgitte and her friend were not in an environment that made them feel safe; they were not among friends, and they were very young. This lack of shelter may account for the bad trip that was about to commence.

> Marijuana is hallucinogenic, right? It's almost like a trip if you smoke really fresh marijuana. It's like tripping. I wasn't prepared for that. I was

in a crowded shop, and people spoke Danish to me and I was supposed to pay for something and then I panicked. It was this feeling of losing control. I was there for two hours. I had real angst. Terrible. Every time she [the women in the shop] opened her mouth, it was like "uahhhuahh" and I was just thinking: "I am Birgitte from Norway. I am in Copenhagen. Why am I in Copenhagen?" It was like when people have lost all memory and keep talking to themselves, crawling back to reality. It was fucked up. I was afraid. I thought, "Now I am crossing over to the other side. I will become crazy, or lose touch with reality." That was the feeling, right? My face was all white and just trying to cling on to something. I don't know what my friend was doing. I remember that at some point I had to block her out.

The fear of going crazy, floating adrift, lost and helpless, is common in bad trip stories. Birgitte was afraid that her trip would last forever, and she desperately tried to reconnect with ordinary reality by reminding herself of her name and nationality, and by ignoring her friend, who was also intoxicated and therefore in no position to lead the way back to normalcy.

All cultures have favored states of consciousness and preferred means to achieve altered consciousness. Some cultures cultivate rituals of possession (Lapassade 1990), in which selected individuals are assisted to make the transition from their ordinary selves to a state of being possessed and then back again. The djinn, demons, or other spirits are invited to take control of a human body to give that body extraordinary powers and capacities. In spirit possession, for example, "it is by allowing oneself to be overcome, taken, infiltrated, or ridden by wild powers that one discovers the resources to go on with life in the face of quotidian hardship and oppression" (Jackson 2007, 148). Radical personality changes, however, are not valued or cultivated among most segments of the population in Western countries. In Norway, for example, there are regular and highly popular ritual occasions for alcohol consumption where individuals are brought to a state where they engage in playful deviance and lose control of themselves (Sande 2002), but spirit possession and psychedelic trips are not central ritual practices. Birgitte was therefore not culturally conditioned to understand and manage the strong effects of the cannabis joint, and this probably contributed to her sense of going crazy. She was becoming increasingly desperate when a stranger came to her rescue.

> What actually happened then was that a guy came over to me and said, "You don't look too well. Come with me." It was a guy that lived there [in Christiania].[3] He probably thought: "Here is a young girl who has come to smoke her head off." So he basically just gave me some food, some water, talked to me, made me relax, got me away from all the people. And then slowly I got better. But the experience has stuck with me. It's just recently, this summer, that I have started smoking hashish again, and I use just a little bit in my joints. Because after that experience, I freaked out every time I even smelled a joint. So, my worst bad trip was on marijuana, definitely. My worst experience with drugs, ever.

Birgitte was saved by a stranger who helped her get back in touch with ordinary reality by bringing her to a calm place and making her focus on everyday trifles such as drinking water and having a conversation. Birgitte thus came back from her trip, but she was not the same anymore. She had become more anxious. However, she had also become wiser and now realized that the purportedly mild drug cannabis is a treacherous substance, which can bring both laughter and horror, good times as well as suffering. Birgitte's bad trip was certainly a dreadful experience, but it provided her with important insights, and it gave her a fascinating story about how she had encountered, fought, and overcome devastating psychedelic forces. This narrative dimension of her life story made her emerge edgier than ever (Tutenges 2012, 137, 142; see also Jackson-Jacobs 2009).

The content of Birgitte's story is closely connected to its form. For example, she uses reported speech. This is a common narrative technique and gives statements more weight by replaying the situation and shifting authority to the person quoted, "even if the person quoted is oneself" (Shuman 2012, 135–37). This makes a story more authentic, especially when told as a personal narrative about a person's own experiences. Narrative rupture makes a story noteworthy, and "having been there" makes it convincing. Together they constitute a good story. The story is also easy to recognize and understand because it has the classical narrative structure outlined by Labov (1972) and includes some of Propp's (1968) narrative characters. The drug is the villain, against which the victim/seeker hero (Birgitte) struggles, and the man that comes to her rescue is the helper. However, the villain is not entirely bad or destructive but a potential source of insight and experience. The content of Birgitte's story would not have been as convincing if it had lacked reported speech and recognizable narrative structure. An edgy life story and identity requires authentic and out-of-the-ordinary personal narratives.

Ambiguous Tragic Stories

Bad trip stories and addiction stories involve one or several individuals who willingly or unwillingly enter into relationships with dangerous forces that wound, bind, or destroy them. Unlike addiction stories, bad trip stories often refer to experiences occurring once in a lifetime. They tend to be told in a serious and confessional tone, and among other functions, they serve as a warning against doors of perception that are best left closed. Merete, for example, told a drug story similar to Birgitte's, in which she was confronted with forces that threatened to overwhelm her: "I smoked pot in New Orleans. I had been to a voodoo museum earlier in the day and was about to go to bed. The hotel room had red plush on the walls, and I was so afraid that I felt I was dying. . . . I was afraid because we were in a very spiritual place. So out of control it was funny, but very uncomfortable."

Drug use destabilizes people's ordinary sense of self and reality (Lapassade 1990, 5). In Merete's case, the destabilization was so intense that she was completely thrown off her feet, leaving her horrified and out of touch with the ordinary world. Here again, we see the theme of losing control, with a main character who is sucked into a frightening "province of reality" that transforms her (Schutz and Luckmann 1973, 3). Kim told a similar story about a bad trip on fly agarics: "I was up in the woods one night and ate fly agarics. I had a bad reaction. But for me, it was important to concentrate on reality, remind myself that it was only a high, you have not become crazy, it's an intoxication and it will pass." Kim used this story about a bad trip to demonstrate that he knew what he was talking about when he said that he stuck to cannabis. The story "I have tried it, it was bad, and you shouldn't do it" is well known in the drug field and usually reflects positively on identity because the use of a particular stigmatized drug is situated in the past. Thus, both good and bad drug experiences have a rich storytelling potential, and telling a story of learning something can transform a bad drug experience into an affirmative self-narrative.

Some stories about addiction and bad trips are state sponsored and warn people against the effects of drugs. However, even these stories are dialogical (Frank 2012), and the very same stories proliferate among active drug users who evaluate events such as addiction and bad trips in a much less dogmatic and more open-ended manner. As Jackson (2002) argues, crossing over to the dark side can be life affirming; dangerous forces are countered and overcome, old habits disrupted, and new insights gained. Maria, for example, told an extensive story about problems she had experienced when using large quantities of drugs, but the point was somehow surprising: "I did too much cannabis and amphetamines, it was crazy, I was completely destroyed. But I have no problems with illegal drugs! I don't see the point in drawing a line between what's good and bad. . . . What's destructive can also be positive, because it helps you break something down." The complicating action of this story, according to Labov's (1972) framework, is that of using drugs and having bad experiences. This may call for an evaluation or coda warning against the use of drugs. Maria's interpretation and that of many other drug users is different: bad experiences can be helpful. Many active drug users' evaluations of tragic drug stories thus reflect Nietzsche's famous dictum: "What doesn't kill you makes you stronger." Both addiction and bad trip experiences may be interpreted in this way. That makes experimenting with drugs more attractive.

Drug Stories as Folktales

The Kuranko people tell stories about meetings with magical creatures (Jackson 1982). Similarly, Arctic Inuit recount myths about animals with human-like characteristics (Henriksen 2009). All societies have stories. In traditional societies, narratives often center upon mythical characters and events that took place a long time ago. Contemporary society has urban myths, but it seems that personal narratives have taken the place of folktales, fairy tales, and myths. This may reflect important changes following secularization, demystification, and individualization; yet, there are still striking similarities in both the structure and function of traditional stories and today's personal narratives. This is particularly evident in drug stories.

Like the Inuit myths (Henriksen 2009, 93), drug stories concern transformation, and like the Kuranko people's narratives, they are "a technique for investigating problems of correct action and moral discernment" (Jackson 1982, 1). Moreover, drug stories and the events of myths must have actually taken place to be worth telling. The authenticity is often secured through the privileged and trusted position of the storyteller; for example, an Inuit elder (Henriksen 2009) or an experienced drug user. After decades of secularization, magical creatures and tradition have been replaced by the self and the importance of personal experiences. Living people have taken the places of gods as the "sources of truth," yet the form, function, and uses of these stories remain the same.

Many folktales portray protagonists who venture into hostile territory to gain a benefit such as wisdom, wealth, or justice (see Jackson 1982, 157–198). This theme is also typical of drug stories. The intake of illegal drugs is commonly narrated as a journey away from the ordinary and into the extraordinary. Depending on the drug, the dosage, luck, and a whole range of other factors, the person undertaking the journey may come back empty-handed, rewarded, or scarred for life. Journeys are fundamentally ambiguous. They represent a negation of the dominating norms and rules of society and can bring about chaos and death. At the same time, they can be revitalizing and therapeutic. Personal drug stories thereby challenge the dominating discourses on drugs, which downplay the pleasures of intoxication and instead create "visions of a consumption characterized by compulsion, pain and pathology" (O'Malley and Valverde 2004, 26). As folktales (Jackson 1982, 20), personal drug stories are less dogmatic and more open to interpretation. We believe that this is an important reason why so many people engage with them. Drug stories question established norms, unsettle official discourses, and invite audiences to take their own stance.

Conclusion

Drug cultures generate and revolve around stories. Many of these stories are well known, even outside contexts of drug use, and can be found in popular movies, books, music, television, and other forms of mass communication. Some drug stories are of little depth and significance. However, as we have attempted to reveal in this article, there are also drug stories that rise far above the banal and touch upon fundamental existential issues, including those concerning the relationship between life and death, reason and madness, control and loss of control, and the good life versus a bad life. Researchers therefore should take drug stories more seriously. Indeed, it is our contention that drug stories have rich potential, not unlike that ascribed to myths (Lévi-Strauss 1964), folktales (Jackson 1982), and other narrative traditions.

Moreover, if people who experiment with drugs are aware of their potential for storytelling, and if these stories are part of established social rituals, this suggests a reflective component of substance use that is downplayed or neglected in much existing research literature. Telling drug stories makes a statement about identity, but to recount drug stories in an authentic and convincing manner, the storyteller needs to have tried the drug in question. The existence, structure, uses, and meaning of drug narratives are therefore crucial to explaining and understanding drug experimentation and use.

Arthur Frank (2012, 36) notes, "people tell the same stories and claim them as their own." After a decade of listening to stories of both illegal and legal drug use, we are left with the same impression. Typical cannabis stories were often about relaxation, eating or laughing excessively, or experiencing alternative states of consciousness. For many participants in this study, the use of cannabis was a good story per se, but for those who used a lot of it, intake of the drug had to be discursively paired with unexpected behavior or consciousness to be a story. In social environments where cannabis was common, other drugs took the place of cannabis in narratives of cultural difference. Moreover, not only are people's stories about the use of particular drugs similar, they are also similar to drinking stories (Tutenges and Rod 2009; Tutenges and Sandberg 2013). Both heavy drinkers and cannabis users, for example, tend to describe periods of intoxication as something to be looked back upon with enjoyment or pride, even when the experiences were bad.

In drug subcultures, drug stories flourish. They are told and retold, and constitute the glue that holds the culture together. Drug stories, however, also have uses in mainstream or conventional society, among people who have never tried any illegal drug. Experiences with illegal drugs can be narrated as contacts with the mythological dark forces of existence. Like the Kuranko villager confronting the dangerous djinn, drug users can proudly report experiences that provide unique insights. Drug use thus adds an exotic or even antagonistic element to a life story, and makes the narrator more edgy, complex, and fascinating. In mainstream society, the narrative use of drug experiences demands that drug use be reserved for special occasions. Illegal drugs must be used in the right way and during the right phases of life to be accepted as life affirming. Conversely, drugs can be embedded in narratives of having lived and experienced the dark side of life in a more destructive way. Common to both narratives, however, is that the story of illegal drug use is best when presented in the past tense. *Having tried* illegal drugs gives the individual access to the narrative potential of illegal drug use without the stigma of *being* an illegal drug user.

NOTES

1. This study was made possible through the financial support of the Research Council of Norway. We also thank Karen Elmeland, Willy Pedersen, and Alex Klein for comments on an earlier version of this chapter.
2. For more information about methods and research design, see the other publications from this project; for example Sandberg and Pedersen (2010), Sandberg (2012b, 2013b), and Pedersen and Sandberg (2012).
3. A neighborhood in Copenhagen renowned for its hippie population and open sale of cannabis.

REFERENCES

Bakhtin, Mikhail. 1981. *The Dialogical Imagination: Four Essays.* Austin: University of Texas Press.

Barth, Fredrik. 1969. *Ethnic Groups and Boundaries.* Bergen, Norway: Universitetsforlaget.

Becker, Howard S. 1953. "Becoming a Marijuana User." *American Journal of Sociology* 59 (3): 235–242.

Campbell, Howard. 2005. "Drug Trafficking Stories: Everyday Forms of Narco-Folklore on the U.S. Mexico Border." *International Journal of Drug Policy* 16 (5): 326–333.

Castaneda, Carlos. 1968. *The Teachings of Don Juan: A Yaqui Way of Knowledge.* Berkeley: University of California Press.

Copes, Heith, Andy Hochstetler, and J. Patrick Williams. 2008. "'We weren't like no regular dope fiends': Negotiating Hustler and Crackhead Identities." *Social Problems* 55 (2): 254–270.

De Fina, Anna. 2003. *Identity in Narrative: A Study of Immigrant Discourse*. Amsterdam: John Benjamins.

Fjær, Eivind Grip. 2012. "The Day after Drinking: Interaction during Hangovers among Young Norwegian Adults." *Journal of Youth Studies* 15 (8): 995–1010.

Fontaine, Astrid, and Caroline Fontana. 1996. *Raver*. Paris: Anthropos.

Frank, Arthur. 2012. "Practicing Dialogical Narrative Analysis." In *Varieties of Narrative Analysis*, edited by James A. Holstein and Jaber F. Gubrium, 33–52. Los Angeles: Sage.

Gauthier, François. 2004. "Rapturous Ruptures: The 'Instituant' Religious Experience of Rave." In *Rave Culture and Religion*, edited by Graham St John, 65–84. London: Routledge.

Gubrium, Jaber F., and James A. Holstein. 2009. *Analyzing Narrative Reality*. London: Sage.

Henriksen, Georg. 2009. *I Dreamed the Animals. Kanieuekutat: The Life of an Innu Hunter*. New York: Berghahn Books.

Holstein, James A., and Jaber F. Gubrium. 2000. *The Self We Live By: Narrative Identity in a Postmodern World*. New York: Oxford University Press.

Jackson, Michael. 1982. *Allegories of the Wilderness: Ethics and Ambiguity in Kuranko Narratives*. Bloomington: Indiana University Press.

———. 1998. *Minima Ethnographica: Intersubjectivity and the Anthropological Project*. Chicago: University of Chicago Press.

———. 2002. *The Politics of Storytelling: Violence, Transgression, and Intersubjectivity*. Copenhagen: Museum Tusculanum Press, University of Copenhagen.

———. 2007. *Excursions*. Durham, NC: Duke University Press.

Jackson-Jacobs, Curtis. 2009. *Tough Crowd: An Ethnographic Study of the Social Organization of Fighting*. PhD dissertation. University of California, Los Angeles.

Järvinen, Margaretha. 2000. "The Biographical Illusion: Constructing Meaning in Qualitative Interviews." *Qualitative Inquiry* 6 (3): 370–391.

Johnson, Ann, and Mike Stax. 2006. "From Psychotic to Psychedelic: The Garage Contribution to Psychedelia." *Popular Music and Society* 29 (4): 411–425.

Labov, William. 1972. *Language in the Inner City: Studies in the Black English Vernacular*. Philadelphia: University of Pennsylvania Press.

Lamont, Michèle, and Virág Molnár. 2002. "The Study of Boundaries in Social Sciences." *Annual Review of Sociology* 28: 167–195.

Lapassade, Georges. 1990. *La Trance*. Paris: PUF.

Lee, Juliet P., and Sean Kirkpatrick. 2005. "Social Meanings of Marijuana Use for Southeast Asian Youth." In *The Cultural/Subcultural Contexts of Marijuana Use at the Turn of the Twenty-first Century*, edited by A. Golub, 135–152. New York: Haworth Press.

Levi-Strauss, Claude. 1964. *Le Cru et le Cuit. Mythologiques I*. Paris: Plon.

Lieblich, Amia, Rivka Tuval-Mashiach, and Tamar Zilber. 1998. *Narrative Research: Reading, Analysis and Interpretation*. Thousand Oaks, CA: Sage.

Loseke, D. 2001. "Lived Realities and Formula Stories of 'Battered Women.'" In *Institutional Selves. Troubled Identities in a Postmodern World*, edited by Jaber F. Gubrium and James A. Holstein, 107–126. New York: Oxford University Press.

McAdams, Dan P. 1993. *The Stories We Live By: Personal Myths and the Making of the Self*. New York: Guilford.

O'Connor, Patricia. 2000. *Speaking of Crime: Narratives of Prisoners*. Lincoln: University of Nebraska Press.

O'Malley, Pat, and Mariana Valverde. 2004. "Pleasure, Freedom and Drugs: The Uses of 'Pleasure' in Liberal Governance of Drug and Alcohol Consumption." *Sociology* 38 (1): 25–42.

Pedersen, Willy. 2008. "Hasjbruk hos unge voksne." *Tidsskrift for Den norske lægeforening* 128: 1825–1828.

Pedersen, Willy, and Sveinung Sandberg. 2012. "The Medicalisation of Revolt: A Sociological Analysis of Medical Cannabis Users." *Sociology of Health and Illness* 35 (1): 17–32.

Peretti-Watel, Patrick. 2003. "Neutralization Theory and the Denial of Risk: Some Evidence from Cannabis Use among French Adolescents." *British Journal of Sociology* 54 (1): 21–42.

Polkinghorne, Donald E. 1991. "Narrative and Self-Concept." *Journal of Narrative and Life History* 1 (2–3): 135–153.

Polletta, Frances, Pang Ching Bobby Chen, Beth Gardner, and Alice Motes. 2011. "The Sociology of Storytelling." *Annual Review of Sociology* 37: 109–130.

Presser, Lois. 2009. "The Narratives of Offenders." *Theoretical Criminology* 13 (2): 177–200.

———. "Getting on Top through Mass Murder: Narrative, Metaphor, and Violence." *Crime Media Cult* 8 (1): 3–21.

Propp, Vladimir. 1968. *Morphology of the Folk Tale*. Austin: University of Texas Press.

Reinarman, Craig. 2005. "Addiction as Accomplishment: The Discursive Construction of Disease." *Addiction Research and Theory* 13 (4): 307–320.

Richardson, Laurel. 1990. "Narrative and Sociology." *Journal of Contemporary Ethnography* 19 (1): 116–135.

Riessman, Catherine K. 2008. *Narrative Methods for the Human Sciences*. Los Angeles: Sage.

Sandberg, Sveinung. 2010. "What Can 'Lies' Tell Us about Life? Notes Towards a Framework of Narrative Criminology. *Journal of Criminal Justice Education* 21 (4): 447–465.

———. 2012a. "The Importance of Culture for Cannabis Markets. Towards an Economic Eociology of Illegal Drug Markets." *British Journal of Criminology* 52: 1133–1151.

———. 2012b. "Is Cannabis Normalized, Celebrated or Neutralized? Analysing Talk as Action." *Addicts Research and Therapy* 20 (5): 372–381.

———. 2013a. "Are Self-Narratives Unified or Fragmented, Strategic or Determined? Reading Breivik's Manifesto in Light of Narrative Criminology." *Acta Sociologica* 56 (1): 65–79.

———. 2013b. "Cannabis Culture. A Stable Subculture in a Changing World." *Criminology and Criminal Justice* 13 (1): 63–80.

Sandberg, Sveinung, and Willy Pedersen. 2010. *Cannabiskultur.* Oslo: Universitetsforlaget.

Sande, Allan. 2002. "Intoxication and Rite of Passage to Adulthood in Norway." *Contemporary Drug Problems* 29 (2): 277–303.

Sarup, Madan. 1996. *Identity, Culture and the Postmodern World.* Edinburgh: Edinburgh University.

Schutz, Alfred, and Thomas Luckmann. 1973. *The Structures of the Life-World.* Vol. 1. Evanston, IL: Northwestern University Press.

Shuman, Amy. 2012. "Exploring Narrative Interaction in Multiple Contexts. In *Varieties of Narrative Analysis,* edited by Jaber F. Gubrium and James A. Holstein, 125–150. Los Angeles: Sage.

Silverman, David. 2006. *Interpreting Qualitative Data: Methods for Analyzing Talk, Text and Interaction.* London: Sage.

Swidler, Ann. 1986. "Culture in Action: Symbols and Strategies." *American Sociological Review* 51 (2): 273–286.

Turner, Victor. 1967. *The Forest of Symbols: Aspects of Ndembu Ritual.* London: Cornell University Press.

Tutenges, Sébastien. 2012. "Nightlife Tourism: A Mixed Methods Study of Young Tourists at a Nightlife Resort." *Tourist Studies* 12 (2): 135–155.

Tutenges, Sébastien, and Morten Hulvej Rod. 2009. "'We got incredibly drunk . . . it was damned fun': Drinking Stories among Danish Youth." *Journal of Youth Studies* 12 (4): 355–370.

Tutenges, Sébastien, and Sveinung Sandberg. 2013. "Intoxicating Stories: The Characteristics, Contexts and Implications of Drinking Stories among Danish Youth." *International Journal of Drug Policy* 24 (6): 538–544.

Young, Jock. 1971. *The Drugtakers: The Social Meaning of Drug Use.* London: MacGibbon and Kee.

Zald, Mayer N. 1996. "Culture, Ideology, and Strategic Framing." In *Comparative Perspectives on Social Movements,* edited by Doug McAdam, John D. McCarthy, and Mayer N. Zald, 261–274. Cambridge: Cambridge University Press.

7

Telling Moments

Narrative Hot Spots in Accounts of Criminal Acts

PATRICIA E. O'CONNOR

Whether story is merely a sequence of events and narrative is the *shaping* of events, we must recognize that the positioning of the teller is crucial, both toward the material told and toward her or his audience, especially in autobiography. Thus, study of autobiographical narrative is inherently dynamic. In studies of narratives, we must be cognizant of the milieu of the telling, the status and particular contexts of participants, and the repercussions of telling. In examining oral life stories of prisoners inside cellblocks and drug addicts in treatment centers, I have been most aware that the events mentioned are sequenced by someone for others, presenting a self for the interviewer, but also making a presentation of the self for the speaker in what I term *telling moments*. Such moments contain *hot spots* composed of a speaker's choices in ways of telling. In the narratives in this chapter I suggest that this presentation of the self can be seen as signaling the reshaping of the self.[1]

Topics and events in stories have meaning to both writers/speakers and readers/listeners. How salience is perceived by the audience can depend greatly on the manner of the telling of the stories. Through sociolinguistic analysis I point out the life story narrator's choices in how she or he narrates and makes these choices available for close analysis. In these narratives that discuss both crimes and change, we can observe not only the shaping of the events but also the signals that show the importance of the events to the speaker. An invitation to tell the story of one's life is an invitation to agency.

Drawing on the premise that "we have no once-and-for-all life story"—that a story or understanding of an event does not stay the same over time and in different circumstances of telling (Presser and

Sandberg, this volume)—I examine narratives of criminal actions that demonstrate that speakers see themselves as capable of change. The data analyzed come from audiotaped life story interviews of nineteen male maximum security prisoners and nineteen male and female drug addicts in recovery. Identities thrust forward (or perceived by the researcher) in the narratives from these life story elicitations are found in segments that I term *hot spots*. Hot spots in narrative indicate epistemic handling through speakers' management of discourse devices, including pausing, listing, repetition, irony, metaphors, enactments, and juxtaposition. These telling moments in narrative are available for analysis by counselors, researchers, and speakers themselves. Thus, narratives become fruitful not only for study but also for effecting rehabilitation. Reactions and responses to such stories, what we can call a community of uptake, could influence and promote not only changed storylines, but also changed lives.[2]

This chapter looks at the narratives by those in total institutions—prisons and drug treatment centers—and examines them via linguistic discourse analysis, psychology, and narratology to demonstrate that the speakers' narratives reveal moments for contemplation. I admit at the outset that this discussion, while drawing from several disciplines of inquiry, cannot do justice to the depths of each. However, interdisciplinary treatment should be seen as a benefit. I am convinced that social problems like crime and addiction will not be solved through the use of any single lens and will benefit from a synthesis of fields. In that spirit I offer this chapter's examination of narratives of those involved in and affected by crime.

Narrative and Its Relation to the Past and Our Conceptions of Understanding

In the case of prisoners and addicted persons, life stories can help us grapple with systems of understanding and help us see how narrative "rewinds" time, allowing for a reconsideration of past actions. By presenting the past in the current discourse, the speaker constructs a showcasing of the past in which the listener and the speaker can begin to examine past actions. Cognitive psychologist Jerome Bruner (1987, 94) notes: "In so far as we account for our own actions and for the human events that occur around us principally in terms of narrative, story, drama, it is conceivable that our sensitivity to narrative provides the major link between our own sense of self and our sense of others in the social world around us." Especially interesting in Bruner's assertion is the recognition of the other as well as the self through narrative ways of knowing. We make stories for presentation and for ratification in the public sphere. Not only the topic or event merits consideration, but also the manner of telling. Narrative theorist Mieke Bal (2009) notes the significant role that a speaker or writer has in shaping the voice of the narrator and choosing the focalizor. In personal narrative when we speak with the pronoun "I" about life, we expect unity in the "who" of seeing (focalizor) and the "who" of telling (narrator). This chapter primarily relies on linguistic discourse analysis by examining the presence of reflexive speech features such as frame breaks (O'Connor 2000), axiom markers and metaphors (Adams, Towns, and Gavey [1995] 2003), verb choices, pronoun shifts (O'Connor 2000), lists (Schiffrin 1988), enactments of dialogue (Tannen 1989), generalizations, exaggerations, and even vagueness in autobiographical narratives. By recognizing such features as part of discourse management by the speakers, we can set up a space for further contemplation not only by researchers in many disciplines, and by counselors and others in criminal justice, but also by speakers themselves.

Data Collection

Teaching inside a maximum security prison starting in 1984 led to my collection of sociolinguistic interviews of over one hundred narratives of crime from nineteen inmates. Stories of drug addiction in that study led to subsequent research into the lives of addicts. My first set of examples comes from that prison data. The second set comes from narratives of eight female drug addicts in a drug treatment center, recorded between 2002 and 2004. The audiotaped life stories last from thirty to ninety minutes. In both the prison and in the treatment centers I had volunteered as a teacher. Along with student volunteers, I provided college credit courses (in the prison) and general writing skills and educational enrichment (in the treatment centers). This long-term service continued for six years prior to data collection in the prison and for four years in the addiction recovery settings. All participants were volunteers who were given anonymity and thus all names presented here are pseudonyms. The prison stories were audiotaped in semiprivate settings in sight lines of guards and other prisoners. Drug treatment interviews were conducted in a private office with only the speaker and myself present, except for one woman's six-month-old. Addicts' stories were transcribed by research assistants with one assistant as the lead to monitor all the transcripts for consistency. Transcripts were then checked by me for accuracy as I had conducted all interviews.

Methodology: Critical Discourse Analysis

These speakers' own stories speak of and resituate their actions within a larger ongoing narrative of crime, retribution, and rehabilitation; a narrative in which we as community members participate. Such data reveal opportunities for close consideration by criminalists, therapists, and speakers themselves as communities confront crime and attempt to reduce recidivism. Presser (2010, 431) suggests that "in-depth qualitative accounts about one's actions—stories—remain the very best data with which researchers might retrieve the meanings that people give to their own violations, including violations that state officials do not know or care about. Simply, our stories draw on the events, symbols, and phenomenological tensions that matter to us." In the narratives I present in this chapter, speakers show what matters. They present themselves in ongoing prior narratives—some are story lines of crime, others of social responsibility—in an intriguing and sometimes volatile mix. Such narratives, while not necessarily justifying crime, do situate crime and the sense of a self within a reasonable set of actions. Thus we find a space for the discipline of narrative criminology as a worthwhile intellectual and practical pursuit and one to which linguistic analysis makes a significant contribution.

Linguistic discourse analysis can provide critical methods and analytical tools for criminologists to adopt in studying criminals' comments on their own actions. By engaging speakers in extended narrative disclosures, we can elicit indicators of meaningful contemplation in reports of significant actions. We can locate signals of thinking about those actions embedded in the manner of telling. Such close analysis also illuminates constructs such as dialects or localized patterns of communication that can bear upon interpretation. When several indicators are used in combination, I assert that a telling moment, or hot spot, results, that is, a site for close analysis in determining pathways to changed behavior. In narrative criminology we seek to examine the larger picture of a criminal situation. We situate the crime, the criminal, and her or his accounts of crime in a larger framework than that usually elicited at stages in the investigation, pretrial, or trial processes. These elements of criminal procedure are all experienced by the criminal, but not always by those of us who study or work within criminal justice. We often experience discrete units or locations: courtroom testimony or confessions in custody, for example. This is due to the intricacies of the criminal investigation and adjudication process. Some of the life stories presented in the following sections are at the far end of this process—those stories of prisoners who are serving long sentences. Other stories here are nearer to the beginning of the process—in the cases of those who have gone into treatment centers in lieu of prison. This chapter showcases tools of analysis that could assist us in our work with a variety of aspects of criminal study in which the *story* of the actions taken details not only the crimes but provides indicators of the criminals' acts of contemplation that shape their stories and behaviors.

Data Analysis: What Prisoner Stories and the Manner of Telling Reveal

The data[3] below show one African American maximum security inmate, whom I give the pseudonym Kingston, discussing some of his life of crime. Analysis of his narrative suggests that Kingston, somewhat like a character in a novel or movie, saw himself inside a familiar and predictable path of criminal behavior going along with his crowd of fellow criminals until he has a life-changing experience. That narrative shows Kingston in a moment of transition.

A Changing Self

Kingston uses several indicators of seeing his actions in an adventure scenario common in popular fiction and movies.[4] In this passage I have asked Kingston if he ever felt in danger of death, a classic query from linguist William Labov (1973). Kingston is discussing a shootout between rival groups. In this first section, he details how he gets the call and goes along to confront a group that is going to strike against his group.

52 KINGSTON: So when I told him I told him
53 that I had got called.
54 My godfathers
55 they had uh/ made/
56 POC: /now this/ was one of your partners?
57 KINGSTON: Yea
58 POC: Oh OK.
59 KINGSTON: Uh . . . so he said, "Well,
60 ain't but one thing for us to do . . .
61 Since they want to carry it to us . . .
62 let's bring it to them first . . ."
63 So he was the type of guy
64 where you didn't say "no" to . . .
65 uh . . . hhh . . . in that type of situation . . .
66 you know . . .
67 So we said, "Yea alright. Cool."

The godfather terminology smacks of movie scenes as does the reference, "So he was the type of guy /where you didn't say 'no' to" (lines 63–64). We might ask whether the person he calls a godfather or the partner commands this sort of acquiescence. Note that in addition to his mention of "the type of guy" Kingston also refers to this decision as "that type of situation" (line 65) a familiar setting in which someone must be ready to choose. The repetition of phrasing increases the attention and thus the involvement of the audience. The "you know" (line 66) while sometimes merely pacing a discourse, also brings in the listener as possible accomplice, you know, who should see it as reasonable to take such decisions.

Kingston's use of constructed dialogue suggests his high evaluation of the retelling as we hear his enactments of the other man saying in lines, "Well, ain't but one thing for us to do . . . / Since they want to carry it to us . . . / let's bring it to them first" (lines 60–62) which is performed as answered with "Yeah alright . . . Cool" (line 67). Enactments of dialogue suggest that the teller is "getting into" his story and thus is highly evaluating both the circumstances and the performance aspect of the retelling. He could have said in a subdued manner "we decided." Instead he manages his story as a performance by showing the audience his version of the memory that includes the dialogue.[5] The dangerous partner, the type of guy who does not back down, sets up the ensuing action as a shared idea with his "us" and "let's" (lines 61–62). The partner indicates himself and Kingston and implies the action of shooting first is reasonable. This act of persuasion is revealed in Kingston's manner of telling using performed speech. His way of creating the scene simultaneously engages and entertains the listener and, I suggest, signals its importance to him.

In the second example we get a play-by-play of the action scene, again suggesting a scenario familiar to us through television and movies.

68 KINGSTON: So we met . . .
69 It was two of em . . .
70 and as we got down there.
71 we parked the car around the corner.
72 on XXX [Street] . . .
73 Coming off of XXX [Street] and come up on YYY Street,
74 That's when they seen us . . .
75 and we didn't know that they had.
76 They had two other guys,
77 down the street so like,
78 it was like we was boxed in . . .
79 And before we knew it,
80 everybody pulled out guns.
81 and everybody was shooting.
82 We were, you know, like,
83 they had a little bit more firepower
84 than we did.
85 Fred had two pistols.
86 I had one,
87 and Lamont had one . . .
88 But I think they had a little bit more,

89 at that particular time.
90 They were hitting the automatics.
91 I'm saying,
92 they were giving like water,
93 cause these are the kind of people
94 they was . . .

In this passage Kingston presents movie-like reportage of a shootout scene as in a western film or a military engagement. After the definitive past action "And that's when they seen us" (line 74), Kingston stops to give explanatory orientation. He notes the opponents have a larger force, what might be achieved through camera angles and danger music if this were on film. Instead of continuing the description of events, however, we have the speaker breaking the action scene, orienting a listener to the firepower danger and analyzing what he has recalled. He says, "But I think they had a little bit more, / at that particular time" (lines 83–84). Such cuing starts with a verb indicating a partial knowledge state—"I think"—that breaks the action while indicating subsequent contemplation. His meta comment "I'm saying" (line 91) shows as well his role in making commentary from a second level of discourse as he recalls the scene in using a water simile. Orientation details decorate the spine, the bare events, of the narrative, indicating, as well, the salience of the memory.

When he returns to talking about the action scene, Kingston notes they are at a marked disadvantage as the others had more "firepower." His dramatic retelling includes asides about weaponry as well as metaphoric sayings that color the scene: "They were hitting the automatics. / I'm saying / they were giving like water" (lines 91–93). Such metaphors and similes signal not only the imagery of many bullets like a stream or shower of water, but also the importance—through amplification via imagery—that he places on the weaponry used. Thus, he indicates a dangerous situation. His "I'm saying" clarifies his teller's stance. He further articulates the danger by noting "these are the kind of people they was" (lines 93–94), implying that trapping and slaughtering would be typical acts by his opponents. His use of such evaluations (Labov 1973) as "kind of people"—similar to "kind of guy" used earlier—shows more of Kingston's management of the discourse that sets up a contrast for his own actions to be revealed later. Here he not only builds up his own precarious situation but also implies more malignant traits for the opposing aggressors. He continues this evaluative depiction, raising the level of suspense via the detail and the imagery, further preparing the listeners for what follows.

> 95 KINGSTON: And now. where I . . .
> 96 I come close death was . . .
> 97 We had to split up . . .
> 98 and . . . the guy that was chasing me,
> 99 that we was exchanging,
> 100 I was exchanging, exchanging shots with . . .
> 101 that was chasing me,
> 102 I fell . . .
> 103 as I was going over a fence in an alley.
> 104 I was going over a fence,
> 105 and I fell . . .
> 106 And he stood right over top of me.
> 107 And he pulled the trigger,
> 108 and and and it jammed.

Again showing contemplation from the stance and positioning of one who is questioned in an interview, Kingston repeats part of the question about danger of death: "I come close to death" (line 96), suggesting he is interpreting this event in the scenario of the interviewer's query. Thus, Kingston frames his story to answer the interviewer's question, but he also uses it to position himself as different from others in danger as we see in his further remarks. This positioning shows him working at two levels, one discursive and one cognitive. His remarks put him inside the interview and also show him grappling with a conception of a self. Several factors show this contemplation. He sets up the danger scene by revealing that he is separated from his partners and tells of other gunfire through euphemistic understatement, noting, "we was exchanging/ I was exchanging, exchanging shots" (lines 99–100). His repetitions of the understatement and his switch to the personally agentive "I" show intensity. He builds the scene as if it were being filmed. Almost as if in a voiceover, he backs up in the storyline to clarify that he was being chased when he fell. Note Kingston's repetitions—"I fell" (lines 102 and 105) and I was "going over a fence" (lines 103 and 104). These slowdown techniques along with additional slow-motion detail—"And he stood right over top of me" and "he pulled the trigger"—occur just before the climax of the scene when he reports that the man's gun jammed. Kingston's stutter stating "and and and it jammed" (line 108) effectively holds the listener's attention through both the signaled intensity of fear and the elongation of time stating the result of an action that would have taken only a second. Bal (2009) observes that slowdowns in narrative build suspense. Such a device here suggests not only a well-told story but also perhaps a difficult and fear-filled memory, one that could be plumbed more deeply in a counseling session. That slowdown preceded a very telling moment in the presentation of self in Kingston's narrative.

Hot Spots

What follows and how it is delivered signal a true hot spot. In the following example we see a significant contemplative frame break where Kingston drops the action scene and relates a recall of contemplation of the action. In O'Connor (2000, 3) I note "frame breaks provide moments of epistemic consideration for thinking about what one knows." Kingston says:

109 And you know like. hhhh.
110 you know . . . people think this is.
111 this is . . . is funny, is a whole cliché,
112 but, you know how you can feel this,
113 you know . . . I felt myself dying.
114 I felt . . . that this would be my last minute.
115 here . . . on earth . . . you know . . .
116 I thought, you know,
117 it's it's amazing
118 how many things can run through your mind,
119 in such a short period of time.
120 I thought,
121 that I hadn't seen my mother that day,
122 you know.

123 I thought that . . .
124 I hadn't seen my son that day.
125 I, I, you know,
126 I thought about so many things
127 on that particular,
128 that that moment . . .

In this long frame break—a stopping of the action scene allowing for a spate of reflection—the utterances reveal how Kingston recalls what he thought at that moment of the man's gun jamming. He turns a second or two of real time into a lyrically drawn memoriam in the retelling. In studies of written stories such a slowdown is a particularly salient device for writers subtly to draw attention to the details of an action. Here, the mental action is depicted in a long retrospective frame break in which Kingston overtly uses metadiscourse to speak about the words he chooses; he notes humorously and with actual laughter "hhhh" (line 109) the idea of seeing one's life pass before one's eyes at a moment of danger and specifically terms it a cliché as he seeks verification with his several statements of "you know" and assigns verification through his "people think this" (line 110) phrasing.

Kingston notes his astonishment of how much can go through the mind in that particular moment (lines 117–119). He also employs a brief shift in pronouns to the "you" rather than the expected autobiographical "I" when he states "how you can feel this, you know" (line 112) Thus, he invites the listener into a shared sense of story. After that drawing-in of the interviewer, he agentively states, "I felt myself dying" (line 113) and amplifies it with an expression about his "last minute. / here . . . on earth . . ." (lines 114–115). Further indication of this as a hot spot is shown as Kingston continues to talk about his mental state, noting "I thought" (lines 116, 120, 123, and 126). In that repetition he is providing a poetic listing of particulars of those he would miss if dead, his mother and his son, and generalities: "so many things." These recollections recalibrate the moment of the pistol being fired and jamming. Such management of discourse shows a speaker at work crafting a narrative and also casting his life experience in the ongoing narratives of others who have narrowly escaped death. Thus, through the elicitation of an extended narrative, we tap into Kingston's view of himself not only as brave, but also vulnerable. His list of those he sees situates him in family, not in crime. While Schiffrin (2006, 156) points out that the genres of narrative and of lists differ—"narratives recount events within temporal structures; lists enumerate items in a hierarchical descriptive structure"—we can see in Kingston's narrative how the two genres interact in shaping the meaning of his life story. At his time of near death he recalls images of his mother and his son and does so in lists of rhyming discourse, further utilizing genres of display. He draws on still more techniques of discourse management as he continues.

Kingston leaves the contemplation to return to the action scene in lines 129 and 130 to report what he then did when he was able to fire at the man who had tried to kill him.

129 And . . . and . . . when. when I when I.
130 when he missed,
131 when it jammed,
132 when it misfired . . . you know.
133 I still had my gun, you know.
134 and I, you know, I said,
135 "Man, you know I could kill you," you know.
136 And he said, "Yea I know . . ."
137 I just couldn't kill him.
138 But he was going to kill me.
139 But I was just couldn't kill him.
140 And uh . . . I just ran on down the alley.
141 And uh. you know that's the closest,
142 I've ever come . . . come to being . . . dead.

In that final passage Kingston uses many narrative techniques. The opponent's action is repeated and restated in clear past tense verbs using synonyms to the effect that the man's shot missed, the gun jammed and misfired, all of which reestablish the action scene, moving forward from the contemplations in the frame break. Kingston once again constructs dramatic dialogue, this time between himself and the man who had tried to shoot him: "'Man, you know I could kill you' you know. / And he said 'yea I know . . .'" (lines 135–136). His enactment signals his own high evaluation of the event and elicits intense involvement from his audience as we can now replay the scene, complete with speaking parts. Kingston's climactic thought in "I just couldn't kill him" (line 137) resets the storyline he has been presenting of himself as an adept gangster caught up in a near-death gunfight. Instead he becomes a benevolent man. The narrative shift has been set up with the frame break passage about being close to death himself. The most Kingston offers by way of explanation is juxtaposition.

137 I just couldn't kill him.
138 But he was going to kill me.
139 But I was just couldn't kill him.

Rather than discuss this change of tactic, this change of heart, Kingston merely states it several times "just couldn't kill him" (lines 137 and 139), leaving the listener and now you to whom I repeat his story to figure out his new storyline.

Signaling through Juxtaposition

African American speaking style has been studied for not only its rich uses of metaphor and stylistic speech, but also for how it puts emphasis on the communicative uptake of the audience. His new behavior, perhaps influenced by images he says "run through your mind" (line 118) leave the audience to do much of the work of interpretation rather than passively receive an analysis. Heath (1983) discusses the roles of speakers and audience in what she terms the plaza stage of ordinary community discourse by African Americans, a type of telling that does not receive rewards in school settings where a speaker/writer is expected to analyze fully and redundantly. Instead African American discourse dramatically offers up episodes for audience uptake as Kingston is doing in this interview (see Smitherman and Baugh 2002; Hamlet 2011; Johnstone 2003; Rickford and Rickford 2000).

The listener is left with much to contemplate. Kingston appears to be seeing himself in a different storyline as a different sort of protagonist—no longer the hardened gangster, but a benevolent man. This narration is sociologically problematic. This presentation is situated in an interview inside the maximum security prison. In that interview with an outsider to the prison hierarchy, Kingston may well be presenting himself in the best of lights, yet dangerously so. By presenting a nonretaliating self he also opens himself up to a show of weakness, a stance to be avoided inside prison. This narrative becomes a site of connection for greater therapeutic uptake by those interested in rehabilitative aspects of imprisonment and, in general, for those interested in how we begin to see ourselves changing. A counselor could note this speaker's narration style, even play it back to the speaker to point out how meaningfully he is portraying his plight and query how that moment of insight did not stop his later criminal acts. Kingston's presentation of what was important in life in that reflective frame break is doubly ironic as it also mirrors all that has been lost as he sits now in prison separated from family and community. His larger narrative of a successful criminal life as seen in movies has been curtailed by this imprisonment, but he is, in his interview narrative, illustrating the process of recasting himself as a more contemplative and agentive being, a strong evaluator in Taylor's (1985) terms. Study of this narrative yields a more contemplative speaker, a man discerning life in the telling of ironic actions with open-ended interpretations. Such discursive practices as seen in Kingston's narrative can be seen in the life stories of others in total institutions. Their narratives contain cues into speakers' considerations of influences, personal actions, and also signal ways of changing patterned behavior.

Data Analysis: Narrative in an Addict's Life Story of Change

In the next examples I locate some of the same methods of presentation as in Kingston's story of criminal actions and inactions. I also note topics broached by an addict in recovery as well as the cues to the significance of the topics through examination of the discourse management of the white female speaker whom I give the pseudonym Marissa.

These data come from my life story study of eight female drug addicts and their conceptions of family and of self while intermittently involved in illegal behaviors.[6] The interview data show how female addicts' narratives often chronicle a series of life events in stories that complement the statistical data obtained from large-scale surveys.[7] Details we can find in life story narratives show how negative family and community influences often preview women's own acts that disappoint others and ultimately themselves in a cycle of desperation. Narratives such as Marissa's show women who have self-medicated with drugs and alcohol and become involved in criminal enterprises of those around them. Marissa recalls her life growing up in the midst of criminal activity in a crack house and her recent life in which she abuses drugs and is arrested for dealing drugs. Her story suggests a criminal pathway, a narrative that shows a seemingly inevitable route into drug use and crime. Thus, a study of her narratives and her management of these stories can yield a partial guide for cross-disciplinary understanding of the details behind the overwhelming growth in drug addiction and its co-occurring criminal behavior that have contributed to the rising incarceration rate of women, and white women in particular, as one of the fastest growing populations in American prisons (Mauer 2013).

I analyze these narratives using discourse analysis to demonstrate the utterance management. I also show the data at the intersection of narrative criminology (Presser 2009, 2010; Sandberg 2010) and narrative medicine (Holmgren et al. 2011). As with Kingston above, hot spots of epistemic understanding are indicated in the speaker's discourse management. Attention to these can help unlock the attractions and triggers of substance abuse and stem pathways to crime, ultimately perhaps leading to ways of changing the self, a key factor in recovery from addiction. Marissa's story of struggle gives us one example of an addict beginning to signal such change. While changing the self is necessary to combat one person's addiction, the observable path toward that change holds out promise for ways to help communities recover from the cyclical social fallout that accompanies addiction.

Marissa is a twenty-four-year-old white woman of some Cherokee ancestry who describes her childhood home in a working-class neighborhood in Virginia that bordered a major highway near Washington, DC. Marissa recalled it at first as an "okay" place, then qualifies this description, showing in her presentation of her life an interesting focalization not only on how she sees her home but also how she thinks others saw it:

48 but it wasn't a very,
49 good neighborhood.
50 To me it was okay,

51 but if you were,
52 somebody else [?] drive by they say "oh that's a bad neighborhood."

Already in Marissa's account we see her stepping outside of the childhood experience to locate what she now sees through a lens of what others would say about this neighborhood, giving us a double focalization. In such a view of her childhood environs, Marissa now invites us to consider, through constructed dialogue, the perspective of outsiders who might "drive by" and label her neighborhood "bad" (line 52). Thus in the words of Gregory (2009) this narrative evinces a more conceptualized experience, something that is now placed in contention with the child's memory of a good or okay place.[8]

She further expands in the next excerpt on the specifics that such a person would note. Marissa shifts from a hypothetical "somebody" witness and instead notes that "you" could see people "selling drugs" (line 60) behind the house. In doing this shift her "you" becomes inclusive of the self as well as generic others (see O'Connor 2000, 103–104). She tells what she recalls:

59 apartments behind my house,
60 you could see people selling drugs,
61 and,
62 doing drugs . . .
63 you know that type of stuff.
64 And,
65 my childhood,
66 I grew up in a um . . .
67 crackhouse . . .
68 My mother,
69 sold drugs,
70 and my father,
71 did too,
72 and they did drugs,
73 and . . .
74 smoked crack,
75 and dealt crack,
76 and shot,

77 the coke,
78 and . . .
79 all that kind of stuff.
80 There was millions and millions of people inside our house,
81 on a constant basis.
82 And violence,
83 and guns,
84 and,
85 stuff like that,
86 type,
87 of environment.

As Kingston did in his telling about the shootout, this speaker uses pronoun switches that increase listener involvement through seeming inclusion in the assessment. Marissa closes in further on the evidence of the bad neighborhood by disclosing that she herself grew up in a crack house. This progression from an outside observer who could view the situation to a "you" that includes a self, to her own personal memory, cues the significance of the memories. Her slow speaking style (as indicated by the punctuation for utterance breaks and longer pauses) adds another aspect of this depiction as she lists the details. Consider the pausing surrounding the remark, "I grew up in a um . . . crack house" (lines 65–67), before the compendium of details of specific actions is strung before the listener (lines 68–79). Such pausing and listing imply contemplation of the scenario. This passage is another hot spot where a combination of devices used in her telling come together and, I suggest, signal a speaker's discernment. Looking back on her early years, Marissa emerges as a "strong evaluator" (Taylor 1985) and thus indicates a more agentive stance.

From viewing others using and selling drugs, Marissa escalates her account of a bad neighborhood (line 68) by telling how each of her parents sells and uses drugs. The drug use moves swiftly in her account from "did drugs" to "smoked crack," and then to "shot coke," asserting a path down more and more dangerously addictive behaviors by moving from the general to the specific as she reveals her understanding of her parents' lifestyle and her proximity to criminal actions.

Signals of Therapeutic Moments

Topics as well as shifts in patterns and tropes in her speech suggest foci for therapeutic moments as they indicate the speaker's reflection on events and on the self. In addition to the slowing down of speech, and shifting from pronoun "I" to "you" above, we can also note here the contrapuntal "you know" (line 63) that pulls the listener in through its generic assumption, a tactic we noted earlier in Kingston's shootout story. Marissa, as did Kingston, generalizes through vague qualifiers and amplifiers "that type of stuff" (line 63), "all that kind of stuff" (line 79), and "stuff like that, type, environment" (line 85–87). Such vagueness reduces details and yet sums up a sadly customary, familiar situation (to her)—life in a crack house.[9] The listener may react negatively, however (as readers now might react), that the exaggerations are sensational. Is her account sensational or is it just how a child saw life and how an adult now contemplates it? We have to consider the double focus of a person who speaks in the present about events she recalled from her childhood past. She is an adult now in the telling but her memories are from a child. The invited narrative thus yields a complex and fruitful place for contemplation and questioning, most useful in therapy.

In recalling growing up in the crack house that complexity is shown as Marissa uses exaggerations about visitors. She says that she endured "millions and millions of people" (line 80) as well as violence and guns. The grand hyperbole to millions situates the narrative back in the focalization of the child Marissa's experience. Discourse in this passage of lists, escalations, and exaggeration signals not only the norm from both childhood and crack house life, but also an older and more reflective speaker's realization of just how that customary life was way out of kilter and actually in a "bad" neighborhood. Thus the passage is replete with signals that indicate her readiness for further discernment, and that can serve as useful cues of starting points for further therapeutic intervention. This hot spot yields pronoun shifts, pauses, lists, generalizations, exaggerations, and shifting focalizations from her child self, generic others, and her adult self.

As her narrative unfolds Marissa tells of her parents' incarceration, during which her life does improve briefly. When her parents lose the house and go to jail, Marissa goes to live with her father's mother. With the grandparents she enjoys a stable life: "my parents were in jail, / and they [grandparents] took care of us. / And I had a good life" (lines 141–143). From out of that crack house low, Marissa's account moves briefly into a peak time, a zone of comfortable assessment, "a good life." However, as analysts of this life, we realize that the respite must have been temporary as we conclude from the environment of the interview: a drug treatment center. Marissa is an addict who obviously did not remain in the brief "good life." After the respite offered by the parents' jail time, we find Marissa reacting in ways that are all too familiar in the lives of addicts and of those who become incarcerated.

Growing Complexity

When Marissa lives again with her parents upon their return from jail, she reports not liking school and quitting in ninth grade. The narrative she tells, more than the statistic of dropping out, is revealed as more complex. Marissa's states:

229 But I just didn't want to go to school. . . .
230 But when I . . .
231 when I was about 15,
232 that's when I, quit school.
233 The ninth grade.
234 Cuz I would . . .
235 my parents, I lived with them,
236 cuz after they got out of jail I went back to live with them.
237 Well we stayed at my grandmother's house for, I think like a year, or something?
238 And then we got, she . . .
239 They got their own apartment,
[240–243 identifying location details omitted]
244 And then um . . .
245 She, they would fight, a lot . . .
246 and I used to always have to,
247 go through that every night=and that's when I was doing drugs,
248 like, that's when I started really, really doing drugs.

249 Like drinking and,
250 smoking weed all the time,
251 all that type /stuff/

An analysis of her discourse choices shows that Marissa uses definitively past tense verbs for part of this statement—"I lived," "I went back," "they got their apartment," "we moved"—and then switches to habitual aspect in her auxiliary verb and adverb choices starting in line 245 when she describes the return of her parents into her life: "they would fight a lot"; "I used to always have to,/ go through that every night" (lines 246–267). These latter phrasings indicate not a specific event, but a usual situation that involved her parents' customary fighting. She continues to amplify adverbially and mark their behavior as habitual: "really really doing drugs" (line 248); smoking marijuana "all the time" (250); and adds a generalized "all that type stuff" (line 251). Such word choices indicate that these actions were far from isolated.

She also reveals that not liking school and using alcohol and drugs were not the sole factors in her quitting school. We see in the following excerpt the effects of her parents' fights and her developing caretaker role.

266 MARISSA: Like when I wouldn't go to school I didn't like going to
    school . . .
267 but the main reason,
268 one main reason was all the time they would,
269 fight,
270 and I'd have to, clean the house up afterwards,
271 and it'd be glass and blood and /all that type of stuff/
272 POC: /your parents' fight/
273 MARISSA: mmhmm.
274 And that's what would keep me up all night . . .
275 was . . .
276 cleaning up after them, fighting.

Thus we find a familiar pattern in the life of children in homes with drug and alcohol abuse as the norm—becoming caretaker for one's own parents. Marissa tells about cleaning up the broken glass and blood from her parents' sprees and fights. She also makes analytical comments noting with several pauses her "main reason" for not going to school as she has stayed "up all night" witnessing the fighting and rectifying the destruction. Her discourse in the interview thus shows contemplation of the past actions of the parents and also of her reactions.

Marissa's later life, however, illustrates her descent into parental patterns, as she relates her own addiction that eventually leads to federal drug charges. Thus she enters into both addiction and into the criminal justice system, seemingly well groomed for this from childhood. She tells of her drug of choice:

352 MARISSA: oxicodone . . .
353 mmhm,
354 like OxyContin but it's not . . .
355 It's /like/
356 POC: /and/ those are prescription drugs?
357 MARISSA: mhmm,
358 mhmm.
359 And,
360 I used to have prescriptions,
361 so . . .
362 I'd want to go to a store and,
363 fill my prescription.
364 That's why,
365 I have charges for that now,
366 federal, federal charges for that.

Marissa's drug use and implied abuse of prescriptions has made her liable for federal charges that carry mandatory sentences in the United States. Pregnant, addicted, and caught for suspicion of selling and misusing prescription opiates and waiting for the federal charges to be filed, she is given the chance to go into residential addiction treatment in lieu of prison. Thus, we find her and her story at a fruitful nexus in the intersection of the juridical and medical worlds. Marissa's own pregnancy gives her an incentive to avoid federal prison, to face her addiction and to get off drugs. My query about her treatment confirms this link.

670 POC: How'd you get into treatment?

671 MARISSA: From, being, in federal court.

672 I couldn't get a bond for release,

673 and I was about to have my, my baby,

674 my son.

675 Aaand I wanted to get in,

676 out of jail,

677 and, the only way I could,

678 is if, they put in a,

679 a treatment center.

680 So that's how I got here.

While Marissa's reasoning for entering treatment is mostly to avoid prosecution, she is now experiencing in treatment a composite look at the self. She is in one of the few treatment centers that allow one to give birth and to keep her baby with her. Perhaps due to the combination of learning more about addiction while parenting her newborn she, like Kingston above, is contemplating ethical considerations. This is something Gregory (2004) says reading narrative promotes. Telling narratives of the self, resituating the self as seen in these autobiographical insights does much the same. Gregory (2004, 282) puts it this way: "The ethical vision of both persons and stories includes all of those actions, thoughts, motives, and attitudes which we feel that we and others *ought* to do or *ought not* to do, and it includes the *ethical criteria* by which we judge ourselves and others to be *good* or *not good*." In treatment, Marissa's life of drug use has paused; she is beginning to review her life and to make ethical considerations. She is learning about changing her way of living, resituating her understandings of the family influences—both biological and environmental factors. She is starting to construct new actions, what Volkow et al. (2011) call new neural pathways. In Marissa's narratives she is demonstrating ways to disengage or healthily resituate toward the family of origin as she builds her future. In treatment she is finding a different model for family through group experiences. Her story indicates she is beginning to take on appropriate responsibility. In her interview she positions herself as a child or younger self in her memories and as an adult recalling them. She also shows how others positioned her whether it be "those driving by," the courts, or her newly influenced self in the social milieu of medical treatment. Thus she shows an awareness of self in society.

Doubts as Signal of Complexity in Change

Yet, should we doubt this narrative? Marissa worries about the same thing. Marissa is troubled by the unfairness of not being trusted or believed by others in treatment, something the public might say are her just deserts as a criminal. She is dealing with constant doubt of her sincerity, a matter also of concern to anyone who hears or reads the narratives of addicts and criminals. Could they merely be conning us? Sandberg (2010) suggests in his analysis of drug addicts' narratives that a positivist notion of the truth has little validity in ethnographic studies. Competing depictions, he suggests, showcase speakers' multiple understandings of situations (458). Sandberg says that "no matter what kind of stories are told, or whether they are true or false, they tell us something important about values, identities, cultures, communities" (455). In the following transcript, Marissa engages us in her worries and shows some growth in her values, as can be observed in her discourse management. Marissa shifts from the pronoun "I" to an engaging "you" and back to the personally agentive "I" in this passage and uses the kind of contemplation upon which treatment providers and criminologists can build.

841 So I mean,
842 that's the hardest thing for me,
843 I think . . .
844 and getting your point across because,
845 you've made yourself,
846 untrusted and not believable,
847 and you gotta pr-,
848 gain all that back.
849 And it's hard when you know what you're talking about,
850 that you're right and stuff and,
851 nobody believes you . . .
852 and you can't blame,
853 I, I can't blame them for not believing so,

In Marissa's uses of "So, I mean" (line 841), "for me" (line 842), and "I think" (line 842), she shows her epistemic considerations, using the first person and verbs depicting cognitive activity as she discerns how difficult she finds it to be believed. She moves next into an inclusive manner of speaking, drawing us into this difficult problematic by using eight second-person pronouns. Marissa shifts to what I see as a self-indicting and simultaneously other-inviting "you" (lines 845–852). She notes how "you've made yourself, / untrusted and not believable" and even repeats "nobody believes you" adding a noticeable pause before assessing that "you can't blame." This part grows even more interesting as she makes a firm shift before finishing that phrase "you can't blame [them]" and shifts to a most agentive "I, I can't blame them for not believing so" (line 853). Such discursive shifts signal the importance she places on ratification of her changes.

Consequently, even in this short passage of consternation we see the complexity of struggles facing a woman who is doing well in recovery after having a most chaotic youth. In Marissa's narratives, we see the addict influenced by both biological and negative environmental experiences in her childhood,[10] interspersed with some high points when removed from such settings, but also plagued by a seemingly inevitable fall into drug use. We see the treatment setting not only expanding the addict's knowledge base but also showing the addict how complex the path is to physical and emotional recovery, and how difficult social recovery is in living with others. When Marissa says with a pause following, "nobody believes you" (line 851), an old way of responding would be to walk out of treatment, to use drugs, and thus to pick up where one left off. Marissa shows she is learning how to face negative reactions rather than simply running from them or blotting them out with oblivion-producing substances. Low self-esteem plagues female addicts.[11] Yet, Marissa relates that she is willing to work to "gain all that back" (line 848). Her understanding of the negative uptake from the community is paramount, whether within the treatment center, in a court, or in prison. Her life story collected in the treatment setting suggests she is becoming a better evaluator of her life, of how others perceive her, and how she can change her reactions to environmental and social factors. The study of her narrative style illustrates how a person begins to recognize that one's self is constituted through a negotiation with the outer world's response to actions and the inner world's contemplation of actions and reactions. A person's struggle to make sense of that tension can be seen in the narration.

Conclusion

How can stories told by addicts or criminals be taken as seriously as the narratives established about them in court? Can we locate change through a speaker's moment of trying to present a believable self while still living inside the world of a juridically criminal self? As a society we must confront the crimes, but we should also promote paths to end more destructive actions toward the community and toward the self. Community uptake must become more than the typical response: "lock them up." Whether one is a recovering addict who is newly navigating sober living or a person residing long term in prison, attention to the individual's opportunity to reconsider the self could lead to enhanced possibilities for positive change. Marissa will have to moderate her goals and work slowly to gain custody of children, decide on whether to renew family ties, and bridge her way into a new way of living in spite of not always being counted credible. This applies doubly so to Kingston, convicted of bank robbery and other crimes. For him to see himself as capable of change, he had to see himself willing to stop a cycle of easy retaliation. In Gregory's (2004) words, Kingston and Marissa have changed what they had previously thought they "ought to do." Kingston's near-death experience when the other man's gun jammed is a key event in how Kingston shifts to reconsider his position and not act on what is expected behavior in a shoot-out scenario. He recounts what makes a person "good" and his telling of that episode indicates he is further contemplating what it takes to change. Marissa's less dramatic decision to learn how to live with others' doubts about her also suggests she is becoming a more contemplative being.

Thus, the narratives examined here showcase the contemplation, the epistemic work that must at least be started in changing a life. Maruna (2001, 8) in his study of self-stories of ex-offenders suggests that these ex-offenders, in order to continue desistance, must "develop a coherent, pro-social identity for themselves." The narrative analysis of criminals' discourse management I have presented alerts us to subtle linguistic devices that indicate the struggles to make change and to find coherence. Inviting such introspection could help facilitate desistance from crime.

How does the linguistic focus assist us in developing a robust area of research into crime? How does discourse analysis enhance narrative criminology? Personal narratives by criminals reveal the lives behind the statistics of other kinds of research. They do not replace quantitative studies. Smaller, qualitative narrative analysis contributes to the larger understandings of aggregate data collections and studies. This discourse analysis yields not only general topics or life events for study, but also elements of a person's management of story that indicate introspection of past situations and past acts. This type of analysis holds out the potential to help individuals work toward changed behavior. Changed actions should be the focus of both prison and drug treatment. At the micro level, each addict, each prisoner, has to confront how to change. Sociolinguistic analysis opens the narrative from a simple topic-centered story to a closer look at how that story is told, how the story is positioned in the individual's life and in ever-expanding circles of community and power.

Life story narratives show each speaker in an individual act of self-contemplation, a reflexive stance, looking back on a life from the current position. We gain a better understanding of the articulation of these stories by unpacking the management of the discourse. These narratives show analyzable depictions of what Presser (2010, 431) notes are "meanings that people give to their own violations." I find these meanings being formed in hot spots where many easily noted devices of discourse management converge—repetitions, pauses, hesitations, enactments, ironic statements, metaphoric phrasings, switches of pronouns, epistemic verbs, metacomments on thinking, lists, and so on. In combination, these elements of the management of the life stories signal the necessary work of a speaker both considering the past and shaping a current life.

Counseling of those who must change can be improved by employing narrative means. The production of life story narratives helps form new ways of seeing the self by placing one's life into ethical visions inside the larger narratives of societies and crime. Those who work or volunteer in the closed settings of prisons and treatment centers have much to contribute to helping change lives whether we are security personnel, therapists, researchers, line staff, and so on. The hot spots I point out in these examples can be readily noted by nonlinguists and assist a variety of workers in rehabilitation and recovery to focus on signals of change.

Analysis of discourse of those in total institutions such as hospitals, treatment centers, and prisons has much to offer.[12] Making sense of all our lives and our work inside closed institutions can be enhanced through a better understanding of the narrative vision that emerges from efforts to make sense of the "chaotic data" that is our world (Gregory 2004, 281).

My sociolinguistic addition to narrative criminology comes through sharing how discourse management can be readily ascertained by nonlinguists to explore how a speaker presents the self in what I think of as "telling moments"—where the speaker presents what matters in the tension-filled and chaotic worlds demonstrated in autobiographical narrative of those in prison and those grappling with addiction. In such a presentation of the self comes the realization of the role of one's self in the midst of making change. Or, as addicts and alcoholics in recovery say, "One must talk the talk, before she walks the walk." Narrative provides just such an opportunity.

NOTES

1. For their insights, I thank attendees at meetings of the American Society of Criminology and the North/South Criminology Conferences in Ireland.
2. For seeing narrative as a means for changing lives, consider Sweeney (2010) on prison reading and Gregory (2009) on stories as sources of "conceptualized experience."
3. These data originally appeared in O'Connor (2000); however, the analysis reflects new considerations and analysis.
4. Transcription conventions: comma = short pause; period = ½ second pause; hhh = laughter; equal symbol = means latching of discourse, that is, quick talking where one expects a pause; parallel lines // indicate two speakers' words overlapping in subsequent lines; POC = author as interviewer; names and places are given pseudonyms or use XXX.
5. Tannen (1989) refers to a speaker's involvement on a continuum from low to high and suggests we call reported speech constructed dialogue.
6. Study approved by Georgetown University IRB-c 03–135C.

7. Substance Abuse and Mental Health Services Administration (SAMHSA) and US Department of Health and Human Services show in 2010 an estimated 22.6 million Americans aged twelve or older were current illicit drug users. Bureau of Justice Statistics notes 51 percent of federal prisoners are drug offenders; 17.8 percent of state prisoners are serving time for drug offenses (Guerino, Harrison, and Sabol 2011, 1). The White House Office on National Drug Policy (2012, 1) highlights a survey that "found that risk factors such as low self-esteem, peer pressure, and depression make girls and young women more vulnerable to substance use as well as addiction, in that females become dependent faster and suffer the consequences sooner, compared to males." See National Center on Addiction and Substance Abuse at Columbia University (2003).

8. Gregory (Gregory 2009, 144) bases his assessments on power of narrative from reading and having vicarious experiences, but notes that our "ethical visions" of our lives and our own stories are informed by this. Marissa is challenging her earlier perceptions of a good life based on more mature readings of it in retrospective thinking.

9. Her uses of "all that kind of stuff" may indicate she assumes her listener, who volunteers in the treatment setting, would be familiar with the details of crack house life.

10. Volkow, Baler, and Goldstein (2011) say best practices require at least two-pronged approaches acknowledging biological and environmental mix, rather than one or the other.

11. See National Center on Addiction and Substance Abuse at Columbia University (2003).

12. See Heidi E. Hamilton (2005), Kathleen W. Ferrara (1994), and Holmgren et al. (2011).

REFERENCES

Adams, Peter J., Allyson Towns, and Nicola Gavey. 1995. "Dominance and Entitlement: The Rhetoric Men Use to Discuss Their Violence towards Women." *Discourse and Society*, 5 (3): 387–406. Repr. in Mary Talbot, Karen Atkinson, and David Atkinson, eds. 2003. *Language and Power in the Modern World*. 184–198. Edinburgh: Edinburgh University Press.

Bal, Mieke. 2009. *Narratology: An Introduction to the Theory of Narrative*. 3rd ed. Toronto: University of Toronto Press.

Bruner, Jerome. 1987. *Actual Minds, Possible Worlds*. Cambridge, MA: Harvard University Press.

Gregory, Marshall. 2004. "Ethical Engagements Over Time: Reading and Rereading David Copperfield and Wuthering Heights." *Narrative* 12 (3): 281–305.

———. 2009. *Shaped by Stories: The Ethical Power of Narratives*. South Bend, IN: University of Notre Dame Press.

Guerino, Paul, Paige M. Harrison, and William J. Sabol. 2011. *Prisoners in 2010*. Washington, DC: Bureau of Justice Statistics. NCJ 236096.

Hamlet, Janice D. 2011. "Word! The African American Oral Tradition and its Rhetorical Impact on American Popular Culture." *Black History Bulletin* 74 (1): 27–31.

Heath, Shirley Brice. 1983. *Ways with Words: Language, Life, and Work in Communities and Classrooms*. Cambridge: Cambridge University Press.

Holmgren, Lindsay, Abraham Fuks, Donald Boudreau, Tabitha Sparks, and Martin Kreiswirth. 2011. "Terminology and Praxis: Clarifying the Scope of Narrative in Medicine." *Literature and Medicine* 29 (2): 246–273.

Johnstone, Barbara. 2003. "Conversation, Text, Discourse." *American Speech*. Supplement 88: 75–98.

Labov, William. 1973. *Language in the Inner City*. Philadelphia: University of Pennsylvania Press.

Maruna, Shadd. 2001. *Making Good: How Ex-Convicts Reform and Rebuild Their Lives*. Washington, DC: American Psychological Association.

Mauer, Marc. 2013. *The Changing Racial Dynamics of Women's Incarceration*. Washington, DC: Sentencing Project.

National Center on Addiction and Substance Abuse at Columbia University. 2003. *The Formative Years: Pathways to Substance Abuse Among Girls and Young Women Ages 8–22*. http://www.casacolumbia.org/articlefiles/380Formative_Years_Pathways_to_Substance_Abuse.pdf.

O'Connor, Patricia. 2000. *Speaking of Crime: Narratives of Prisoners*. Lincoln: University of Nebraska Press.

Presser, Lois. 2009. "The Narratives of Prisoners." *Theoretical Criminology* 13 (2): 177–200.

———. 2010. "Collecting and Analyzing the Stories of Offenders." *Journal of Criminal Justice Education* 21 (4): 431–446.

Rickford, John R., and Russell J. Rickford. 2000. *Spokensoul: The Story of Black English*. New York: John Wiley.

Sandberg, Sveinung. 2010. "'What can lies tell us about life?': Notes Toward a Framework of Narrative Criminology." *Journal of Criminal Justice Education* 21 (4): 447–465.

Schiffrin, Deborah. 1988. *Discourse Markers*. New York: Cambridge University Press.

———. 2006. *In Other Words: Variation in Reference and Narrative*. New York: Cambridge University Press.

Smitherman, Geneva, and John Baugh. 2002. "The Shot Heard from Ann Arbor: Language Research and Public Policy in African America." *Howard Journal of Communications* 13 (1): 5–24.

Substance Abuse and Mental Health Services Administration. 2011. *Results from the 2010 National Survey on Drug Use and Health: Summary of National Findings*. NSDUH Series H-41, HHS Publication No. (SMA) 11–4658. Rockville, MD: Substance Abuse and Mental Health Services Administration. http://www.samhsa.gov/data/NSDUH/2k10NSDUH/2k10Results.htm#1.1.

Sweeney, Megan. 2010. *Reading Is My Window: Books and the Art of Reading in Women's Prisons*. Chapel Hill: University of North Carolina Press.

Tannen, Deborah. 1989. *Talking Voices: Repetition, Dialogue and Imagery in Conversational Discourse*. Cambridge: Cambridge University Press.

Taylor, Charles. 1985. *Human Agency and Language*. Cambridge: Cambridge University Press.

Volkow, Nora D., Ruben D. Baler, and Rita Z. Goldstein. 2011. "Addiction: Pulling at the Neural Threads of Social Behavior." *Neuron* 69 (4): 599–602.

White House Office of National Drug Control Policy. 2012. *Women Girls, Families and Substance Abuse*. http://www.whitehouse.gov/ondcp/women-children-families.

PART III

Storytelling, Creative and Reflexive

8

The Shifting Narratives of Violent Offenders

FIONA BROOKMAN

In truth, in talk it seems routine that, while firmly standing
on two feet, we jump up and down on another.
—Goffman (2007, 398)

I recently watched the video-recorded interrogation of Jermaine,[1] a
young black man who had shot and killed a young white man during
a robbery in Washington, DC. I wanted to see how the two detectives
managed to persuade the suspect to waive his Miranda rights and, as
the detectives put it, "tell his story." Through trickery and deceit (which
involved lies, plot suggestion, and redirecting the conversation) they
carefully set the stage for him to confess in detail to the robbery homicide. They judged his account (by other corroborating evidence) to be
truthful and he was ultimately convicted of first-degree murder and sentenced to thirty-three years imprisonment. Of particular interest for this
chapter, is that, despite the gravity of the offense and the potential for
this young man to claim self-defense (he was himself attacked by the
ultimate victim and another man, and fired two warning shots before he
killed the victim), he appeared more concerned to uphold his identity
as a tough guy. For example, he was affronted when the detectives suggested that perhaps he was scared at one point and replied, "Hell no . . . I
wasn't scared of them dudes." In short, the dominant persona presented
throughout his narrative was one of the tough street guy, as he stated:
"I've done this and I have to deal with it now like a man."

Amongst other things, this experience reminded me of the very powerful role of self-image in the creation of narratives—that is, the importance of narrative identity. This young man was particularly committed
to a gangster narrative (Sandberg 2009b), one with which he likely was
well acquainted. Nevertheless, he shifted from a narrative of gangster-

ism to victimhood (drawing upon conventional neutralizations) at various points throughout the interview, most notably when discussing the murder itself.

This chapter draws principally upon three case studies of violent offenders. In presenting detailed extracts from these interviews I aim to illustrate how narratives shift between different discourses during interview and to consider what might cause these multilingual, and seemingly contradictory, accounts. More broadly, I consider the implications of shifting accounts for narrative criminology. If, as I suggest, the narratives of violent offenders are constantly shifting, how can we makes sense of past and (potentially) future offending?

Background: Narrative Accounts and Narrative Identity

In the following section I consider three interconnected issues: What do we already know about how offenders present themselves through narrative? In what ways do the peculiarities of research methodologies and broader research agendas impact upon the kinds of narrative retrieved from offenders? And finally, in what ways have (and can) such narratives been understood in relation to broader discourses?

How Offenders Present Themselves through Narrative

It is now well established that offenders present themselves in a multitude of ways. A large body of literature broadly focuses upon the ways that offenders neutralize or in some way excuse or justify their offending behavior and present positive self images (e.g., Scott and Lyman 1968; Sykes and Matza 1957; for an overview, see Maruna and Copes 2005). It is probably fair to say that this stance has dominated the criminological and sociological literature on accounts and self-presentation. For example, Presser (2004) interviewed twenty-seven violent male offenders and found that they all claimed an identity as morally decent *in the present*. How they arrived at such decency varied. Some told a *return narrative* (from offender back to the good person they were before); others told a *stability narrative* (of an essentially consistently good person) and, yet others told *elastic narratives* (stories of change that were contradictory or vague).

However, some research clearly demonstrates a somewhat reverse kind of narrative whereby offenders embrace a violent identity and are less likely to offer exculpatory accounts for their misdeeds. Athens (1974) demonstrated some time ago that offenders readily embrace violent self-images. He gathered data on the self-images of violent offenders at the time of their offenses and revealed that most of the fifty-eight offenders held violent (or incipiently violent) self-images, and a small number held nonviolent self-images. He went on to argue that the self-images of violent criminals are always congruent with their violent criminal actions (Athens 1997, 68).

More recently, Topalli (2005) discovered that persistent violent street offenders felt no need to neutralize their law-breaking behavior when accounting for their crimes, apparently because they were so committed to a subcultural code of violence. Their accounts did nevertheless contain justifications for breaking subcultural codes—such as snitching or talking to the police (i.e., they neutralized being good rather than being bad). Similarly, Garot (2010) found that juveniles use an extensive set of excuses or justifications for *not* retaliating, a primary tenet of the code. They claim that violence is not always needed in such circumstance, especially if the opponent is weak physically or the slight is too small (see also Copes et al. 2013).

Research Agendas and the Nature of the Data Retrieved

In various ways each of the criminological studies considered above differed in their methodologies and focus, undoubtedly impacting the kinds of narrative retrieved and, ultimately, the kind of analysis adopted to interpret the narratives. Some (e.g., Topalli) spoke to active offenders whilst others (e.g., Athens) conducted interviews with incarcerated offenders, while Presser's research included both incarcerated and free (though not ostensibly active) offenders. Some of the studies required interviewees to provide narratives of self in the present, while others looked to their narrative identity in the past. Had Athens asked his offenders to provide descriptions of their self-images at the time of interview (instead of at the time of offending) he would likely have elicited quite different responses. For example, incarcerated offenders, particularly those undergoing cognitive therapy, are often encouraged to think of themselves and their acts in particular ways that may color their narratives in a broad range of contexts.[2] Finally, some of the narratives generated arose from explorations of specific acts of violence, others from conversations about the offender's life or self. In summary, there are various ways in which the research design of a project can shape the data retrieved. In this chapter, I am particularly interested to explore the distinction between narratives of *acts* and narratives of *self* or what I would like to term *action narratives* and *reflection narratives*. I explore whether violent offenders draw upon different discourses during action and reflection narratives and, more broadly, the mixing of, and movement between, distinct discourses during offender talk.

Narratives, Discourse, and Interdiscursivity

Narratives are embedded in, and emerge from, discourses.[3] These are the broader structural and cultural constraints on, or enablers of, the production of meaning (Fairclough 2003; Foucault 1972). Discourses are enabling in that they "make available positions for subjects to take up" (Hollway 1984, 236). At the same time, however, language is used under particular cultural, historical, and institutional contingencies (Moita-Lopes 2006, 293). As Bamberg (2004, 226) states, "subjects position themselves in relation to discourses by which they are positioned." Put another way, people have a limited repertoire of language from which to select (consciously or subconsciously) to explain their actions and present themselves.

Scholars responsible for the aforementioned studies tend to view criminal's narratives as embedded either in conventional discourses or subcultural discourses (Sandberg 2009a). For example, narratives that employ the use of neutralizations are generally embedded in conventional discourse, while those that speak to street codes, toughness, and reputation emerge from subcultural discourse. However, recent evidence of a more complex picture reveals that offenders may draw upon different, seemingly competing discourses when constructing their identity through narrative: they tell conflicting stories (Sandberg 2010). Of note, Sandberg (2009b) identified two contradictory discourses both used by ethnic minority drug dealers in a street drug market in Oslo, Norway. Specifically, he described the street drug dealers as "bilingual" in that they drifted between an oppression and gangster discourse when accounting for their crimes. Through oppression discourse they justified their offending as a necessity due to their inability to find paid work combined with the affects of racism and discrimination. By contrast, through gangster discourse they provided presentations of self as tough men and good fighters who never snitched. Sandberg (2009b, 538) suggested that "similar interdiscursivity"[4] may have been "systematically excluded in previous research in order to obtain a more coherent theoretical framework."

In summary, until recently, the dominant approach to the analysis of life stories and offenders' narratives has been inspired by narrative psychology and has involved the search for "a unified and coherent self-narrative" (Sandberg 2013, 72). As the aforementioned review illustrates, there is mounting evidence that such an approach may be at best restrictive and at worst misleading; narratives are not always ordered in such ways. Criminologists have variously described the incoherent and nonunified character of offenders' accounts as elastic narratives (Presser 2008), inconsistent story lines (Brookman et al. 2011a), or interdiscursivity (Sandberg, 2009b). In keeping with ethnomethodology (e.g., Garfinkel 1967), these researchers acknowledge that value is to be found in unraveling the fragmented nature of narrative and highlighting the strategic shifts between different and sometimes competing self-narratives.

Data and Research Methodology

This chapter draws largely upon three case studies involving two violent female offenders and one violent male offender. All of the participants were incarcerated in prisons in the United Kingdom at the time of the research and interviews took place in private rooms within the respective prisons and with the informed consent of the interviewees. Interviewees were provided with information sheets and consent forms prior to agreeing to take part in the research. The information sheet outlined the aims of the study and what kinds of themes and questions would be put to interviewees for discussion. For example, they were told that I was interested in understanding what factors led to their involvement in particular acts of violence as well as in gathering their views on the causes of violence. They were also told that I wanted to discuss in detail at least one act of serious violence that they had perpetrated. At the start of each interview I revisited these issues to ensure that the participants fully understood the aims and purpose of the study and their role in it, and to reassure them of the procedures in place to ensure confidentiality. I assured them that their identities would remain anonymous and that nothing of what they revealed during the interview would be passed on to the prison authorities, police, or any other agency or individual.[5] As part of the process of confidentiality and anonymity, I asked the interviewees to create pseudonyms, which are used throughout the chapter. Interviews lasted on average eighty minutes. Each interview was recorded with the permission of the inmate and subsequently transcribed verbatim.

The case studies are used as detailed examples of the links between self-image and narrative. More broadly, however, the interpretations and conclusions that I draw are based on my experiences of having interviewed over 50 violent offenders and my analysis of the verbatim transcripts of over 160 interviews with violent offenders. My decision to draw from a small number of case studies in this chapter was to allow the space to present as much as possible of the offenders' narrative (i.e., to forego breadth for the sake of depth). This is particularly important given that I wish to demonstrate the complexities, shifts, and twists of individual narratives.

Over the years, the interview transcripts have been analyzed for various projects and in different ways (sometimes thematically by hand, at other times with the assistance of the qualitative software package NVivo). For the purpose of the current chapter each transcript was revisited and analyzed by hand. Two distinct sections of narrative were extracted for detailed analysis: (a) narratives pertaining to the actual enactment of violence and (b) narratives that contained reflections and explanations of the violent act as well as broader narratives of self (i.e., self-image). Sometimes these boundaries are blurred where interviewees interweaved the two (e.g., they offered neutralizations for their involvement in a violent act while describing the detail of the act). Nevertheless, it was possible to identify these broadly discrete segments of narrative.

There are various conventions regarding the analysis of narrative. For example, Labov and Waletzky (1967) suggest that narrative is comprised of six discernable structures that serve specific communicative functions. Most narrative scholars in the social sciences have tended to adopt Labov's model for the purposes of analysis. However, their model suggests a structure and coherence that I contend may be somewhat artificial or misleading. Although I have used their model as an overarching guide to approach the reading of narrative, I also draw upon the principles of dialogical narrative analysis (DNA) that borrows heavily from the work of Bakhtin (1981). Frank (2012, 35) eloquently outlines five commitments of DNA, including, of particular relevance to this chapter, DNA's interest "in hearing how multiple voices find expression within any single voice" and, relatedly, an appreciation that narratives are at once both subjective (i.e., belong to the teller) and external (i.e., are borrowed and shaped from preexisting stories). "We humans are able to express ourselves only because so many stories already exist for us to adapt, and these stories shape whatever sense we have of ourselves. Selfhood always trades in borrowed goods" (36). DNA, then, acknowledges the interconnectedness between narrative and identity but, above all, recognizes that individual narratives are multivoiced.[6]

The Discourses of Violent Men and Women

In the case studies that follow I consider offenders' narratives of violent acts and of self and explore to what extent these various accounts are congruent or in conflict. In short, I ask, are the narratives coherent and consistent or fractured and inconsistent?

Jane

Age twenty-eight at the time of the interview, Jane had over forty criminal convictions, mostly for violent offenses such as grievous bodily harm, kidnapping, robbery, false imprisonment, and various weapons charges. Jane talked in detail about two acts of violence, including robbing a man by hitting him over the head with a hammer and kidnapping and torturing (with three accomplices) a young female. Jane had a number of prominent scars on her arms and hands, the result of self-harm. Here is her narrative of the kidnapping and prolonged torture of a young woman.

NARRATIVE OF A VIOLENT ACT

> A girl owed me ten pound for drugs. I had three codefendants and
> we took her in my house and against her will took some money off
> her and her jewelry and beat her up and kept her there for a few
> hours. They didn't like her anyway and she was passing down the
> road and that I just said I would call her in and see what she had to
> say. Nothing was planned it just went, you know what I mean, one
> thing after the other and it just got out of hand like. . . . I called her
> over to my house and I hit her and her eye come out really, really
> bad and I thought, "I gone a bit far here so I can't let her go." Things
> then went from bad to worse like . . . it went on for hours. Do you
> know what I mean? Shaved her hair off and broke her ribs with a
> hammer, made her drink bleach. It was quite a big case, do you know
> what I mean?

Jane opens with minimizing language (e.g., "took *some* money off her"
and "kept her there for *a few* hours") though shortly afterward provides
fuller and less sanitized detail about the precise nature of the attack,
almost bragging about the status of the case ("it was quite a big case").
Her repeated use of the term *just* can be read as a limiter or minimizer
(McKendy 2006). While she takes responsibility as the instigator of
the attack (and uses the first-person pronoun "I" throughout), she also
adopts deflecting or passivizing language (O'Connor 1995) when she
says that "*it* got out of hand" and "*things* went from bad to worse." Both
phrases suggest that the event took on a life of its own that was somehow beyond Jane's control. By pointing to the unplanned nature of the
attack she aligns herself with conventional discourse where spontaneous
violence is distinguished from planned violence and viewed less harshly
(Hochstetler et al. 2010). The tensions within the narrative between
agency or personal responsibility and external contributory factors
become further evident as the conversation progresses:

FIONA: Why did it spiral like that?
JANE: Don't know. We were just, I don't know. We were out of control.
I just don't know. I don't know. Obviously she owed me money but
I would never have . . . things just got out of hand. I think people
were showing off in front of people and she lost her sense of being a

person like. I just went overboard. The four of us were, yeah, "bigging" ourselves up.

Jane struggles to account for her actions when probed further. Her repeated use of the phrase "I don't know" perhaps illustrates her genuine inability to explain in terms that she feels the listener may relate to. Alternatively, as O'Connor (1995) suggests, epistemic utterances such as "I don't know what made me do it" may illustrate both evaluation and speculation regarding the criminal act and on personal agency. In any event, what is clear is that Jane draws upon contrasting discourses during her account. She points to the outstanding debt ("she owed me money") and thus draws upon subcultural discourse that places a premium upon retaliation as an acceptable and often necessary response to disrespect (Anderson 1999; Brookman et al. 2011b; Jacob and Wright 2006). However, in the same breath she suggests that such behavior should not have prompted this response ("I would never have") alluding to her alignment to more conventional discourses that would disavow such a grave and violent response. She puzzles her way through by focusing upon the group dynamics that provided the fuel and momentum for the prolonged attack. Jane now uses "we" much more often (though she does return to the first person in the final sentence) and suggests that the group dynamic played a critical role in the ensuing violence. Nevertheless, despite some attempt at minimization and deflection she presents a fairly damming portrayal of her role in the event, as these further excerpts illustrate:

FIONA: Did you think at any time, "we should stop this"?

JANE: Yeah, from the beginning. I remember when I hit her and her eye really came up bad I just thought, "I have gone too far."

FIONA: Why didn't you stop then?

JANE: I was frightened she would go to the police. My intention then was to kill her. Do you know what I mean? I just thought when I hit her and it come out huge I thought I'm gonna go back to jail and I thought, "right, you can't go now."

Once again, Jane oscillates between conventional and subculture discourse. She states that she had gone "too far" (conventional) yet also expresses her intention to kill. Contemplating murder to avoid imprisonment is clearly embedded in a gangster, rather than mainstream, discourse. It is also noteworthy that Jane was given the opportunity to continue to narrate the event in the first person plural and, thereby, temper her individual responsibility but instead returned to the first person singular, choosing to point to her agency. Jane's frequent use of the tag question "do you know what I mean" throughout her narrative implies her desire to solicit support and understanding from the listener (see McKendy 2006, 487). Despite the fluctuations between discourses, what emerges as particularly prominent in Jane's account of this violent act, up to this point, is her desire to present herself as violent and to resist a marginalized status. The remainder of her description, of the final moments of the event, reveals further shifts in narrative:

> JANE: My friends had to go a couple of hours later; it was just me and her. They went and I was on my own with her. She was sitting in the chair and I said, "just go and get out." And she ran out the back door like.
>
> FIONA: Why did you then let her go?
>
> JANE: I was on a comedown like, do you know what I mean? I was left on my own and my baby was upstairs and I wanted it to end. I had sobered up a bit and come down off the drugs, do you know what I mean?

To begin with, Jane explains freeing her victim by continuing the theme of group dynamics; the crime ends as the group disperses. Her friends having gone, "bigging up" and any thrills associated with the enactment of group violence perhaps became redundant. However, she then adds a new, as yet untold, piece of information when she states that she was "on a comedown." This phrase of course reveals a great deal. She now positions her actions as somewhat beyond her control. She, partially at least, rejects responsibility for the violence blaming it on her consumption of drugs and alcohol and her resultant altered mental state. This classic denial-of-responsibility technique of neutralization (Sykes and Matza 1957) is embedded in conventional discourse. She and I knew immediately that a "comedown" follows the up or high associated with drug and alcohol consumption and that it is commonplace to explain away errant and abhorrent behavior by pointing to the effects of mind-altering substances (Brookman 2013). In Scott and Lyman's (1968, 48) terms, she offers an "appeal to defeasibility" in that her full mental capacity was temporarily voided. In summary, Jane's narrative of this one violent act meanders between subcultural discourse (retaliation for a debt owed) and conventional discourse (blame apportioned to group dynamics and drug consumption).

NARRATIVE SELF-IMAGE

As outlined earlier, how offenders depict themselves is not always in alignment with how they depict particular acts of violence. This is because offenders strive to overcome the stigma associated with their offending (Goffman 1971) and to claim an identity "as morally decent in the present" (Presser 2004, 86). Jane, however, does not attempt to present herself as a changed person. She claims an identity in the present as a violent person, thereby embedding herself quite firmly within a violent subculture.

> FIONA: Would you say you are a violent person?
>
> JANE: Oh yeah. Takes a lot more for my temper to go when I am straight but it just takes a lot more for it to go when I am straight. I am vicious. It's difficult [to explain]. In the area I grew up my family had quite a reputation for being violent and that, but I felt I had to live up to that and I had something to prove so that's how it started. I had to live up to the reputation of them, and then I had to live up to the reputation I built myself. I couldn't let myself be walked over.
>
> FIONA: How do you feel now?
>
> JANE: I could never go back there to live . . . I would never go back. I wouldn't want to. I want a fresh start, nothing to do with any of that.

In this narrative Jane unequivocally embraces a violent self-image (I *am* vicious). She does not claim to have changed, speaking of herself in both the past and present as violent and under varying conditions (i.e., "straight" or under the influence). She draws upon the classic cultural-level "formula story" (Loseke 2007) to narrate this aspect of her life.[7] Specifically, Jane points to having a particular "street" reputation that necessitates responding to disrespect with violence (Anderson 1999;

Brookman et al. 2011b). On the face of it, then, she self-presents as violent. However, on closer reading there are subtle tensions in her account. For example, she identifies criminogenic forces in her family background and social environment (e.g., having to live up to the reputation "of them," her family) and targets this for change (i.e., her desire for a "fresh start"). This is a sentiment more akin to a return narrative (Presser 2004, 87) than an authentically and committed violent person and points to Jane's efforts to reject a violent self-image. By situating herself as a product of her environment she draws upon an oppression or disadvantage discourse and perceives herself as being acted upon rather than acting.

In summary, Jane's narrative of a violent act and of her self combine several contrasting discourses. She moves between conventional and gangster discourses in almost equal proportions when describing the violent act but appears more committed to a gangster discourse when describing her self. Despite Jane's self-defined viciousness she, nevertheless, weaves in disadvantage discourse when reflecting upon how she became a violent person. Turning now to Nicola, we discover a narrative less aligned with subcultural discourse and rather more complex and fractured in its telling.

Nicola

Nicola was twenty-six at the time of the interview. She had eleven convictions including shoplifting, various drug-related offenses, multiple armed robberies, assault on a police officer, and public disorder. She was a petite and softly spoken woman.

NARRATIVE OF A VIOLENT ACT

NICOLA: We went into the shop and pretended to look at something because there was a customer in there and we waited for him to go and then Jim showed her the gun and got her into the back and I get the keys and lock it from the inside and put the sign up. The woman was hysterical, she was terrified. I tried to calm her down.

FIONA: How did you try to calm her down?

NICOLA: I ended up taking off my hat and that because I was trying to look at her and reassure her and that. She thought I was some evil sick bitch. I remember before when I worked in nursing homes—

that was a job I loved—sometimes, just by a look you give them
you can comfort them without saying anything, just a look that says
everything is okay. I remember during that robbery it was as if I was
trying to be me as I would normally be, forgetting that it was me that
was causing all the stress. Trying to reassure her that it would all be
alright but not getting back that thing in return, that look that would
give me the satisfaction of knowing I had comforted somebody. How
could she accept comfort from me?

Nicola uses a number of terms that serve to minimize the violent elements of this offense (such as "showed her the gun") and provides several examples of how she tried to ease the victim's fear (i.e., in her use of the terms "comfort," "reassure," and "calm"). At several junctures Nicola interrupts the narrative of the armed robbery with reflection in what Goffman (1974) calls a "frame break." For example, instead of completing the description of the robbery, she describes the victim's response and her efforts to help the victim. Later, when elaborating upon how she tried to calm the victim, she again engages in a discourse maneuver that breaks from the main story to tell the listener about her work in a nursing home. In this way Nicola does not just provide an account, she also guides the listener's interpretation of her throughout (see O'Connor 1995). She presents her behavior as out of the ordinary when she states "I was trying to be me, as I *normally* would be." The suggestion is that the normal Nicola is kind and caring (not violent and frightening) and her reference to having worked in nursing homes serves to prove her naturally caring disposition. She (rather unusually for a violent offender) describes how the victim acted and felt (hysterical and terrified) and "steps outside" to view herself as the victim must have (as an "evil, sick bitch"), ending with the rhetorical question, how could she accept comfort from me? This self-reflexive and self-critical position creates a narrative that positions Nicola as outside and separate from the earlier (criminal) person—a morally decent person.

Later in the interview, Nicola extends her depictions of how nonauthentic a robber she was to include her partner-in-crime, stating: "There was a documentary made about him when he was known as the gentleman bank robber and stuff because of his nature and stuff. I don't want to make excuses or say that it is alright but it's like, we were as nice as you can be." As Hochstetler et al. (2010) observe, depictions of being nice during the commission of crime helps offenders to project a nonviolent self and distances themselves from the authentically violent. Nicola's reference to the documentary adds credibility to her claims acting as an authoritative corroboration of her position.

NARRATIVE SELF-IMAGE

In narrating her identity, Nicola engages in what Segal (1991, 126–128) terms "alienness"—the experience of distancing of self from one's past or current actions, emotions, beliefs, or even the totality of one's life. She suggests that the person during the period of violent offending was simply not the real Nicola.

> NICOLA: Because it was in England, I felt it wasn't real. I would never have dreamed of doing it in Scotland because it would have been real and I would have had family around me. . . . It wasn't real life. It was like I had taken on a role and character and I was playing it out.
> FIONA: When did you start taking on the role?
> NICOLA: When I first met them. I was drinking a lot and out of my face and I had split up with my girlfriend and I was acting like I was cool but I wasn't. It was very much his influence. I am my own person and I can't say I didn't enjoy it in the beginning but now . . . I can't believe it. I can't believe I was capable for doing these things but I look back and it's not real but obviously it is real and I done it.

Nicola draws upon numerous distinct discourses in a matter of seconds when presenting her self. For example, her references to the influence of alcohol and a personal loss suggest victimhood and loss of control and draw upon conventional and vulnerability discourse, whereas her statement that she "was cool" and the phrase "I can't say I didn't enjoy it" are clearly embedded in subcultural and specifically what I have termed thrills discourses that recognize the allure, excitement, and risks associated with violent crimes, such as armed robbery (Katz 1988; Lyng 2004). In addition, Nicola oscillates between narratives of choice and agency ("obviously I am my own person") to those of external control ("it was very much his influence") within the very same sentence. She presents herself as both an agent and an undergoer (Bamberg

2010) and moves between narratives of acceptance and resistance of her personal responsibility.

Nicola presents a dual-person identity that she demarcates both temporally and culturally. She recognizes, for example, that what is perceived as cool is situationally dependent when she states "I was acting like I was cool but I wasn't." That is, she indicates that, back then, she saw herself as cool; now, on reflection, she does not. Simultaneously she seems to acknowledge that her coolness, even at the time of her criminality, was only associated with a particular subculture (e.g., gangsters and armed robbers) and that many in society would not have shared this view. In Goffman's (1963) terms she was engaging in "two-headed" role-play.

Overall, Nicola's narrative is littered with attempts to establish a nonviolent self. However, she has to confront the reality of having committed numerous armed robberies, which by anyone's reckoning fall fairly high up on the scale of violent offending. In order to do this she persistently distances herself from the person of the past and reconceptualizes her personal biography such that the bad person is not the real or true self (Maruna 2001). In this way Nicola offers a return narrative of "moral transformation back to the essentially good person the narrator was, prior to his [or her] violent offences" (Presser 2004, 86; see also Henry 1976). Furthermore, through a process of "self-other differentiation" (Bamberg 2012) she portrays both herself and her criminal partner as distinct from other armed robbers, suggesting that they were not authentically violent individuals.

Nicola's action and reflection narratives are fairly congruent. In both cases she works to present herself as a good person who committed violent acts—as sensitively and kindly as possible—but who is not *really* a violent person. While her narrative of the act draws wholly upon conventional discourse, her narrative of self is more complex. Here she occasionally makes space for some personal responsibility (McKendy 2006) and her account is also interspersed with vulnerability discourse as well as snippets of subcultural discourse when she acknowledges that her involvement in armed robberies was fun and that she *was* cool.

Paul

Paul was twenty-six when I interviewed him. He had served half of a fourteen-year prison sentence for the robbery and murder of an elderly man in his home. He had prior convictions for arson, criminal damage, and vehicle theft. He had also committed credit card fraud and burglary. In his narrative, Paul states the murder was orchestrated by his codefendant's hatred of the victim whom, he claimed, was a pedophile. Paul had already explained that their intentions were to "get the victim drunk" and then rob him when he fell asleep. This plan had gone awry when the victim became uneasy and "sensed danger."

NARRATIVE OF A VIOLENT ACT

PAUL: My codefendant said, "get upstairs then" and as he knew the bloke I thought, well I didn't know what he was gonna do, this is totally new to me, um, so they went upstairs, and I just started to ransack the place downstairs . . . and then there was movement upstairs, banging going on, as if furniture is being moved and I just went upstairs, 'cos it was getting louder and louder, and the bloke was tied up on the bed. The bedroom was smashed up, it was in total disarray. It seemed as if I stood there for about five minutes in shock, but it was only a few seconds, and he said, my co-d said, "grab this," so I grabbed this telephone cord and put it around his neck, literally five seconds, and then I said, "come on, let's get out of here." I could see blood over the top of his head and my codefendant went out of the room, and I stood at the doorway and looked back at the man and I could see he was still breathing, his head was moving from side to side and I thought he'll be OK.

What starts out as a fairly sanitized account of the murder that minimizes Paul's direct and active role, soon changes.

FIONA: Did you pull the cord around his neck then?
PAUL: It was around his neck and I pulled it.
FIONA: So it was already around his neck?
PAUL: Yea. Um and then like I say we left but.
FIONA: Why did you do that?
PAUL: It was, um, just to see what it was like, um . . .
FIONA: To see what it was like?
PAUL: Um, how can I put it? I looked at him and, um, I just felt, how can I put it, like a sensation run through me. Even though what I was

doing was bad, I felt good, I don't know if you can understand that, um, I felt good and obviously afterwards, you know, I felt terrible about it, but at the time, when I was actually doing, the actual, putting everything else to one side, me, flex and him, um, the feeling for what I was doing, you know.

Paul provides three contradictory accounts of the murder.[8] First, he presents a scenario wherein his codefendant orchestrated the key events of the crime and plays the central role in assaulting and incapacitating the victim, and instructing Paul to tighten the cord. Paul presents himself as the hapless victim of a plot to kill, drawing upon conventional neutralizations: he was told to grab the chord, he was in shock, he didn't mean for this to happen (i.e., the victim was alive when he left him) and this kind of situation was "new" to him. However, when pressed further about the actual moment of the murder, he describes a pleasurable sensation when tightening the cord around the victim's neck ("I felt good"; "me, flex and him") and narrates an almost existential magical event involving distinctive "sensual dynamics" (Katz 1988, 4–5; see also Lyng 2004).

Paul tries to deflect the listener away from the critical moment of the strangulation by skipping quickly to the point at which both offenders leave the house ("and then like I say, we left"). However, as part of the co-production of the story, Paul is pulled back to the fatal act and ultimately describes his feelings at the time. His repeated use of the epistemic utterance "how can I put it" suggests that he is struggling to relate this particular aspect of the event—perhaps because it is genuinely hard for him to speak of it, or perhaps because he does not wish to alienate me, the listener. Paul provides direct quotes from the exchange between himself and his codefendant (e.g., "my co-d, 'grab this'") bringing the offense to life but also perhaps adding a sense of authenticity to his account.

Embedded within these contrasting accounts are different discourses. For example, he begins by drawing wholly upon conventional discourse, neutralizing and sanitizing his role and responsibility. However, he ends on a rather different note, drawing upon subcultural discourse regarding the pleasures or seduction of crime. Finally, his reference to "obviously" feeling terrible afterwards draws upon conventional and institutional discourses and positions him as a remorseful or repentant individual, rather than a monster who continues to take pleasure in his crime.

NARRATIVE SELF-IMAGE

Paul constructs his self-image by juxtaposing his own perception of self with perceptions of him held by his immediate family and close friends.

> You know people have said that what I did was totally out of the blue, totally, that's not Paul, that's not me, I'm not that kind of person, but in myself and in my heart of hearts, I put my hands up to it, I felt myself that I was going down that path, a downward spiral, and I knew that at the end of it I was gonna end up doing something bad; didn't know what, didn't know when, didn't know who, I just knew.

This narrative blends an interesting mix of inevitable downward spiraling ("felt myself going") and predictability ("I knew") with a foreboding hint of unknown ("didn't know what . . . when . . . who"). There is the sense that he was forewarned that something bad was coming and may have been able to make the choice to not continue along that path. His reference to "heart of hearts" suggests a deep inner self that was authentically bad and contrasted with his more public persona and concealed his true self. His account is almost the reverse of Nicola in that he seems to be claiming an authentically violent self-image. Paul also draws upon responsibilization or prison discourse when he states, "I put my hands up to it"—as if confessing there and then to the murder. Of all three violent offenders presented in this chapter, Paul seems the most torn between two worlds. Evidence of his two-headed role-playing is revealed when he explains his decision to plead not guilty:

> I went not guilty all the way on both crimes. I was like caught in, um, two things really. My family were putting a lot of pressure on me. As soon as I got arrested they immediately believed, and took it upon themselves to believe, that I was innocent, they couldn't think that I was involved in anything like this and a part of me, um, knew I did it, but a part of me wasn't sure, you know.

Paul suggests that innocence was imposed upon him by his family and in doing so denies his agency. He goes so far as to suggest that he became unsure of whether he had in fact committed the murder. This is in stark contrast to his early revelations regarding the pleasures experienced during the offense.

Paul's description of the murder itself is contradictory, pulling from quite different discourses. He initially draws upon classic neutralizations but later meanders between pathological and subcultural discourses.[9] In part, his discourses develop in response to further questioning and illustrate how narrative evolves in situ; they are dynamic and coproduced (Frank 2010). For example, we may never have heard about the pleasurable sensations that he experienced during the final moments of the murder had I not repeatedly asked him to explain further. He presents a complex appraisal of his self-image, suggesting an inner bad core over which he had little control (drawing upon positivistic and pathological discourse); but he also interweaves responsibilization discourse with conventional neutralization.

Conclusion

The narratives presented in this chapter illustrate that offenders generally provide complex narratives of their lives and past acts of violence. They can shift, from one breath to the next, from a gangster narrative to one of vulnerability, or from a narrative of agency and responsibilization to one of structural disadvantage. Oftentimes these narratives seem in conflict, and sometimes they are. All this may seem messy or contradictory, I wish to suggest that this is how narratives are made. Moreover, researchers ought not to smooth over the bumpy contours, and instead pay special attention to the narrative flotsam and jetsam. Before I consider the implications of this for narrative criminology, I want to reflect a little more closely upon some of the nuanced differences that emerge in offender narratives and some of the causes of interdiscursivity.

Action and Reflection Narratives

The case studies considered here illustrate that both action narratives (concerning the enactment of violence) and reflection narratives (concerning self and identity) draw upon and shift between different discourses—notably conventional, institutional, subcultural, gangster, oppression, pathological, and victimhood discourses. Most of the violent offenders, initially at least, minimized the levels of harm and violence enacted. When pressed, some talked in detail about how doing harm felt to them in the moment (à la Katz 1988). Put another way, while violent offenders neutralize, excuse, and justify, they may also relive the excitement and pleasures. Encouraging offenders to go back to the moment and openly express the experiential nature of violence is quite different from asking them to simply explain their crimes. The former allows offenders to express the appeal of crime; the latter is more likely to elicit excuses and justifications. Reflection narratives are even more complex. They are much more all-encompassing in that they require that the interviewees metaphorically gaze back at their reflection in the mirror and consider who they *are* or who they *were* or both. This distinction is important. Depending upon how questions are framed and phrased, interviewees may deliver narratives of present self (who are you?) or narratives of past selves (who were you?). Alternatively, they may provide narratives of past acts (what have you done?) or, in the case of active offenders, narratives of current acts (what do you do?). It is my contention that each of these narratives is subtly distinct. Moreover, it is not always clear whether researchers seek to unravel action or reflection narratives, or to disentangle the offender's identity in the past or the present. Needless to say, offenders often offer both in order to juxtapose the past (bad) self with the present (good) self. Understanding whether we are retrieving action or reflection narratives and at what point in the offender's life history may help us to discern whether an offender presents a changed self, is trying to contest and mend an earlier narrative of self, or is trying to keep a particular narrative going (see Giddens 1991).

Athens (1997, 54) notes, "one of the most vital facts that can be known about human beings is how they see themselves, their self-portraits. Of course, sufficient attention must always be paid to the date when the self-portrait was painted." Athens required his offenders to cast their minds back in time and to describe their self-images at the time of the violent offenses. Given that fact it is perhaps unsurprising that he generally found congruence between actors' self-images and their violent criminal actions. In contrast, the narratives explored in this chapter include references to past and present self-images as well as violent acts and have revealed less alignment. Hence, as illustrated in table 8.1, different discourses are called forth throughout these different narratives.

The fact that Sandberg (2009b) identified two juxtaposed discourses of gangster and oppression in his research may, in part, be due to him having tapped into both action and reflection narratives. His Norwegian drug dealers justified their offending as a necessity due to their inability to find paid work combined with the affects of racism and discrimination. By contrast, through gangster discourse they provided presentations of self as tough men and good fighters who never snitched. The former are narratives about offending (action), the latter about self (reflection). This distinction between action and reflection narratives is but one of the myriad of factors relevant to understanding the production and nature of narrative.

Table 8.1: Discourses Adopted by Violent Offenders During Action and Reflection Narratives.

Pseudonym	Action Narratives	Reflection Narratives
Jane	Conventional (considerable) Subcultural (considerable)	Gangster (extensive) Disadvantaged (limited)
Nicola	Conventional (extensive)	Conventional (extensive) Vulnerable (partial) Thrill-seeking (partial) Subcultural (partial)
Paul	Conventional (extensive) Victimized (partial) Pathological (partial) Subcultural (minimal)	Responsibilization/institutional (partial) Pathological (partial) Conventional (partial)

Perhaps we should not be surprised that narratives are so malleable; as Dean and Whyte (1958) argue, behavior, opinions, and values are in flux. So too, then, are the accounts that offenders provide to explain behavior and values. Incoherent narrative is a reflection of the fact that the speaker is fully aligned to neither conventional nor subcultural codes but rather drifts between the two (see Sandberg 2009b). While some offenders are more embedded in and committed to a criminal lifestyle and may speak more to gangster discourse, they nevertheless are not hermetically sealed off from wider society and immune from broader discourses. Hence, even the most authentically violent offenders will often present themselves and their violence in ways that are complex and seemingly contradictory.

Finally, that stories are fractured and at times incoherent and even shift during an interview may be, in part at least, foundational—that is the way that stories are. The teller's voice is "one voice amongst many" (Bakhtin 1981, 261) as he or she naturally draws upon a cultural reservoir of discourses (some extensive, others more limited) in order to make sense of actions and self. That researchers have identified (and continue to search for) coherence says more about our predilection to find order amongst chaos than the existence of coherence itself. It also speaks to researchers' desire to find one voice.

The Implications of Shifting Narratives for Narrative Criminology

How are we to make sense of offender accounts when the meaning of stories and the stories themselves are moving targets? As the aforementioned discussion has illustrated, there is evidence that the interdiscursivity observed in offender's accounts is both foundational (i.e., that is how stories are made) and the result of external forces (e.g., the product of the methodologies that researchers employ and the broader context within which accounts are elicited). Narrative criminologists have an opportunity to develop techniques that help to illuminate interdiscursivity.

To begin with, narrative criminologists can fine-tune and utilize methodologies that are sensitive to the dialogic nature of narrative production. For example, we might aim to interview an incarcerated offender multiple times using different researchers to gauge the role and impact of the interviewer. Interviewers could actively vary their interview styles from neutral on one hand to challenging on the other (see Presser 2004). Relatedly, we might compare the narratives that are produced in the traditional one-to-one interview setting with those told in groups. Riessman (2008, 123) suggests that stories told in group contexts are generally less rehearsed and lack the neat boundaries of research interviews. They can take the form of performance pieces, "performed for (and with) an audience that includes the investigator" (ibid.). What discourses dominate and what alternatives arise under such conditions as different members of the group interject, agree, or challenge the narrative of another member? Finally, given the often-made point that offenders narrate the responsibilization discourse of prison (McKendy 2006; Guo 2012), researchers working within prisons might consider techniques for carefully identifying the extent of this discourse and whether alternative discourses easily emerge. For example, researchers could listen into the narratives of offenders during cognitive therapy and compare these to the accounts of identical issues generated during research interviews. Alternatively, one might ask questions during an interview that encourage offenders to speak to different imagined audiences (e.g., prison therapist, family member, or best friend) and then ask, which of these accounts are you most comfortable with and why?

Alternatively, directly accessing the conversations that offenders engage in with a range of different people may assist in gauging how (and why) narratives actually shift. We might assume that criminals are more likely to adopt gangster discourse when conversing among themselves (than with, say, representatives of the Criminal Justice System (CJS) but this may not be the case. To these ends, detailed ethnographic studies are more likely to access the gamut of one's narratives. There may also be much to learn from the "small stories" of offenders told in passing, for, as Bamberg (2012, 102) notes, "identity is navigated as much in the small stories . . . prompted in ordinary interaction as it is presented in extended accounts of biographical material."

Greater awareness and detailing of the changes in position or footing that emerge during the interview (Goffman 2007) could also be of benefit. Audio-visual recording of accounts may provide a useful additional route to analyzing how narratives emerge in interaction (see Bamberg 2010). In addition, we might ask offenders to write down their reflections in response to some framing questions and compare the written to the oral. This may be fruitful as it would remove the moment-to-moment reframing due to the presence of the researcher and perhaps help to lessen coproduction.[10]

Just as offenders' narratives are made up of multiple voices drawn from various cultural and intuitional stories, so too the researcher's analysis of narrative is multilayered and dependent upon one's exposure to particular modes of analysis and cultural exposure to particular stories. Hence, what I might interpret on reading a particular segment of narrative is partly my particular take on it but also intimately connected to my stock of knowledge and my own narrative repertoires. Further, the position from which I make sense of and engage in conversation will be, in part, the product of many of my personal attributes such as gender, age, race, and status.[11] In short, researchers see different things in narratives. Reflexively interrogating one's own influence on the production and interpretation of narrative data is, therefore, an important ongoing consideration for narrative criminologists.

Narrative criminologists can strive to think more carefully about the range of discourses that are available to particular categories of offenders (i.e., what sorts of discourses have they been exposed to?) as well as thinking about the broader political or historical genres that may infuse their talk (see Reissman 2008). Gubrium and Holstein (1998, 180) claim that ownership of narrative in contemporary life is "increasingly mediated by widely available communicative frameworks" and is more "diffusely proprietary than ever." They specifically refer to self-help groups and talk shows, but one might add to these various social media sites such as Facebook, Twitter, and Tumblr—all of which provide a backdrop for the emergence and adoption of new narrative discourse. Narrative criminologists can interrogate how these new postmodern forms of communication infuse offender talk.

Above all, those of us interested in the multilingual nature of offender accounts ought to pay particular attention to so-called narrative debris, which includes false starts, inconsistencies, self-interruptions, repetition, disfluencies, and various kinds of verbal stumbling (McKendy 2006). We should seek out (not analyze out) the multivoiced nature of offenders' narratives while trying to locate the broader discourses that inform offenders' stories of their past, present, and future.

The final challenge for narrative criminology is to navigate a fine balance between searching for the messages that can reasonably be garnered from offender[12] narratives while acknowledging that, from the perspective of DNA at least, we must not assume the final word on behalf of our participants; for they are forever able to adjust their narratives, bringing in new voices and abandoning the old ones as they make further sense of their lives.

NOTES

1. This is a pseudonym.
2. To illustrate, McKendy (2006, 475) argued, "Now more than ever, the official institutional frame of the prison screens out sociologically oriented accounts, i.e. ones which bring into view the external forces that shape and condition the behaviour of the individual." See also Guo (2012).
3. Scholars have used various terms to describe discourses including master narratives (Bamberg 2004) and metanarratives (Somers 1994)
4. Wu (2011, 96) has described interdiscursivity as "the mixing of diverse genres, discourses, or styles associated with institutional and social meanings in a single text."
5. Interviewees were aware that confidentiality would not apply if they (a) mentioned something that showed a significant and previously undetected risk to themselves or another or (b) provided specific and identifying details that could link them to a serious offense (such as murder) that had not previously been disclosed.
6. See also Moita-Lopes (2006) on positioning in narratives and Riessman (2008) on dialogic/performance analysis.
7. Formula stories refer to "narratives of typical actors engaging in typical behaviours within typical plots leading to expectable moral evaluations" (Loseke 2007, 664). These widely circulated stories help people create and perpetuate symbolic codes. For example, when someone asserts that hard times lead them to commit property crime so that a listener might assume that they were stealing to be able to afford food, they rely on a formula story constructed to capture, in a few words, how persons like them make familiar choices (see Brookman et al. 2011a).
8. It is also not clear whether he put the cord around the victim's neck (as stated in the opening statement) or whether it was already around the victim's neck before he was told to tighten it (as he subsequently states).
9. I distinguish pathological discourse from gangster or subcultural discourses not to judge the pathological nature of the offender but, rather, to highlight that the vivid narrative of the pleasures associated with lethal or sublethal violence is distinct from gangster discourse that emphasizes skill, daring, and hardness.
10. Coproduction can probably never be completely overcome in that there is always an imagined and anticipated audience for whom the narrator or writer performs even in their physical absence.
11. Maltz and Borker (2007), for example, argue that American men and women come from different sociolinguistic subcultures that lead to their adoption of different conversational styles. It follows, that they likely also interpret talk differently. Gumperz (1977) has also identified differences in conversational inference among those of different speech cultures.
12. Or, for that matter, victims of crime or agents of the criminal justice system.

REFERENCES

Anderson, Elijah. 1999. *Code of the Street: Decency, Violence, and the Moral Life of the Inner City*. New York: Norton.

Athens, Lonnie. 1974. "The Self and the Violent Criminal Act." *Urban Life and Culture* 3 (1): 98–112.

———. 1997. *Violent Criminal Acts and Actors Revisited*. Urbana and Chicago: University of Illinois Press.

Bakhtin, Mikhail. 1981. *The Dialogic Imagination. Four Essays by M. M. Bakhtin*. Edited by M. Holquist. Translated by C. Emerson and M. Holquist. Austin: University of Texas Press.

Bamberg, Michael. 2004. "Narrative Discourse and Identities." In *Narratology Beyond Literary Criticism*, edited by J. C. Meister, T. Kindt, W. Schernus, and M. Stein, 213–237. New York: Walter de Gruyter.

———. 2010. "Who Am I? Narration and Its Contribution to Self and Identity." *Theory and Psychology* 21 (1): 1–22.

———. 2012. "Narrative Practice and Identity Navigation." In *Varieties of Narrative Analysis*, edited by James A. Holstein and Jaber F. Gubrium, 99–124. Los Angeles: Sage.

Brookman, Fiona. 2013. "Accounting for Homicide and Sub-Lethal Violence." In *In Their Own Words: Criminals on Crime An Anthology*, 6th ed., edited by P. Cromwell, 175–192. Oxford: Oxford University Press

Brookman, Fiona, Trevor Bennett, Andy Hochstetler, and Heith Copes. 2011b. "The 'Code of the Street' in the Generation of Street Violence in the UK." *European Journal of Criminology* 8 (1): 17–31.

Brookman, Fiona, Heith Copes, and Andrew Hochstetler. 2011a. "Street Codes as Formula Stories: How Inmates Recount Violence." *Journal of Contemporary Ethnography* 40 (4): 397–424.

Copes, Heith, Fiona Brookman, and Anastasia Brown. 2013 "Accounting for Violations of the Convict Code." *Journal of Contemporary Ethnography* 34 (10: 841–858.

Dean, John. P., and William. F. Whyte. 1958. "How Do You Know If the Informant Is Telling the Truth?" *Human Organization* 17 (2): 34–38.

Fairclough, Norman. 2003. *Analysing Discourse: Textual Analysis for Social Research*. London: Routledge.

Foucault, Michel. 1972. *The Archaeology of Knowledge and the Discourse on Language*. New York: Pantheon.

Frank, Arthur. 2005. "What Is Dialogical Research, and Why Should We Do It?" *Qualitative Health Research* 15 (7): 964–974.

———. 2012. "Practicing Dialogical Narrative Analysis." In *Varieties of Narrative Analysis*, edited by James A. Holstein and Jaber F. Gubrium, 33–50. Los Angeles: Sage.

Garfinkel, Harold. 1967. *Studies in Ethnomethodology*. Englewood Cliffs, NJ: Prentice Hall.

Garot, Robert. 2010. *Who You Claim. Performing Gang Identity in School and on the Streets*. New York: New York University Press.

Giddens, Anthony. 1991. *Modernity and Self-Identity: Self and Society in the Late Modern Age*. Stanford, CA: Stanford University Press.

Goffman, Erving. 1963. *Stigma: Notes on the Management of Spoiled Identity*. Englewood Cliffs, NJ: Prentice Hall.

———. 1971. *Relations in Public: Microstudies of the Public Order*. New York: Basic Books.

———. 1974. *Frame Analysis*. New York: Harper and Row.

———. 2007. "Footing." In *A Cultural Approach to Interpersonal Communication*, edited by L. Monaghan and J. E. Goodman, 396–399. Oxford: Blackwell.

Gubrium, Jaber. B., and James, A. Holstein. 1998. "Narrative Practice and the Coherence of Personal Stories." *Sociological Quarterly* 39 (1): 163–187.

Guo, Jing-Ying. 2012. "'Anyone in my shoes will end up like me': Female Inmates' Discourse of Responsibility for Crime." *Discourse and Society* 23 (1): 34–46.

Henry, Stuart. 1976. "Fencing with Accounts: The Language of Moral Bridging." *British Journal of Law and Society* 3 (1): 91–100.

Hochstetler, Andy, Heith Copes, and Patrick Williams. 2010. "That's Not Who I Am: How Offenders Commit Violent Acts and Reject Authentically Violent Selves. *Justice Quarterly* 27 (4): 492–516.

Hollway, Wendy. 1984. "Gender Difference in the Production of Subjectivity." In *Changing the Subject: Psychology, Social Regulation, and Subjectivity*, edited by J. Henriques, W. Hollway, C. Urwin, C. Venn, and V. Walkedine, 227–263. London: Methuen.

Jacobs, Bruce, and Richard Wright. 2006. *Street Justice: Retaliation in the Criminal Underworld*. Cambridge: Cambridge University Press.

Katz, Jack. 1988. *Seductions of Crime: Moral and Sensual Attractions in Doing Evil*. New York: Basic Books.

Labov, William, and Joshua Waletzky. 1967. "Narrative Analysis: Oral Versions of Personal Experience. In *Essays on the Verbal and Visual Arts*, edited by J. Helms, 12–44. Seattle: University of Washington Press.

Loseke, Donileen. 2007. "The Study of Identity as Cultural, Institutional, Organizational, and Personal Narratives: Theoretical and Empirical Integrations." *Sociological Quarterly* 48 (4): 661–688.

Lyng, Stephen. 2004. "Crime, Edgework, and Corporeal Transaction." *Theoretical Criminology* 8 (3): 359–375.

Maruna, Shadd. 2001. *Making Good: How Ex-Convicts Reform and Rebuild Their Lives*. Washington, DC: American Psychological Association.

Maruna Shadd, and Copes Heith. 2005. "What Have We Learned from Five Decades of Neutralization Research" *Crime and Justice: A Review of Research* 32: 221–320.

McKendy, John. 2006. "I'm Very Careful about That: Narrative and Agency of Men in Prisons." *Discourse and Society* 17 (4): 473–502.

Moita-Lopes, Luiz Paulo. 2006. "On Being White, Heterosexual, and Male in a Brazilian School: Multiple Positioning in Oral Narratives." In *Discourse and Identity*, edited by Anna de Fina, Deborah Schiffrin, and Michael Bamberg, 288–313. Cambridge: Cambridge University Press.

O'Connor, Patricia E. 1995. "Speaking of Crime: 'I don't know what made me do it.'" *Discourse and Society* 6 (3): 429–456.

Presser, Lois. 2004. "Violent Offenders, Moral Selves: Constructing Identities and Accounts in the Research Interview." *Social Problems* 51 (1): 82–101.

———. 2008. *Been a Heavy Life: Stories of Violent Men*. Urbana and Chicago: University of Illinois Press.

Riessman, Catherine K. 2008. *Narrative Methods for the Human Sciences*. Los Angeles: Sage.

Sandberg, Sveinung. 2009a. "A Narrative Search for Respect." *Deviant Behaviour* 30 (6): 487–510.

———. 2009b. "Gangster, Victim, or Both? The Interdiscursive Construction of Sameness and Difference in Self-Presentations." *British Journal of Sociology* 60 (3): 523–542.

———. 2010. "What Can 'Lies' Tell Us about Life? Notes Towards a Framework of Narrative Criminology." *Journal of Criminal Justice Education* 21 (4): 447–465.

———. 2013. "Are Self-Narratives Unified or Fragmented, Strategic, or Determined? Reading the Manifesto of A. B. Breivik in Light of Narrative Criminology." *Acta Sociologica* 56 (1): 69–83.

Scott, Marvin. B., and Stanford M. Lyman. 1968. "Accounts." *American Sociological Review* 33 (1): 46–61.

Segal, Jerome. 1991. *Agency and Alienation: A Theory of Human Presence*. Savage, MD: Rowman and Littlefield.

Somers, Margaret R. 1994. "The Narrative Constitution of Identity: A Relational and Network Approach." *Theory and Society* 23 (5): 605–649.

Sykes, Graham, and David Matza. 1957. "Techniques of Neutralization: A Theory of Delinquency." *American Sociological Review* 22 (6): 664–670.

Topalli, Volkan. 2005. "When Being Good Is Bad: An Expansion of Neutralization Theory." *Criminology* 43 (3): 797–835.

Wu, Jianguo. 2011. "Understanding Interdiscursivity: A Pragmatic Model." *Journal of Cambridge Studies* 6 (2–3): 95–115.

9

Narrative Criminology and Cultural Criminology

Shared Biographies, Different Lives?

KESTER ASPDEN AND KEITH J. HAYWARD

For I stole things which I already had in plenty and of better
quality. Nor had I any desire to enjoy the things I stole, but
only the stealing of them and the sin. There was a pear tree
near our vineyard, heavy with fruit, but fruit that was not
particularly tempting either to look at or to taste. A group
of young blackguards, and I among them, went out to knock
down the pears and carry them off late one night, for it was
our bad habit to carry on our games in the streets till very
late. We carried off an immense load of pears, not to eat—
for we barely tasted them before throwing them to the hogs.
Our only pleasure in doing it was that it was forbidden. . . .
The malice of the act was base and I loved it—that is to say I
loved my own undoing, I loved the evil in me.
—St. Augustine, Bishop of Hippo

Set against today's many true crime autobiographies—the type of
sensationalist, tell-all accounts of life as a violent gangster or football
hooligan that stare down at us from the shelves of main street and air-
port bookshops—the confession of a theft of pears by St. Augustine in
AD 397 seems entirely innocuous, innocent even. Yet, if we leave aside
the important distinction that exists between the reverent contrition of
Augustine and the self-aggrandizement associated with, say, contemporary "hooli-lit" (Fischer 2006), it is clear that, as long as society has
recognized the concept of crime, a shadow process of making sense of
criminal transgression has followed through autobiographical narrative exploration. Surprising, then, that twentieth-century criminology

had so little to say about first-person narratives. There were, of course, one or two brief moments of exception: most famously the detailed and compelling life histories of criminals and delinquents developed and produced by the Chicago School sociologists in the 1930s (e.g., Shaw 1930; Landesco 1933; Sutherland 1937); and much later, the ongoing revival of interest in first-person life narratives that accompanied the desistance approach to offender rehabilitation (e.g., Maruna 1997; Gadd and Farrall 2004). Despite these developments and their valuable contributions to dispositional theory building, it remains the case that autobiographical accounts and humanistic life histories have rarely penetrated the carefully patrolled hinterlands of mainstream criminology.

Thankfully this is now changing. The early twenty-first century has seen a revival of interest in both biography and life history (Goodey 2000; Shover 2012), and the more general relationship between subjective worldviews, human agency, storytelling, and etiology. For example, the recent emergence of psychosocial criminology (Gadd and Jefferson 2007) places considerable emphasis on the latent or unconscious meanings embedded in offenders' stories. Likewise, the emerging field of existentialist criminology (Crewe and Lippens 2009; Hardie-Bick and Lipens 2011) is also interested in internal conversations and the project of the self. The most significant development, of course, and the reason for this collection, has been the rise of narrative criminology (Presser 2009; Sandberg 2009). Narrative criminology is a bespoke disciplinary subvariant that looks at how offenders create a storied identity and in the process construct the self through a series of narratives that they use to make sense of their world and their surroundings. Reflecting the wider narrative turn that took place in psychology, sociology, and social theory during the 1990s (Bruner 1987; McAdams 1993, 1999; Ricoeur 1992), narrative criminologists adopt a catholic position regarding the self-narrative, seeing it not only as a receptacle for both perfect and imperfect factual representations but also as an avenue for the imaginative rendering of self. This inclusive, some might say overly permissive, position means that the raw material for their analyses extends well beyond the immediate biographical detail contained in qualitative interviews, autobiographies, reports, ethnographic case study notes, and other written sources, to include chronicles, expositions, metaphors, dialogue, popular discourses, and arguments.

This renewed interest in narrative also extends to cultural criminology. Simply stated, cultural criminology is a well-established theoretical, methodological, and interventionist approach to the study of crime that places crime and its control squarely in the context of culture; that is, it views crime and the agencies and institutions of crime control as cultural products—as creative constructs (see Ferrell et al. 2014; Hayward and Young 2012). Cultural criminology's focus is intentionally broad and avowedly interdisciplinary; what is of most importance here is its fundamental interest in how individuals strive to resolve certain psychic and emotional conflicts that are themselves spawned by the contradictions and peculiarities of contemporary life (Hayward 2004, 9). In exploring this question, cultural criminology shares with narrative criminology a scholarly and moral commitment to inquire into people's lived experiences. It thus shares an interest in examining the cultural trail that individuals leave behind, the transgressions, the flawed decisions, the cultural and personal artifacts and traces of a life lived that help us understand human behavior; hence cultural criminology's dictum that it "uses the 'evidence' of everyday existence, wherever it is found and in whatever form it can be found; the debris of everyday life is its 'data'" (Presdee 2000, 15).

This chapter builds on this overlapping intellectual terrain by constructing a series of theoretical and practical bridges between narrative and cultural criminology. The chapter proceeds in two parts. It starts by excavating the putative narrative criminology implicit within cultural criminology's established interests in biography, (auto)ethnography, existentialism, and phenomenology. The second half of the chapter takes a more reflexive, methodological turn by zeroing in on a number of key issues and dilemmas that challenge both the individual offender/transgressor involved in the process of autobiographical narrative construction and the analyst—be they of a cultural or narrative criminological persuasion—whose task it is to interpret (and on occasion interpolate) this data for the purposes of theoretical extrapolation. Importantly, these issues—which include questions concerning the role of truth, selectivity, and artful creativity in the process of narrative construction/ interpretation—will not be dealt with systematically or didactically; instead, they will be approached in a more oblique fashion through (and this is entirely intentional) a form of autobiographical narrative. One of us (Aspden) will reflect on his own biographical history; a narrative arc that includes life as an incarcerated youth offender, a doctoral student at the University of Cambridge, and most recently an award-winning nonfiction crime writer. Only one element of this backstory will be scrutinized: like St. Augustine all those centuries ago, the focus will be on a moment of youthful criminality, albeit one a good deal more serious than the theft of a few overripe pears.

First, however, we will turn to the shared biographies of narrative and cultural criminology and how their mutual concerns might help us better understand and analyze the complex and interconnected nature of individual values, emotions, and identities.

Shared Concerns, Overlapping Foci

We are all products of everyday life and as such we all have everyday stories. . . . It is here in the hazy ephemeral "being" of everyday life, where "all that is solid melts into air," that social excavation must take place as we concern ourselves with social lives already formed. . . . (Auto)biography is the raw material, our raw material; it cannot stand on its own, it needs to be "worked on."
—Mike Presdee (2004, 43)

You don't have to delve too deeply into recent work in the burgeoning field of narrative criminology to appreciate the influence of cultural criminology. For example, in a recent article on Anders Behring Breivik, the Norwegian neo-Nazi terrorist, Sveinung Sandberg (Sandberg et al. 2014, 291), one of the leading proponents of the narrative approach, states that any theoretical framework for understanding such attacks must include "cultural criminology's emphasis on reading action as narrative," and that his goal with this article was to actively "combine insights from cultural and narrative criminology." Likewise, in the introduction to this book, the editors highlight cultural criminology as one of "the two established criminological traditions closest to our project," commenting that, although "narrative criminology's explicit emphasis on discourse and its methodological commitment to studying discourse seem to differentiate it from cultural criminology . . . cultural criminology's insistence on the seductions of crime is something narrativists can get behind, by understanding those seductions as mediated by language" (Presser and Sandberg, introduction, this volume). These are positive early steps toward a promising and mutually beneficial relationship, but they remain just that—first steps. In this section we aim to explore certain aspects of this fledgling liaison by bringing into sharper relief a number of overlapping criminological interests and shared disciplinary concerns that animate both approaches. In doing so, we also hope to identify what aspects of narrative criminology are likely to be of most use to cultural criminologists and what aspects might prove more difficult to integrate.

Both approaches share a fundamental interest in the etiology of crime and especially the existential currents and phenomenological specificities that surround the decision to engage in or desist from offending. However, this shared interest also illustrates what is perhaps the most fundamental difference between narrative/psychosocial criminology and cultural criminology. Although both criminologies are clearly interested in first-person explanations of crime and violence, narrativists choose to focus on discursive retrospection (e.g., Presser 2012), while cultural criminologists—so far at least—have remained committed to a criminology that seeks to understand the visceral immediacy and experiential thrill of crime and transgression.

In their efforts to privilege the story, narrative criminologists utilize a host of theoretical approaches. Depending on the article you read, you might find a narrativist drawing upon cognitive processes or psychotherapeutic notions of a unified self, stressing the value of Sykes and Matza's (1957) "techniques of neutralization" and other theories traditionally associated with subcultural or collective action, or even relying on the prewritten narratives allied with cultural structuralism. Whatever approach is used, one thing is for certain: it will be as part of an inherently *constructivist project*. Here again, the narrative approach overlaps with early North American cultural criminology (see Ferrell and Sanders 1995), which also drew heavily on theories of social construction. However, while cultural criminologists have always balanced this interest with more empirical forms of criminological analysis, including an emphasis on ethnographic immediacy, narrativists exist exclusively and unapologetically in the discursive realm, insisting that the only appropriate data is that which is available in a material (i.e., a discursive or language) form. Thus, when Presser and Sandberg discuss cultural criminological works such as Jack Katz's (1988) seductions of crime or Stephen Lyng's (2004) concept of edgework, they are keen to stress that *doing* should not be privileged over *speaking* (this volume, 13). In other words, according to Presser and Sandberg the nascent narrative possibilities associated with cultural criminology's focus on existential motivations remain nascent precisely because the attention is tipped too far in favor of the action itself instead of focusing on the subsequent interpretation of the act or one's interpretation of one's life.[1] Even when the act is acknowledged as symbolically important, it is only "something narrativists can get behind" if the (seductive) act is "mediated by language" (Presser and Sandberg, this volume).

In contrast, cultural criminologists focus on "the perceptual context" (Ferrell 1999, 405), or more simply, the reality of emotional experiences—at least in the sense that they feel real to the person experiencing them. The meaning and character of brute facts associated with criminality—for example, waving a gun in someone's face, victimizing a cell mate, snorting a line of cocaine, or igniting a flare at a football match—are necessarily shaped in and through a narrative (whether constructed by the agent or narrative analyst); however, the fact remains that the rawness and reality of the transgressive act produces biographical moments that cannot be denied. Indeed, for cultural criminology the task is to capture these moments and, following Katz, to understand their emotional meaning and seductive allure.[2] Consequently, for Katz, Lyng, and other cultural criminologists, what is of most importance is the criminal act itself, or more accurately the *moment of transcendence* it affords. Subsequent reflections—be they ex post facto storied reconfigurations or stories that precede action (see Presser 2013; Tutenges and Sandberg 2013)—are certainly valuable tools for ascertaining meaning, but it is the here and now of the transgressive act that matters more to cultural criminologists than the here and now of the narration. Cultural criminologists, then, are wary of a narrativist retreat into the intertextual language games associated with postmodern analysis.[3] Focusing on "multiple interpretations of one narrative" and viewing a narrative as "a multidimensional space where different genres, discourses, and vocabularies merge and clash" (Presser and Sandberg, this volume) may have its uses in the constructivist process, but it also runs the risk of turning the search for narrative themes into a metacommentary with little reference to the urgent project of public criminology.

This different approach to etiology manifests itself in a number of ways, even when common ground is apparent. For example, although both criminologies understand that a criminal narrative will always be a work in progress—partial, finite, unfinished—their search for the unarticulated, missing elements takes different forms. For narrative and psychosocial criminologists, the issue is what lies beneath the surface of the articulated account: the negative and destructive psychodynamic meanings and symbols that are hinted at in the data but that require subsequent excavation and interpretation. For their part, cultural criminologists recognize that while the criminal act may be pure, it is almost always emblematic of wider socio-cultural and psycho-dynamics forces that are only partially understood by the transgressor. This is a subtle difference but an important one. Consider, for example, two recent pieces of (cultural) criminological research, both of which actively employ the term *narrative* in their analyses, and both of which journey beyond the discursive.

Curtis Jackson-Jacobs, one of Katz's former PhD students, outlines a cultural criminological account of street brawling as storied action. Drawing on the themes of risk-taking, hegemonic masculinity, and Erving Goffman's (1967) concept of reputational consequences, Jackson-Jacobs (2004, 243) describes how the eighty-five young male street fighters he studied in Tucson, Arizona, use peer-group violence to manage "competing narrative gratifications and narrative threats." He claims that "fighters intend their brawls to make good stories that reveal themselves as charismatic, 'strong' or 'courageous' characters. And so they enact storylines that they expect will both test their character and be applauded by audiences" (232). Jackson-Jacobs arrives at his conclusion that fighting—and especially taking a beating—provides a means of constructing a positive narrative about oneself during moments of extreme public ordeal through a mix of firsthand ethnography and transcribed interviews. In this sense, this study is clearly something narrativists can get behind because each act of violence is indeed mediated by language—a straightforward example, then, of narrative criminology's assertion that speaking and acting are equally important when it comes to the process of data collection. However, it is not quite that simple. In his conclusion, Jackson-Jacobs also points to a series of "tentative hypotheses" that also need consideration; including the sensibilities associated with "late modern consumerism," "affluent leisure cultures," and "mass-mediated entertainment," all of which he suggests are unarticulated "frames of reference to explain and construct behavior" (243).

This unspoken dimension of narrative construction features even more prominently in Simon Winlow and Steve Hall 2009. The authors' preferred method is the unstructured interview, so once again there is plenty of material data to analyze; this time on relatively successful criminals whose stock-in-trade is the street-level violence that accompanies professional criminality in Britain's postindustrial urban landscapes. Adhering more closely to the psychosocial approach (Walkerdine et al. 2001; Gadd and Jefferson 2007) than to narrative criminology, Winlow and Hall set out to show how "violent men often address unfolding social interaction as a means of taking control of painful and humiliating memories, rewriting the past and rehabilitating the self from its previous failures" (2009, 288). Biographical narrative construction, then, is once again the task at hand; but just like with Jackson-Jacobs's sample of street brawlers, it is a task made more complex by a social context in which capitalist consumer culture clouds preexisting forms of identity construction. In Winlow and Hall's words, these men now have to deal with new and unfamiliar forms of "introspection, guilt and self doubt which have never before been such active constituents of human experience" (289). The narratives of these men are thus shrouded by cultural sublimation and dogged by a structural shadow that they can neither recognize nor fully articulate. Like their hypermasculine counterparts in Tucson, Winlow and Hall's street criminals speak comprehensively about their violent acts, but remain incapable of grasping the totality of their material or historical circumstance.[4]

Despite acknowledging the importance of psychodynamic determinants, Hall and Winlow never quite throw off the "pull" of social structure in the form of impactful processes such as industrial downsizing, chronic job insecurity, the lure of consumerism, and so on. Here their position is redolent of cultural criminology. While cultural criminologists do not totally ignore matters psychodynamic, they typically prefer to situate the act of transgression in a broader socio-structural context, recognizing as one of us has stated elsewhere that "motives are cultural products [and] not essences revealed" (Ferrell et al. 2008, 23). Indeed, the cultural criminological position on this has already been articulated:

Men and women create culture, give meaning to their lives, and attempt to solve the problems which face them, as viewed from their own particular cultural perspective, albeit in a moral and material world not of their own making. None of this rules out the mechanistic mores of habit and here we follow Matza (1969)—the ability to act "as if" determined and the leap of bad faith that this entails. Human behavior is shaped by the actors themselves. It is not merely the unfolding of preordained essences which have been encoded in some DNA sequence, or in the psychoanalytical drama of phallus and breast set in some conjectured encounter early in the family or the steady causal dominance of broken home or childhood poverty stretching through the actor's life. . . . Rather moral careers are contingent on the present, and the past appears to hold sway only when there has been a continuity of experience or a process of self-fulfillment where powerful actors reinforce notions of a fixed self and powerless subjects come to believe these narratives. . . . To postulate that human beings are narrative creators who constantly rewrite and reshape their personal narratives does not imply a lack of unity of the self but the very opposite. (Ferrell, Hayward, and Young 2008, 23)

It is this position, this fusion of both foreground *and* background determinants that allows cultural criminologists to stray outside the confines of the offender's written or spoken account. As a consequence they are clearly less inhibited about extrapolating from the criminal act and grounding certain forms of criminal behavior in structural and sociocultural conditions (e.g., Ferrell 1992, 118–119; Young 2003; Hayward 2004, 152–166). We will now leave behind the issues of etiology and existential motivation and turn to the ultimate objective of (biographical/autobiographical) narrative construction.

If, as Mike Presdee (2004, 43) asserts, "(auto)biography is the raw material, our raw material" that "cannot stand on its own, it needs to be 'worked on,'" the question we must ask is, to what end? It is a question that once again highlights a fundamental difference between the approaches: specifically, whether narrative construction should begin and end with personal reflection and exploration, or whether it should serve a more social or public function? Expressed in a disciplinary language, should narrative criminology continue to favor the individual approach to self-understanding associated with narrative psychology, or should it widen its approach to include the more autoethnographic sociological approach favored by cultural criminologists?

Historically, cultural criminology's position on data collection for the purposes of narrative construction has been very different to that adopted by narrativists. Because of its strong emphasis on ethnography (Hamm and Ferrell 1998), the few cultural criminologists interested in creating something akin to a personal narrative have been preoccupied with interactional and situational issues relating to either the researcher's emotions (Ferrell et al. 2001) or concerns about "hierarchies of knowledge production" (Kane 2004, 304). More recently, however, this position has expanded to include a *verstehen*-oriented, autoethnographic approach (Jewkes 2011; Ferrell 2012; Denzin 2014) designed specifically to enhance researcher reflexivity and improve personal testimony. At one level, autoethnography is similar to autobiographical sociology (Friedman 1990) in that both seek to situate microsocial events in a broader social context.[5] However, autoethnography goes one step further than autobiographical sociology. As Jeff Ferrell (2012, 220) states in a recent essay on the subject, autoethnography "transcends autobiography" by linking personal experience with social and structural circumstance as a means of unlocking understanding of public issues.

Consider the recent attempt by cultural criminologists Carl Root, Jeff Ferrell, and Wilson Palacios (2013) to construct an autoethnographic narrative about an act of unwarranted police violence experienced by one of the authors (Root) in May 2009. Using official records, medical files, and court transcripts, alongside Root's diary and personal notes, and drawing on Norman Friedman's three core questions of autobiographical sociology—What happened to me and why did it happen? In what ways was my experience similar to and different from others involved? What is the larger sociological significance of the experience?—the authors show that autoethnographic narrative construction, apart from serving a cathartic and psychotherapeutically useful function, can also have wider sociological and political applicability. In this case, Root's reconstructed narrative helped cast light on the ambiguity surrounding excessive force in police-citizen encounters and added to the theoretical knowledge of "*verstehen*-oriented cultural victimology" (Ferrell et al. 2008, 190–191).

Our discussion so far has illustrated common ground that exists between narrative and cultural criminology. It also has highlighted some enduring differences that remain unresolved. In short, whether it is a question of how action is interpreted or read or whether narratives should serve a wider public/social function, the issue boils down to how much analytical weight criminologists are prepared to afford storytelling and storied action. So far, narrative criminologists have done a good job of presenting their case, and especially pointing out how reflective first-person narratives can challenge the purported realism to which other theories of criminal behavior are bound (Presser 2009; 2012). The key thing now is for narrative criminologists to try to avoid some of the bear traps that have tripped up narrativists in other disciplines. In particular, narrative criminologists have to ensure that the enterprise does not deteriorate into a poststructural language game concerned only with stories about reality and not reality itself. This is not to say that telling stories about stories is not important,[6] but rather that problems can emerge when interest in narratives becomes less about the stories themselves and more about how they are told (see Plummer 1995).

Thankfully, recent work produced by key figures in the field suggests that this is unlikely. For example, in her paper on the Tennessee spree killer, David Adkisson, Lois Presser uses the traditional Labovian model of narrative analysis (see Labov and Waletzky 1967) to analyze Adkisson's homicide/suicide note and other discursive statements and interview comments. Her findings make for an interesting case study on the discursive construction of motivation, but they also highlight the value of narrative criminology for theory building. Consider the following statement about what motivated Adkisson to embark on his campaign of mass murder:

> The challenge my evidence poses to strain theory is especially encapsulated in the fact that David [Adkisson] was selective about his rage: he directed it toward liberals, Democrats, Marxists, Blacks, and gay people. In contrast, he was not especially angry at the prospective employers who denied him work. He did not believe in blaming owners and other people of means: "It's wrong to vilify people like that." Whereas he saw himself as a victim of age discrimination in the workplace, he said that such practices are "just business." I told him that his angry feelings toward those who denied him work struck me as quite muted compared with his anger toward his political nemeses. He responded that his work-related frustrations were "more all-encompassing." (Presser 2012, 15)

In an important augmentation of strain theory, Presser shows how, through narrative sleight-of-hand, Adkisson has collapsed the personal and the political to such an extent that he can no longer correctly identify the true source of his status frustration. Such a statement speaks volumes about how once traditional narratives associated with class and economic opportunities have been replaced by ones now aligned with a more recent relativistic cultural politics. This sort of reimagining of early twentieth-century criminological theories for the late modern world is the type of theoretical development that dispositional criminologists of all stripes should get behind.

Similarly insightful is Sandberg's (2013) recent paper on the manifesto of Anders Behring Breivik. After pouring over Breivik's fifteen-hundred-page terrorist manifesto, Sandberg outlines four creative self-narratives adopted by Breivik at various points in the text: the professional revolutionary, the evangelist, the pragmatic conservative, and the social and likeable person. In a careful and subtle reading of the document, Sandberg recognizes that these narratives are not just simple neutralizations but also attempts to fabricate a unified self through a series of heroic personas (something akin to what Frank van Gemert [2014] describes as the "pose," a stance one adopts in a story "in order to send a message to the other"). Furthermore, these narratives are most pronounced when filtered through emotional outpourings ("Only once has 'the evangelist' appeared [during the trial] for example, when a rather pompous movie he had made about the threat of Islam and posted on YouTube was shown in court. Then he lost control over his emotions and wept" [Sandberg 2013, 79]). Here Sandberg's work on narrative closely resonates with theoretical developments in terrorism studies; in particular analysis of terrorist diaries, biographies, and online proclamations in which the terrorist actor casts himself in the role of hero or the avenging martyr (Roy 2008; Sageman 2004). It is this focus on the conjunction of narrative and emotions (and in a subsequent article on Breivik, Sandberg's claim that terrorist narratives are formed from a "cultural bricolage" that also includes more general "cultural stories" [Sandberg et al. 2014]), that is appealing to cultural criminology, not least because work on this very subject in relation to terrorist emotions is already well underway within the field (see Cottee 2009; Cottee and Hayward 2011).

As these examples suggest there is much to be gained by continuing to develop the close ties that already seem to exist between narrative and cultural criminology. Certainly the time is right for like-minded culturally informed criminologists to work together, not least because our discipline is currently confronted by a number of challenges in the form of the rising influence of criminologies predicated on rational calculation, crude social positivism, and other forms of self-styled "scientific" criminology. Indeed, as Maruna and Matravers (2007, 430) suggest, today's criminology affords a diminishing amount of space for detailed analysis of offender motivations and emotions: "Gone are the complexities, the conflicts, the contradictions, the insecurities and confusions that all of us struggle with as vulnerable, sensitive, emotional beings, replaced by a sort of 'stick figure' of the over-socialized individual or the rational actor." The time, then, to contribute to a culturally sensitive narrative criminology capable of challenging crime-beyond-agency and crime-as-choice theories with all their explanatory limitations is now.

We recognize that this chapter so far has been concerned exclusively with quite technical, intradisciplinary matters. As cultural criminologists we also recognize that we have a duty to stimulate and provoke disciplinary discussion through engaging humanistic real-world examples. To that end, we now shift gears and turn to the process of narrative construction and specifically Aspden's attempt to make sense of his own teenage crime. Modern autobiography, we have seen, started with St. Augustine and a crime story—"the most momentous fruit-theft in the history of salvation" (Shanzer 1996, 45). Aspden's middle-aged ruminations on a moment of youthful criminality belong to this long tradition of confessional literature. In what follows he attempts to bring elements of his story—including the story of his struggle to tell that story—into a fruitful dialogue with criminology.

An Author's Reflections on the Making of a Personal Offender Narrative

My example seems very unreal from a distance of almost thirty years. I now think and write about crime rather than do it. It was my first and only time in prison. "Why would I want to read about you robbing the local off-license?" one friend asked when I told her I was writing a memoir. I like to think that St. Augustine would have got it. And it is a question no cultural criminologist would ask.

I was a disenchanted researcher in his mid-thirties when I first heard about cultural criminology. It was the spring of 2003 and my friend Keith Hayward invited me along to a conference he had organized on the subject. I remember an impassioned address by Mike Presdee, an excoriation of administrative criminology by Jock Young, and a moody treatment of a recent murder case by Phil Cohen, which he described as "popular criminology." There was a strong feeling in the hall that criminology had taken a wrong turn; that it had become the servant of the criminal justice industry; that it was wedded to statistical methods at the expense of human inquiry; that emotion, passion, and excitement had gone.

I should admit that I wasn't an immediate convert to cultural criminology. An academic historian, I was unfamiliar with the names Presdee celebrated in his presentation: Merton, Becker, Katz, Ferrell. I was on the outside of a club and wondered what these interdisciplinary disputes had to do with the world beyond. The conference also caught me at a bad time. My girlfriend, a journalist, had just been assigned to cover the war in Iraq. I was drinking heavily, trying to block out dark thoughts. My work was giving me little satisfaction. I was looking at a future of disconnected fixed-term research posts. I probably was a little envious that day at London University, seeing my good friend at the center of this exciting new project.

In hindsight, I can put that time of my life in a more positive frame. It was when the germ of the idea for a memoir of youth began to form. Not long after that conference, I devised a module on the history of crime, policing, and punishment. Also in 2003, on a trip to County Durham, I sat in a car outside the young offenders' institution where I had served time as a teenager. Finally, on a visit to the National Archives, I chanced upon documents relating to the case of David Oluwale, a Nigerian brutalized by Leeds policemen at the end of the 1960s, and started work on my own popular criminology (Aspden 2007). I left academic life in 2004, moved to Russia to rejoin my girlfriend, and tried to start a writing career.

It wasn't until after the publication of my book on the Oluwale case that I started on my memoir. All I had to work with were some fragments of memories—you couldn't call it a narrative—and a yellowing, crumpled newspaper clipping headlined "Boy Raider Pointed Gun," dated Saturday November 16, 1985. In addition to tracing sources that would help me get back to those days—a cache of twenty-five letters I wrote to a friend from prison being the best find—I asked friends, family, and others who had dealings with me to share their memories and thoughts on my crime. One of those was my former probation officer. She remembered me because I was not her usual client: I was a grammar school–educated boy from an affluent part of York. She had had few middle-class clients before, certainly none whose first offense was attempted armed robbery. "I was trying to make conversation and you weren't having any of it," she recalled of our first meeting at Deerbolt Youth Custody Centre. "I didn't know what was going in your head."

I do not need to persuade cultural and narrative criminologists of the value of first-person offender narratives, although many criminologists remain skeptical. Some are disinclined to believe offender accounts, suspecting that they are mostly self-serving exercises (Presser 2009, 181); others assert that real crime is not much of a story at all, urging that criminologists direct their attention toward crime prevention rather than the motivations and inner lives of offenders. The crime story, according to one influential text, boils down to: "He saw, he took, and he left. He won't give it back" (Felson and Boba 2010, 3).

Cultural criminologists, by contrast, want to insist on the rich individual and social dramas that can be played out through crime, even in the case of apparently mundane crimes. Against those who would see the offender as a rational agent, weighing up the relative advantages and disadvantages of criminal activity, cultural criminologists (following Katz 1988) have wanted to emphasize the expressive, emotive, exciting, and even seductive nature of certain forms of transgression. Crime is seen less as a rational or utilitarian activity than as a phenomenon that uplifts, excites, thrills, and purifies (Hayward 2007; 2012). Narrative criminology also shares this commitment to humanize the offender, and is equally set against such reductive accounts of human action and behavior.

Writing from within the cultural criminological tradition, Hayward has highlighted some key concerns, but also points of contact, with narrative criminology. I have my preferences, but I am a writer not a criminologist with a particular theoretical commitment. A memoir should only attempt to tell the story of a life as truthfully as possible; it is not the best vehicle for refuting or adding support to particular theories. On the face of it, though, my memoir project would seem to have close affinities with the preoccupations of the narrativists. Narrative criminology is interested in the overarching life story, and the way in which the subject narrates that life. My memoir is an attempt to understand how I came to the point when I thought that crime was the solution to my troubles. It ranges across the events of a long stretch of life, evaluating and reflecting on past acts.

Narrativists believe that we construct our lives as stories, asserting that narrative itself is constitutive of reality. Hayward's concern that discourse about stories could become more important to narrativists than the content of the story—the stories themselves—would presumably be brushed away as a false distinction. Furthermore, narrativists assert that the "factual basis" of the narrative—the "what actually happened"—is beside the point (Presser 2009, 190–191). Though some of these stronger epistemological claims of narrative criminology make me uneasy—the "what actually happened" is of supreme importance to me—I don't dispute the importance of stories in the construction of self-identities, for good or ill. The most fascinating and novel claim of narrative criminology is that stories themselves are instrumental in instigating harmful action. More firmly established is the claim that stories may be instrumental in effecting desistance from harmful action (Presser 2009, 178; Presser and Sandberg, this volume). Maruna's (2001) celebrated research found that ex-offenders who "made good" were those who could fashion a positive self-story. The successful desisters were those skilled at "constructing positive illusions"; those who failed to make a coherent narrative out of their lives were vulnerable to depression, anxiety, or other problems (7). Again, what matters is not the truth or falsity of the story, but rather that it is a convincing tale of change.

Much of this chimes with my experience. There was a time in my life, in the years after my release and into my twenties, when "constructive positive illusions" was probably more helpful than painful self-examination. The story I told myself was that I had fallen to the bottom, that I was exiled from my community and peers. This self-story drove my ambitions to *show* people. I told myself that I had risen above those peers who had washed their hands of me. On January 10, 2001, the fifteenth anniversary of my imprisonment, I reflected in a letter to my girl-friend that going into the shop and brandishing a gun was the best thing that could have happened to me. At the same time, I was aware that the relative success I enjoyed in life wasn't because of some superior moral character or some heroic overcoming of a bad start. Parental financial support as much as intelligence had been the reason I was able to go to Cambridge University to do graduate work. When I began writing my memoir, it was in the hope that I might be able to fashion a more honest story of change.

Although my memoir is concerned with many aspects of my life and not just the single criminal episode, it seems worthwhile narrowing the focus to consider some of the challenges I have encountered in narrating the criminal event, and to look at it using insights from cultural and narrative criminology.

Before I read Katz and the criminologists inspired by his work, I was struggling to make sense of my experiences. I could not see or recognize myself in the academic texts on youth justice, focused as they were on background factors, defects in offenders' psychological development, social environments, and so on. Instead, films like Alan Clarke's *Scum* and *Made in Britain*, novels like *Brighton Rock* and *A Clockwork Orange*, and music by The Smiths and Morrissey provided the stories that helped me make sense of my experiences. Cultural criminology's emphasis on the thrilling nature, excitement, and emotion of crime was therefore appealing to this ex-offender-turned memoirist. Katz wanted to put the individual offender and the emotions back into the study of crime. He wanted to put the criminal act itself at the center—the moment of transgression—and only then consider the background factors. Under the influence of Katz, the *how* of the criminal act became the starting point of my inquiry. The crime, unlike other parts of my past, was something solid to grab, something fixed in time, ending on a certain date—January 10, 1986—with court and imprisonment. There was a narrative arc inherent in the criminal justice process.

I thought of armed robbery as the most sexy of crimes. When I was twelve or thirteen, I read the book the movie *Bonnie and Clyde* was based on and was aroused by a description in the first couple of pages where Clyde is looking up from the street at the naked Bonnie behind the window. I later saw the movie and thought Faye Dunaway was the sexiest woman alive, particularly in the scene when Bonnie first gets to handle Clyde's gun. There were other sources for my fascination with the figure of the armed robber. In my teens I read the book, saw the movie, and bought the record of *The Harder They Come*, which filled me with romantic ideas of the "rude boy." My favorite group were The Clash, who had songs such as "Safe European Home" (with the line, "No one knows what the rude boy knows") and "Bankrobber." The armed robber was someone outside and above society. Several months before my raid, it would have been mid-1985, I was impressed by an armed robber on the BBC's *Crimewatch* program. There was a hint of admiration in the way the presenters talked about the man they dubbed Mr. Cool: professional yet audacious, firm but polite, smartly dressed with smooth dark hair. This solitary lone raider fascinated me.

I had money worries in the lead-up to the robbery attempt. I had lost my morning cleaning job at Homebase after stealing a pound from a coworker's coat. I dreaded the thought of having to approach my parents again for pocket money. The weekend of my robbery there was a party in another town that I wanted to attend. A girl I was crazy about was going to be there. I had to be at this party, but I was completely broke. I had no idea what I might get from a robbery, but I had it in my mind that one hundred pounds would be a good yield. I persuaded a friend who collected replica guns to lend me his latest purchase and started looking for a likely target. I would go for a small shop away from the main streets. I found a shop that seemed ideal. Best of all it was run by a woman on her own.

It is extremely difficult to recapture the excitement of the criminal moment. I sometimes wish that I possessed the skills of a great novelist or poet, but capturing or evoking such moments is a challenge for all writers—whether memoirist, criminologist, or ethnographer. I returned to the scene of my crime on a number of occasions hoping somehow to get back in the skin of that teenage offender. The first time I went back I found that the off-license had gone and the property turned into a residence. The old shop doorway had been bricked up. I tucked myself into a narrow alleyway that I had stood in on a cold November night in 1985, a good point from which to see goings-on in the shop.

One memory that had stayed with me over the years, and that was confirmed in one of the letters I wrote from prison, was that I had a song in my head as I set out to raid the off-license that evening. The song was "The Bottom Line" by Big Audio Dynamite, an upbeat tune. I felt emboldened by the words: "When you reach the bottom line, the only thing to do is climb." As I crossed the river at Scarborough Bridge—roughly the halfway point between my home and the off-license—I felt this surge of conviction that I was taking control of my life. I also know that as I stood on that cold street corner waiting anxiously to make my raid I was no longer hearing "The Bottom Line."

With closing time approaching I knew I had to act. I pulled the scarf further up my face and the gun from my trousers. I chose to launch my attack just after an elderly female customer entered the shop. I could not have been in there more than thirty seconds. The shopkeeper asked me whether the gun was real and fumbled with the till. The elderly woman pushed by me to leave the shop. I heard shouting on the street. I fled without the cash and did not stop running till I was almost home.

I imagined that mine would be a story of a boy in war with his upbringing. This disjuncture between middle-class, Catholic background, and the inner turbulence I felt seemed to offer rich narrative possibilities. I believed that I had all I needed to make sense of my crime, that I could become my own historian. Instead, the biographical material grew and unexpected new themes emerged.

It may surprise criminologists to learn that it took me so long to think about masculinity—a theme very much at the forefront of the concerns of narrative criminologists. In her study of men convicted of violent crimes, Presser identified a common narrative: the embattled, lone hero defying great odds, essentially moral—self-righteously so—in the face of a hostile society. These were men who, when telling about their crimes, reveled in their bravery and heroism (Presser 2008). "Masculinity challenges" for such men were a necessary aspect of doing masculinity (Presser 2008, 146–147).

Perhaps one way of reading my crime is to see it as an attempt to assert a stronger, more potent sense of male identity. I hated the feeling of being disregarded—by teachers, the girls at school, and my parents. I felt trapped in a skinny, unattractive body and sought an escape. I drank, I took hallucinogenic drugs, but nothing changed inside. I felt that I had special qualities and despaired that nobody seemed to recognize them. I wanted to become the maker of my own story.

Perhaps my story is just a common one of youthful transgression—some would no doubt think it a mundane tale. Perhaps the value of a life story such as mine might not lie in its originality; the interest might lie in the step-by-step, detailed account of one individual's idiosyncratic struggle for a more sure sense of masculine identity. Such narratives would not only seek to capture the thrilling and uplifting nature of transgression but also the underlying desperation, sadness, and pathos.

The day after my raid, a few hours before my arrest, I was on my way to the train station to meet a girl. We were going to go to the party together that evening. She was a friend of the girl I was crazy about and I thought that arriving with her—an attractive, artsy blonde—would raise my credibility. Waiting for her train, I saw a placard at the newspaper stand with the headline "Boy Raider Pointed Gun." I bought a copy and read a story about my crime, right there on the front page. I was mortified by the police description: "Very thin build. Black greasy hair." I could see only those words, missing the line that should have been a warning that my freedom was going to be short-lived: "Is not thought to be dangerous."

Putting down these thoughts on paper, I am painfully aware that I am seven years into my memoir. I have come close to tears and have had to fight the urge to throw my laptop out of my apartment window. Yet the memoir will not go away quietly. Somewhere in all my jumble of thoughts, notes, and broken drafts I believe there is a new story to tell; perhaps this new story will simply illuminate an old truth—a truth found in the first great confessional story told by St. Augustine: that a single "youthful indiscretion, one moment of excitement and transgression, can reverberate for a lifetime" (Webber 2007, 155).

Conclusion

This chapter is divided into two parts; each one independently authored, and each one approaching the particular and developing relationship that now exists between cultural and narrative criminology. The first part is authored by a theoretical criminologist, and as such focuses on the rather technical task of teasing out the common intellectual ground and theoretical differences that exist between these two areas of dispositional criminological theory. The second part strikes a more reflective tone, and approaches the interface between cultural and narrative criminology from the perspective of a one-time criminal offender who now makes his living as a biographer, historian, and memoirist, someone for whom the construction of narrative is almost a daily process. Although technically coauthored, in truth it is the work of two separate pens; with drafts swapped across time zones between England and Cuba. However, despite our separate approaches and our very different epistemological relationship to the concept of the criminal narrative, what is interesting is that we both alighted on very similar strengths and weaknesses of the narrative approach. Moreover, we both came to realize—independently and collectively—that what is important is not that one approach is better than the other, but that, as Presser and Sandberg have asserted, their respective strengths are enhanced when employed together.

It is in this spirit that we conclude by stating what kind of criminology we would like to see, and perhaps even contribute to, in the future. We imagine a mix of cultural, narrative, and psychosocial approaches, that is both historically informed and publicly oriented. It would want finely detailed complex narratives, stories that relate private troubles to public issues (Mills 2000, 226) and break down the dichotomies of social/individual, inner/outer, rational/emotional, and foreground/background. Our criminology would try to stay close to the idiosyncratic details of the individual life, aware of "how everything, even the most seemingly idle comment or glance, is part of a practical course of action, a project, the innovative execution of a recipe, an effort to do a certain kind of social thing" (Katz 2002, 259). It would be a criminology that recognizes that all of us—researchers and researched—live the crime story in some way (Presdee 2004). Perhaps what we are ultimately describing is a critical, humanistic criminology that we can all get behind.

NOTES

1. Elsewhere this difference has been articulated by Lois Presser (2009, 186) when she states that the "narrative possibilities" in Katz's *Seductions of Crime* are less likely to be of use to narrative criminologists because—unlike, for example, the narratives of Shadd Maruna's (2001) informants, which concern entire lives—Katz's narratives (intentionally) tend to begin and end at the crime scene.

2. This difference in focus is brought out nicely by Sandberg (2013, 71) when he states: "'If street offenders are only asked about crime, violence and illegal drugs,

for example, they will often present a relatively coherent code of the street'
(Anderson 1999). Asking about family, upbringing and children can bring forth a
quite different self-narrative."

3. This point is further illustrated when one considers how narrativists and cultural
criminologists have engaged with Henry and Milovanovic's (1996) constitutive
criminology. While cultural criminology has adopted a fairly skeptical stance
toward some of constitutive criminology's more baroque postmodern postula-
tions (see Hayward 2004, 155–156), narrativists have enthusiastically embraced
the constitutive approach; with Presser and Sandberg (this volume, 12), for
example, championing its "emphasis on discursive action" and its "insights on the
dialectics of crime and discourse."

4. It is possible that a close narrative analysis might turn up some of the discursive
residue of these circumstances, especially if the focus was placed on narrative
habitus.

5. "Autobiographical sociology also helps to highlight the *linkages* between the way
the same person is simultaneously like all and some other persons, as well as
individualistically like no other ones, in various social situations, processes, and
phenomena" (Friedman 1990, 64).

6. For example, in his groundbreaking work on apostates from Islam, Simon Cottee
(2015) documented how his entire sample claimed to have had subconscious or
subliminal doubts about Islam from childhood. Postulating the concept of
"subliminal doubt," Cottee is right to suggest that what is important about this
discovery is not whether it is true, but that his entire sample independently
asserted it. Such continuity across biographical narratives can prove extremely
useful for theory-building purposes.

REFERENCES

Aspden, Kester. 2007. *Nationality: Wog, the Hounding of David Oluwale*. London:
Jonathan Cape.

Augustine. 2006. *Confessions*. 2nd ed. Translated by F. J. Sheed. Introduction by Peter
Brown. Indianapolis, IN: Hackett.

Borchgrevink, Aage. 2013. *A Norwegian Tragedy: Anders Behring Breivik and the Mas-
sacre on Utoya*. Cambridge, UK: Polity Press.

Bruner, Jerome. 1987. "Life as Narrative." *Social Research* 54 (1): 11–32.

Cottee, Simon. 2009. "The Jihadist Solution." *Studies in Conflict and Terrorism*. 32 (12):
1117–1134.

———. 2015. *The Apostates*. Oxford: Oxford University Press.

Cottee, Simon, and Keith J. Hayward. 2011. "Terrorist (E)Motives: The Existential Attractions of Terrorism." *Studies in Conflict and Terrorism* 34 (12): 963–986.

Crewe, Don, and Ronnie Lippens. 2009. *Existentialist Criminology*. London:
Routledge-Cavendish.

Denzin, Norman. 2014. *Interpretive Autoethnography*. Thousand Oaks, CA: Sage.

Felson, Marcus, and Rachel Boba. 2010. *Crime and Everyday Life*. 4th ed. London: Sage.

Ferrell, Jeff. 1992. "Making Sense of Crime: Review Essay on Jack Katz's Seductions of Crime." *Social Justice* 19 (3): 110–123.

———. 1999. "Cultural Criminology." *Annual Review of Sociology* 25 (1): 395–418.

———. 2012. "Autoethnography." In *The Sage Handbook of Criminological Research Methods*, edited by D. Gadd, S. Karstedt, and S. Messner. London: Sage.

Ferrell, Jeff, and Mark Hamm. 1998. *Ethnography at the Edge*. Boston, MA: Northeastern.

Ferrell, Jeff, Keith Hayward, and Jock Young. 2014. *Cultural Criminology: An Invitation*. London: Sage.

Ferrell, Jeff, Dragon Milovanovic, and Stephen Lyng. 2001. "Edgework, Media Practices, and the Elongation of Meaning." *Theoretical Criminology* 5 (2): 177–202.

Fischer, Tibor. 2006. "Savage, Violent, Drunk—and Misunderstood." *The Daily Telegraph*, July 23.

Friedman, Norman L. 1990 "Autobiographical Sociology." *American Sociologist* 21 (1): 60–66.

Gadd, David, and Stephen Farrall. 2004. "Criminal Careers, Desistance, and Subjectivity: Interpreting Men's Narratives of Change." *Theoretical Criminology* 8 (2): 123–155.

Gadd, David, and Tony Jefferson. 2007. *Psychosocial Criminology: An Introduction*. London: Sage.

Gemert, Frank van. 2014. "Biographies of Criminals, and Why Criminologists Should Write Them." Unpublished manuscript.

Goffman, Erving. 1967. *Interaction Ritual*. New York: Pantheon.

Goodey, Jo. 2000. "Biographical Lessons for Criminology." *Theoretical Criminology* 4 (4): 473–498.

Hardie-Bick, James, and Ronnie Lippens. 2011. *Crime, Governance, and Existential Predicaments*. Basingstoke, UK: Palgrave-Macmillan.

Hayward, Keith J. 2002. "The Vilification and Pleasures of Youthful Transgression." In *Youth Justice: Critical Readings*, edited by John Muncie, Gordan Hughes, and Eugene McLaughlin, 80–93. London: Open University Press.

———. 2004. *City Limits: Crime, Consumer Culture, and the Urban Experience*. London: Glasshouse.

———. 2007. "Situational Crime Prevention and Its Discontents: Rational Choice Theory Versus 'The Culture of Now.'" *Social Policy and Administration* 41 (3): 232–250.

———. 2012. "A Response to Farrell." *Social Policy and Administration* 46 (1): 21–34.

Hayward, Keith J, and Jock Young. 2012. "Cultural Criminology." In *The Oxford Handbook of Criminology*, 5th ed., edited by M. Maguire, R. Morgan, and R. Reiner, 113–137. Oxford: Oxford University Press.

Henry, Stuart, and Dragan Milovanovic. 1996. *Constitutive Criminology*. London: Sage.

Jackson-Jacobs, Curtis. 2004. "Taking a Beating: The Narrative Gratifications of Fighting as an Underdog." In *Cultural Criminology Unleashed*, edited by K. J. Hayward, J. Ferrel, W. Morrison, and M. Presdee, 231–244. London: Cavendish.

Jewkes, Yvonne. 2011. "Autoethnography and Emotion as Intellectual Resources: Doing Prison Research Differently." *Qualitative Inquiry* 18 (1): 63–75.

Kane, Stephanie. 2004. "The Unconventional Methods of Cultural Criminology." *Theoretical Criminology* 8 (3): 303–321.

Katz, Jack. 1988. *Seductions of Crime*. New York: Basic Books.

———. 2002. "Start Here: Social Ontology and Research Strategy." *Theoretical Criminology* 6 (3): 255–278.

Labov, William, and Joshua Waletzky. 1967. "Narrative Analysis: Oral Versions of Personal Experience." In *Essays on the Verbal and Visual Arts*, edited by J. Helms, 12–44. Seattle: University of Washington Press.

Landesco, John. 1933. "The Life History of a Member of the 42 Gang." *Journal of Criminal Law and Criminology*. 23 (6): 964–998.

Lyng, Stephen. 2004. *Edgework*. London: Routledge.

Maruna, Shadd. 1997. "Going Straight: Desistance from Crime and Life Narratives of Reform." In *The Narrative Study of Lives*, vol. 5, edited by A. Lieblich and R. Josselson, 59–93. London: Sage.

———. 2001. *Making Good: How Ex-Convicts Reform and Rebuild Their Lives*. Washington, DC: American Psychological Association.

Maruna, Shadd, and Matravers, Amanda. 2007. "*N*=1: Criminology and the Person." *Theoretical Criminology* 11 (4): 427–442.

McAdams, Dan. 1993. *Stories We Live By*. New York: Morrow.

———. 1999. "Personal Narratives and the Life Story." In *Handbook of Personality: Theory and Research*, edited by L. Pervin and O. John, 478–500. New York: Guildford Press.

Mills, C. Wright. 2000. *The Sociological Imagination*. Oxford and New York: Oxford University Press.

Plummer, Ken. 1995. *Telling Sexual Stories*. London: Routledge.

Presdee, Mike. 2000. *Cultural Criminology and the Carnival of Crime*. London: Routledge.

———. 2004. "The Story of Crime: Biography and the Excavation of Transgression." In *Cultural Criminology Unleashed*, edited by K. J. Hayward, J. Ferrel, W. Morrison, and M. Presdee, 41–48. London: Cavendish.

Presser, Lois. 2008. *Been a Heavy Life: Stories of Violent Men*. Urbana and Chicago: University of Illinois Press.

———. 2009. "The Narratives of Offenders." *Theoretical Criminology* 13 (2): 177–200.

———. 2012. "Getting on Top through Mass Murder: Narrative, Metaphor, and Violence." *Crime, Media, Culture* 8 (1): 3–21.

Ricoeur, Paul. 1992. *Oneself as Another*. Chicago: University of Chicago Press.

Root, Carl, Jeff Ferrell, and Wilson Palacios. 2013. "Brutal Serendipity: Criminological *verstehen* and Victimization." *Critical Criminology* 21 (2): 141–155.

Roy, Olivier. 2008. "Al Qaeda in the West as a Youth Movement: The Power of a Narrative." http://www.ceps.eu/book/al-qaeda-west-youth-movement-power-narrative.

Sageman, Marc. 2004. *Understanding Terror Networks*. Philadelphia: University of Pennsylvania Press.

Sandberg, Sveinung. 2009. "A Narrative Search for Respect." *Deviant Behavior* 30 (60): 487–510.

———. 2013. "Are Self-Narratives Strategic or Determined, Unified or Fragmented? Reading the Manifesto of Anders Behring Brevik." *Acta Sociologica* 56 (1): 69–83.

Sandberg, Sveinung, A. Oksanen, L. E. Berntzen, and T. Kiilakoski. 2014. "Stories in Action: The Cultural Influence of School Shootings on the Terrorist Attacks in Norway." *Critical Studies on Terrorism* 7 (2): 277–296.

Shanzer, Danuta. 1996. "Pears before Swine: Augustine, *Confessions* 2.4.9." *Revue des Études Augustiniennes* 42: 45–55.

Shaw, Clifford. 1930. *The Jack Roller: A Delinquent Boy's Own Story*. Chicago: Chicago University Press.

Shover, Neal. 2012. "Life Histories and Autobiographies as Ethnographic Data." In *The Sage Handbook of Criminological Research Methods*, edited by D. Gadd, S. Karstedt, and S. Messner, 11–23. London: Sage.

Sutherland, Edwin. 1937. *The Professional Thief*. Chicago: Chicago University Press.

Tutenges, Sébastien, and Sveinung Sandberg. 2013. "Intoxicating Stories: The Characteristics, Contexts, and Implications of Drinking Dtories among Danish Youth." *International Journal of Drug Policy* 24 (6): 538–544.

Walkerdine, Valerie, Helen Lucey, and June Melody. 2001. *Growing Up Girl: Psychosocial Explorations of Gender and Class*. Houndmills, UK: Palgrave.

Webber, Craig. 2007. "Background, Foreground, Foresight: The Third Dimension of Cultural Criminology?." *Crime Media Culture* 3 (2): 139–157.

Winlow, Simon, and Steve Hall. 2009. "Retaliate First: Memory, Humiliation, and Male Violence." *Crime, Media, Culture* 5 (3): 285–304.

Young, Jock. 2003. "Merton with Energy, Katz with Structure." *Theoretical Criminology* 7 (3): 389–414.

10

Narratives of Tax Evasion

The Cultural Legitimacy of Harmful Behavior

CARLO TOGNATO

In recent years a number of European countries have come dangerously close to defaulting on their sovereign debt. They have responded to the pressures of the financial markets by carrying out draconian measures to bring their national accounts under control. The magnitude of the adjustments made to avert the prospect of a default has peremptorily brought onto the agenda of many European countries the question of whether the sacrifices imposed on their respective societies have been fairly distributed among all citizens. This discussion, in turn, has drawn public attention to the phenomenon of tax evasion. In this regard, Italy must be singled out. Not only does it have the largest sovereign debt in the European Union in absolute terms—second only to Greece relative to GDP—but it also has the largest tax evasion problem. In 2011 evaded taxes reached approximately 17 percent of its GDP.

In Italy, traditionally, no particular social stigma has been attached to tax evaders. Rather, they have often drawn sympathy, or at least met the understanding, of many of their fellow citizens. As Italy approached the abyss of a sovereign debt crisis toward the end of 2011, a different public discourse about tax evasion increasingly set in. Surveys showed that public perceptions of tax evasion had become more disapproving.[1] Thus, analysts referred to an ongoing cultural shift as far as Italian tax culture was concerned. In this chapter I will analyze that shift and suggest that the analysis of that phenomenon may contribute to the development of narrative criminology at different levels. More precisely, at an empirical level, I will shift the analysis beyond offenders' talk and concentrate on the discourses and narratives that in the public sphere legitimize or undermine societal responses to harmful behavior.

This inquiry, in turn, will allow me to bring the concepts of symbolic function and cultural performance more to the forefront of narrative criminology. I will then show that Alexander's cultural pragmatics, and neo-Durkheimian cultural sociology more generally, can be useful to the intellectual project of narrative criminology. I will conclude by recapitulating my argument and by suggesting that a shift in focus to the issue of legitimation of harmful behavior in the public sphere may place narrative criminology in a better position to appreciate the geopolitical horizon of cultural standards on harmful behavior and possibly capture why, to modify cultural responses to harmful behavior at home, it might also be necessary in some cases to address cultural responses on harmful behavior far away from home and vice versa.

Narrative Criminology, Symbolic Function, and Cultural Performance

Narrative criminology recently has brought stories to the center of criminological reflection (Presser 2009; Presser 2012; Sandberg 2010). Criminologists traditionally have regarded narrative either as a record of criminal behavior or as a subjective interpretation of it. Narrative criminologists take a different approach. They treat narratives as a constitutive dimension of human experience, thus recognizing that narratives can exercise an autonomous effect on harmful action by instigating, sustaining, or deterring it.

Narrative criminologists acknowledge that the stories offenders tell and that end up shaping their behavior, are embedded in culture and are influenced by it. In this book, for example, Jennifer Fleetwood (chapter 2, this volume) shows that the story of the woman led astray and taken advantage of resurfaces in the stories that women sentenced for drug smuggling told her in an Ecuadorian prison, while Sandberg and Tutenges (chapter 6, this volume) report that stories of meeting with dark forces, which are available in Western and non-Western cultures, loom in the background of bad trip stories by drug users. Sometimes background cultural resources shaping offenders' stories belong to the horizon of interpretation of specific institutional settings. Ugelvik (chapter 1, this volume), for example, shows how in prison culture the trope of the rapist shapes inmates' stories about who is a proper criminal and who, instead, should be marginalized on moral grounds. In other cases, background cultural resources are common currency within society at large or even across societies. While narrative criminologists accept that the cultural resources explicitly used in offenders' stories or implicitly evoked from their cultural background can be used strategically by tellers to achieve their goals, they also recognize that, irrespective of the tellers' rhetoric or narrative competence (Sandberg 2013), such cultural resources are not indefinitely malleable and therefore still constrain what tellers can say and how they can say it.

So far, narrative criminologists have focused on offenders' talk and street or violent crimes. This chapter focuses on white-collar crime and, in particular, on the discourses and narratives which in the public sphere legitimize or undermine societal responses against harmful behavior. This, in turn, brings two concepts to the forefront of narrative criminology: symbolic function and cultural performance.

Stories do not only shape the meaning of harmful action. Sometimes, they also fulfill an important *symbolic function*, which crucially influences social responses to harmful action and does not have to do with boundary maintenance between groups. For example, if tax evaders are represented as immoral fathers that provide poisoned bread to their children, they will be seen to infringe upon a very important moral prohibition in a society in which family constitutes a core building block of collective identity, and, consequently, their behaviors will be met with moral outrage and greater social demand for a firmer crackdown. If, instead, tax evasion is represented as an amoral behavior that merely reflects the existing institutional incentives, then experts will be called in to reengineer dispassionately those incentives; the general public will hardly get involved because harmful action at that point will not be perceived as a fundamental threat to society, but rather as a technical matter. In the former case, stories link harmful action to the symbolic center of society and transform it into a matter of collective identity, thereby casting the social battle over harmful behavior into a confrontation between good and evil. In the latter case, stories locate harmful behavior in the profane realm of technical evaluation. Social reactions to harmful action at that point walk the terrain of careful rational analysis. Hence, the symbolic function I am talking about here has to do, potentially, with the shift of harmful behavior onto the symbolic center of society

(Shils 1975), and therefore with its transformation into a mark or a threat to the collective identity of society.

Acknowledging symbolic function, in turn, brings us to the issue of cultural performance. To determine whether some discourses and narratives are successfully carrying out the symbolic function of linking or de-linking harmful behavior from the center, narrative criminologists must ascertain whether they convincingly turn harmful behavior in the eyes of the general public into a matter of collective identity, or, alternatively, whether they persuasively keep it on a strictly technical turf. Now, being persuasive is not only a matter of symbolic coherence for those discourses and narratives. A good theater script, after all, can still fail to persuade because of the poor performance of the actors, or the disappointing mise-en-scène on the part of the director, or because the work has been performed for the wrong audience. To be convincing, as a consequence, all the elements that make up the cultural performance of the stories that seek to link harmful behavior to collective identity must fuse together in a coherent fashion.

Bringing cultural performance into narrative criminology surely builds on what is currently present within this field, but it also introduces something new. Narrative criminologists, for example, already recognize that narrative is enacted in real-life situations and that therefore the oral and gestural renderings of stories are also important (Presser 2009, 178). Yet, the concept of cultural performance deriving from Alexander's cultural pragmatics, on which I will dwell in the next section, brings to narrative criminology one important innovation: a different understanding of authenticity. Presser (2009, 179–181) addresses the issue of authenticity as she discusses the tradition within criminological research that takes narrative as a record of reality. In that case, authenticity has to do with the factual truth of the narrative. Since narrative criminology recognizes, instead, that narrative shapes behavior—irrespective of whether it is true or not— Presser concludes, its authenticity no longer matters. The notion of authenticity that cultural sociologists working on cultural performance employ is different from the one Presser draws on and yet it still matters a great deal to narrative criminology. It has to do not with truth but rather with verisimilitude; what matters is not whether narratives actually reflect a true reality but whether they manage to carry meaning over to their audiences in a convincing manner; in other words, whether the points they make *appear* real. A story may tell something that really happened but it may not sound and look real and hence it will not be believed. In that case reality looks inauthentic simply because the conditions under which the story is told or performed before its audience make it unconvincing. The reverse holds: a story may be a total fabrication and yet it may appear totally authentic to its audiences.

A narrative criminology that hews to the importance of symbolic function and performance is also bound to capitalize on the rich body of scholarship that has so far been produced on a number of fronts. More precisely, it may tap into the extensive literature on narrative cultural identity (Loseke 2007) to yield a much more fine-grained characterization of the symbolic center of society. It may draw from the literature about the social construction of social problems to identify more closely both the social-structural circumstances under which claim-making may support the transformation of harmful behavior into a matter of collective identity as well as the variety of frames that may intervene along that process (Loseke 2003).[2] It may then capitalize on the existing literature about the use of collective action frames in political mobilization (Snow et al. 1986; Snow and Benford 1992; Gamson 1992; 1995; Gamson and Meyer 1996; Snow 2004; Snow and Benford 2000; Polletta 2006; 2011), and about the need to situate framing in culture and language (Steinberg 1998; 1999; Johnston 2002; Skillington 1997; Sandberg 2006). Finally, by bringing in the body of scholarship on framing as well as the growing literature on storytelling in policy, politics, and protest, narrative criminologists may progressively sharpen their analysis of the symbolic strategies actors tap into for the purpose of making harmful behavior into a matter of collective identity (Polletta et al. 2011).

Narrative Criminology and the Strong Program in Cultural Sociology

The application of Alexander's cultural pragmatics to narrative criminology connects the paradigm with an exciting theoretical development in neo-Durkheimian cultural sociology. Over the past three decades the Strong Program in Cultural Sociology has built on the later Durkheim of *The Elementary Forms of Religious Life* to make sense of the lasting role of culture in modern societies. As Smith and Alexander (2005, 26) have pointed out, Durkheim's homological understanding of religious and social life allowed him to acknowledge the power and compulsion of social symbols in modern social life, the transformation of value conflicts into struggles between the sacred and the profane, the capability of pollution and purity to orient social action, and the lasting power of ritual within modern societies. The Strong Program also has recognized that the Durkheimian framework falls short of recognizing that the experience of meaning today is much more unstable and contingent than in traditional societies and the framework must be extended to capture that change in experience (Smith and Alexander 2005, 26). Alexander's (2006) theory of social action as performance responds to that specific need.

Building on Shils (1975), the Strong Program acknowledges that modern societies still have a sacred center and that all spheres of social life are symbolically linked to it. It is the activation of such latent linkages, which is a matter of cultural performance, that makes it possible for social action to exit the profane realm of routine function and enter the sacred space of collective identity (Tognato 2012). Drawing on Parsonian theory (Parsons and Smelser 1957, chap.7; Parsons and Bales 1955, 353–396; Smelser 1959; 1963), Alexander (1988, 180) also reads the activation of those linkages as a process of *generalization* "away from the specificity of everyday social life," by virtue of which social action is no longer about antagonistic interests, but rather about the very foundations of society.

At the beginning of the 1990s the Strong Program had a cultural-structural orientation, and focused on the influence of symbols, cultural codes, narratives, discourses, and narrative genres on social action. Then, it turned its attention to the pragmatic contexts within which action occurs—first by focusing on ritual, then on drama, and at the end, more generally, on cultural performance.

Some of the elements of the Strong Program are already present in current narrative criminology. Like neo-Durkheimian cultural sociologists, for example, Sandberg and Tutenges (this volume) recognize that myth still plays a role in contemporary society. The need to address both the pragmatic and the cultural-structural circumstances under which stories unfold, in turn, has also been acknowledged by narrative criminologists. Sandberg (2013, 2010) and Presser (2010), for example, understand offenders' stories as drawing from a variety of background cultural resources and reflecting a social context within which offenders exercise their agency.

After addressing the potential for convergence between narrative criminology and the Strong Program in Cultural Sociology, I will now show in what way the narrative criminology I have outlined in the first part of this chapter can account for the way societies go about legitimizing harmful behavior or undermining public responses to it. For the sake of concreteness, I will do so by addressing the shift in public narratives about tax evasion that took place in Italy between 2011 and 2012.

Research Methodology

In Italy tax evasion has traditionally been widespread, if not endemic within vast segments of Italian society. For a long time many Italians have tolerated, sympathized with, and sometimes even envied tax evaders. However, before the prospect of a sovereign debt crisis in 2011 narratives of tax evasion started to shift. I will identify three discursive moves with reference to this shift: from deflecting responsibility to accepting it; from justifying it to condemning it; and from the profane realm of routine economic life to the sacred space of collective identity, or, as Shils (1975) puts it, from the periphery to the symbolic center of society.

For this study I have drawn empirical data from the mass media. As Smith (2005, 50, 52) points out, the stories that appear in the media are intended for the general public and in democracies the media are the space where popular concerns are both shaped and expressed. In other words, they indirectly reflect public opinions and cannot be reduced to a mere mirror of elite or professional understandings. Furthermore, in print media "cultural codings and narratives are formed and justifications made most explicit in our society" (Smith 2005, 53). Following Smith, I therefore have focused on the corpus of hundreds of articles published over the past five years about, or with reference to, tax evasion in the major Italian newspapers (*Il Corriere della Sera, La Repubblica, Il Sole 24Ore, Il Messaggero, Il Fatto Quotidiano, Il Giornale, Libero,* and *La Stampa*).

From Deflecting to Accepting Responsibility

For a long time many Italians have taken pride in outsmarting the system and tax evaders have received a rather lenient or even sympathetic representation in media reports.[3] Consider two examples: One offers a portrait of tax evaders as *furbetti* (cheeky), an attribute that indicates a mix of cleverness and cheekiness, the other that of wreckless yet charming "bad boys."[4]

In Italy parents address their children as furbetti when they detect some minor fault on their part. "Non fare il furbetto" (don't be *furbetto* [cheeky]) serves as an admonition: "Don't expect I have not seen what you are up to!" At the same time, the admonition betrays a hint of admiration on the part of the parents for the fact that their child has defied their authority or control in a clever way. The situation also implies that parents will not punish the child for his fault with the tacit understanding that the child will seek to behave adequately on future occasions, but it also leaves open the possibility that parents might not punish future misbehavior and will instead be won over again by the cleverly cheeky behavior of their child. So, the portrait of tax evaders as *furbetti* implicitly understands tax evasion as a social interaction in which state authorities see but don't want to see, and maybe will continue to not want to see; tax evaders know that and therefore know that they will get away with harmful behavior in the present and possibly in the future. Also, their complacent description as *furbetti* does not assign responsibility to them.

When not described as *furbetti*, tax evaders in public narratives are identified as so-called bad boys—wreckless, dangerous, and yet charming. For example, in an interview with Andrea Ghiotto, a businessman who bribed tax inspectors from the Italian Financial Police on behalf of several entrepreneurs, Andrea Pasqualetto reports in the *Corriere del Veneto* that when he turned up at his interviewee's doorstep, Ghiotto opened the door wearing "camouflage shorts, yellow Ray-Ban glasses on his head, and a trolley always ready to take off" and showed the face of a "rascal, frank, amoral, direct, and even likeable."[5] After describing Ghiotto's criminal behavior, Pasqualetto's narrative then dwells on the sex parties Ghiotto organized to please tax inspectors, shares that one of the participating escorts had also been at one of Berlusconi's infamous "bunga-bunga" parties, and then elaborates on Ghiotto's fondness for women. The portrait of a wreckless and yet charming bad boy is therefore woven into the background picture of an Italian society in which political leaders have a certain taste for parties (and rule-breaking).

As the economic crisis deepened in Italy, the context within which narrators have referred to tax evaders as *furbetti* started to change and became more disapproving. The use of the term *furbetti* was seen within stories about public investigations that led to their discovery and prosecution. The new cultural tempo of those stories, as a result, has been *furbetto, ma non troppo* (but not too much), since a *furbetto* that has been caught and punished can no longer be qualified as such. Yet, irrespective of its discursive context, the reference to tax evaders as *furbetti* retained some ambivalent complacency which is why it was increasingly replaced or openly contested by public authorities. In summer 2012, for example, Prime Minister Mario Monti publicly urged the news on Italian public TV to avoid using the term *furbetti* with reference to tax evaders.

Observers therefore have recognized more frequently that tax evaders are not so smart as they would think or have others think, as they do not only damage others but ultimately damage themselves. Bystanders within society, as a result, should recognize that and stop sympathizing with them. Lorenzo Tomasin, for example, referred to tax evasion as a betrayal of the community in the *Corriere del Veneto*. "People have understood that by deceiving tax authorities, they are not deceiving Roma, a faraway state, but . . . our own municipality, our children."[6] And Marco Bonet offered, in the same newspaper, that people were starting to see tax evasion as a theft against the community instead of something that deserves a medal or the award of knighthood.[7] The fact that these journalists spoke from the Veneto section of the *Corriere della Sera* was quite suggestive. After all, Veneto, the northeastern region of Italy, has traditionally been the beacon of a flourishing economy based on small and medium-sized enterprises, among which tax compliance has never been high. The region has traditionally supported Berlusconi's party and the Northern League and has customarily been very sensitive over the issue of tax evasion. Thus, seeing repeated instances in public discourse of distancing from tax evasion was a sign of the changing attitudes and moods on this issue.

From Justifying to Condemning Tax Evasion

Justifications of tax evasion have varied from affirming the good faith of the tax evader to suggesting that tax evaders are forced into it by others, to affirming the morality of tax evasion as an act of resistance against intolerable state oppression. For example, Andrea Ghiotto, the business-man previously mentioned, told an interviewer: "I felt I was part of a system within which I thought I had no obligation to pay taxes. I was investing everything on sport. I saw it [investing on sport] as a sort of charity and hence I did not think it was fair to pay more." In addition, he pointed out, many companies are bound to evade taxes if they want to survive in the market because they have to compete with companies that evade and hence can afford to sell their goods cheaper.[8] Other stories, in turn, depicted tax authorities as a Big Brother.[9] Prime Minister Silvio Berlusconi, for example, cast taxation in this way, thus presenting him-self as an apologist of tax evasion. Whenever the tax burden gets above 50 percent, evasion is a form of "legitimate self-defense," an act dictated by morals, he stated.[10] One should not feel any guilt for evading taxes under those circumstances: indeed, it is a "natural right in the very heart of people."[11] In 2006 Berlusconi stigmatized Finance Minister Visco for taking an aggressive stance on tax evasion. "Visco," Berlusconi said in parliament, "wants the total control of taxpayers" and plans to turn the state "into a big Inquisitor."[12] More recently, Berlusconi dedicated one of his many jokes to the topic of tax evasion: "Two bandits enter an office and shout: 'This is a robbery.' An employee comments: 'Thank God, I thought they were tax inspectors.'"[13]

Between 2011 and 2012 different narratives of condemnation of tax evasion started to challenge the above-mentioned narratives of jus-tification more assertively within the Italian public sphere. Tax eva-sion was presented as an act against both the community and family. It was referred to as a crime and a serious moral trespass. Occasion-ally, it was even equated with absolute evil. In August 2011, with the help of the advertising firm Saatchi and Saatchi, the Italian Treasury and Equitalia launched a campaign against tax evaders on television, radio, and posters in all major Italian railway stations as well as in the Milan and Rome airports. One ad urged: "No more living at other people's expenses." Another claimed: "Whoever evades taxes is a social parasite."[14] A television ad showed a sequence of slides, each one featuring the photo of a different microscopic parasite with the final slide showing the close-up of a man. The caption clarified his identity: "tax evader = parasite of society." The head of a provincial section of Equitalia played along with this message when he stressed that "the black economy is heaven for tax evaders but hell for those who comply with their tax obligations."[15] In an interview with Vatican Radio, Prime Minister Monti thus insisted that tax evaders not only hurt their fellow citizens. They also "provide poisoned bread for their children" because the latter will end up living in a country that will no longer be sustainable. On a different occasion Monti struck further and referred to tax evaders as thieves who slip their hands into the pockets of honest citizens.[16] The president of the Conference of Italian Bishops, Cardinal Bagnasco, in turn, stated that tax evasion is morally wrong as it is linked to a rogue form of individualism that leads people to disengage from community and ultimately promotes injustice,[17] while Alessandro Russello, director of the *Corriere del Veneto*, pushed this point even further by proposing a parallel between a man who just had been found to have evaded his tax obligations completely in spite of owning forty-two houses and two million euros in savings certificates, and Nazi organizer Adolf Eichmann. In his article, Russello invoked Hannah Arendt's "banality of evil" to interpret the phenomenon of tax evasion in Italy.[18]

From the Periphery to the Symbolic Center

The shift in public narratives of tax evasion in Italy from 2011 to 2012 went through two passages: from deflecting to accepting responsibility and from justifying to condemning tax evasion. Public narratives, however, underwent yet another important shift: from the periphery to the symbolic center of Italian society which transformed tax evasion into a matter of collective identity, one that could therefore shake the very foundations of Italian society.

As Shils (1975, 3) points out, modern societies still have a sacred center that comprises their ultimate and irreducible transcendent core. Such a sacred center defines their very identity as well as the ultimate structure of reality and works as a source of legitimacy for the members of society and the institutions that establish relationships with it.[19] Narratives may locate tax evasion at variable distances from the symbolic center of society. Saying, for example, that the fight against tax evasion is a matter of adequate institutional design locates it away from the center within the peripheral realm of routine technical evaluation. This is precisely what Bruno Tinti did in an article in *Il Fatto Quotidiano* when he voiced his skepticism about the 2011 advertising campaign against tax evaders, which defined them as social parasites. He insisted that the fight against tax evasion was an institutional matter that called for some virtuous political elite, effective control over taxpayers, and "effective and fearsome punishments" for tax evaders.[20] In contrast, saying that it is an act of responsibility and care for one's own family, particularly in a familistic culture, places the issue toward the center of society.

The very core of Italian political culture—notwithstanding differences between northern and southern Italy—has often been described as lacking the kind of civism that characterizes American democracy (Putnam, Leonardi, and Nanetti 1993). Loyalty in Italy has traditionally been more important than liberty and merit. Group affiliations, particularly family ties, have counted more than individuals.[21] These elements have shaped Italian cultural understanding of agency, social relations, and political institutions. After the collapse of the First Republic at the beginning of the 1990s, however—as a result of the Clean-Hands Operation that a pool of public prosecutors in Milan unleashed against various national political leaders on corruption charges—many hoped that the Second Republic would do away with the local familistic culture and its organic understanding of society and organizations. The long stream of corruption and recent sex scandals that have marked the life of the Second Republic has revealed, instead, that this change never took place. A more liberal political culture, one that would lay greater emphasis on individual rights and responsibilities, never firmly established itself as a mark of Italian identity. Instead, the more traditional familistic culture continued to be hegemonic.

As the father is not only the leader of the family but also a moral authority and the guardian of the health of his family, the narrative articulation of Italian familistic identity has drawn on the symbolic constellations of the family, of medicine and hygiene, and of religion. Casting tax evasion within any of these three semantic fields has therefore signaled the ongoing drift of this issue into the field of collective identity. The narration of tax evasion as a form of social parasitism in the advertising campaign mentioned above is a typical example in this respect.

The Cultural Performance of Narratives of Tax Evasion

So far I have addressed the narrative shifts that took place between 2011 and 2012 in Italy over the issue of tax evasion at the symbolic level. However, even if we assume that the stories that are told are symbolically coherent, we cannot be assured that their meaning will be conveyed to their audiences. Actors posing as priests leading a crusade against tax evasion, or as good fathers who provide bread for their children, or as doctors who have at heart the good health of the social body, will still need to authentically perform those roles. And to do so, it will not be sufficient to rely on effective scripts that skillfully condense relevant background cultural understandings of priestly devotion, fatherly responsibility, and medical expertise. The actors that interpret those scripts also need to fine-tune their roles. The staging of their performance must be appropriate to the audience. In the end, the audience for which they will enact their roles must be right for the performance, since not all performances are necessarily appropriate for all audiences. In short, the cultural performance of their stories will need to be coherent to be convincing.

Following Alexander (2006, 29), a cultural performance is a process of social interaction in which direct participants and observers seek to achieve a common understanding of the situation. When the parties involved feel that such a process of interaction conveys meaning in an authentic manner, then they will buy into that meaning and share it. To understand how a cultural performance manages to be persuasive, Alexander breaks it down into its analytical components, just as if it were a stage play: the script or the story that actors tell; the background cultural resources, such as symbols, tropes, codes, and discourses that the story may evoke; the actors; the audiences for which the performance of the story is being staged; the mise-en-scène or the staging of the performance; the means of symbolic production, from the clothing to the means that transmit the performance to the audiences; and finally, social power, which prefilters the texts, audiences, actors, means of symbolic production, and staging that will in the end be allowed to make up the performance. When these elements come together in a coherent fashion, or when they *fuse* with one another, to use Alexander's (2006) term, the cultural performance will come across as authentic and thus convincing.

An eye to cultural performance is important to understand the contingency and variability—even within relatively short periods of time—of the effects of narrative on both harmful behavior and responses to harmful behavior. As I suggested earlier, Italy experienced an increasing narrative shift between 2011 and 2012 that legitimized a more aggressive crackdown on tax evasion. Equitalia, the Italian tax collection agency, was at the forefront of the new crusade against tax evaders. By the end of December 2011 that crusade had achieved the support of the general public; only a few months later, however, new events showed that its cultural legitimacy could not be taken for granted.

At the end of 2011 Equitalia staged a series of dramatic tax inspections at Cortina, the elite winter resort in the Italian Alps, which sparked considerable media attention. The reactions to Equitalia's reviews on the part of the media, politicians, and the public were quite polarized. Some complained that the inspections had transformed Cortina into the "Gomorra of the Dolomites."[22] Others, instead, praised the timing and the skillful staging of the inspections: nobody could accuse Equitalia of practicing an indiscriminate form of terror, they said.[23] At that stage two alternative stories about the inspections were told and enacted in the public sphere and competed to persuade the Italian public about their respective points. One tried to convey the idea that Equitalia was the oppressive agent of an unchecked Leviathan. The other sought to present Equitalia as an instrument of social justice that, albeit late, was finally doing its job.

To assess the persuasiveness of the two stories, it is necessary to examine the analytical components of their respective cultural performances. I will focus on the stories, the background collective resources evoked by the stories, the actors enacting the stories, the audiences, and the staging. Also, I will discuss the extent to which such elements coherently came together, or whether they actually fused with one another.

In the performance against Equitalia, which sought to present the agency as an arm of an oppressive Leviathan, the script pledged a sincere commitment to the fight against tax evasion and insisted that entrepreneurs and the supporters of a free market and wealth generation must join that fight because tax evasion is a form of unfair competition. The objection to the inspections in Cortina, the script added, was therefore directed more against the method, which featured the inspections as a public spectacle for Italian and foreign media, rather than against their substance. If this part of the script managed to make sense, its other component—which attacked Attilio Befera, the head of Equitalia, for seeking the public spotlight and for acting like a politician rather than a civil servant—failed in that respect. The public dramatization of the inspections, after all, was an important part of the signaling game Equitalia set out for the purpose of increasing deterrence of tax evasion. Since it made sense from a technical standpoint, Equitalia's inspections did not necessarily have to cue that Befera was politically motivated.

In spite of the overall internal coherence of the story that sought to equate Equitalia with an oppressive Leviathan, the script ultimately fell short of fusing the actors, the staging, and the audiences that made up that cultural performance. In the performance of "Equitalia = Leviathan," the leading actors staging the story belonged to the center-right coalition. They were very close to those socio-economic segments of the Italian public among which tax evasion is recognizably endemic, and in some cases they were considered to be unconditionally, almost fanatically supportive of Silvio Berlusconi, who had never shown particular enthusiasm for the fight against tax evasion and was facing a court procedure for tax crimes at the time. As a result, any criticism on their part against Equitalia would come across as ill-intentioned and self-interested. To argue authentically that Equitalia was the expression of a Leviathan, it would have been necessary to cast a whole different set of actors, possibly drawn from those socio-economic segments of Italian society that were instead recognized to be most tax compliant. Only in that case would their call for Equitalia to be less oppressive have been more credible. The staging of the performance, then, did not help, either. Actors often spoke to journalists in interviews that took place in the symbolically polluted palaces of national Italian politics or alternatively on the relatively shielded stages of Italian TV talk shows, which have become iconic expressions of the dramatic distance in Italian politics between words and actual behavior on the part of politicians.

The alternative performance of Equitalia as an instrument of justice, in contrast, was more convincing. Although Equitalia has repeatedly come under the spotlight in previous years for vexing taxpayers, the story Equitalia enacted was particularly compelling from a narrative standpoint compared to the one put forward by the performance "Equitalia = Laviathan." First, it stressed that only a few businesses in Cortina (fewer than 4 percent) had been targeted by the inspections based on prior analysis of suspicious tax reports. They did not constitute a generalized attack on the population. The inspections were not indiscriminate, contrary to the accusation that they hit like a terrorist attack. Finally, in an interview for a popular talk show, *Piazza Pulita*, the head of Equitalia, Attilio Befera, spoke ironically of the effects of those inspections. They turned out to be extraordinarily beneficial to the affected businesses, he said. For example, on that day one restaurant the inspectors examined had revenues three times higher than that reported the same day of the previous year and a jeweler's turnover was four times higher. Obviously, Befera's ironic remark was meant to imply that such businesses had been evading taxes and that therefore the inspections were warranted and actually paid off. Structurally speaking, that ironic line in Befera's script was a winner. Let me explain why.

In general, the fight against tax evasion in Italy has tapped into melodramatic and tragic narratives. More precisely, melodramatic narratives have been used to instigate a reaction on the part of public opinion against tax evasion; they have sought to represent the struggle on the part of those few heroes in society committed to the rule of law and to the service of their community against tax evaders, who abuse the tolerance of their fellow citizens and insult their intelligence. Tragic narratives, in turn, have served the purpose of inspiring a fatalistic acceptance either of the failure on the part of the state in its struggle against tax evasion or, later, a fatalistic acceptance of the fact that the fiscal crisis was bringing down the state, and therefore it was time for everyone to start paying taxes. These narratives have laid out the stories of those heroes that have tried to challenge the unjust order of the Italian immoral cosmos and have finally had to accept its inevitability, or, alternatively, they have told the story of those heroes who have tried to resist the oppressive power of the Italian state and in the end have had to submit to it. Occasionally, the battle against tax evasion has been narrated in ironic terms, but only to express the bitterness and powerlessness of taxpayers vis-à-vis tax evaders.

The use of irony on the part of Befera, as a consequence, is innovative. It is not only culturally savvy but also quite subversive. After all, Italian political culture traditionally has placed value on loyalty, obedience, patience, acceptance of arbitrariness, and the self-absolving nature of power. Befera's words constituted a deliberate breach of that cultural syntax. Not only was he suggesting that those who did not pay taxes would be targeted—however powerful they might be and however untouchable they might feel—but he also ridiculed them by suggesting that he actually contributed through the inspections to their business. And in so doing, he pushed a powerful key in Italian familistic culture. If social relations in Italy are about outsmarting anyone who does not belong to one's own inner circle of solidarity, and if outsmarting the other, whatever one does to achieve it, is *the* cultural practice to gain sympathy and admiration on the part of the generalized other, then Befera played that exact game. In a way, Befera cheated the cheaters with his ironic line. His narrative outsmarted tax evaders by turning their own logic onto themselves.

As I have already pointed out, it is not sufficient for a story to be internally coherent or to cohere with the background culture. The other elements of the cultural performance must also fuse with the story. The staging of the inspections clearly helped the performance of Equitalia's legitimate war against tax evasion. The Italian media showed and talked about the tax inspectors entering luxurious hotels and restaurants or prestigious jeweler shops in Cortina, or inquiring about tax declarations in the streets of Cortina with the drivers of Ferraris and Porsches. The view of privilege on the stand, projected by that staging, legitimized Equitalia's action at a time of growing distance between the wealthy and powerful and the average Italian citizen, including the plethora of small entrepreneurs making up the backbone of the Italian economy and not particularly sympathetic to a ruthless crackdown on tax evasion, yet desperately struggling with the deepening economic crisis.

As an actor on stage, Befera's professional biography also contributed to making more persuasive his role as a civil servant acting above particularistic interests—as opposed to that of an ill-intentioned bureaucrat in pursuit of a political career with one of the political coalitions. After all, Befera's professionalism had been recognized over more than a decade by both center-right and center-left governing coalitions, thereby indicating that his service had been inspired by the pursuit of the general interest.

Narratives of Tax Evasion, Cultural Performance, and Contingency

Even if during the 2011 Christmas holidays Equitalia managed to draw sympathy on the part of large segments of the Italian public, such a gain turned out to be relatively short-lived. The effects of shifts in cultural representations on public perceptions of tax evasion can be more contingent than one might think or hope.

In March 2012 a small entrepreneur set himself on fire in front of the Bologna section of Equitalia, leaving three letters on the floor: one for the community, one for his wife, and one for the tax commission.[24] In the letter to the tax commission he restated his honesty, declared he had paid his taxes,[25] and asked the commission to leave his wife in peace.[26] Such a new story about Equitalia smudged with human blood revived the earlier story about Equitalia as a ruthless Leviathan, which had not managed to persuade the Italian public on the occasion of the Cortina inspections.

This time, the ritual of self-immolation on the part of the entrepreneur brought together the elements of the cultural performance of Equitalia as a bloodthirsty Leviathan in a more coherent, more authentic, and hence more persuasive fashion. The story about the man burning in flames leaving his letters on the floor of that square powerfully evoked the background cultural scripts of the desperate but still caring husband and father who had one last concern for his beloved, even in his final moments. In a familistic culture this strikes a rather sensitive chord. Most importantly, however, the supporters of the crackdown on tax evasion had resorted to the image of the caring father to support their own battle. Remember, for example, that Prime Minister Monti had reprimanded tax evaders as fathers who provide with poisoned bread for their children, thereby implying that tax compliance would instead stand as an attribute of good fatherhood. The story about the self-immolation of the entrepreneur, and particularly the letters he wrote to and in defense of his family, indicated, however, that caring fathers are not necessarily on one single side in the struggle over tax evasion and therefore reclaimed for those upholding the equation between Equitalia and a ruthless Leviathan a powerful symbol of Italian familistic culture that Equitalia and its supporters had been trying to monopolize.

The staging of this new story on the part of the "Equitalia = blood-thirsty Leviathan" front was also more effective than on the occasion of its earlier resistance against the Cortina inspections. If earlier Equitalia had used convincingly the proverbial stage at Cortina to appear in the eyes of the public as an instrument for social justice, now the mark of burnt fuel on the pavement of the square where a human body laid in flames questioned the limits that instruments of justice should reach. Furthermore, the new stage was in Bologna, which is located within the most tax-compliant region in Italy, the very same region where entrepreneurs and the working class have traditionally managed to work together cooperatively for decades. The fact that people in Bologna could sympathize with the victim rather than with Equitalia countered the perception that only tax evaders and their sympathizers could side against Equitalia.

The actors involved in this performance also fused with the new script more coherently. The self-immolation of the entrepreneur, after all, vividly set the contrast between an annihilated and powerless human being and the footprint of his burnt body on the ground on one hand, and the impersonal all-powerful bureaucracy of Equitalia, now tainted with his blood, on the other. In contrast, at Cortina, Equitalia took part in the performance not as an impersonal all-powerful bureaucracy but rather through the direct intervention of tax inspectors, hence persons, who were out to question wealth and power.

In the end, as a result of this case of self-immolation, Equitalia came under increasing attack. When in May 2012 a bomb exploded in the building of the Bologna section of Equitalia, public reaction to the attack did not unequivocally side with Equitalia. On the contrary, journalist Dario Di Vico remarked in the *Corriere della Sera* that the attackers were occasionally represented as "modern-day Robin Hoods, friends of the small enterprise." Beppe Grillo, a comedian, founder of a new party, and rising star in the Italian political scene, encouraged the public to try to understand the motives of the attackers and demanded the end of Equitalia.[27] The employees of Equitalia, in turn, complained in the Italian media that the state and their fellow citizens had left them alone. In the end, between 2011 and 2012, a shift occurred in public narratives about tax evasion; that shift, however, did not per se establish once and for all the legitimacy of public responses against tax evasion, simply because the performative effects of that narrative shift turned out to be both unstable and quite contingent. A look at the cultural performance of those narratives within the Italian public sphere has allowed me to show why this was the case.

Conclusion

Narrative shifts in the representation of tax evasion in Italy have played a role in supporting the crackdown on tax evasion. Their effectiveness, however, has not been automatic and has depended on the performative circumstances under which narratives about tax evasion have been told and enacted in the Italian public sphere.

In Italy, traditionally no particular social stigma has been attached to tax evaders. As the country approached the abyss of a sovereign debt crisis toward the end of 2011, a different public discourse about tax evasion set in. Surveys have shown that particularly since 2011 public perceptions of tax evasion have changed and many analysts have talked about an ongoing cultural shift as far as Italian tax culture is concerned. Here, I have suggested that a look at the cultural shift in Italian tax culture can contribute to the development of narrative criminology at an empirical, conceptual, and theoretical level by respectively shifting the focus of the analysis to white-collar crime and, more importantly, to the discourses and narratives that in the public sphere legitimize or undermine societal responses against harmful behavior; by bringing two concepts—that of symbolic function and that of cultural performance—closer to the forefront of narrative criminology; and by connecting narrative criminology with both some exciting theoretical developments in recent neo-Durkheimian sociology and Alexander's cultural pragmatics.

By taking these directions, new research opportunities may open up before narrative criminology. Presser (2009, 189–190) has stressed that narrative can explain passive tolerance of harmful action on the part of bystanders and that criminologists have paid quite curiously little attention to this. This chapter tries to address her point by taking on those cultural processes that in the public sphere legitimize or undermine societal responses against harmful behavior. With such processes as a key pivot of the future research agenda of their emerging field, narrative criminologists will be able to contribute new insights into a broad spectrum of issues that range from tax evasion to global business mal-practices, to the war on drugs, to transitional justice regimes and the treatment of war crimes and crimes against humanity, to the war on terror. Turning the study of the cultural legitimation of harmful behavior into a focus of the intellectual project of narrative criminology will open up a window onto a whole new set of issues that so far has been overlooked completely by scholars.

Social responses against harmful behavior, in turn, often involve a double standard. People are frowned upon if they evade taxes at home; yet, quite often their practices of tax evasion abroad, particularly in the developing world, are not regarded with the same severity. Companies are expected to uphold social, environmental, and transparency standards at home; yet, all too often, they have been excused by broad segments of their own societies when they do so in the Global South. To protect societies in the North from the public health implications of drug consumption, illegal crops in the South are being sprayed with chemicals whose effects on the health of local communities are questionable. To foster peace negotiations abroad, some societies that hold a very tough line against terrorism expect other societies to free terrorists. Finally, to preempt terrorist attacks, people who do not normally accept restrictions of their liberties at home are willing to relax their posture and restrict the liberties of others, particularly if those others live in the South. What is interesting about this double standard is that it might be a constitutive dimension of existing cultural standards of legitimacy on harmful behavior.[28] By making cultural legitimacy a focus of their analysis, narrative criminologists have a chance not only to delve into the nature and operation of such standards at home, but they may also establish whether and to what extent standards at home and standards far from home are actually coconstituting each other. They may check whether standards are actually as double as they look to some, whether they are always that way or need to be that way and, if not, under what circumstances cultural standards of legitimacy on harmful behavior end up being double standards. Most importantly, however, shedding light on the geopolitical horizon of cultural standards on harmful behavior may enable narrative criminologists to understand why, to modify cultural responses on harmful behavior at home, it also might be necessary to address cultural responses on harmful behavior far away from home, and vice versa.

NOTES

1. In February 2012 a poll by the Istituto Demopolis for *La7*, one of the major Italian TV channels, found that 63 percent of Italians believed that tax evasion is unacceptable, even in spite of the high tax burden, whereas three years before half of the respondents had justified it. See "Evasione fiscale, l'Italia cambia idea," *Otto e Mezzo, La7*, February 14, 2012, http://www.la7.it/ottoemezzo/ pvideo-stream?id=i510976.

2. Claim-making refers to the articulation of claims that bear on someone else's interests (Lindekilde 2013). It may rely on storytelling or it may occasionally tap into alternative forms of expression that are not necessarily channeled through narrative. Stories, in turn, may simply describe some occurrence and may not necessarily seek to establish causality or, for example, demand, criticize, protest, or blame. Frames, on their part, are interpretative structures that organize experience and orient action (Snow 2013). They can convey stories about the realms of experience they help interpret and organize but also, like picture frames, their way of demarcating such realms goes beyond storytelling and reminds us of the way iconicity organizes the interpretation of reality.

3. Rachel Donadio and Elisabetta Povoledo, "Italy Tries Raising the Social Stigma on Tax Evaders," *New York Times*, December 24, 2011, http://www.nytimes.com/ 2011/12/25/world/europe/italy-tries-to-raise-the-social-stigma-on-tax-evasion. html?pagewanted=all.

4. "Mense scolastiche e asili gratis Il Comune scopre 53 'furbetti' *Padova, evasione: 300 controlli, 20 segnalazioni alla Guardia di Finanza*," *Corriere del Veneto*, October 9, 2009, http://corrieredelveneto.corriere.it/veneto/notizie/cronaca/2009/ 9-ottobre-2009/mense-scolastiche-asili-gratis-comune-scopre-53- furbetti-1601858800743.shtml; "Evasione fiscale, è record nel Salento 'Tolleranza zero contro i furbi," *Corriere del Mezzogiorno*, June 8, 2010, http:// corrieredelmezzogiorno.corriere.it/napoli/notizie/economia/2010/22-giugno-2010/ evasione-fiscale-record-salentotolleranza-zero-contro-furbi-1703244195363.shtml.

5. Andrea Pasqualetto, "Andrea Ghiotto, il superevasore 'Escort e mazzette, mi sentivo intoccabile,"' *Corriere del Veneto*, January 1, 2010, http://corrieredelveneto. corriere.it/veneto/notizie/cronaca/2010/14-giugno-2010/andrea-ghiotto- superevasore-escort-mazzettemi-sentivo-intoccabile-1703194520145.shtml.

6. Lorenzo Tomasin, "La politica contro i maxi evasori," *Corriere del Veneto*, February 2, 2011, http://corrieredelveneto.corriere.it/veneto/notizie/ politica/2011/11-febbraio-2011/politica-contro-maxi-evasori-via-privacy-giusto- fare-nomi-181444014290.shtml.

7. Marco Bonet, "Non per morale ma per legge," *Corriere del Veneto*, February 2, 2011, http://corrieredelveneto.corriere.it/veneto/notizie/cronaca/2011/ 26-agosto-2011/non-morale-ma-legge-1901366486789.shtml.

8. Dario Di Vico, "Andrea Ghiotto, il superevasore 'Escort e mazzette, mi sentivo intoccabile,"' *Corriere del Veneto*, January 1, 2010, http://corrieredelveneto.

corriere.it/veneto/notizie/cronaca/2010/14-giugno-2010/andrea-ghiotto-superevasore-escort-mazzettemi-sentivo-intoccabile-1703194520145.shtml.

9. "Il nuovo patto: Comuni 'spie' del Fisco *Accordo con l'Anci, saranno compensati con il 30 per cento del denaro recuperato*," *Corriere del Veneto*, November 14, 2009, http://corrieredelveneto.corriere.it/veneto/notizie/economia/2009/25-giugno-2009/nuovo-patto-comuni-spie-fisco-1601501464633.shtml.

10. "Programmi di evasione," *La Repubblica*, March 18, 2009, http://www.repubblica.it/2003/k/rubriche/cartacanta/18-marzo-09/18-marzo-09.html?ref=search.

11. Ibid.

12. "Quando Silvio strizzava l'occhio ai furbi," *La Repubblica*, June 2, 2010, http://www.repubblica.it/politica/2010/06/02/news/le_frasi_di_berlusconi_sull_evasione_fiscale-4511069/index.html?ref=search.

13. Sergio Rizzo and Gian Antonio Stella, "L'evasiva lotta all'evasione," *Corriere della Sera*, August 31, 2011, http://www.corriere.it/editoriali/11_agosto_31/l-evasiva-lotta-all-evasione-sergio-rizzo-gian-antonio-stella_347e05bc-d38f-11e0-85ce-5b24304f1c1c.shtml.

14. Cristina Lacava, "'Evasore parassita,' lo spot delle Entrate, *La campagna dal 9 agosto su giornali, radio e tv*. '*Stop a chi vive a spese di altri*,'" *Corriere della Sera*, April 14, 2011, http://www.corriere.it/economia/11_agosto_08/spot-anti-evasione_922e495c-c1d2-11e0-9d6c-129de315fa51.shtml.

15. "Evasione, cambio di rotta," *Corriere della Sera*, January 21, 2012, http://brescia.corriere.it/brescia/notizie/cronaca/12_gennaio_21/evasione-1902959010416.shtml.

16. "Monti: 'Inammissibili sacrifici se c'è chi evade Mani in tasca agli italiani? Le mettono altri,'" *Corriere della Sera*, January 7, 2012, http://www.corriere.it/politica/12_gennaio_07/napolitano-rigore-equita-coesione-sociale_e6b69a5c-390e-11e1-af60-0a4a95cfbebb.shtml.

17. "Bagnasco: individualismo genera evasione fiscale e corruzione," *ASCA— Notiziario Generale*, March 8, 2012, http://www.asca.it/news-Bagnasco__individualismo_genera_evasione_fiscale_e_corruzione-1132129-POL.html.

18. Alessandro Ruscello, "L'uomo che incarna il male," *Corriere del Veneto*, February 16, 2012, http://corrieredelveneto.corriere.it/veneto/notizie/cronaca/2012/16-febbraio-2012/uomo-che-incarna-male-1903303804076.shtml.

19. Shils (1961, 117) defines the center as "a phenomenon of the realm of values and beliefs. It is the centre of the order of symbols, of values and beliefs, which govern the society. . . . The central zone partakes of the nature of the sacred. . . . The centre is also a phenomenon of the realm of action. It is a structure of activities, of roles and persons, within the network of institutions. It is in these roles that the values and beliefs which are central are embodied and propounded."

20. Bruno Tinti. "Quei ridicoli spots contro l'evasione fiscal." *Il Fatto Quotidiano*, August 16, 2011.

21. On one occasion the *Washington Post* referred to tax evasion in Italy as one aspect of a more cultural model, which is characterized by a dramatic lack of civism and a pervasive reach of nepotism. See Federico Rampini, "'Siete sempre il malato d'Europa,' Usa scettici sulla rinascita italiana," *La Repubblica*, July 2, 2012, http://www.repubblica.it/economia/2012/07/02/news/siete_sempre_il_malato_d_europa_usa_scettici_sulla_rinascita_italiana-38362636/index.html?ref=search.

22. Emanuele Imperiali, "Zaia: Cortina non è Gomorra, gli evasori fiscali cercateli al Sud," *Corriere del Mezzogiorno*, January 6, 2012, http://corrieredelmezzogiorno.corriere.it/napoli/notizie/politica/2012/6-gennaio-2012/zaia-cortina-non-gomorra-evasori-fiscali-cercateli-sud-1902766634844.shtml.

23. Pierluigi Battista, "Vacanze di Natale. E questa volta non è un film," *Corriere della Sera*, January 5, 2012, http://www.corriere.it/cronache/12_gennaio_05/vacanze-di-natale-no-film-battista_2b81a92e-3766-11e1-8a56-e1065941ff6d.shtml.

24. Deborah Dirani, "L'imprenditore che si è dato fuoco era accusato di evasione fiscale," *Il Sole 24Ore*, March 29, 2012, http://www.ilsole24ore.com/art/notizie/2012-03-29/restano-gravi-imprenditore-fuoco-091844.shtml?uuid=Ab0GuiFF&fromSearch.

25. Deborah Dirani, "Imprenditore edile si dà fuoco davanti all'agenzia delle Entrate di Bologna," *Il Sole 24Ore*, March 28, 2012, http://www.ilsole24ore.com/art/notizie/2012-03-28/ustionato-per-debiti-142913.shtml?uuid=AbnnaNFF.

26. "Tre lettere in tasca. Agli esattori: 'Lasciate stare mia moglie,'" *Il Sole 24Ore*, March 28, 2012, http://www.ilsole24ore.com/art/notizie/2012-03-29/restano-gravi-imprenditore-fuoco-091844.shtml?uuid=Ab0GuiFF&fromSearch.

27. Dario Di Vico, "I silenzi allarmanti della política su una vera campagna terroristica," *Corriere della Sera*, January 3, 2012, http://www.corriere.it/politica/12_gennaio_03/silenzi-politica_4a801224-35d2-11e1-8614-09525975e917.shtml.

28. Go (2013) and Bhambra (2007) provide useful insights for reflecting on the potentially global horizon of local cultural responses against harmful behavior.

REFERENCES

Alexander, Jeffrey. 1988. "Culture and Political Crisis: 'Watergate' and Durkheimian Sociology." In *Durkheimian Sociology: Cultural Studies*, edited by Jeffrey Alexander, 187–223. Cambridge: Cambridge University Press.

———. 2006. "Cultural Pragmatics: Social Performance between Ritual and Strategy." In *Social Performance*, edited by Jeffrey Alexander, Bernhard Giesen, and Jason Mast, 29–90. Cambridge: Cambridge University Press.

Alexander, Jeffrey, Ron Jacobs, and Philip Smith, eds. 2012. *The Oxford Handbook of Cultural Sociology*. Oxford: Oxford University Press.

Alexander, Jeffrey, Philip Smith, and Steven Sherwood. 1993. "Risking Enchantment: Theory and Methods in Cultural Studies." *Culture* 8 (1): 10–14.

Bhambra, Gurminder. 2007. *Rethinking Modernity: Postcolonialism and the Sociological Imagination*. Basingstoke, UK: Palgrave-Macmillan.

Gamson, William. 1992. "The Social Psychology of Collective Action." In *Frontiers in Social Movement Theory*, edited by Aldon Morris and Carol Mueller, 53–76. New Haven, CT: Yale University Press.

———. 1995. "Constructing Social Protest." In *Social Movements and Culture*, edited by Hank Johnston and Bert Klandermans, 85–106. Minneapolis: University of Minnesota Press.

Gamson, William, and David Meyer, 1996. "Framing Political Opportunity." In *Comparative Perspectives on Social Movements*, edited by Doug McAdam, John McCarthy, and Mayer Zald, 275–290. Cambridge: Cambridge University Press.

Fleetwood, Jennifer. 2014. "In Search of Respectability: Narrative Practice in a Women's Prison in Quito, Ecuador." Chapter 2 in this volume.

Go, Julian. 2013. "For a Postcolonial Sociology." *Theory and Society* 42 (1): 25–55.

Johnston, Hank. 2002. "Verification and Proof in Frame and Discourse Analysis." In *Methods of Social Movement Research*, edited by Bert Klandermans and Suzanne Staggenborg. Minneapolis: University of Minnesota Press.

Loseke, Donileen. 2003. *Thinking about Social Problems: An Introduction to Constructionist Perspective*. 2nd ed. Piscataway, NJ: Transaction Books.

———. 2007. "The Study of Identity as Cultural, Institutional, Organizational and Persornal Narratives: Theoretical and Empirical Integrations." *Sociological Quarterly* 48 (4): 661–688.

Parsons, Talcott, and Robert Bales, eds. 1955. *Family, Socialization, and Interaction Process*. New York: Free Press.

Parsons, Talcott, and Neil Smelser. 1957. *Economy and Society*. New York: Free Press.

Polletta, Francesca. 2006. *It Was Like a Fever: Storytelling in Protest and Politics*. Chicago: University of Chicago Press.

Polletta, Francesca, Pang Ching Bobby Chen, Beth Gharrity Gardner, and Alice Motes. 2011. "The Sociology of Storytelling." *Annual Review of Sociology* 37 (1): 109–130.

Presser, Lois. 2009. "The Narratives of Offenders." *Theoretical Criminology* 13 (2): 177–200.

———. 2010. "Collecting and Analyzing the Stories of Offenders." *Journal of Criminal Justice Education* 21 (4): 431–446.

———. 2012. "Getting on Top through Mass Murder: Narrative, Metaphor, and Violence." *Crime, Media, Culture* 8 (1): 3–21.

Putnam, Robert, Robert Leonardi, and Raffaella Nanetti. 1993. *Making Democracy Work*. Princeton, NJ: Princeton University Press.

Sandberg, Sveinung. 2006. "Fighting Neo-liberalism with Neo-liberal Discourse: ATTAC Norway, Foucault, and Collective Action Framing." *Social Movements Studies* 5 (3): 209–227.

———. 2010. "What Can 'Lies' Tell Us about Life? Notes towards a Framework of Narrative Criminology." *Journal of Criminal Justice Education* 21 (4): 447–465.

———. 2013. "Are Self-Narratives Unified or Fragmented, Strategic or Determined? Reading Breivik's Manifesto in Light of Narrative Criminology." *Acta Sociologica* 56 (1): 69–83.

Sandberg, Sveinung, and Sébastien Tutenges. 2014. "Meeting the Djinn: Stories of Drug Use, Bad Trips, and Addiction." Chapter 6 in this volume.

Shils, Edward. 1961. "Centre and Periphery." In *The Logic of Personal Knowledge: Essays Presented to Michael Polanyi on His Seventieth Birthday, 11th March 1961*. London: Routledge and Kegan Paul.

———. 1975. *Center and Periphery. Essays in Macrosociology*. Chicago: University of Chicago Press.

Skillington, T. 1997. "Politics and the Struggle to Define: A Discourse Analysis of the Framing Strategies of Competing Actors in a 'New' Participatory Forum." *British Journal of Sociology* 48 (3): 493–513.

Smelser, Neil. 1959. *Social Change in the Industrial Revolution*. Chicago: University of Chicago Press.

———. 1963. *Theory of Collective Behavior*. New York: Free Press.

Smith, Philip. 2005. *Why War? The Cultural Logic of Iraq, the Gulf War, and Suez*. Chicago: University of Chicago Press.

Smith, Philip, and Jeffrey Alexander. 2005. "Introduction: The New Durkheim." In *The Cambridge Companion to Durkheim*, edited by Jeffrey Alexander and Philip Smith, 1–39. Cambridge: Cambridge University Press.

Snow, David. 2004. "Framing Processes, Ideology, and Discursive Fields." In *The Blackwell Companion to Social Movements*, edited by David Snow, Sarah Soule, and Hanspeter Kriesi, 380–412. Malden, MA: Blackwell.

———. 2013. "Frame." In *Blackwell Encyclopedia of Sociology*, edited by George Ritzer. Blackwell Publishing, 2007. Blackwell Reference Online. http://www.sociologyencyclopedia.com/subscriber/tocnode. html?id=g9781405124331_yr2010_chunk_g978140512433112_ss1–64.

Lindekilde, Lasse. 2013. "Claims-making." In *The Wiley Blackwell Encyclopedia of Social and Political Movements*, edited by David A. Snow, Donatella Della Porta, Bert Klandermans, and Doug McAdam. DOI: 10.1002/9780470674871. wbespm027.

Snow, David, and Robert Benford. 1992. "Master Frames and Cycles of Protest." In *Frontiers in Social Movement Theory*, edited by Aldon Morris and Carol Mueller, 133–155. New Haven, CT: Yale University Press.

———. 2000. "Mobilization Forum: Clarifying the Relationship between Framing and Ideology." *Mobilization* 5 (1): 55–60.

Snow, David, Burke Rochford, Steven Worden, and Robert Benford. 1986. "Frame Alignment Processes, Micromobilization, and Movement Participation." *American Sociological Review* 51 (4): 464–481.

Steinberg, Marc. 1998. "Tilting the Frame: Considerations on Collective Action Framing from a Discursive Turn." *Theory and Society* 27 (6): 845–872.

———. 1999. "The Talk and Back Talk of Collective Action: A Dialogic Analysis of Repertoires of Discourse among Nineteenth-Century English Cotton Spinners." *American Journal of Sociology* 105 (3): 736–780.

Tognato, Carlo. 2012. "Culture and the Economy." In *The Oxford Handbook of Cultural Sociology*, edited by Jeffrey Alexander, Ronald Jacobs, and Philip Smith, 117–156. Oxford and New York: Oxford University Press.

Ugelvik, Thomas. 2015. "The Rapist and the Proper Criminal: Exclusion of Immoral Others as Narrative Work on the Self." Chapter 1 in this volume.

Conclusion

Where to Now?

LOIS PRESSER AND SVEINUNG SANDBERG

It would be easy enough to categorize narrative criminology as an organizational advance, an assembling of research involving stories related to crime, and to pronounce once again the importance of stories as data. But narrative criminology is far more innovative and vital than that, a fact underscored by the studies shared in this book. Narrative criminology conceives of a world where experience is always storied and where action advances or realizes the story. This vision produces new understandings of harm as well as new and difficult questions.

Do stories motivate harm or do they simply legitimize it? In other words, do stories run hot or cold? Do they affect the storyteller or other people or both? We tell many stories, all day long. Which stories are relevant to harmful action? Can we know in advance of the action? How can we, as researchers, collect the relevant stories? For that matter, how can we pin down any stories when they do not sit still for analysis but rather are always generated in and through social encounters? If our stories are collectively sourced, what choices do we—*can* we—make in constructing them? In this final chapter, drawing on the chapters that came before, we map the future of narrative criminology as one in which these problematics are confronted theoretically and methodologically.

The Call of Stories

Narrative criminology contests the popular notion that stories only rationalize past action. Boldly, it professes that stories also *inspire* action. Stories give action some meaning that leads the would-be actor on—a sacred mission in the case of Keeton's early white Americans (chapter

5) or a struggle against Italy's tax agency as a cruel bully in Tognato's study of that nation's shifting tax culture (chapter 10). Although further research is needed, one of two basic mechanisms seems to operate. The story leads the would-be actor on in the sense of giving her a very good suggestion of what to do next. That is, the story charts an acceptable, legitimate path. Alternatively, the story's meaning entices audiences and storytellers to live according to its plotline. Those enticements are affective as well as practical—the story captivates those engaged in it—hence the erotic connotation of being "led on" is apropos.

Stories Legitimate

Stories provide a culturally feasible path of action. The implication here, whether stated or not, is that motivation is a prior event; the actor simply requires legitimation to proceed. This perspective is compatible with techniques of neutralization, conceived as definitions favorable to law violation. The motivation comes from elsewhere, say, anticipated rewards, whereas the neutralization—which we see as embedded in a self-story—makes the act all right to do. The plotlines of stories relate action to values or to generally held norms. Ugelvik's incarcerated men (chapter 1) draw moral boundaries between themselves and rapists in prison, in doing what he calls ethical work on the self. Similarly, female offenders in the work of Fleetwood (chapter 2) and Miller and colleagues (chapter 3) used traditional constructions of gender when describing, respectively, drug smuggling and meth use.

In this light, stories are a sort of moral lubricant. As Hayden White (1987, 12) puts it, "the reality that lends itself to narrative representation is the conflict between desire and the law." Thus, in Keeton's analysis of the forced migration of the Cherokees in nineteenth-century America (chapter 5), stories referencing biblical themes got the white populace on board with a policy at odds with collective principles of fairness and freedom. The story of Jacob and Esau, for example, consecrated the dominance of white Americans over the Native Americans. In the case of mass harm, leaders may well have psychic or material reasons that they set aside in order to relate a story that arouses sympathies of others (Presser 2013). Hence a reminder that stories promote action by storytellers *and* by listeners and that the story probably works differently for each; indeed, they may be different stories. Still, speakers may come to believe what they say, however cynical they were in the first instance.

Stories Captivate

The other possible mechanism for narrative effects posits stories as motivating. Specifically, stories captivate us. In *Seductions of Crime* Katz (1988) tells the story of the murderer, an outsider who comprehends that something sacred has been defiled and seeks to avenge that defilement: he (for it is usually a he) must shed blood lest the world remain in moral disarray. The project of enacting the narrative grabs hold of him, its violent conclusion something he was "headed toward" (309). Whereas Katz's senseless murderers seek to vanquish darkness itself, Sandberg and Tutenges's (chapter 6) drug users cast themselves as the adventurer brave enough to approach the edge of its potential darkness. The protagonist will desist from use before the story reaches the part where return to the light is impossible.

Sandberg and Tutenges's work showcases the seductions of less dramatic crimes. Does the perpetrator of even more mundane actions likewise operate under a spell nurtured by stories? Actually, quite common actions such as speeding and overeating are even more automatic than the aforementioned, and thus the actor may be even more spellbound while engaged in them. What about harms such as theft or other cheating, which seem guided by rational choice and hence presumably a lucid mind? Stories may not lure us in the same way. And yet, are we ever free from the influence of *some* story—now one that promotes harm, now one that promotes civility? Not according to a postmodern perspective on narrative capture, which blurs the line between narrative and experience. On that view, narrated experience is the only kind there is. We live in the narrated world; we liberate ourselves from one story only to enter another.

Ways Forward

Narrative criminology is still in the making. Some vital tasks need doing, including expanding the methodological toolkit, distinguishing crime-relevant narratives and their effects, scrutinizing storytelling in context, exploring the relationship between narrative and cultural and socioeconomic structures, and identifying implicit narratives in text, talk, and events.

Expanding the Toolkit

Narrative criminologists have isolated harm-relevant narratives while doing ethnographic fieldwork (Ugelvik, chapter 1; Fleetwood, chapter 2) and autoethnography (Aspden and Hayward, chapter 9), and through interviews (Brookman, chapter 8; Miller, Carbone-Lopez, and Gunderman, chapter 3; O'Connor, chapter 7; Sveinung and Tutenges, chapter 6; Victor and Waldram, chapter 4), media reports (Tognato, chapter 10), and archival material (Keeton, chapter 5). Within narratives, objects of attention have included recognizable tropes, character types, plot lines, and genre choices. Narrative criminologists take advantage of a multitude of possibilities for doing more fine-grained and detailed narrative analysis than has been common in criminology thus far.

We anticipate still more analytical angles and approaches inspired by semiotics, linguistics, and ethnomethodology. Working closely with cultural criminology we anticipate more studies of media narratives and the way these circulate and imbue the various stories we tell (Hall et al. 1978). We also foresee closer attention to language use, following leads such as O'Connor's sociolinguistically inspired work (chapter 7; see also O'Connor 2000) and studies situated within discourse analysis, cultural sociology and structural anthropology. Narrative criminologists might, for example, study the role of nominalization (Fairclough 1992), nodal points (Laclau and Mouffe 1985), symbolic boundary drawing (Lamont and Molnár 2002) and floating signifiers (Levi-Strauss 1987) in constructing the excusable harm and the insignificant or blameworthy victim.

Narrative criminology can also be a fruitful location for reflexive studies of the discipline itself. What stories does the discipline tell and to what effect? Like other institutions (e.g., the mass media, the state) and certain subcultures, social science is one of the main narrators in the field of crime. There is an ongoing and reciprocal relationship between the narratives of offenders, the narratives of state agencies, and the narratives of the social sciences: witness the fact that these are often different versions of the same story.

Relatedly, we would stress that narrative criminology potentially relates to stories concerning a variety of harming and helping actions by governments, intellectuals, and regular folk. Examples include justifications of harm (e.g., to so-called illegals) by ordinary actors and accounts of social movements that mobilize for social justice. Narrative criminology is thus poised to make good on critical criminology's promise of deconstructing and challenging the violation of bodies and spirits and not just the violation of law (Presser 2013).

Distinguishing Relevant Narratives and Their Effects

It will do little good in the world to simply infer the relevant stories of crime/harm after the fact. Close research attention to the variety of stories that people tell about themselves is necessary to clarify which of these matter to the analyst. We need more research that is creative in identifying criminogenic stories. Similarly, we must tap into the narratives told *prior to* a criminal action being committed. The story someone tells after they have committed a crime is not the very story they told just before committing a crime, and which can be said to have caused that crime. Victor and Waldram (chapter 4) examine the narratives of sex offenders that orient their future behavior, following Maruna's (2001) example of theorizing relationships between narrative and desistance versus persistence. Turning to harmful actions that are patterned, where the storytelling and the harmdoing co-occur, is another way to substantiate that narrative sustains harm. Tognato's study of income tax fraud (chapter 10) is exemplary in this regard. The crime is embedded within a particular discursive environment, and shifts in offending can be mapped onto discursive shifts.

Narrative criminology emerges from a qualitative research tradition. Data are open-ended and most analysts derive textual results from them. For making claims as to causal impact, the toolkit must include quantitative approaches as well. Franzosi (2004, 2012) describes a framework for doing quantitative narrative analysis (QNA), allowing thousands of texts and text units to be coded for a narrative structure that answers the basic questions who, what, when, where, and why. QNA allows the researcher to determine the representativeness of story themes, metaphors, and entire plots in large sets of narrative data, and to statistically relate these to harm. Quantitative techniques such as QNA will also enable analysts to evaluate the nesting of narratives within other narratives.

Fragmented Narratives and Meaningful Paradoxes

Most narratives are open-ended. They contain fragments, ironic allusions, and play: they are given to a plurality of interpretations. Characters can be difficult to pin down as either good or bad. In fact, frequently several stories are told and character evaluations generated simultaneously. In stark contrast to the epistemological grounding of most quantitative research, postmodern perspectives emphasize the fragmented nature of narrative (Sandberg 2013). In line with such a view, Brookman (chapter 8) delineates the multiple, at times even contradictory discourses that perpetrators of violence draw upon. The offenders she interviewed shifted between a narrative of gangsterism and one of victimhood to assign meaning to their actions.

Narratives have been described as inconsistent (Brookman, chapter 8), elastic (Presser 2008), flexible (Maruna 2001), and interdiscursive (Sandberg 2009; 2012). Stories have "multiple and often contradictory meanings and evaluations, depending upon audience characteristics" (Loseke 2012, 256). Stories' dialogical character (Frank 2012) likely explains why they lend themselves, more than other forms of discourse, to multiple interpretations and thus why their influence is hard to pin down. Mainstream criminologists tend to treat these contradictions as a methodological problem, but narrative criminologists mine discursive contradictions for meaning. Real-world narratives generally contain more chaos, ambiguity, and shorter sequences than traditional narrative analysis is able to reveal. We suggest that narrative criminologists continue to study narrative fragmentation and the dialogical character of narratives and contradictions as vehicles of innovation and tools for narrative transmission by individuals and group.

Gaps, silences, and contradictions in text are especially instrumental in producing hegemonies; one might even say that hegemony mainly operates *through* gaps and silences, and contradictions. Presser (2013) has found that a certain kind of incoherence, which she calls a power paradox, promotes harm. In her research on various forms of harmful action, narratives that legitimize the harm feature a protagonist morally licensed to do harm that is at the same time necessary and inevitable. The settings within which we tell and hear ambiguous stories must be considered in any analysis to make meaning out of the ambiguous text.

Storytelling Situations

The study of narrative practice or situated narratives is yet another crucial direction for narrative criminology (see Fleetwood, chapter 2; Ugelvik, chapter 1). The nature of a particular narrative is always a function of "the social and circumstantial context of the narrative and the structure of motivation that sustained the narrative transaction between the teller and his audience" (Herrnstein Smith 1981, 184). Indeed, Tognato (chapter 10) reminds us that we gain insight into the effects of stories by attending to their public performance.

While narrative researchers typically acknowledge that the interview is a social event where data are coconstructed and thus both interviewer and interviewee influence narrative outcomes, studies of stories told in natural contexts remain uncommon. Few scholars have studied the continuous flow of narratives in a social field, and thus the way criminogenic stories are made up, taken up, exaggerated, molded, or rejected. The closest we get to these kinds of narrative studies are ethnographies of criminal milieus, but these seldom emphasize narrative. We must read a narrative approach into them to appreciate the influence of stories.

The same story can have different meanings and receptions in different social contexts. Close relationships, local cultures, statuses, jobs, and organizations, for example, can be viewed as narrative environments, shaping stories in "locally preferred ways" (Gubrium and Holstein 2009, 227). So-called narrative ethnography (Gubrium and Holstein 2008) will illuminate the constructing and embedding of criminogenic stories within the kinds of social contexts that actually nurture crime, such as in the company of one's peers. We believe narrative criminologists should both do more ethnography and explore and analyze interviews as storytelling situations with their own characteristics (see Presser 2004).

Our times call for studies of web-based storytelling. New developments online and in social media raise several challenges for narrative scholars. Storytellers in electronically mediated contexts have limited control over their stories and the meanings of those stories. Accountability for coherence is limited. We expect that today's social actors, at least in mediated environments, are inclined to take even more liberties with "interpretive ambiguity" (Polletta and Lee 2006, 715) than in other historical periods and in other settings and to hold less allegiance to consistency in stories of self, given the rapid-fire pace and collaborative character of storytelling online. Future studies in narrative criminology could explore the foundations of harm that get laid through collaborative story production on blogs, message boards, and social media sites such as Twitter and Facebook. What is the nature of self-stories and storytelling that promote, for example, online bullying or music piracy? What organizational and institutional narratives shape these criminogenic stories?

Structures Beyond Stories

Narratives are embedded in storytelling situations, but they also emerge from and are shaped by cultural and material structures. Enigmatically, stories are both unique to individuals ("my story") and based on a finite number of prevailing forms ("the same old story"). Whereas we fashion stories out of the particulars of our experiences, basic story forms and constituent discursive devices (e.g., metaphors) are shared. Besides, our stories must resonate with at least some interlocutors, for "to stray too far from the familiar is to risk unintelligibility" (Polletta 2006, 169). And thus we necessarily draw from a common pool of stories. Despite this formidable constraint, storytellers get creative by taking liberties with story forms and particulars. As Holstein and Gubrium (2000, 120) put it, "discursive practice complicates discourse-in-practice."

Scholars have looked to the influential templates within which we construct "our stories." They have pondered formula stories (Loseke 2001), cultural narratives (Singer 2004), and master narratives (Mishler 1995). We suggest that narrative analysis needs an even broader understanding of cultural context, as the gestalt of meaning within which stories get told and understood. Foucault's (1972) all-encompassing (system or order of) discourse is one way to grasp cultural context, but other conceptualizations are also potentially fruitful. The task before us is to map the discursive landscape of a given culture within which crime or harmful action takes place, and to locate criminogenic narratives along this landscape.

Fleetwood (chapter 2), Miller et al. (chapter 3), and Aspden and Hayward (chapter 9) maintain that narrative analysis should take structures beyond the discursive into account. Fleetwood and Miller and colleagues, for example, emphasize the shape that gender gives to narrative. Clearly, narrative resources are not equitably distributed, and not all stories can be narrated by everyone (Polletta 2006). Sandberg and Pedersen (2009) argue that some highly marginalized groups of offenders will have difficulties in self-presenting as other than "gangster" or "victim." A similar narrative dilemma faces the sex offenders of Victor and Waldram's research (chapter 4) in telling their lives to others and to themselves as well. Social and economic exclusion is intertwined with one's narrative repertoire and with how a narrative from it is received.

Whereas narrative criminologists fruitfully explore how gender, ethnicity, class, nationality, and stigmatized status are linked to repertoires and reception of narratives, the paradigm also holds that marginalization and oppression—no less than criminalized harms—are discursively *constituted* by storytelling. Narrative criminology contributes a view of social distinctions as storied.

Furthermore, narrative criminologists ought not and need not ignore the big material things in the social world, structures that impress us with their weightiness and stability such as global capitalism, the World Bank, and various laws. These can all be scrutinized through a narrative lens. Norman Fairclough, one of the founders of critical discourse analysis, is helpful in that regard. In his 1992 book *Discourse and Social Change* he states that analysts should attend to three things. They should study text such as a story's grammar—the passive voice, the choice of pronouns, and the like. At one level up, they should study discursive practice, such as the story's productive context, its genre, and the characters that inhabit it—tragedy or comedy, badass or hero. Lastly, they should study the story as an instance of sociopolitical phenomena. Tackling each of these tasks, we see a future for a *critical* narrative criminology as exposing the stories that, inter alia, bring injustice and devastation into being.

Narratives beyond Narrative

In this concluding chapter, we find ourselves returning to certain fundamentals, including what we take to be narratives. The word narrative, as noun or adjective, typically refers to something explicitly said or written. Research data are therefore typically extracts of transcribed field notes, interviews, or archived texts. However, narratives need not be verbalized to influence action. Actors tell *themselves* stories, which may be considered a basic feature of internal human experience (Hurlburt et al. 2013). In addition and of particular sociological significance, actors take certain culturally preferred stories for granted and do not bother to articulate them. Indeed, taken-for-granted narratives may be the most impactful insofar as they dominate patterns of thought and action. Therefore, we call on narrative criminologists to explore nontraditional discursive expressions. We have three such expressions in mind.

First, cognitive cues or tropes can be studied as indicators of hidden or taken-for-granted stories, only hinted at in talk and text. Rapists (Ugelvik, chapter 1), drug mules (Fleetwood, chapter 2), drug users (Miller et al., chapter 3, Sandberg and Tutenges, chapter 6) and white-collar offenders (Tognato, chapter 10) all allude to narratives they presume to be shared, which seem not to require recounting. We submit that these sorts of allusions indeed stand in for cultural stories. That is, what we often recognize as narratives are in many cases mere fragments—cues directing the audience's attention in particular, familiar directions. We ought to look for these cues to stories and reconstruct the narratives they refer to as part of our analysis. We might combine studies of full and partial narratives with studies of cues/tropes, images, and events to get the fullest understanding of the narratives at play in a particular social situation or environment.

Second, images both tell stories and mobilize story making on the part of audiences. Narrative criminologists might explore these processes further, as visual narrative analysis (Riessman 2008). Images can reveal taken-for-granted and dominant narratives. They can also call forth stories people fear telling or for which they lack a vocabulary. The diverse feelings that images provoke among spectators—astonishment, revulsion, outrage, admiration, confusion, and apathy—make them key sites for observing processes of meaning making. The cultural turn in criminology has paved the way for inquiry into issues of representation, including what is now described as visual criminology (Carrabine 2012; Brown 2014). Narrative criminologists are inclined to view all forms of representation—image, narrative, trope, and so on—as interrelated and mutually reinforcing.

Finally, whereas narratives tell about action, the reverse is also true: actions tell stories. We choose actions for the contribution they make to our autobiographies in the making (Jackson-Jacobs 2004). With that idea in mind, narrative criminology touches ground with cultural criminology, potentially sharing the latter's emphasis on the self-representational project of the offender including in the moment of offending (Aspden and Hayward, chapter 9). In cases where harm-doers either do not realize or do not wish to expose their full narrative repertoire, narrative analysis of events can be a way to reveal the cultural bricolage that is harmful action (Sandberg et al. 2014). This emphasis on narratives as dramatized opens up new areas for narrative criminological research.

Whether analysts seek to demystify the story that is action or the story that cultivates action, whether they work with the aura or germ of a story or, at the other extreme, with a story that announces itself on arrival, their best efforts in narrative criminology stand to advance narrative interventions for the sake of greater justice and less harm in the world. Such is the highest achievement of any project in criminology.

REFERENCES

Brown, Michelle. 2014. "Visual Criminology and Carceral Studies: Counter-Images in the Carceral Age." *Theoretical Criminology* 18 (2): 176–197.

Carrabine, Eamonn. 2012. "Just Images: Aesthetics, Ethics and Visual Criminology." *British Journal of Criminology* 52 (3): 463–489.

Fairclough, Norman. 1995. *Critical Discourse Analysis*. London: Longman Group Limited.

———. 1992. *Discourse and Social Change*. Cambridge, UK: Polity Press.

Foucault, Michel. 1972. *The Archaeology of Knowledge*. New York: Pantheon Books.

Frank, Arthur. 2012. "Practicing Dialogical Narrative Analysis." In *Varieties of Narrative Analysis*, edited by James A. Holstein and Jaber F. Gubrium, 33–52. Los Angeles: Sage.

Franzosi, Roberto. 2004. *From Words to Numbers: Narrative, Data, and Social Science*. Cambridge: Cambridge University Press.

———. 2012. "On Quantitative Narrative Analysis." In *Varieties of Narrative Analysis*, edited by James A. Holstein and Jaber F. Gubrium, 75–98. Los Angeles: Sage.

Gubrium, Jaber F., and James A. Holstein. 2008. "Narrative Ethnography." In *Handbook of Emergent Methods*, edited by Sharlene Hesse-Biber and Patricia Leavy, 241–264. New York: Guilford.

———. 2009. *Analyzing Narrative Reality*. London: Sage.

Hall, Stuart, C. Critcher, T. Jefferson, J. Clarke, and B. Roberts. 1978. *Policing the Crisis: Mugging, the State, and Law and Order*. London: Macmillan.

Herrnstein Smith, Barbara. 1981. "Narrative Versions, Narrative Theories." In *American Criticism in the Post-Structuralist Age*, edited by Ira Konigsberg, 162–186. Ann Arbor: Michigan Studies in the Humanities.

Holstein, James A., and Jaber F. Gubrium. 2000. *The Self We Live By: Narrative Identity in a Postmodern World*. New York: Oxford University Press.

Hurlburt, Russell, Christopher L. Heavey, and Jason M. Kelsey. 2013. "Toward a Phenomenology of Inner Speaking." *Consciousness and Cognition* 22 (4): 1477–1494.

Jackson-Jacobs, Curtis. 2004. "Taking a Beating: The Narrative Gratifications of Fighting as an Underdog." In *Cultural Criminology Unleashed*, edited by Jeff Ferrell, Keith Hayward, Wayne Morrison, and Mike Presdee, 231–244. London: Glasshouse Press.

Laclau, Ernesto, and Chantal Mouffe. 1985. *Hegemony and Socialist Strategy: Towards a Radical Democratic Politics*. London: Verso.

Loseke, Donileen R. 2001. "Lived Realities and Formula Stories of 'Battered Women.'" In *Institutional Selves: Troubled Identities in a Postmodern World*, edited by Jaber F. Gubrium and James A. Holstein, 107–126. New York: Oxford University Press.

———. 2012. "The Empirical Analysis of Formula Stories." In *Varieties of Narrative Analysis*, edited by James A. Holstein and Jaber F. Gubrium, 251–272. Los Angeles: Sage.

Maruna, Shadd. 2001. *Making Good: How Ex-Convicts Reform and Rebuild Their Lives*. Washington, DC: American Psychological Association.

O'Connor, Patricia E. 2000. *Speaking of Crime: Narratives of Prisoners*. Lincoln: University of Nebraska Press.

Polletta, Francesca. 2006. *It Was Like a Fever: Storytelling in Protest and Politics*. Chicago: University of Chicago Press.

Polletta, Francesca, and John Lee. 2006. "Is Telling Stories Good for Democracy? Rhetoric in Public Deliberation After 9/11." *American Sociological Review* 71 (5): 699–723.

Presser, Lois. 2004. "Violent Offenders, Moral Selves: Constructing Identities and Accounts in the Research Interview." *Social Problems* 51 (1): 82–101.

———. 2008. *Been a Heavy Life: Stories of Violent Men*. Urbana and Chicago: University of Illinois Press.

———. 2013. *Why We Harm*. New Brunswick, NJ, and London: Rutgers University Press.

Sandberg, Sveinung. 2009. "Gangster, Victim, or Both? Street Drug Dealers' Interdiscursive Construction of Sameness and Difference in Self-Presentations." *British Journal of Sociology* 60 (3): 523–542.

———. 2012. "Is Cannabis Normalized, Celebrated or Neutralized? Analysing Talk as Action." *Addiction Research and Theory* 20 (5): 372–381.

———. 2013. "Are Self-Narratives Unified or Fragmented, Strategic or Determined? Reading Breivik's Manifesto in Light of Narrative Criminology." *Acta Sociologica* 56 (1): 65–79.

Sandberg, Sveinung, and Willy Pedersen 2009. *Street Capital: Black Cannabis Dealers in a White Welfare State*. Bristol, UK: Policy Press.

Sandberg, Sveinung, Atte Oksanen, Lars Erik Berntzen, and Tomi Kiilakoski. 2014. "Stories in Action: Cultural Influences of School Shootings on the Terrorist Attacks in Norway." *Critical Studies on Terrorism* 7 (2): 277–296.

Singer, Jefferson A. 2004. "Narrative Identity and Meaning Making Across the Adult Lifespan: An Introduction." *Journal of Personality* 72 (3): 437–460.

White, Hayden. 1987. *The Content of the Form: Narrative Discourse and Historical Representation.* Baltimore, MD: Johns Hopkins University Press.

ABOUT THE CONTRIBUTORS

KESTER ASPDEN has a doctorate in history from Cambridge University and has taught history of crime at the University of Leeds. He is better known, however, for his nonfiction writing. In 2008 he won the prestigious Crime Writers' Association Non-Fiction Dagger Award for his book *Nationality: Wog–The Hounding of David Oluwale*, published by Jonathan Cape (Random House). He is currently working on his new book, an autobiography of his troubled youth. Whilst engaged on this project, he has been a visiting fellow at the Centre for Criminology, University of Oxford, and also at the Centre for Life-Writing Research, King's College London.

FIONA BROOKMAN is Professor of Criminology at the University of South Wales, UK. Her research and publications are mainly focused on homicide and violence, qualitative research methods, and the police investigation of homicide. She is the author of *Understanding Homicide* (2005) and is widely published in leading journals including the *British Journal of Criminology* and the *Journal of Contemporary Ethnography*. She contributes regularly to prestigious edited collections, including the *Oxford Handbook of Criminology* (2012). She is currently undertaking research into homicide investigation.

KRISTIN CARBONE-LOPEZ is Associate Professor in the Department of Criminology and Criminal Justice at the University of Missouri–St. Louis. Her research focuses on gender and the connections between crime and victimization across the life course. Her recent publications appear in *Criminology, Journal of Research in Crime and Delinquency, Journal of Interpersonal Violence, Journal of Quantitative Criminology,* and *Signs: Journal of Women in Culture and Society.*

JENNIFER FLEETWOOD is Lecturer in Criminology at the University of Leicester, UK. Her research focuses on women's offending, especially in the drug trade, as well as globalization. She is also interested in qualitative research including ethnography and feminist methods. Her first book, *Women in the International Drug Trade*, was published in 2014.

MIKH V. GUNDERMAN is a doctoral candidate in the Department of Criminology and Criminal Justice at the University of Missouri–St. Louis. He received his bachelor of science and master of science in Criminology and Criminal Justice from Appalachian State University. His research interests include qualitative methods, gender, criminological theory, and restorative justice.

KEITH J. HAYWARD is Professor of Criminology at the University of Kent, UK. He has published widely in the areas of criminological theory, cultural criminology, spatial and social theory, popular culture, and terrorism and fanaticism. He is the author, coauthor, or editor of nine books, the most recent being the second edition of *Cultural Criminology: An Invitation* (2015).

ROBERT M. KEETON is Assistant Professor of Criminology and Criminal Justice at Lincoln Memorial University. He earned his PhD (2012) in Sociology from the University of Tennessee with a specialization in criminology. His research takes a critical perspective on atrocity crime, criminal justice ethics, and public policy. Current projects explore the influence of rhetoric on Indian removal, genocide, and other forms of public policy. Influenced by classical philosophies of democracy and individual rights, the goal of his research is to uncover the social and cultural forces that shape public policy, especially that which negatively impacts less powerful social groups.

SHADD MARUNA is Professor and Dean of the School of Criminal Justice at Rutgers Newark. Previously, he has worked at Queen's University Belfast, the University of Cambridge, and the University at Albany, State University of New York. His book *Making Good: How Ex-Convicts Reform and Rebuild Their Lives* was named the Outstanding Contribution to Criminology by the American Society of Criminology in 2001.

JODY MILLER is Professor in the School of Criminal Justice at Rutgers University. Her research examines how inequalities of gender, race, and class shape women's experiences of crime and victimization. She is the author of *Getting Played: African American Girls, Urban Inequality, and Gendered Violence* (NYU Press 2008) and *One of the Guys: Girls, Gangs, and Gender* (2001).

PATRICIA E. O'CONNOR is a sociolinguist and Associate Professor of English at Georgetown University. Her work in prisons, jails, and drug treatment centers situates her narrative research. Author of *Speaking of Crime* (2000), coauthor of *Literacy Behind Bars* (1994), coeditor of *Reflections* special issue on Prison Literacies (2004), editor of the "Discourse and Violence" volume of *Discourse and Society* (1995), she also contributed to *Discourse and Silencing* (2003) and *Critical Discourse Analysis: Theory and Interdisciplinarity* (2007).

LOIS PRESSER is Professor of Sociology at the University of Tennessee. Guided by critical criminology, cultural sociology, and social constructionism, she has published extensively on harm, discourse, identity, narrative, and restorative justice, and is the author of *Why We Harm* (2013) and *Been a Heavy Life: Stories of Violent Men* (2008).

SVEINUNG SANDBERG is Professor in the Department of Criminology and Sociology of Law, University of Oslo. His research focuses on processes of marginalization, violence, masculinity and illegal drugs often using a narrative or discourse analytical approach. His work has appeared in journals such as *Sociology, British Journal of Sociology, British Journal of Criminology, Theoretical Criminology,* and *Sociology of Health and Illness.*

CARLO TOGNATO is Associate Professor at the Department of Sociology and Director of the Center for Social Studies at the National University of Colombia, Bogotá. He is also Fellow at the Indo-Pacific Governance Research Centre at the University of Adelaide and Faculty Fellow at the Centre for Cultural Sociology at Yale University. His research focuses on cultural economic sociology. In 2012 he published *Central Bank Independence: Cultural Codes and Symbolic Performance* on the role of culture in monetary affairs. His next, forthcoming book, *Rethinking Cultural Agency: The Significance of Antanas Mockus*, concerns the role of creative practices in public policy.

SÉBASTIEN TUTENGES is Associate Professor at the Centre for Alcohol and Drug Research, Aarhus University. His research focuses on drugs, tourism, and transgression, often using a narrative or a phenomenological approach. It has appeared in journals such as *Addiction*, *International Journal of Drug Policy*, *Journal of Youth Studies*, and *Tourism Management*.

THOMAS UGELVIK is Associate Professor at the Department of Sociology at the University of Tromsø. His main research interest is in prisons and other places of incarceration and he is currently working on an ethnographic study of state power with a particular focus on immigration detention. He is the author of *Power and Resistance in Prison: Doing Time, Doing Freedom* (2014).

JANICE VICTOR is a postdoctoral research fellow with the Indigenous Peoples' Health Research Centre at First Nations University of Canada in Prince Albert, Saskatchewan. She completed her dissertation on the role of agency and moralities in the treatment and community integration of men convicted of sexual offenses in the Department of Psychology at the University of Saskatchewan. She is now investigating how participation in arts-based health interventions affects the well-being and decolonization of Indigenous youth.

JAMES B. WALDRAM is a medical and psychological anthropologist, and Professor in the Department of Psychology and the Department of Archaeology and Anthropology, at the University of Saskatchewan. His books include *The Way of the Pipe: Aboriginal Spirituality and Symbolic Healing in Canadian Prisons* (1997) and *Hound Pound Narrative: Sexual Offender Habilitation and the Anthropology of Therapeutic Intervention* (2012).

INDEX

Absent presence, 52

Abstract, 2, 151

Abuse, child, 76, 89, 103

Account, 53–54

Accountability: for coherence, 294; gender and, 72

Action: complicating, 2, 151–52, 162, 167; social, 42, 71, 91, 129, 265; in structured action theory, 7, 17n4

Action narratives: complexity of, 226; dramatized, 297; street brawling as, 241–42; of violent offenders, 210, 212, 214–28, 227

Addiction: conceptions of understanding and, 175–76; in drug stories, 151–53, 159–62, 166; methamphetamine, 85–87; telling moments and, 175–76, 187–98; treatment for, 194–97. *See also* Women drug addicts

Adkisson, Jim David, 245–46

Adulthood, early movement into, 76–79

African American speaking style, 187

Agency: external factors and, 214–16, 220–21; first person singular and, 216; gender inequality and, 77; invitation to, 174; of prisoners, 35; of sex offenders, 100, 108; theoretical context of, 8–11; of violent offenders, 214–16, 220–21, 224–25; of women methamphetamine users, 77, 88–89; of women offenders, 42–43, 57, 59–62

Alcohol, 164, 193, 216, 220

Alexander, Jeffrey, 260, 263–65, 272–73, 279

Alienness, 220

Althusser, Louis, 34–35

Ambiguous tragic narratives, 166–67

Apocalyptic narratives, 131

Appeal to defeasibility, 217

Arendt, Hannah, 270

Armed robbery, 251–53

Athens, Lonnie, 16n4

Atrocity crimes: defined, 128; narrative criminology and, 127–31

Audit selves, 53–56

Augustine (saint), 235, 238, 247–48, 254

Authenticity: of cultural performance, 263–64, 272–76; of reported speech, 165; self and, 108–18; of storyteller, 156–58, 168; truth and, 263–64

Authentic self: moral regulation influencing, 116–17; self-narrative and, 104, 107; sex offenders and, 96–97, 101, 104, 107, 109, 115–19; violent, 224

Authoethnography, 244, 290

Autobiographical narratives: of Augustine, 235, 238, 247–48, 254; cultural criminology and, 235–37, 243–44, 247; narrative criminology and, 235–37, 243–44, 247, 290; objective of, 243–44; true crime, 235; youthful crime, 238, 247–54

Autobiographical sociology, 244, 256n5

Autonomy, 52

Axiom markers and metaphors, 176

Bad trip drug stories, 151–53, 160, 162–67

Bakhtin, Mikhail M., 10, 213, 228

Bal, Mieke, 176, 183

Stability narrative, 208
State-sponsored drug stories, 152, 167
Stigma: against drugs, 74, 159, 167, 170;
    against immoral others, 38; self, 105–6,
    109, 113; against sex offenders, 97,
    100–101, 104–10, 113; tax evasion and,
    260, 279; against women offenders,
    47–52, 57
Story, 16n1, 158, 174; call of, 287–89; capti-
    vation by, 289; claim-making and, 264,
    281n2; formula, 217, 231n7, 294; legiti-
    mation by, 288–89; as moral lubricant,
    288; structures beyond, 294–95. *See
    also* Drug stories
Storyteller, authentic, 156–58, 168
Storytelling situations, 293–94
Strain theories, 7, 246
Street criminals, 242, 255n2
Strong Program in Cultural Sociology,
    264–66
Structuralism, cultural, 9–10
Structured action theory, 7, 17n4
Structures, beyond stories, 294–95
Subculture discourse, 215–18, 220–21, 223,
    227
Subject position, 43–44, 58–62
Subliminal doubt, 256n6
Survivors, 77
Sykes, Gresham, 6, 39n5, 42, 115, 239
Symbolic boundary work, 158–59
Symbolic function: defined, 262; narrative
    criminology and, 261–66, 279
Synopticism, 108–10, 113–18

Tax evasion narratives: collective identity
    and, 262–66, 270–72; contingency and,
    277–79; cultural performance and, 16,
    261–66, 272–79; cultural pragmatics
    and, 261, 263–64, 279; from deflecting
    to accepting responsibility in, 267–68,
    270; double standard in, 280; Equitalia
    and, 269–70, 273–78; evil in, 269–70;

furbetti in, 267–68; irony in, 275–76;
    in Italy, 260, 266–79, 283n21; from
    justification to condemnation, 269–70;
    melodramatic, 275; from periphery
    to symbolic center, 270–72; public
    narratives about, 260, 266–73, 277–79,
    281n1, 291; self-immolation in, 277–78;
    stigma and, 260, 279; Strong Program
    in Cultural Sociology and, 264–66;
    symbolic function and, 261–66, 279;
    tragic, 275
Taylor, Charles, vii
Techniques of self, 27–28
Teenage rebellion, 77
Telling moments: addiction and, 175–
    76, 187–98; changing self and, 174,
    178–83, 188, 198; community uptake
    and, 175, 186–87, 197–98; complex-
    ity and, 192–98; contemplation and,
    175–78, 181–83, 185–87, 190–91, 194–
    96, 198–99; crime and, 174–87, 198;
    critical discourse analysis and, 177–
    78, 188; defined, 174; doubts about,
    196–98; ethics and, 195, 199, 201n8;
    hot spots and, 174–75, 178, 183–
    86, 190–91, 199–200; overview of,
    174–75; signaling through juxtaposi-
    tion, 186–87; therapeutic moments
    signaled in, 191–92; women drug
    addicts and, 187–98
Terrorism, 246, 280
Therapeutic moments, signals of, 191–92
Thinking errors, 5–6
Thrills discourses, 220, 227
Tomasin, Lorenzo, 268
Toolkit, of narrative criminology, 92,
    290–91
Tough guy identity, 207
Tragic narratives: ambiguous, 166–67;
    drug stories, 16, 151–52, 159–60, 162,
    166–67; tax evasion and, 275
Transcendence, in crime, 240

Women offenders (*cont.*)
    gender and, 42–44, 47–56, 59–62;
    misrecognition of, 50–52; narrative
    practice among, 15, 42–62, 288; pro-
    test selves of, 48–52, 55; relationships
    of, 52, 57, 59, 61; religion and, 58–59;
    resistance by, 55–56; respectability
    sought by, 52, 54–55, 60; situating
    narratives of, 47–52, 288; special
    consideration of, 42; stigmatized,
    47–52, 57; victimhood and, 50–52,
    60
Word narrative, 295–96
Working self, 118–19
Written narrative, 229

Young, Jock, viii, 248
Youthful crime, 238, 247–54

Lightning Source UK Ltd.
Milton Keynes UK
UKOW04f1008051215

264157UK00003B/104/P